Anthropological Perspectives on Aging

UNIVERSITY PRESS OF FLORIDA

Florida A&M University, Tallahassee
Florida Atlantic University, Boca Raton
Florida Gulf Coast University, Ft. Myers
Florida International University, Miami
Florida State University, Tallahassee
New College of Florida, Sarasota
University of Central Florida, Orlando
University of Florida, Gainesville
University of North Florida, Jacksonville
University of South Florida, Tampa
University of West Florida, Pensacola

ANTHROPOLOGICAL PERSPECTIVES ON
AGING

Edited by Britteny M. Howell and Ryan P. Harrod

UNIVERSITY PRESS OF FLORIDA
Gainesville / Tallahassee / Tampa / Boca Raton
Pensacola / Orlando / Miami / Jacksonville / Ft. Myers / Sarasota

Frontis: Art by Sally Carraher, PhD

Copyright 2023 by Britteny M. Howell and Ryan P. Harrod
All rights reserved
Published in the United States of America.
28 27 26 25 24 23   6 5 4 3 2 1

Library of Congress Cataloging-in-Publication Data
Names: Howell, Britteny M., editor. | Harrod, Ryan P., editor.
Title: Anthropological perspectives on aging / edited by Britteny M. Howell and Ryan P. Harrod.
Description: Gainesville : University Press of Florida, 2023. | Includes bibliographical references and index. | Summary: "Taking a holistic approach to the study of aging, this volume uses biological, archaeological, medical, and cultural perspectives to explore how older adults have functioned in societies around the globe and throughout human history"—Provided by publisher.
Identifiers: LCCN 2022031541 (print) | LCCN 2022031542 (ebook) | ISBN 9780813069593 (cloth) | ISBN 9780813068909 (paperback) | ISBN 9780813070346 (pdf) | ISBN 9780813072579 (epub)
Subjects: LCSH: Aging—Research. | Aging—Physiology. | Older people—History. | Older people—Social conditions. | Aging—Social aspects. | Anthropology—Study and teaching. | Gerontology—Research. | BISAC: SOCIAL SCIENCE / Anthropology / Cultural & Social | SOCIAL SCIENCE / Archaeology
Classification: LCC HQ1061 .A5875 2023 (print) | LCC HQ1061 (ebook) | DDC 305.26072—dc23/eng/20220721
LC record available at https://lccn.loc.gov/2022031541
LC ebook record available at https://lccn.loc.gov/2022031542

The University Press of Florida is the scholarly publishing agency for the State University System of Florida, comprising Florida A&M University, Florida Atlantic University, Florida Gulf Coast University, Florida International University, Florida State University, New College of Florida, University of Central Florida, University of Florida, University of North Florida, University of South Florida, and University of West Florida.

University Press of Florida
2046 NE Waldo Road
Suite 2100
Gainesville, FL 32609
http://upress.ufl.edu

Contents

List of Figures vii
List of Tables ix
Acknowledgments xi

1. Introduction 1
   Britteny M. Howell and Ryan P. Harrod

PART I. EVOLUTIONARY AND BIOLOGICAL PERSPECTIVES ON AGING

2. Reproductive and Social Aspects of Aging in Non-Human Primates 11
   Joyce A. Parga

3. Human Adaptability to Age-Related Biological Changes 27
   Ryan P. Harrod and Alyssa Willett

4. Biocultural Perspectives on Aging: Importance of the Microbiome 46
   Melissa K. Melby, Ankita Kansal, and Mark Nichter

5. Aging and Childcare: A Biocultural Approach to Grandmothering in Ukraine 77
   Sofiya Shreyer and Julie Hemment

6. Menopause: A Lifespan Perspective with a Focus on Stress 96
   Peteneinuo Rulu and Lynnette Leidy Sievert

PART II. MEDICAL AND CULTURAL PERSPECTIVES ON AGING

7. Age-Related Changes in Human Skin: Impacts on Health and Perceptions of Attractiveness 117
   Heather L. Norton

8. How Old Is Your Patient? A Medical Anthropological Approach to Age   136
   Suzan Yazıcı and Nilüfer Korkmaz Yaylagül

9. The Importance of Traditional Foods and Subsistence Activities for Healthy Aging in Alaska Native Communities   152
   Britteny M. Howell, Ruby L. Fried, and Vanessa Y. Hiratsuka

10. Caring for Karma: Death, Rebirth, and the Other "Successful Aging" on the Roof of the World   172
    Jing Wang

11. The Aging Body in Islam: Exploring the Experiences of Older, Dying Muslims in the United States   191
    Cortney Hughes Rinker

12. Dementia and the Divided Personhood in China   209
    Yan Zhang

13. Generativity, Gender, and a Good Old Age among Urban-Dwelling Older Yoruba People in Southwest Nigeria   228
    Ojo Melvin Agunbiade

PART III. ANTHROPOLOGICAL THEORY AND METHODS FOR RESEARCHING AGING

14. Conceptualizing Frailty in the Quick and the Dead   249
    Douglas E. Crews and Kathryn E. Marklein

15. Methodological Issues in Participatory Research with Older Adults   271
    Jean J. Schensul

16. Recruiting Participants for Dementia Research without Saying "Dementia": A Site Study in Central Mexico   298
    Eric E. Griffith

17. Future Directions for an Anthropology of Aging   314
    Britteny M. Howell and Ryan P. Harrod

List of Contributors   321
Index   325

Figures

4.1. Microbiome-Mediated Pathways   52
4.2. Gut Microbiome-Bone Axis   55
4.3. Gut Microbiome-Brain Axis   57
4.4. Social-Ecological Factors Influencing Aging   63
15.1. Depression Conceptual Model   278
15.2. Good Oral Health Model Based on Older Adult Input   279
15.3. The Areas That People Needed the Most Improvement   288
15.4. Improvements in Gingival Index and Plaque Scores   289
15.5. Commemorative Poster of GOH Study Staff   291

Tables

4.1. Factors and Changes Associated with Aging, Effects on Microbiome and Health, and Alternatives   66
6.1. Prevalence of Hot Flashes in India   102
14.1. Skeletal Biomarkers and Frailty Score   261
14.2. Monastic and Non-Monastic Cemetery Sites   262
14.3. Skeletal Frailty by Cemetery Context within Each Age Group   263
14.4. Frequencies of Adult Males with Observed Skeletal Conditions   263

Acknowledgments

Partial financial support for the publication of this book was provided by an Institutional Development Award (IDeA) from the National Institute of General Medical Sciences of the National Institutes of Health (NIH) under grant number 2P20GM103395. The coeditors also wish to thank the anonymous peer-reviewers for helping to improve this manuscript.

The coeditors of this volume also greatly appreciate the custom frontispiece by Dr. Sally Carraher that was created for this book project. Sally Carraher is a health anthropologist from Alaska focusing on community-engaged scholarship and advocacy. She is a self-taught artist who draws subjects of all ages, genders, body types and sizes, skin tones, and abled and disabled bodies. *Older Adults Playing Cards* displays several details that are nods to cultures, communities, and features discussed in this volume.

We wish to express gratitude to the board of directors and to our acquisitions editor, Mary Puckett, at the University Press of Florida for believing strongly in this work and making the publication of this book a reality.

1

Introduction

BRITTENY M. HOWELL AND RYAN P. HARROD

Although aging is a human universal, the pace and intensity of age-related biological and cultural changes that occur throughout the life course are variable around the world. Older adulthood is often defined as commencing around age 60, resulting in many people spending nearly four decades of their lives in this stage. In fact, age-related changes are so heavily influenced by environmental, genetic, sociocultural, and political-economic variables that older adulthood is the most heterogeneous phase in one's life span. The chapters in this volume will provide some key examples of these variations that exist for older adults around the world.

In this book, we suggest that anthropological perspectives provide a lens through which we can view the process of advancing age as a biological and cultural experience that varies by time and place. In this way, *aging* is viewed as more than a series of physiological declines with increasing years; it is also a complicated process of change and adaptation throughout the life course (Rose et al. 2012). In contrast, *senescence* involves changes at the cellular level (Bribiescas 2020; Crews 2007, 2003), a concept first demonstrated by Hayflick and Moorhead (1961). Senescence is the process by which cells no longer proliferate, but this definition is not sufficient to explain the reasons for this phenomenon to occur (von Zglinicki, Wan, and Miwa 2020). Although there are still gaps in our knowledge regarding the science of aging, integrating our biological understanding of physical changes with the lived experiences of growing older can help anthropologists understand more deeply the variation in aging outcomes and experiences.

For example, one common myth that continues to be perpetuated, but could easily be dispelled with a biocultural anthropological perspective on aging that utilizes cross-cultural and archaeological case studies, is that in the ancient past humans rarely lived past age 30. In reality, high infant mortality rates tend bring down the average age at death, while some individuals lived well into their seventies or eighties (Cave and Oxenham 2016). Additionally, skeletal aging estimates are just that, *estimates*, often based on signs of deterioration like tooth and skeletal wear patterns (Uhl 2012). Because humans are so variable, especially throughout human prehistory, many skeletal remains demonstrating such signs of wear will be given broad age estimates, such as "40+" or "50+" years of age, rather than more specific ranges such as 40–49 and 50–59 years of age. Such misconceptions of the anthropological data render the full life span of older adults in the past "invisible" (Cave and Oxenham 2016), as if it were rare for an individual to live past age 30, thus demonstrating the need for a more holistic anthropology of aging to realize that old age has likely always existed.

The anthropology of aging is a relatively new subfield of anthropology, arising in its own right in the 1960s. Since that time, anthropologists around the globe have contributed much to the ethnographic literature on the process and experience of aging. Likewise, several significant reviews have been written about the history of the cultural anthropology of aging (see, for example, Cohen 1994; Fry 1981; Nydegger 1981; Perkinson and Solimeo 2014; Sokolovsky 2020). However, the unique positionality of anthropology as a holistic social science, including biological variation spanning the human past and present, is often neglected in such literature reviews that tend to focus on the medical or cultural aspects of aging in the present, rather than including anthropology's biological and archaeological contributions. A truly holistic anthropology of aging should include biological, archaeological, medical, and cultural perspectives of aging, for humans and our closest primate relatives. This is the beauty of anthropology; it is a field that allows us to "tack" across related disciplines (Park and Littleton 2013), such as evolutionary biology, primatology, history, and public health, to create a deeper intellectual framework for understanding human aging.

Theories of Aging

To appreciate a holistic anthropology of aging, let us look at some theories of the aging process. This section of the chapter is not meant to provide an exhaustive overview of the numerous theories that have been proposed to explain the process of aging. Instead, we examine a few key pieces of literature, including the work of several anthropologists in this area.

Chmielewski (2017, 259) and da Costa and colleagues (2016, 91) highlight a review conducted nearly two decades before their own reviews, where Medvedev (1990) considered over three hundred different theories developed to explain aging. With so many theories, researchers have had to create categories that cluster them under larger topics. For example, da Costa and colleagues (2016) have developed three categories of aging (program, damage, and combined); Pandit and colleagues (2016) describe four main categories (evolutionary, molecular, cellular, systemic, and multi-approach); while anthropologist Chmielewski (2017) has created three categories (programmed, quasi-programmed, and non-programmed); and anthropologist Bribiescas (2020) combines evolutionary and life-history approaches to consider three main theories (pleiotropy, rate of living, and disposable soma).

Despite these different classification schemas, many theories of aging suggest that senescence is adaptive for human populations by eliminating post-productive aged individuals who would compete for resources. Anthropologists Bribiescas (2020) and Chmielewski (2017) discuss several theories of aging, including the "rate of living hypothesis," which is focused on body size and basal metabolic rate (BMR) as factors in aging outcomes. Such cellular and molecular theories of aging focus on specific processes like mutations, epigenetic and genetic changes, degeneration of cells, free radicals, or caloric changes throughout the life course. These theories of aging also tend to focus on cellular damage and the gradual degeneration of the organism as the result of decreasing selective pressures on post-reproductive individuals (da Costa et al. 2016). However, these theories do not shed light on why humans have such prolonged post-reproductive life spans in the first place, or why aging looks so different across the animal kingdom.

We highlight these reviews of different theories of aging published within the last five years to emphasize how little the scientific community still knows about the process of human and non-human primate aging, despite our understanding of biochemistry, cellular biology, genetics, and zoology. As da Costa and colleagues (2016, 91) note, the reality is that "gerontologists may have to face the possibility that there may not be a universal cause of aging valid for all living organisms." Despite our inability to identify and explain the exact mechanisms that cause aging, we can still clearly recognize that there are great disparities in aging outcomes across the globe and over time.

Life course theory is arguably the most commonly used conceptual framework in the social and behavioral analysis of aging (Elder, Johnson, and Crosnoe 2003). This framework takes a longitudinal approach to life histories, utilizing ethnographic and other life record data, to investigate the variation that exists between individuals and groups of people in the past and present. The life course perspective is especially well-suited to anthropological analysis because it (1) assumes that aging is a process that occurs from birth to death, rather than simply focusing on the lives of older adults; (2) includes the analysis of cross-cultural age-norms of the past and present; and (3) incorporates the study of older adults' perceptions of, and experiences with, the aging process (Climo 1992; Passuth and Bengston 1988). Although anthropologists have long been interested in the life course, much early anthropological research has focused on childhood, adolescence, and rites of adulthood. Older adults in these early ethnographies served mainly as informants and culture-bearers rather than the focus of investigations into the lived experiences of older adults and the processes of aging. Life course theory, in which researchers document how life pathways and social experiences influence the course of development and aging in historical and geographic contexts, provides just one possible pathway by which anthropologists can contribute to the conversation on aging.

Another fruitful theory on an anthropology of aging is political-economy. Political-economic theories on aging, pioneered by Carroll Estes (1982; Estes et al. 1982), argue that aging experiences can only be understood in terms of the social conditions provided by society at large (Portacolone and Herd 2018). Political and economic conditions often limit access to resources, creating unequal labor distributions and other structural inequalities that cause premature aging as well as other adverse outcomes (Estes and Associates 2001). The importance of this theoretical approach is that it acknowledges that aging is more than a biological process that happens in a vacuum, and that each individual's experience with growing older will be based on their place and role in their society. In the following chapters, biological, life course, and political-economy frameworks, as well as other theories, contribute to anthropological perspectives on aging.

Themes in the Book

This text constitutes a holistic look at aging from multiple anthropological lenses. A mixture of review articles, conceptual pieces, and original research, this book aims to elucidate the pathways through which human culture, behavior, and belief come to affect the aging process. Because the theoretical framework for this manuscript takes a holistic approach to the anthropology of aging, these chapters likewise take a global perspective. Rather than focusing too heavily on U.S. content, the locale of these chapters ranges from Alaska to Tibet and aims to introduce the reader to the wide range of aging experiences and frameworks for studying such experiences. The book begins by considering the evolutionary and biological perspectives on aging through an anthropological lens (Part I), followed by the medical and cultural perspectives on aging (Part II), and finally anthropological theory and methods for researching aging (Part III). In chapter 2, Joyce Parga reviews the vast literature on non-human primates, focusing on the reproductive and social changes that occur as a result of aging. A glimpse into the aging of our closest animal relatives helps to frame one of science's biggest questions regarding aging: Why do humans experience prolonged post-reproductive life spans? Parga addresses this question, as well as the grandmother hypothesis, in terms of decreased fertility and other social changes that both male and female non-human primates experience as they age. This concept suggests that post-reproductive females (and males) play an important role in the caregiving and knowledge transmission necessary for a productive younger generation, a concept that also appears in Sofiya Shreyer and Julie Hemment's biocultural approach to grandmothering in Ukraine (chapter 5) and Peteneinuo Rulu and Lynnette Leidy Sievert's life span perspective on menopause (chapter 6). Likewise, Britteny Howell et al. (chapter 9) and Ojo Melvin Agunbiade (chapter 13) provide a deeper look at the role of such intergenerational teaching and learning (generativity) among Alaska Native and Yoruba Elders, respectively.

A biocultural perspective appears throughout several chapters in this text, tying together such concepts as human adaptability to age-related changes (chapter 3), the importance of the human microbiome for healthy aging (chapter 4), the role of childcare for grandmothers in Ukraine (chapter 5), the effects of stress on menopause (chapter 6), and how skin aging affects health and perceptions of attractiveness (chapter 7). These chapters demonstrate important linkages between biological age-related changes and their effects on the health of human populations. These chapters review the literature and provide important ethnographic examples of how to utilize a biocultural anthropological perspective on aging.

Chapters 9–14 all address the complicating factors surrounding how different populations of people define *healthy aging*. In fact, chapter 8 takes a step back to ask the question: Do we know our participants' chronological age, and does it truly matter? Suzan Yazıcı and Nilüfur Korkmaz Yaylagül situate the current medical practice in Turkey within a tumultuous history that affected accurate birth record-keeping, resulting in incorrect age estimations that can have implications for medical care and treatment recommendations. This raises the question: How can we define healthy aging in locations where "age" itself may hold different meanings? Such a question takes us from Turkey (chapter 8), the United States (chapters 9 and 11), Tibet (chapter 10), China (chapter 12), Nigeria (chapter 13), and Mexico (chapter 16) to seek understanding of how older adults conceptualize the aging process. While Howell et al. (chapter 9) demonstrate the importance of generativity and engaging in subsistence activities and food procurement for defining healthy aging among Alaska Natives in the face of Westernizing influences, the same question produces different results in Jing Wang's study in Tibet (chapter 10), where a good old age is defined as increasing (inter)dependence between generations and renewed interest in religious devotion. In fact, increasing religiosity expressed among older adults links chapters 10, 11, and 13 in a common thread. While older Tibetans are trying hard to increase their chances for a positive rebirth, older Muslims are reinterpreting how they view religion and aging in terms of the neoliberal values they must negotiate in the United States, and older adults in Nigeria are focusing their spirituality in terms of "avoiding wickedness" and increasing engagement in generative teaching experiences (chapter 13).

Meanwhile, Yan Zhang (chapter 12), Douglas Crews and Kathryn Marklein (chapter 14), and Eric Griffith (chapter 16) utilize an anthropological lens in looking at some of the less desirable aspects of aging, such as cognitive changes and increasing frailty. Zhang suggests that in China the concept of dementia is so highly stigmatized that older adults may lose their "personhood," and Griffith demonstrates that in Mexico older adults with dementia are virtually impossible to locate, since individuals and medical providers alike avoid using this unfavorable term. Avoiding cognitive decline and frailty is a common component of how most older adults define healthy aging, from Nigeria to Alaska and everywhere in between, but Crews and Marklein situate our understanding of frailty in the archaeological record. They point out that indicators of frailty vary greatly between living populations and skeletonized samples, and they put forth a methodology for finding common ground between "the quick and the dead," among biomedical providers and bioarchaeological researchers alike.

Their work opens up Part III of this volume on the methodological and theoretical concerns regarding an anthropology of aging. After Crews and Marklein's discussion of measuring frailty, Jean Schensul (chapter 15) posits several methodological considerations for anthropologists conducting research with older adults. Focusing on participatory approaches rich with examples from her experiences engaging older adults with the research process, Schensul's chapter foreshadows the ways that Griffith described working with local gatekeepers, and in locally accepted frameworks of aging, in Mexico (chapter 16). We conclude the book with a discussion of some possible future avenues for an anthropology of aging that will take us into the next phase of inquiry.

The authors of these chapters each elucidate the ways in which biological, medical, archaeological, and cultural anthropology have informed their work. Whether through anthropological methods or the use of holistic theories, these works establish how the experience of aging varies in time and place to deepen our understanding of advancing age. Such in-depth research on aging provided by anthropologists can assist researchers, students, and practitioners in a variety of fields to "tack" across disciplines to address societal issues such as reducing age discrimination and improving health outcomes throughout the life course.

References

Bribiescas, Richard G. 2020. "Aging, Life History, and Human Evolution." *Annual Review of Anthropology* 49: 101–121.

Cave, Christine, and Marc Oxenham. 2016. "Identification of the Archaeological 'Invisible Elderly': An Approach Illustrated with an Anglo-Saxon Example." *International Journal of Osteoarchaeology* 26(1): 163–175.

Chmielewski, Piotr. 2017. "Rethinking Modern Theories of Ageing and Their Classification: The Proximate Mechanisms and the Ultimate Explanations." *Anthropological Review* 80(3): 259–272.

Climo, Jacob J. 1992. "The Role of Anthropology in Gerontology: Theory." *Journal of Aging Studies* 6(1): 41–55.

Cohen, Lawrence. 1994. "Old Age: Cultural and Critical Perspectives." *Annual Review of Anthropology* 23(1): 137–158.

da Costa, João P., Rui Vitorino, Gustavo M. Silva, Christine Vogel, Armando C. Duarte, and Teresa Rocha-Santos. 2016. "A Synopsis on Aging—Theories, Mechanisms and Future Prospects." *Ageing Research Reviews* 29: 90–112.

Elder, Glen H., Monica Kirkpatrick Johnson, and Robert Crosnoe. 2003. "The Emergence and Development of Life Course Theory." In *Handbook of the Life Course*, edited by J. T. Mortimer and M. J. Shanahan, 3–19. New York: Springer.

Estes, Carroll L. 1982. "Austerity and Aging in the United States: 1980 and Beyond." *International Journal of Health Services* 12(4): 573–584.

Estes, Carroll L., and Associates. 2001. *Social Policy and Aging: A Critical Perspective*. Thousand Oaks: Sage Publications.

Estes, Carroll L., James H. Swan, and Lenore E. Gerard. 1982. "Dominant and Competing Paradigms in Gerontology: Towards a Political Economy of Ageing." *Ageing & Society* 2(2): 151–164.

Fry, Christine L. 1981. "Anthropology and Dimensions of Aging." In *Dimensions: Aging, Culture, and Health*, edited by C. L. Fry, 1–11. New York: Praeger.

Hayflick, Leonard, and Paul S. Moorhead. 1961. "The Serial Cultivation of Human Diploid Cell Strains." *Experimental Cell Research* 25(3): 585–621.

Medvedev, Zhores A. 1990. "An Attempt at a Rational Classification of Theories of Ageing." *Biological Reviews of the Cambridge Philosophical Society* 65(3): 375–398.

Nydegger, C. 1981. "Gerontology and Anthropology: Challenge and Opportunity." In *Dimensions: Aging, Culture, and Health*, edited by C. L. Fry, 293–303. New York: Praeger.

Pandit, Dina N., R. R. Singh, and S. P. Srivastava. 2016. "A Review of Theories Regarding Ageing." *Journal of Biological Engineering Research and Review* 3(1): 21–25.

Park, Julie, and Judith Littleton. 2013. "Tacking between Disciplines: Approaches to Tuberculosis in New Zealand, the Cook Islands, and Tuvalu." In *When Culture Impacts Health*, edited by C. Banwell, S. Ulijaszek, and J. Dixon, 157–166. New York: Elsevier.

Passuth, P. M., and V. L. Bengston. 1988. "Sociological Theories of Aging: Current Perspectives and Future Directions." In *Emergent Theories of Aging*, edited by B. J. Birren and V. L. Bengston. New York: Springer Publishing.

Perkinson, Margaret A., and Samantha L. Solimeo. 2014. "Aging in Cultural Context and as Narrative Process: Conceptual Foundations of the Anthropology of Aging as Reflected in the Works of Margaret Clark and Sharon Kaufman." *Gerontologist* 54(1): 101–107.

Portacolone, Elena, and Pamela Herd. 2018. "The Political Economy of Aging in the 21st Century: The Influence of Carroll Estes' Scholarship in Social Gerontology." *Innovation in Aging* 2 (Suppl. 1): 368–369.

Rose, Michael R., Thomas Flatt, Joseph L. Graves, Lee F. Greer, Daniel E. Martinez, Margarida Matos, Laurence D. Mueller, Robert J. Shmookler Reis, and Parvin Shahrestani. 2012. "What Is Aging?" *Frontiers in Genetics* 3: 134.

Sokolovsky, Jay. 2020. *The Cultural Context of Aging: Worldwide Perspectives*. 4th ed. New York: Praeger Publishers/Greenwood Publishing Group.

Uhl, Natalie M. 2012. "Age-at-Death Estimation." In *Research Methods in Human Skeletal Biology*, edited by Elizabeth A. DiGangi and Megan K. Moore, 63–90. Oxford: Academic Press.

von Zglinicki, Thomas, Tengfei Wan, and Satomi Miwa. 2020. "Senescence in Post-Mitotic Cells: A Driver of Aging?" *Antioxidants and Redox Signaling* Ahead of Print. doi.org/10.1089/ars.2020.8048.

I

Evolutionary and Biological Perspectives on Aging

2

Reproductive and Social Aspects of Aging in Non-Human Primates

JOYCE A. PARGA

As our closest living relatives, non-human primates (hereafter, primates) have been used as models for investigating different aspects of human aging, including changes to social behavior, physiological declines, and the progression of disease (Erwin and Hof 2002; Emery Thompson, Rosati, and Snyder-Mackler 2020). Models for human aging have come from every major primate group, including apes (Emery Thompson et al. 2020), monkeys (Tardif 2019), and prosimians (Languille et al. 2012). Because the literature on primate aging is voluminous and a full treatment is beyond the scope of this work, this chapter will be limited to a review of reproductive senescence in both male and female primates, and it will discuss some of the differences in social behavior exhibited by aged primates.

Reproductive Aging in Female Primates

Female primate reproduction across the life span typically shows an inverse U-shaped distribution, with fertility being highest in prime-aged females (non-adolescent adult females not yet showing signs of aging), and lower in very young and old females (Caro et al. 1995; Pusey 2012). Female reproductive decline can take many forms. With advanced age, females can begin to show irregular hormonal cycling or cycles lacking ovulation, as in howler monkeys (Raño, Valeggia, and Kowalewski 2018), macaques (Nozaki, Mitsunaga, and Shimizu 1995), and tamarins (Tardif and Ziegler 1992). Old females frequently have lower conception and birth rates than younger females (Altmann et al. 2010; Borries, Sommer, and Srivastava 1991; Hrdy 1981; Koyama et al. 1992; van Noordwijk and van Schaik 1987). Older females can also show increased rates of spontaneous abortions and stillbirths (Packer, Tatar, and Collins 1998; Roof et al. 2005) and can give birth to infants having poorer survival than offspring born to younger, prime-aged mothers (Gagliardi et al. 2007; Hoffman et al. 2010; Robbins et al. 2006). This trend of poorer survival of infants born to older females can be especially true for females of low social status (Silk et al. 1981). Where more than one offspring is born per pregnancy, litter size can be smaller for old females, as in common marmosets (Smucny et al. 2004) and ruffed lemurs (Tidière et al. 2018). Females of some species can also cease to produce offspring near the end of their lives, as has been documented among Japanese macaques (Pavelka and Fedigan 1999), vervet monkeys (Atkins et al. 2014), and blue monkeys (Cords and Chowdhury 2010).

Among Milne-Edwards's sifaka, reproductive decline among older females was found to be both tooth wear–determined and rainfall-mediated (King et al. 2005). In this species, aged females with significant tooth wear were able to continue reproducing until they reached old age, but infants of these older mothers only survived if rainfall was high during lactation seasons (King et al. 2005; Wright et al. 2008). Analysis of the feces of a dentally senescent individual showed poorer ability to reduce food particle size than for younger individuals in their dental prime (King et al. 2005; Wright et al. 2008). These findings underscore the importance to lactating mothers of food processing efficiency for maximal extraction of moisture and nutrition. However, such relationships are often specific to a particular species or environment. For example, in the ring-tailed lemur, some older females show evidence of severe tooth wear and tooth loss (Cuozzo and Sauther 2006; Sauther, Sussman, and Cuozzo 2002), but the presence and degree of wear does not predict infant survival (Cuozzo et al. 2010).

Despite the reproductive disadvantages to females of reaching old age, certain social benefits may accrue to older female primates that can help offset the reproductive costs associated with aging. For example, older female langurs are more likely to successfully compete with other females in the group and rise in rank, and these older females show superior success in rearing offspring (Borries, Sommer, and Srivastava 1991). Additionally, males of some species preferentially show mate choice for old females who continue to be reproductively successful, which has been found among ring-tailed lemurs (Parga 2006) and chimpanzees (Muller, Emery Thompson, and Wrangham 2006).

Is Menopause Unique to Humans?

Reproductive senescence in women and the phenomenon of menopause have been the focus of numerous studies (Broekmans et al. 2007; Leidy Sievert 2001, 2014; Peccei 2001). Menopause is the permanent cessation of menses and ovarian cycling due to the depletion of oocyte stores (Leidy 1994; Soules et al. 2001). Whether menopause exists for any primate aside from humans has been a topic of discussion for decades (Caro et al. 1995; Fedigan and Pavelka 2011; Graham, Kling, and Steiner 1979; Johnson and Kapsalis 1998; Nishida, Takasaki, and Takahata 1990; Pavelka and Fedigan 1991; Pavelka et al. 2018; Takahata, Koyama, and Suzuki 1995; Videan et al. 2006; Walker and Herndon 2008). As such, this topic deserves further explanation here.

First, it should be noted that the disagreement about whether primates other than humans experience menopause only applies to monkeys and apes (Erwin and Hof 2008). Because female prosimians such as lemurs do not menstruate (Dixson 2012), using the permanent cessation of menses to indicate menopause does not work for these primates. Therefore, research has considered instead whether prosimians experience a permanent cessation of ovarian cycling similar to what human women experience in menopause. Available evidence suggests that female prosimians do not appear to experience a post-reproductive life span (Taylor 2008). For example, in the ring-tailed lemur, although infants born to some older females have decreased survival, females can produce infants until they die (Gould, Sussman, and Sauther 2003; Ichino et al. 2015; Koyama et al. 2001; Parga and Lessnau 2005). Similarly, in diademed sifakas, there is no evidence for a post-reproductive life span, and females are capable of reproducing well into old age (Pochron, Tucker, and Wright 2004; Richard et al. 2002).

In contrast, several authors have argued that some monkeys and apes experience a reproductive cessation akin to human menopause, citing as evidence a lack of infant production for a percentage of older females for a number of years prior to death, data on older females experiencing irregular cycles or anovulation, or data demonstrating the cessation of menstruation (Gilardi et al. 1997; Nishida et al. 2003; Sommer, Srivastava, and Borries 1992).

However, the short length of the post-reproductive life span in non-human primates relative to humans—and the fact that this post-reproductive life span typically applies to such a small percentage of older females in any particular monkey or ape species—has led several researchers to conclude that the reproductive decline seen in many older female monkeys and apes is fundamentally different from the cessation of reproduction in women that occurs in mid-life (Alberts et al. 2013; Emery Thompson et al. 2007; Fedigan and Pavelka 2011; Peccei 2001). Moreover, cycles that are irregular and lack ovulation in older monkey and ape females are often seen in captivity and/or among exceptionally old females at an age long after which most wild individuals of those species would have died—leading to the conclusion that menopause is a rare trait only experienced by humans and some whales, among mammals (Ellis et al. 2018; Johnstone and Cant 2019; Pavelka et al. 2018). Some authors have used the term "menopause" to describe the decline in reproduction in older female primates but concede that the cessation of reproduction in such species differs from human menopause by occurring much later in the maximum life span of primates than in our own species (Borries and Koenig 2008).

Reproductive Aging in Male Primates

The declining reproductive potential of older male primates is evidenced in many ways, including in physiological declines, less successful mating behavior, and decreased reproductive success (production of infants) compared to younger males. With respect to physiological effects of aging, just as human males show reproductive senescence (Bribiescas 2006, 2010), some of the same signs of reproductive aging can be seen in non-human primate males. For example, older male primates can show declines in various measures of sperm quality (Hernández-López et al. 2012) and tend to pass more genetic mutations to their offspring than younger males (Thomas et al. 2018; Venn et al. 2014; Wang et al. 2020). Older male primates can also experience declines in testosterone (Beehner et al. 2009; Muller 2017; Tardif et al. 2008), which could have negative effects on the sexual behavior of older males.

Behavioral data collected on mating in species as varied as lemurs (Parga 2013) and chimpanzees (Muller 2017) show decreased sexual performance of older, relative to younger, males. In the ring-tailed lemur, older males require a greater number of mounts and more time spent in mounts than younger males before reaching ejaculation (Parga 2013), which can potentially put older males at a distinct reproductive disadvantage in male-male competition if older males physically lose access to females before they are able to ejaculate. In rhesus macaques, older males perform fewer instances of mounting and ejaculation than younger males (Robinson et al. 1975; Phoenix and Chambers 1982; but see Milich et al. 2020). Moreover, female primates may be less inclined to prefer older males as mates, which can result in lower mating success for older males (Huffman and Takahata 2012).

In addition to documenting declines in the sexual performance and mating success of older males, there are other indicators that older male primates experience difficulty in reproductive competition against younger males. In mandrills, older males show high fecal glucocorticoid (stress hormone) levels during the mating season when there is a greater influx of new males (Charpentier et al. 2018); at this time, "mature" male mandrills appear to be under greater nutritional stress than younger males—a difference likely caused by male-male competition (Oelze et al. 2020). Because male primates are typically most successful in various forms of male-male competition when they are in their physical prime, male reproductive success often shows a peak, before and after which reproductive success is lower. In savanna baboons, males show a peak in reproductive success (measured as number of infants sired) in early adulthood that corresponds to a peak in male dominance status, after which there is a rapid decline in these traits that is accompanied by lower testosterone levels and declining body condition with increasing age (Altmann et al. 2010).

Therefore, although there may be some exceptions, the general trend among primates is for older males to have reduced reproduction relative to younger (prime-aged) males. Exceptions may be found in some cases where older males can still successfully compete via various mechanisms, such as the formation of coalitions with alpha males who concede mating opportunities to older males in exchange for their coalitionary support (Muller et al. 2020). However, studies that use genetic analyses to measure paternity overwhelmingly reveal that older males sire fewer offspring than younger males who are in their prime (Alberts, Buchan, and Altmann 2006; Bercovitch et al. 2003; Dubuc, Ruiz-Lambides, and Widdig 2014; Wroblewski et al. 2009), occasionally even when old males show high rates of mating behaviors and retain high dominance rank (Milich et al. 2020). Clearly, experiencing decreased reproductive potential is a pervasive feature of aging for older male primates.

Behavioral and Social Differences

Behavioral adjustments are commonly seen among aged primates due to physiological limitations imposed by senescence. Older individuals may spend more time resting and sleeping (Corr 2003; Pavelka 1990; Nakamichi 1984; Veneema et al. 1997) and tend to engage in less costly forms of locomotion (Almeling et al. 2017). In captive mouse lemurs, older individuals spend more time in nests than younger individuals (Terrien, Perret, and Aujard 2010).

Older individuals are also frequently described as being less socially active than younger individuals (Corr, Martin, and Boysen 2002; Machanda and Rosati 2020). Older individuals may be more peripheral to the group or may spend more time alone (Nakamichi 1984; Overdorff et al. 1999; Taylor 1998a, 1998b, 2008), and may spend less time in mutual grooming (Huffman 1990; Almeling et al. 2016; Picq 1992). Older individuals may also be less likely than younger individuals to initiate affiliative interactions (Taylor 2000, 2008) or may selectively prefer to approach other old individuals for social interactions (Veneema et al. 1997).

Circulating stress hormones can be increased in older individuals (Altmann et al. 2010; Sapolsky and Altmann 1991), and older individuals can show higher rates of stress-related behaviors, such as yawning (Veneema et al. 1997). Overall, aged individuals may be less able to compete against peers, and as a result may avoid competition in group-living species by occupying less centralized spatial positions in the group (Almeling et al. 2017; Hrdy 1981; van Noordwijk and van Schaik 1987). Conversely, other studies show that aged individuals are not always less socially active than other individuals (McGuire 2017; Pavelka 1990, 1991; Tarou et al. 2002).

Some studies posit a beneficial role that older female primates can provide to their adult offspring and even grand-offspring (Pavelka, Fedigan, and Zohar 2002), such as triadic agonistic support in langurs (Borries 1988) or infant-carrying by grandmothers in ring-tailed lemurs (McGuire 2017). Indeed, the "grandmother hypothesis" has been suggested as an adaptive explanation for menopause in humans, whereby older women may gain a greater fitness advantage by aiding daughters in caring for grand-offspring than by continuing to reproduce into old age themselves (Hawkes 2003). Although menopause appears to be a distinctly human phenomenon (Pavelka et al. 2018), having a grandmother present in the group can positively affect the dominance status of non-human primate granddaughters, as in Japanese macaques (Chapais et al. 1997). The presence of a grandmother may also deter the evictions of female relatives in species with high intra-group competition, such as the ring-tailed lemur (Soma and Koyama 2013). Older individuals can also benefit their groupmates through their superior ecological knowledge, such as in the vervet monkey, a species in which older females are particularly successful at leading group progressions to foraging sites (Lee and Teichroeb 2016).

Discussion

This chapter has briefly summarized findings on reproductive and behavioral changes experienced by aged male and female non-human primates. Evidence shows that male and female primates experience reproductive senescence, with older individuals experiencing declines that can include lower reproductive rates, higher offspring mortality, and the propensity for passing a greater number of genetic mutations to offspring. Behavior can likewise display marked changes in older primates, manifesting in such differences as increased time spent resting, the use of less energetically costly forms of locomotion, and decreased grooming or proximity to others compared to younger individuals.

However, the primate order is so diverse that it is difficult to easily generalize the effects of aging across primates or even within any single taxonomic group. The effects of aging can be species- or even population-specific, and results may differ broadly depending on the research site. Nonetheless, although there are many disadvantages of senescence (e.g., reproductive decline), aging can provide special advantages to older individuals and to the social groups to which they belong, such as superior ability to rear offspring, social aid provided to relatives, and unique ecological knowledge. With the number of long-term field (Kappeler and Watts 2012) and captive studies of primates increasing, our available sample sizes of old individuals of known ages (or known age classes) will grow, and with them, our understanding of the myriad effects of aging on primate physiology, reproduction, and behavior (see also Harrod and Willett, this volume).

Aging research of all kinds will be of ever-increasing utility as the world's human elderly population continues to grow (He, Goodkind, and Kowal 2016). Research on aging in non-human primates can serve as a valuable counterpoint, as many of the changes associated with human aging are mirrored in non-human primates, while dissimilarities help reveal important differences in our evolutionary trajectories. Insights learned from primate aging research can be applied for the benefit of our own species as well as for the care of aged primates in captivity. However, in an era when a striking number of primates are under threat of extinction (Estrada et al. 2017), many wild primate populations may disappear before we are able to glean all we can about these species to whom we are so closely related.

Acknowledgments

I thank the editors, Britteny Howell and Ryan Harrod, for the opportunity to contribute to this volume and for their excellent comments that helped improve the manuscript. I also thank the reviewers for providing comments that increased the clarity of this work. For facilitating research that fostered my interest in aging and its effects on primate behavior and reproduction, I acknowledge the generous support of the American Museum of Natural History, the E.J. Noble Foundation, the Wildlife Conservation Society, and the St. Catherines Island Foundation and staff. During the research and writing of this chapter, support was received from California State University, Los Angeles (Office of Research, Scholarship and Creative Activities).

References

Alberts, Susan C., Jason C. Buchan, and Jeanne Altmann. 2006. "Sexual Selection in Wild Baboons: From Mating Opportunities to Paternity Success." *Animal Behaviour* 72(5): 1177–1196. https://doi.org/10.1016/j.anbehav.2006.05.001.

Alberts, Susan C., Jeanne Altmann, Diane K. Brockman, Marina Cords, Linda M. Fedigan, Anne Pusey, Tara S. Stoinski, Karen B. Strier, William F. Morris, and Anne M. Bronikowski. 2013. "Reproductive Aging Patterns in Primates Reveal that Humans are Distinct." *Proceedings of the National Academy of Sciences* 110(33): 13440–13445. https://doi.org/10.1073/pnas.1311857110.

Almeling, Laura, Holger Sennhenn-Reulen, Kurt Hammerschmidt, Alexandra M. Freund, and Julia Fischer. 2017. "Social Interactions and Activity Patterns of Old Barbary Macaques: Further Insights into the Foundations of Social Selectivity." *American Journal of Primatology* 79(11): e22711. https://doi.org/10.1002/ajp.22711.

Almeling, L., Kurt Hammerschmidt, Holger Sennhenn-Reulen, Alexandra M. Freund, and Julia Fischer. 2016. "Motivational Shifts in Aging Monkeys and the Origins of Social Selectivity." *Current Biology* 26(13): 1744–1749. https://doi.org/10.1016/j.cub.2016.04.066.

Altmann, Jeanne, Laurence Gesquiere, Jordi Galbany, Patrick O. Onyango, and Susan C. Alberts. 2010. "Life History Context of Reproductive Aging in a Wild Primate Model." *Annals of the New York Academy of Sciences* 1204(1): 127–138. https://doi.org/10.1111/j.1749-6632.2010.05531.x.

Atkins, Hannah M., Cynthia J. Willson, Marnie Silverstein, Matthew Jorgensen, Edison Floyd, Jay R. Kaplan, and Susan E. Appt. 2014. "Characterization of Ovarian Aging and Reproductive Senescence in Vervet Monkeys (*Chlorocebus aethiops sabaeus*)." *Comparative Medicine* 64(1): 55–62.

Beehner, Jacinta C., Laurence Gesquiere, Robert M. Seyfarth, Dorothy L. Cheney, Susan

C. Alberts, and Jeanne Altmann. 2009. "Testosterone Related to Age and Life-History Stages in Male Baboons and Geladas." *Hormones and Behavior* 56(4): 472–480. https://doi.org/10.1016/j.yhbeh.2009.08.005.

Bercovitch, Fred B., Anja Widdig, Andrea Trefilov, Matt J. Kessler, John D. Berard, Jörg Schmidtke, Peter Nürnberg, and Michael Krawczak. 2003. "A Longitudinal Study of Age-Specific Reproductive Output and Body Condition among Male Rhesus Macaques, *Macaca mulatta*." *Naturwissenschaften* 90(7): 309–312. https://doi.org/10.1007/s00114-003-0436-1.

Borries, C. 1988. "Patterns of Grandmaternal Behavior in Free-Ranging Hanuman Langurs (*Presbytis entellus*)." *Human Evolution* 3(4): 239–260. https://doi.org/10.1007/BF02435856.

Borries, Carola, and Andreas Koenig. 2008. "Reproductive and Behavioral Characteristics of Aging in Female Asian Colobines." In *Primate Reproductive Aging: Cross-Taxon Perspectives*, edited by Sylvia Atsalis, Susan W. Margulis, and Patrick R. Hof, 80–102. Basel: S. Karger AG. https://doi.org/10.1159/000137686.

Borries, Carola, Volker Sommer, and Arun Srivastava. 1991. "Dominance, Age, Reproductive Success in Free-Ranging Female Hanuman Langurs (*Presbytis entellus*)." *International Journal of Primatology* 12(3): 231–257. https://doi.org/10.1007/BF02547586.

Bribiescas, Richard G. 2006. "On the Evolution, Life History, and Proximate Mechanisms of Human Male Reproductive Senescence." *Evolutionary Anthropology* 15(4): 132–141. https://doi.org/10.1002/evan.20087.

Bribiescas, Richard G. 2010. "An Evolutionary and Life History Perspective on Human Male Reproductive Senescence." *Annals of the New York Academy of Sciences* 1204: 54–64. https://doi.org/10.1111/j.1749-6632.2010.05524.x.

Broekmans, Frank J., Erik A. H. Knauff, Egbert R. te Velde, Nick S. Macklon, and Bart C. Fauser. 2007. "Female Reproductive Ageing: Current Knowledge and Future Trends." *Trends in Endocrinology and Metabolism* 18(2): 58–65. https://doi.org/10.1016/j.tem.2007.01.004.

Caro, T. M., D. W. Sellen, A. Parish, R. Frank, D. M. Brown, E. Voland, and M. Borgerhoff Mulder. 1995. "Termination of Reproduction in Nonhuman and Human Female Primates." *International Journal of Primatology* 16(2): 205–220. https://doi.org/10.1007/BF02735478.

Chapais, Bernard, Carole Gauthier, Jean Prud'Homme, and Paul Vasey. 1997. "Relatedness Threshold for Nepotism in Japanese Macaques." *Animal Behaviour* 53(5): 1089–1101. https://doi.org/10.1006/anbe.1996.0365.

Charpentier, M.J.E., L. Givalois, C. Faurie, O. Soghessa, F. Simon, and P. M. Kappeler. 2018. "Seasonal Glucocorticoid Production Correlates with a Suite of Small-Magnitude Environmental, Demographic, and Physiological Effects in Mandrills." *American Journal of Physical Anthropology* 165(1): 20–33. https://doi.org/10.1002/ajpa.23329.

Cords, Marina, and Shahrina Chowdhury. 2010. "Life History of *Cercopithecus mitis stuhlmanni* in the Kakamega Forest, Kenya." *International Journal of Primatology* 31(3): 433–455. https://doi.org/10.1007/s10764-010-9405-7.

Corr, Judith. 2003. "Social Behavior in Aged Rhesus Macaques." *Collegium Antropologicum* 27(1): 87–94.

Corr, Judith A., Leslee J. Martin, and Sarah T. Boysen. 2002. "Comparative Models of Cognitive Decline in Aging Great Apes." In *Aging in Nonhuman Primates*, edited by Joseph M. Erwin and Patrick R. Hof, 196–208. Basel: Karger.

Cuozzo, Frank P., and Michelle L. Sauther. 2006. "Severe Wear and Tooth Loss in Wild Ring-tailed Lemurs (*Lemur catta*): A Function of Feeding Ecology, Dental Structure, and Individual Life History." *Journal of Human Evolution* 51(5): 490–505. https://doi.org/10.1016/j.jhevol.2006.07.001.

Cuozzo, Frank P., Michelle L. Sauther, Lisa Gould, Robert W. Sussman, Lynne M. Villers, and Cheryl Lent. 2010. "Variation in Dental Wear and Tooth Loss among Known-Aged, Older Ring-tailed Lemurs (*Lemur catta*): A Comparison between Wild and Captive Individuals." *American Journal of Primatology* 72(11): 1026–1037. https://doi.org/10.1002/ajp.20846.

Dixson, Alan F. 2012. *Primate Sexuality: Comparative Studies of the Prosimians, Monkeys, Apes, and Human Beings*, 2nd ed. Oxford: Oxford University Press. https://doi.org/10.1093/acprof:osobl/9780199544646.001.0001.

Dubuc, Constance, Angelina Ruiz-Lambides, and Anja Widdig. 2014. "Variance in Male Lifetime Reproductive Success and Estimation of the Degree of Polygyny in a Primate." *Behavioral Ecology* 25(4): 878–889. https://doi.org/10.1093/beheco/aru052.

Ellis, Samuel, Daniel W. Franks, Stuart Nattrass, Michael A. Cant, Destiny L. Bradley, Deborah Giles, Kenneth C. Balcomb, and Darren P. Croft. 2018. "Postreproductive Lifespans Are Rare in Mammals." *Ecology and Evolution* 8(5): 2482–2494. https://doi.org/10.1002/ece3.3856.

Emery Thompson, Melissa, Alexandra G. Rosati, and Noah Snyder-Mackler. 2020. "Insights from Evolutionarily Relevant Models for Human Ageing." *Philosophical Transactions of the Royal Society B* 375(1811): 20190605. https://doi.org/10.1098/rstb.2019.0605.

Emery Thompson, Melissa, James H. Jones, Anne E. Pusey, Stella Brewer-Marsden, Jane Goodall, David Marsden, Tetsuro Matsuzawa, et al. 2007. "Aging and Fertility Patterns in Wild Chimpanzees Provide Insights into the Evolution of Menopause." *Current Biology* 17(24): 2150–2156. https://doi.org/10.1016/j.cub.2007.11.033.

Emery Thompson, Melissa, Stephanie A. Fox, Andreas Berghänel, Kris H. Sabbi, Sarah Phillips-Garcia, Drew K. Enigk, Emily Otali, Zarin P. Machanda, Richard W. Wrangham, and Martin N. Muller. 2020. "Wild Chimpanzees Exhibit Humanlike Aging of Glucocorticoid Regulation." *Proceedings of the National Academy of Sciences* 117(15): 8424–8430. https://doi.org/10.1073/pnas.1920593117.

Erwin, Joseph M., and Patrick R. Hof, eds. 2002. *Aging in Nonhuman Primates*. Basel: Karger.

Erwin, Joseph M., and Patrick R. Hof. 2008. "Menopause and Reproductive Senescence in Comparative Context." In *Primate Reproductive Aging: Cross-Taxon Perspectives*, edited by Sylvia Atsalis, Susan W. Margulis, and Patrick R. Hof, 4–16. Basel: S. Karger AG.

Estrada, Alejandro, Paul A. Garber, Anthony B. Rylands, Christian Roos, Eduardo Fernandez-Duque, Anthony Di Fiore, K. Anne-Isola Nekaris, et al. 2017. "Impending Extinction Crisis of the World's Primates: Why Primates Matter." *Science Advances* 3(1): e1600946. https://doi.org/10.1126/sciadv.1600946.

Fedigan, Linda Marie, and Mary S. M. Pavelka. 2011. "Menopause: Interspecific Comparisons of Reproductive Termination in Female Primates." In *Primates in Perspective*, 2nd ed., edited by Christina J. Campbell, Agustín Fuentes, Katherine C. MacKinnon, Simon K. Bearder, and Rebecca M. Stumpf, 488–498. New York: Oxford University Press.

Gagliardi, Christine, John R. Liukkonen, Kathrine M. Phillippi-Falkenstein, Richard M. Harrison, and H. Michael Kubisch. 2007. "Age as a Determinant of Reproductive Success among Captive Female Rhesus Macaques (*Macaca mulatta*)." *Reproduction* 133(4): 819–826. https://doi.org/10.1530/REP-06-0323.

Gilardi, Kirsten V. K., Susan E. Shideler, Celia R. Valverde, Jeffrey A. Roberts, and Bill L. Lasley. 1997. "Characterization of the Onset of Menopause in the Rhesus Macaque." *Biology of Reproduction* 57(2): 335–340. https://doi.org/10.1095/biolreprod57.2.335.

Gould, Lisa, R. W. Sussman, and Michelle L. Sauther. 2003. "Demographic and Life-History Patterns in a Population of Ring-tailed Lemurs (*Lemur catta*) at Beza Mahafaly Reserve, Madagascar: A 15-Year Perspective." *American Journal of Physical Anthropology* 120(2): 182–194. https://doi.org/10.1002/ajpa.10151.

Graham, Charles E., O. Ray Kling, and Robert A. Steiner. 1979. "Reproductive Senescence in Female Nonhuman Primates." In *Aging in Nonhuman Primates*, edited by Douglas M. Bowden, 183–202. New York: Van Nostrand Reinhold Company.

Hawkes, Kristen. 2003. "Grandmothers and the Evolution of Human Longevity." *American Journal of Human Biology* 15(3): 380–400. https://doi.org/10.1002/ajhb.10156.

He, Wan, Daniel Goodkind, and Paul Kowal. 2016. "An Aging World: 2015." U.S. Census Bureau, International Population Reports, P95/16–1. Washington, DC: U.S. Government Publishing Office.

Hernández-López, Leonor, Ana L. Cerda-Molina, Guillermo Díaz-Díaz, Roberto Chavira-Bolaños, and Ricardo Mondragón-Ceballos. 2012. "Aging-Related Reproductive Decline in the Male Spider Monkey (*Ateles geoffroyi*)." *Journal of Medical Primatology* 41(2): 115–121. https://doi.org/10.1111/j.1600-0684.2011.00528.x.

Hoffman, Christy L., James P. Higham, Adaris Mass-Rivera, James E. Ayala, and Dario Maestripieri. 2010. "Terminal Investment and Senescence in Rhesus Macaques (*Macaca mulatta*) on Cayo Santiago." *Behavioral Ecology* 21(5): 972–978. https://doi.org/10.1093/beheco/arq098.

Hrdy, Sarah Blaffer. 1981. "'Nepotists' and 'Altruists': The Behavior of Old Females among Macaques and Langur Monkeys." In *Other Ways of Growing Old*, edited by Pamela T. Amoss and Stevan Harrell, 59–76. Stanford, CA: Stanford University Press.

Huffman, Michael A. 1990. "Some Socio-Behavioral Manifestations of Old Age." In *The Chimpanzees of the Mahale Mountains: Sexual and Life History Strategies*, edited by Toshisada Nishida, 237–255. Tokyo: University of Tokyo Press.

Huffman, Michael A., and Yukio Takahata. 2012. "Long-Term Trends in the Mating Relationships of Japanese Macaques at Arashiyama, Japan." In *The Monkeys of Stormy Mountain: 60 Years of Primatological Research on the Japanese Macaques of Arashiyama*, edited by Jean-Baptiste Leca, Michael A. Huffman, and Paul L. Vasey, 71–86. Cambridge: Cambridge University Press.

Ichino, Shinichiro, Takayo Soma, Naomi Miyamoto, Kaoru Chatani, Hiroki Sato, Naoki Koyama, and Yukio Takahata. 2015. "Lifespan and Reproductive Senescence in a Free-Ranging Ring-tailed Lemur (*Lemur catta*) Population at Berenty, Madagascar." *Folia Primatologica* 86(1–2): 134–139. https://doi.org/10.1159/000368670.

Johnson, Rodney L., and Ellen Kapsalis. 1998. "Menopause in Free-Ranging Rhesus Macaques: Estimated Incidence, Relation to Body Condition, and Adaptive Significance." *International Journal of Primatology* 19(4): 751–765. https://doi.org/10.1023/A:1020333110918.

Johnstone, Rufus A., and Michael A. Cant. 2019. "Evolution of Menopause." *Current Biology* 29(4): R112–R115. https://doi.org/10.1016/j.cub.2018.12.048.

Kappeler, Peter M., and David P. Watts., eds. 2012. *Long-Term Field Studies of Primates*. Berlin: Springer. https://doi.org/10.1007/978-3-642-22514-7.

King, Stephen J., Summer J. Arrigo-Nelson, Sharon T. Pochron, Gina M. Semprebon, Laurie

R. Godfrey, Patricia C. Wright, and Jukka Jernvall. 2005. "Dental Senescence in a Long-Lived Primate Links Infant Survival to Rainfall." *Proceedings of the National Academy of Sciences* 102(46): 16579–16583. https://doi.org/10.1073/pnas.0508377102.

Koyama, Naoki, Masayuki Nakamichi, Ryo Oda, Naomi Miyamoto, Shinichiro Ichino, and Yukio Takahata. 2001. "A Ten-Year Summary of Reproductive Parameters for Ring-tailed Lemurs at Berenty, Madagascar." *Primates* 42(1): 1–14. https://doi.org/10.1007/BF02640684.

Koyama, Naoki, Yukio Takahata, Michael A. Huffman, Koshi Norikoshi, and Hisayo Suzuki. 1992. "Reproductive Parameters of Female Japanese Macaques: Thirty Years Data from the Arashiyama Troops, Japan." *Primates* 33(1): 33–47. https://doi.org/10.1007/BF02382761.

Languille, S., S. Blanc, O. Blin, C. I. Canale, A. Dal-Pan, G. Devau, M. Dhenain, et al. 2012. "The Grey Mouse Lemur: A Non-Human Primate Model for Ageing Studies." *Ageing Research Reviews* 11(1): 150–162. https://doi.org/10.1016/j.arr.2011.07.001.

Lee, Hillary C., and Julie A. Teichroeb. 2016. "Partially Shared Consensus Decision Making and Distributed Leadership in Vervet Monkeys: Older Females Lead the Group to Forage." *American Journal of Physical Anthropology* 161(4): 580–590. https://doi.org/10.1002/ajpa.23058.

Leidy, L. E. 1994. "Biological Aspects of Menopause: Across the Lifespan." *Annual Review of Anthropology* 23: 231–253. https://doi.org/10.1146/annurev.an.23.100194.001311.

Leidy Sievert, Lynnette. 2001. "Aging and Reproductive Senescence." In *Reproductive Ecology and Human Evolution*, edited by Peter T. Ellison, 267–292. New York: Aldine de Gruyter.

———. 2014. "Anthropology and the Study of Menopause: Evolutionary, Developmental, and Comparative Perspectives." *Menopause* 21(10): 1151–1159. https://doi.org/10.1097/GME.0000000000000341.

Machanda, Zarin P., and Alexandra G. Rosati. 2020. "Shifting Sociality During Primate Ageing." *Philosophical Transactions of the Royal Society B: Biological Sciences* 375(1811): 20190620. https://doi.org/10.1098/rstb.2019.0620.

McGuire, Katie Marie. 2017. "The Social Behavior and Dynamics of Old Ring-Tailed Lemurs (*Lemur catta*) at the Duke Lemur Center." MA thesis, University of Colorado Boulder.

Milich, Krista M., Angelina Ruiz-Lambides, Elizabeth Maldonado, and Dario Maestripieri. 2020. "Age Negatively Impacts Reproduction in High-Ranking Male Rhesus Macaques on Cayo Santiago, Puerto Rico." *Scientific Reports* 10: 13044. https://doi.org/10.1038/s41598-020-69922-y.

Muller, Martin N. 2017. "Field Endocrinology of Nonhuman Primates and Humans." *Hormones and Behavior* 91: 36–51. https://doi.org/10.1016/j.yhbeh.2016.09.001.

Muller, Martin N., Melissa Emery Thompson, and Richard W. Wrangham. 2006. "Male Chimpanzees Prefer Mating with Old Females." *Current Biology* 16(22): 2234–2238. https://doi.org/10.1016/j.cub.2006.09.042.

Muller, Martin N., Nicholas G. Blurton Jones, Fernando Colchero, Melissa Emery Thompson, Drew K. Enigk, Joseph T. Feldblum, Beatrice H. Hahn, et al. 2020. "Sexual Dimorphism in Chimpanzee (*Pan troglodytes schweinfurthii*) and Human Age-Specific Fertility." *Journal of Human Evolution* 144: 102795. https://doi.org/10.1016/j.jhevol.2020.102795.

Nakamichi, Masayuki. 1984. "Behavioral Characteristics of Old Female Japanese Monkeys in a Free-Ranging Group." *Primates* 25(2): 192–203. https://doi.org/10.1007/BF02382391.

Nishida, Toshisada, Nadia Corp, Miya Hamai, Toshikazu Hasegawa, Mariko Hiraiwa-Hasegawa, Kazuhiko Hosaka, Kevin D. Hunt, et al. 2003. "Demography, Female Life History, and Reproductive Profiles among the Chimpanzees of Mahale." *American Journal of Primatology* 59(3): 99–121. https://doi.org/10.1002/ajp.10068.

Nozaki, Masumi, Fusako Mitsunaga, and Keiko Shimizu. 1995. "Reproductive Senescence in Female Japanese Monkeys (*Macaca fuscata*): Age- and Season-Related Changes in Hypothalamic-Pituitary-Ovarian Functions and Fecundity Rates." *Biology of Reproduction* 52(6): 1250–1257. https://doi.org/10.1095/biolreprod52.6.1250.

Oelze, Vicky M., Alice M. Percher, Gontran Nsi Akoué, Nory El Ksabi, Eric Willaume, and Marie J. E. Charpentier. 2020. "Seasonality and Interindividual Variation in Mandrill Feeding Ecology Revealed by Stable Isotope Analyses of Hair and Blood." *American Journal of Primatology* 82(12): e23206. https://doi.org/10.1002/ajp.23206.

Overdorff, Deborah J., Adina M. Merenlender, Pierre Talata, Albert Telo, and Zoe A. Forward. 1999. "Life History of *Eulemur fulvus rufus* from 1988–1998 in Southeastern Madagascar." *American Journal of Physical Anthropology* 108(3): 295–310. https://doi.org/10.1002/(SICI)1096-8644(199903)108:3<295::AID-AJPA5>3.0.CO;2-Q.

Packer, C., Marc Tatar, and Anthony Collins. 1998. "Reproductive Cessation in Female Mammals." *Nature* 392(6678): 807–811. https://doi.org/10.1038/33910.

Parga, Joyce A. 2006. "Male Mate Choice in *Lemur catta*." *International Journal of Primatology* 27(1): 107–131. https://doi.org/10.1007/s10764-005-9006-z.

———. 2013. "Male Reproductive Senescence in the Ring-Tailed Lemur (*Lemur catta*)." *American Journal of Physical Anthropology* 150(S56): 216. https://doi.org/10.1002/ajpa.22247.

Parga, Joyce A., and Robert G. Lessnau. 2005. "Female Age-Specific Reproductive Rates, Birth Seasonality, and Infant Mortality of Ring-tailed Lemurs on St. Catherines Island: 17-year Reproductive History of a Free-Ranging Colony." *Zoo Biology* 24(4): 295–309. https://doi.org/10.1002/zoo.20062.

Pavelka, Mary S. McDonald. 1990. "Do Old Female Monkeys Have a Specific Social Role?" *Primates* 31(3): 363–373. https://doi.org/10.1007/BF02381107.

———. 1991. "Sociability in Old Female Japanese Monkeys: Human versus Nonhuman Primate Aging." *American Anthropologist* 93(3): 588–598. https://doi.org/10.1525/aa.1991.93.3.02a00030.

Pavelka, Mary S. M., and Linda Marie Fedigan. 1991. "Menopause: A Comparative Life History Perspective." *Yearbook of Physical Anthropology* 34: 13–38. https://doi.org/10.1002/ajpa.1330340604.

Pavelka, Mary S. McDonald, and Linda Marie Fedigan. 1999. "Reproductive Termination in Female Japanese Monkeys: A Comparative Life History Perspective." *American Journal of Physical Anthropology* 109(4): 455–464. https://doi.org/10.1002/(SICI)1096-8644(199908)109:4<455::AID-AJPA3>3.0.CO;2-Z.

Pavelka, Mary S. MacDonald, Linda M. Fedigan, and Sandra Zohar. 2002. "Availability and Adaptive Value of Reproductive and Postreproductive Japanese Macaque Mothers and Grandmothers." *Animal Behaviour* 64(3): 407–414. https://doi.org/10.1006/anbe.2002.3085.

Pavelka, Mary S. M., Lauren J. N. Brent, D. P. Croft, and Linda M. Fedigan. 2018. "Post-Fertile Lifespan in Female Primates and Cetaceans." In *Primate Life Histories, Sex Roles, and Adaptability: Essays in Honour of Linda M. Fedigan*, edited by Urs Kalbitzer and Katharine M. Jack, 37–55. Cham: Springer. https://doi.org/10.1007/978-3-319-98285-4_3.

Peccei, Jocelyn Scott. 2001. "Menopause: Adaptation or Epiphenomenon?" *Evolutionary Anthropology* 10(2): 43–57. https://doi.org/10.1002/evan.1013.

Phoenix, C. H., and K. C. Chambers. 1982. "Sexual Behavior in Aging Male Rhesus Monkeys." In *Advanced Views in Primate Biology*, edited by A. B. Chiarelli and R. S. Corruccini, 95–104. Berlin: Springer-Verlag. https://doi.org/10.1007/978-3-642-68300-8_8.

Picq, Jean-Luc. 1992. "Aging and Social Behaviour in Captivity in *Microcebus murinus*." *Folia Primatologica* 59(4): 217–220. https://doi.org/10.1159/000156664.

Pochron, Sharon T., W. Troy Tucker, and Patricia C. Wright. 2004. "Demography, Life History, and Social Structure in *Propithecus diadema edwardsi* from 1986–2000 in Ranomafana National Park, Madagascar." *American Journal of Physical Anthropology* 125(1): 61–72. https://doi.org/10.1002/ajpa.10266.

Pusey, Anne. 2012. "Magnitude and Sources of Variation in Female Reproductive Performance." In *The Evolution of Primate Societies*, edited by John C. Mitani, Josep Call, Peter M. Kappeler, Ryne A. Palombit, and Joan B. Silk, 343–366. Chicago: University of Chicago Press.

Raño, Mariana, Claudia R. Valeggia, and Martin M. Kowalewski. 2018. "Aged Black-and-Gold Howler Monkey Female (*Alouatta caraya*): A Sign of Reproductive Senescence?" *Folia Primatologica* 89(2): 101–110. https://doi.org/10.1159/000485975.

Richard, Alison F., Robert E. Dewar, Marion Schwartz, and Joelisoa Ratsirarson. 2002. "Life in the Slow Lane? Demography and Life Histories of Male and Female Sifaka (*Propithecus verreauxi verreauxi*)." *Journal of Zoology* 256(4): 421–436. https://doi.org/10.1017/S0952836902000468.

Robbins, Andrew M., Martha M. Robbins, Netzin Gerald-Steklis, and H. Dieter Steklis. 2006. "Age-Related Patterns of Reproductive Success among Female Mountain Gorillas." *American Journal of Physical Anthropology* 131(4): 511–521. https://doi.org/10.1002/ajpa.20474.

Robinson, J. A., G. Scheffler, S. G. Eisele, and R. W. Goy. 1975. "Effects of Age and Season on Sexual Behavior and Plasma Testosterone and Dihydrotestosterone Concentrations of Laboratory-Housed Male Rhesus Monkeys (*Macaca mulatta*)." *Biology of Reproduction* 13(2): 203–210. https://doi.org/10.1095/biolreprod13.2.203.

Roof, Katherine A., William D. Hopkins, M. Kay Izard, Michelle Hook, and Steven J. Schapiro. 2005. "Maternal Age, Parity, and Reproductive Outcome in Captive Chimpanzees (*Pan troglodytes*)." *American Journal of Primatology* 67(2): 199–207. https://doi.org/10.1002/ajp.20177.

Sapolsky, Robert M., and Jeanne Altmann. 1991. "Incidence of Hypercortisolism and Dexamethasone Resistance Increases with Age among Wild Baboons." *Biological Psychiatry* 30(10): 1008–1016. https://doi.org/10.1016/0006-3223(91)90121-2.

Sauther, Michelle L., R. W. Sussman, and F. Cuozzo. 2002. "Dental and General Health in a Population of Wild Ring-tailed Lemurs: A Life History Approach." *American Journal of Physical Anthropology* 117(2): 122–132. https://doi.org/10.1002/ajpa.10016.

Silk, Joan B., Cathleen B. Clark-Wheatley, Peter S. Rodman, and Amy Samuels. 1981. "Differential Reproductive Success and Facultative Adjustment of Sex Ratios among Captive Female Bonnet Macaques (*Macaca radiata*)." *Animal Behaviour* 29(4): 1106–1120. https://doi.org/10.1016/S0003-3472(81)80063-2.

Smucny, Darlene A., David H. Abbott, Keith G. Mansfield, Nancy J. Schultz-Darken, M. Emilia Yamamoto, Anuska Irene Alencar, and Suzette D. Tardif. 2004. "Reproductive Output, Maternal Age, and Survivorship in Captive Common Marmoset Females (*Cal-

lithrix jacchus)." *American Journal of Primatology* 64(1): 107–121. https://doi.org/10.1002/ajp.20065.

Soma, Takayo, and Naoki Koyama. 2013. "Eviction and Troop Reconstruction in a Single Matriline of Ring-tailed Lemurs (*Lemur catta*): What Happened When 'Grandmother' Died?" In *Leaping Ahead: Advances in Prosimian Biology*, edited by Judith Masters, Marco Gamba, and Fabien Génin, 137–146. New York: Springer. https://doi.org/10.1007/978-1-4614-4511-1_16.

Sommer, Volker, Arun Srivastava, and Carola Borries. 1992. "Cycles, Sexuality, and Conception in Free-Ranging Langurs (*Presbytis entellus*)." *American Journal of Primatology* 28(1): 1–27. https://doi.org/10.1002/ajp.1350280102.

Soules, Michael R., Sherry Sherman, Estella Parrott, Robert Rebar, Nanette Santoro, Wulf Utian, and Nancy Woods. 2001. "Stages of Reproductive Aging Workshop (STRAW)." *Journal of Women's Health & Gender-Based Medicine* 10(9): 843–848. https://doi.org/10.1089/152460901753285732.

Takahata, Yukio, Naoki Koyama, and Shigeru Suzuki. 1995. "Do the Old Aged Females Experience a Long Post-Reproductive Life Span?: The Cases of Japanese Macaques and Chimpanzees." *Primates* 36(2): 169–180. https://doi.org/10.1007/BF02381343.

Tardif, Suzette D. 2019. "Marmosets as a Translational Aging Model—Introduction." *American Journal of Primatology* 81(2): e22912. https://doi.org/10.1002/ajp.22912.

Tardif, S. D., and T. E. Ziegler. 1992. "Features of Female Reproductive Senescence in Tamarins (*Saguinus* spp.), a New World Primate." *Journal of Reproduction & Fertility* 94(2): 411–421. https://doi.org/10.1530/jrf.0.0940411.

Tardif, Suzette D., Arrilton Araujo, M. Fatima Arruda, Jeffrey A. French, M. Bernardete C. Sousa, and M. Emilia Yamamoto. 2008. "Reproduction and Aging in Marmosets and Tamarins." In *Primate Reproductive Aging: Cross-Taxon Perspectives*, edited by Sylvia Atsalis, Susan W. Margulis, and Patrick R. Hof, 29–48. Basel: S. Karger AG.

Tarou, Loraine R., Mollie A. Bloomsmith, Michael P. Hoff, Joseph M. Erwin, and Terry L. Maple. 2002. "The Behavior of Aged Great Apes." In *Aging in Nonhuman Primates*, edited by Joseph M. Erwin and Patrick R. Hof, 209–231. Basel: Karger.

Taylor, L. L. 1998a. "Behavior and Reproduction in Aged Lemurs." *American Journal of Physical Anthropology* 105(S26): 217. https://doi.org/10.1002/(SICI)1096-8644(1998)26+<207::AID-AJPA18>3.0.CO;2-Y.

———. 1998b. "Social Isolation and Aged Lemurs." *American Journal of Primatology* 45(2): 210–211. https://doi.org/10.1002/(SICI)1098-2345(1998)45:2<209::AID-AJP8>3.0.CO;2-%23.

———. 2000. "Social Behavior of Aged Lemurs." *American Journal of Physical Anthropology* 111(S30): 300. https://doi.org/10.1002/(SICI)1096-8644(2000)111:30+<282::AID-AJPA19>3.0.CO;2-N.

Taylor, Linda. 2008. "Old Lemurs: Preliminary Data on Behavior and Reproduction from the Duke University Primate Center." In *Elwyn Simons: A Search for Origins*, edited by John G. Fleagle and Christopher C. Gilbert, 319–334. New York: Springer.

Terrien, J., M. Perret, and F. Aujard. 2010. "Gender Markedly Modulates Behavioral Thermoregulation in a Non-Human Primate Species, the Mouse Lemur (*Microcebus murinus*)." *Physiology & Behavior* 101(4): 469–473. https://doi.org/10.1016/j.physbeh.2010.07.012.

Thomas, Gregg W. C., Richard J. Wang, Arthi Puri, R. Alan Harris, Muthuswamy Raveendran, Daniel S. T. Hughes, Shwetha C. Murali, et al. 2018. "Reproductive Longevity Predicts Mutation Rates in Primates." *Current Biology* 28(19): 3193–3197.e1-e5 https://doi.org/10.1016/j.cub.2018.08.050.

Tidière, Morgane, Xavier Thevenot, Adamantia Deligiannopoulou, Guillaume Douay, Mylisa Whipple, Aurélie Siberchicot, Jean-Michel Gaillard, and Jean-François Lemaître. 2018. "Maternal Reproductive Senescence Shapes the Fitness Consequences of the Parental Age Difference in Ruffed Lemurs." *Proceedings of the Royal Society B: Biological Sciences* 285(1886): 20181479. https://doi.org/10.1098/rspb.2018.1479.

van Noordwijk, Maria A., and Carel P. van Schaik. 1987. "Competition among Female Long-tailed Macaques, *Macaca fascicularis*." *Animal Behaviour* 35(2): 577–589. https://doi.org/10.1016/S0003-3472(87)80284-1.

Veenema, H. C., B. M. Spruijt, W. H. Gispen, and J.A.R.A.M. van Hooff. 1997. "Aging, Dominance History, and Social Behavior in Java-Monkeys (*Macaca fascicularis*)." *Neurobiology of Aging* 18(5): 509–515. https://doi.org/10.1016/S0197-4580(97)00107-3.

Venn, Oliver, Isaac Turner, Iain Mathieson, Natasja de Groot, Ronald Bontrop, and Gil McVean. 2014. "Strong Male Bias Drives Germline Mutation in Chimpanzees." *Science* 344(6189): 1272–1275. https://doi.org/10.1126/science.344.6189.1272.

Videan, Elaine N., Jo Fritz, Christopher B. Heward, and James Murphy. 2006. "The Effects of Aging on Hormone and Reproductive Cycles in Female Chimpanzees (*Pan troglodytes*)." *Comparative Medicine* 56(4): 291–299.

Walker, Margaret L., and James G. Herndon. 2008. "Menopause in Nonhuman Primates?" *Biology of Reproduction* 79(3): 398–406. https://doi.org/10.1095/biolreprod.108.068536.

Wang, Richard J., Gregg W. C. Thomas, Muthuswamy Raveendran, R. Alan Harris, Harshavardhan Doddapaneni, Donna M. Muzny, John P. Capitanio, Predrag Radivojac, Jeffrey Rogers, and Matthew W. Hahn. 2020. "Paternal Age in Rhesus Macaques is Positively Associated with Germline Mutation Accumulation but Not with Measures of Offspring Sociability." *Genome Research* 30(6): 826–834. https://doi.org/10.1101/gr.255174.119.

Wright, Patricia, Stephen J. King, Andrea Baden, and Jukka Jernvall. 2008. "Aging in Wild Female Lemurs: Sustained Fertility with Increased Infant Mortality." In *Primate Reproductive Aging: Cross-Taxon Perspectives*, edited by Sylvia Atsalis, Susan W. Margulis, and Patrick R. Hof, 17–28. Basel: S. Karger AG.

Wroblewski, Emily E., Carson M. Murray, Brandon F. Keele, Joann C. Schumacher-Stankey, Beatrice H. Hahn, and Anne E. Pusey. 2009. "Male Dominance Rank and Reproductive Success in Chimpanzees, *Pan troglodytes schweinfurthii*." *Animal Behaviour* 77(4): 873–885. https://doi.org/10.1016/j.anbehav.2008.12.014.

3

Human Adaptability to Age-Related Biological Changes

RYAN P. HARROD AND ALYSSA WILLETT

Humans experience an inevitable process of physiological change as they get older. Rockstein (1968, 124) states that "the process of aging is a universal phenomenon. That is to say, cats or dogs or horses or rabbits all grow old in a similar way, so that an old dog has graying hair, may even develop cataracts, and shows slow decline in muscular reaction, as well as in nervous function." However, the biology of human aging is a complex process, and its precise nature is still not well understood and is continually debated among researchers in different academic disciplines. In the last half decade, there have been numerous articles published in the disciplines of anthropology (Chmielewski 2017; Bribiescas 2020), biochemistry (Hartl 2016; Dodig et al. 2019; Stenvinkel and Shiels 2019), cellular biology (McHugh and Gil 2018; Schmeer et al. 2019; Son and Lee 2019), epigenetics and genetics (Wagner 2019; Reynolds et al. 2020), and zoology (Pandit et al. 2016; Thompson et al. 2020), trying to identify the causes and processes of aging and senescence.

In this chapter, we will briefly summarize common biological changes, consider how the human experience of aging is a biocultural experience, and highlight how health and wellness practices allowed humans to adapt to, and mitigate against, age-related degeneration. While we cannot consider the full spectrum of the biological changes associated with human aging in this chapter, our primary focus is on changes that can be inferred from the analysis of human skeletal remains. The intent is to emphasize how cultural adaptations to biological aging have been customary throughout human history by comparing evidence of past approaches of mitigating the effects of aging with current approaches.

The Biology of Aging

Defined in the introduction to this volume, the term "senescence," while often used interchangeably with "aging," is actually a distinct biological process (Adams 1969; Rose 1991; Rosen et al. 1999; Crews 2003). Given that the focus of this chapter is on human cultural adaptations to bodily changes associated with growing older, we have opted to focus primarily on the concept of aging. Crews defines aging as the "passage of time" (2007, 367) that includes the "social, behavioral, cultural, lifestyle, and biological changes that occur as individuals grow older in a particular social setting" (2003, 5). Ongoing research on cellular senescence continues to reveal that senescent cells have variable effects and developmental onset depending on the organ in which they are found (Adams 1969; Herranz and Gil 2018). While the causal relationship is still debated, cellular senescence is crucial for understanding the biological processes behind neurological decline, loss of musculoskeletal function, organ failure, cardiovascular disease, and a compromised immune system (McHugh and Gil 2018). However, Adams (1969, 1240) has argued that we can really only perceive the changes related to senescence when multiple changes occur in the body that are indicative of getting older (gray hair, wrinkled skin [see Norton, this volume], the non-traumatic loss of teeth, or the development of arthritis), some of which we can see on the bones.

Common Biological Changes

As humans age, they are at higher risk for developing what researchers have called age-related diseases and geriatric syndromes, or a group of medical conditions that older adults are at more risk of developing (Flacker 2003; Rikkert et al. 2003; Inouye et al. 2007; Kane et al. 2012; Franceschi et al. 2018). Rikkert and colleagues (2003, 84) compare the meaning of the terms "syndrome" and "disease," with the former associated with an unknown and the latter with a known cause, and argue that these syndromes are not as clearly defined as other medical conditions. Franceschi and colleagues (2018) suggest that many age-related diseases are also unknown and that the distinction between them and a syndrome, while distinct from a medical perspective, is ambiguous as they are both the result of age-related changes. Scholars have argued that improving medical treatment has led to an increase in medical conditions in general as people live longer (see Crews 2005 for an in-depth discussion of this trend). However, a longitudinal analysis of aging between 1990 and 2010 found that people in Jerusalem were living longer but the onset of age-related medical conditions was delayed by more than a decade, suggesting that a longer life is not directly associated with poor health (Jacobs et al. 2012). However, the experience of aging is not the same for all individuals, as studies that consider lower socioeconomic status clearly demonstrate (Franse et al. 2017; Rausch et al. 2019).

Age-related conditions can include disorders such as anorexia and malnutrition (Landi et al. 2018), urinary incontinence (Lawhorne et al. 2008), impaired sleep (Dean et al. 2017), sarcopenia or progressive muscle loss (Cruz-Jentoft et al. 2010), dental problems (van der Putten et al. 2014), and delirium (Lauretani et al. 2020). The progressive loss of muscle mass and strength is correlated with disability and decreased quality of life. Injury or illness may be the impetus for decreased physical activity that leads to decreased muscle mass and strength, furthering inactivity and lessening independence (Santilli et al. 2014; Morais 2018). Medical conditions associated with aging often overlap with one or more medical conditions present in an individual. Casado (2012, 229) notes that the researchers working in the gerontological community did not consider falls "a medical problem until they were included in a list of geriatric syndromes," but the risk of falling is increased by reduced muscle mass (Yeung et al. 2019). Age-related medical conditions are related to the concept of frailty, which is an increased susceptibility to stress, reduced activity-levels, and body mass reduction (Fried et al. 2001; Fulop et al. 2010; Fedarko 2011).

Bioarchaeological Perspectives on Aging

We focus on bioarchaeological analyses of skeletal material because bones and teeth are typically all that remain from the bodies of people in past societies (Behrensmeyer and Hill 1980; Lyman 1994; Haglund and Sorg 1997). Mummified tissue can also shed light on the past, but this type of preservation is far less common (Aufderheide 2003). In bioarchaeology, researchers try to determine the cause of changes to the skeleton by assessing age, sex, known or suggested occupation, or the presence of a disease like diffuse idiopathic skeletal hyperostosis (DISH) (Burt et al. 2013; Cawley and Paine 2015; Agarwal 2019). Through differential diagnosis (Ortner 1991, 2012), several different categories of skeletal changes associated with aging populations have been identified, including osteoarthritis (OA) and rheumatoid arthritis (RA), joint disorders like *osteochondritis dissecans*, degenerative disc disease and other changes to the spine, or a general loss of bone density as with osteoporosis.

To differentiate how these skeletal changes might be related to aging, it is crucial to understand bone remodeling. Researchers have shown that the remodeling of the skeletal system changes through the lifetime, with a decline in bone formation as we age (Marks and Hermey 1996; Marks and Odgren 2002). The relationship between changes in the muscles and bone remodeling is complex, involving mechanical forces and the endocrine system (Karsenty 2012; Brotto and Bonewald 2015); nevertheless, these are clearly interconnected systems. For example, the geriatric syndrome of sarcopenia has been closely associated with the development of OA and osteoporosis (Milte and Crotty 2014; Locquet et al. 2019; O'Brien and McDougall 2019). Additionally, O'Brien and McDougall (2019) show a reciprocal relationship between frailty and OA, with frailty being a risk factor for OA, but OA may also increase the likelihood of frailty. The pathway between geriatric syndromes and skeletal pathology may not necessarily be causal, however, which may be the case for an individual who has both sarcopenia and osteomalacia. Osteomalacia (increased softening of the bone) is associated with vitamin D deficiency and overall malnutrition, but a reduction in vitamin D can also occur as we age, and can lead to sarcopenia (Uchitomi et al. 2020). Clearly, these are complicated processes.

Other limitations researchers face include identifying when past peoples experienced an event, correlating the skeletal indicator of disease or trauma with a particular etiology, and determining whether the state of the bones means the person was healthy or not (Wood et al. 1992; Wright and Yoder 2003; DeWitte and Stojanowski 2015; McFadden and Oxenham 2020). For example, as we age we are at increased risk for gait disorders and associated falls (Blake et al. 1988). The Centers for Disease Control (CDC) in 2018 indicated that over 27 percent of adults over the age of 65 had reported falling one time or more, totaling more than 35 million falls (Moreland et al. 2020). Yet falls also occur as a result of a range of accident-related and occupational activities (Kemmlert and Lundholm 2001). The problem with associating aging with trauma is that in general people are more likely to have traumatic injuries over the life span. Being older may not be the reason you have higher rates of trauma. It is possible that living an active life was the culprit.

Osteoporosis and OA are often associated with age, but they both can be the result of a number of other factors (Domett et al. 2017; Agarwal 2019). OA can also result from trauma, certain genetics, nutritional changes, and physical activity or lack thereof (Spector et al. 1996; Ghosh and Smith 2002; Berenbaum et al. 2018). Accepting that osteoporosis and OA are multifactorial, there is still a higher incidence and increased severity of these two skeletal changes with age (Anderson and Loeser 2010; Loeser 2017; O'Brien and McDougall 2019). OA is "often accepted as a part of getting older and as inevitably getting worse" (Hammond 2014, 1217).

While OA is a leading cause of pain and disability worldwide today (Neogi 2013; Hammond 2014), rheumatoid arthritis (RA) is an autoimmune disease that can lead to inflammation and muscle mass loss, which are different from the processes that cause sarcopenia (Hammond 2014). RA is not a medical condition associated with old age, but as it progresses in severity it is more likely to be visible on the skeleton on an older individual. It begins with soft tissue inflammation that progresses to deformed small joints that may then erode bony structures, eventually leading to dislocation, or fusion (Atchinson and Powers Dirette 2017, 432), which has also been studied in bioarchaeological contexts (Rothschild et al. 1992; Inoue et al. 1999; Biehler-Gomez and Cattaneo 2018).

Fragility-related fractures are injuries caused by trauma or disease, with osteoporosis and osteoarthritis as common contributing conditions (Atchinson and Powers Dirette 2017). Falls are the leading cause of fractures in older adults, with the most reported fractures being in the spine, hip, and distal portion of the forearm (Chung and Spilson 2001; Stubbs et al. 2014; Freire Junior et al. 2017). Other common fragility fractures in old age are injuries involving the hip joint, specifically breaks at the proximal end of the femur and involving the femoral neck or trochanters (Atchinson and Powers Dirette 2017). This is the most serious type of fracture for older adults, often leading to disability and death (Atchinson and Powers Dirette 2017). OA is a risk factor for fracture, and OA of the hip has the poorest outcome, often requiring surgical intervention within five years of onset (Hammond 2014). Brance and colleagues (2021) have found a correlation between RA and sarcopenia, and female patients that had both had higher rates of fragility-related fractures. Finally, the development of osteoporosis or generalized bone loss (NIH 2006) also increases the risk of fragility fractures (Agarwal 2019, 385). A person with osteoporosis may fracture a bone through normal movement, leading to decreased movement and further bone loss (NOF 2020).

Current and Past Health and Wellness Approaches to Aging

As we age and experience a higher likelihood of sarcopenia, osteoporosis, tooth loss, and traumatic injuries like fragility fractures, humans are more likely to need additional support from family or community members to maintain daily activity levels, acquire proper nutrition, treat illness, and heal from injuries. However, every individual ages differently, and self-care should not be underestimated. Kaufman (1994) has highlighted the balancing act that medical professionals, families, and older adults in the United States face when considering care while trying to prevent the loss of self-control and over-surveillance of their daily lives. To understand how humans help aging individuals with geriatric syndromes adapt, we will look to modern approaches from the discipline of occupational therapy.

Occupational therapy is focused on helping people do the tasks and activities (occupations) they need and want to do through adaptive, restorative, educational, and advocative approaches (Fisher 2013). According to the American Occupational Therapy Association (AOTA), adults face challenges related to continued engagement in desired activities as they age—for biological reasons such as dementia/cognitive decline, chronic conditions like diabetes or arthritis, vision impairment, changes in ability after stroke or heart disease, and general loss of strength and stamina (AOTA 2020). Occupational therapists work with older adults to find ways of being as independent as possible while still being safe by teaching adaptive strategies for activities of daily living (ADLs). Today's intervention programs focus on independence through community mobility (transportation), falls prevention, home modifications to support aging in place, and strategies for adjusting to changes in cognition and mental health later in life (AOTA 2020).

Within the field of occupational therapy, culture is thought of as the aspects of a person that comprise a client's identity, an integral part of understanding who a person is and how to interact with that client (Matuska and Barrett 2019). Client perceptions of age-related changes are influenced by culture, leading to reactions to age-related change that impact engagement in physical activity. Anthropological research has shown that cultural beliefs about age-related changes can shape responses in adaptive and maladaptive ways (see, for example, Howell and Bardach 2018). The behaviors aging adults acquire in response to biological changes can support or hinder functional health outcomes (Matuska and Barrett 2019).

Socioeconomic status may further impact the role of culture on age-related changes both today (see, for example, Franse et al. 2017) and in the past (see, for example, Yaussy 2019). Populations living in low-income, high-density, urban environments may experience difficulty engaging in certain activities. Older adults may be at increased risk in outdoor occupations such as taking a walk, due to exposure to environmental pollutants. They may feel unsafe as lone pedestrians, and unsafe sidewalks may increase the likelihood of falls (Huang et al. 2012; Kerr et al. 2012; Zandieh et al. 2016; Howell et al. 2020). Nutrition augmentation and physical activity are current intervention approaches used to manage and prevent sarcopenia, osteoporosis, and osteoarthritis (Santilli et al. 2014; Gutiérrez Robledo and Pérez-Zepeda 2018; Greco et al. 2019). Limited access to adequate nutrition, specifically vitamin D, and physical activity are among the social determinants of health that affect outcomes of individuals with, and at risk for, decreased muscle mass, strength, and skeletal frailty (Brennan Ramirez et al. 2008).

While the discipline of occupational therapy is relatively recent, humans have been practicing this type of healing for a long time as they cared for members of the community and even modified their "built environment" (Battles 2011, 111). These changes to community and landscape are key to the theory of occupational adaptation (Grajo et al. 2018; Grajo 2019). Occupational adaptation "is a product of engagement and participation in occupations; a transaction with the environment; a manner of responding to change, altered situations, and life transitions; and a manner of forming identity" (Grajo 2019, 634). Schkade and Schultz (1992, 831) describe the three elements of occupational adaptation: 1) the person "made up of three systems: sensorimotor, cognitive, and psychosocial"; 2) the occupational environment, which includes places where people "work, play and leisure, and self-maintenance"; and 3) the interaction between the person and their environment. Grajo (2019) states that occupational adaptation is a normative human process that happens when a person has the desire to master an occupation within a specified context—including physical, social, cultural, personal, temporal, and virtual contexts—in the face of an event that has disrupted that occupation. An event may be illness, injury, natural disaster, or violence that leads to a change in the ability of an individual or group of people to engage in chosen occupations that support health and well-being.

In this chapter, we focus on age-related processes and their impacts on individuals. For example, an aging individual could fall and fracture a hip or suffer a traumatic brain injury. This individual is a part of the community, with roles to fulfill and daily activities to complete that allow for participation and continuation of roles. The individual, with help and as a self-care process, will learn to adapt the way chosen occupations are done to continue participation in desired activities. The community might help by building a ramp in place of steps, creating an ambulatory device, and assisting with activities of daily living while the individual learns new ways to live. The aging individual will be influenced by their adaptive capacity, which can be thought of as tools in a toolbox related to physical, cognitive, and social capacities (Grajo 2019). Where an older individual may have less physical strength, he or she could rely on life experience, expertise, and social ties within the community. In a recent study, Toledano-González and colleagues (2019) found that occupational therapy on the group level had a positive effect on the well-being and self-efficacy of older adults, and we would argue that this same approach was taken in past cultures in the form of community-based approaches to aging. For example, Sneed (2020) notes the bioarchaeological evidence of age-related changes and loss of mobility as support for ways that the ancient Greeks considered disability when they developed ramps for accessibility in the healing sanctuaries.

Studies questioning how well people age have found that engaging in occupations, specifically participating in chosen and meaningful activities, is associated with longevity (Wright-St Clair et al. 2012). Types of occupations that people find meaningful can be influenced by aspects of their culture. A person from the United States, a largely individualistic culture, may find doing a handicraft independently meaningful, while an elder Maori person from a more collectivist culture might find connecting with family more meaningful than doing an activity independently (Hayman et al. 2012). Cultural diversity influences how one defines an occupation of deep purpose that promotes wellness; the key is choice and engagement in the chosen activity (Torres 2003; Wright-St Clair et al. 2012).

Self-care and caring for others are considered occupations that may be therapeutic in and of themselves (AOTA 2020). Self-care involves ensuring both bodily and mental health. Wilcock and Townsend (2019) find that health is supported and maintained when people can engage in a variety of occupations within the home, school, workplace, and community life. The model developed by Tilley (2015) called the "Bioarchaeology of Care" is useful for assessing family and community contributions in the past. While it varies cross-culturally in how it is expressed and why, depression is a growing problem for older adults who no longer find a sense of worth. The World Federation of Occupational Therapy declares that it is a human right for people to participate in a range of occupations that enable them to flourish (Townsend and Marval 2013). A person's understanding of health and engagement in health maintenance is shaped by the culture specific to that person, and health-related occupations are most effective when the activities are aligned with that person's culture (Cohn and Crepeau 2019; AOTA 2020). Occupations that lead to health and well-being are often tied to cultural identity and traditional practices of ritual and ceremony (Balick and Lee 2005; Gomes et al. 2011; Quinlan 2011). Ethnomedicine is a field focused on different societies' ideas of health and illness, and can be thought of as "one's culture of medicine" (Quinlan 2011, 381). The field of ethnomedicine can help trace how people used medicine in the past to treat age-related changes, as well as how traditional medicine is currently used to treat some age-related changes like arthritis (Gomes et al. 2011; Yu et al. 2016; Lardjam et al. 2018; Savinaya et al. 2019; Babu et al. 2020).

A History of Treating the Aging Body

Cultural adaptation to, and mitigation against, the decline in health and the development of cognitive, musculoskeletal, and nutritional disability is arguably something humans have been engaged with for thousands of years (see, for example, Tilley 2015; Cunha 2016; Tornberg and Jacobsson 2018). Cunha states that care in the past is not surprising given that "our large brain and cooperative behavior, and pair bonding among other things" (2016, 656), as well as the fact that non-human primates have been shown to care for each other (Matsumoto et al. 2016). When a health issue arises, "adults of any culture will consider the nature of their (or a dependent's) problem and weigh it against their cultural understanding of the sickness and mental repertoire of appropriate treatments to try" (Quinlan 2011, 391).

While there are numerous examples of family and community helping aging adults adapt to age-related changes and geriatric syndromes, most of these we cannot identify in the past using human skeletal remains or archaeological evidence. For example, vision problems would have been present in the past. In the United States, occupational therapists work with older adults to both enhance the accessibility of the environment to accommodate vision loss and promote social awareness of these changes (McGrath et al. 2017). One could see how cultures might have adapted to reduced vision in the past through way-finding strategies such as landmarks that provide orientation cues, and well-structured paths with tactile markings. For example, Laes (2018) discusses the role that the blind played in the Roman world and notes that many people with low vision were recorded in texts engaging in activities of the period, from aging generals and senators who were losing their sight, to street beggars who were intentionally blinded. In ancient communities, many "individuals were expected to contribute to the best of their ability, even those who were completely blind had an abundance of possibilities. Within a familiar environment it was quite possible to perform manual tasks" (Laes 2018, 103). Adaptation to reduced mobility included use of assistive devices, such as canes and splints, and reorganization of living spaces to decrease physical demands. While not related to aging, archaeologists have discussed the use of assistive devices in the past, such as splints in the U.S. Southwest over seven hundred years ago (Morris 1924; Willett and Harrod 2017) and the presence of a prosthetic toe in Egypt approximately twenty-five hundred years ago (Brier et al. 2015).

While many geriatric syndromes have biological consequences that we cannot identify in the past using human skeletal or mummified remains, it may be possible to infer malnutrition, sarcopenia, and dental problems because they leave traces on the body. For example, an older adult with a healed hip fracture could inform anthropologists about a change in lifestyle. Such an injury often necessitates a change in weight-bearing activity and the use of an ambulatory device while recovering (Maher 2014). In this case, one may see a leg length discrepancy, a cane/ambulatory device, bolstering objects, a change in living space to decrease physical demands, and possible evidence of gait change (Sneed 2020, 1018).

Decreases in function of sensory systems, cardiovascular and musculoskeletal functions, and cognition are universal issues for aging adults. The degree of decline varies from person to person but is profoundly influenced by social, economic, and environmental factors (Bonder and Goodman 2019, 1057). Research indicates that physical activity is an effective intervention for prevention and management of sarcopenia, osteoporosis, osteoarthritis, rheumatoid arthritis, and rehabilitation after illness and trauma (Santilli et al. 2014; Yoo et al. 2018). Purposeful physical exercise for health benefits is a relatively new concept. Researchers have argued that physical activity was a normal part of everyday life up until relatively recently (Berenbaum et al. 2018). Bioarchaeological research looking at different cultures in the past have found that the majority of people within a specific society were involved in strenuous activity (see, for example, Hawkey and Merbs 1995; Porčić and Stefanović 2009; Havelková et al. 2011; Woo and Sciulli 2011). Sands (2010, 27) suggests that physical activity is a part of religious, social, and cultural expression, along with subsistence practices (see also Howell et al., this volume).

Ethnomedical research, particularly ethnopharmacology and ethnobotany, has found that approximately 85 percent of traditional medicines are plant-based (Gomes et al. 2011; Quinlan 2011). Plants used to make medicines involve the physical activity of gathering and processing, with some requiring ritual practice involving dance and song (Quinlan 2011; Babu et al. 2020). Babu and colleagues (2020) interviewed chiefs, priests, Vaidas, herbal practitioners, older adults, and educated youths of the Andhra Pradesh region in India, finding that eighty-four species of plants are used for the treatment of OA. These plants are prepared in a specific way and ingested at designated times for a prescribed duration. It is important to note that elders were sought out for information, which differs from Western biomedical culture in that older patients often seek diagnosis and treatment from doctors who are younger.

Occupational therapy is founded on the premise that humans are occupational beings, meaning that they require a variety of activities, both chosen and necessary, to live healthy lives (Townsend and Marval 2013). It is possible that physical activity in the form of religious, social, and cultural expression satisfied humans in the way of occupations they wanted to perform, and that subsistence activities satisfied humans in the way of occupations. Berenbaum and colleagues (2018) state that OA is more common today than it was in the past because of increased metabolic disorders, dietary changes, and decreased physical activity.

Conclusion

Occupations, or the way humans occupy their time, can be therapeutic and used to restore function. As humans age, occupations may be lost or adapted. When an occupation is completely lost, risk factors for physical inactivity and reduced quality of life become greater, leading to increased symptoms of aging. Indeed, healthy aging is based on much more than avoiding disease and disability, maintaining mental and physical function, and sustaining active engagement in life.

While humans age like all other animals, we are unique in the ways we adapt to the changes associated with getting older. As biocultural beings (Goodman and Leatherman 1998; Dufour 2006), humans have developed the capacity to mitigate age-related changes and establish cultural support systems that can help people continue to be active members of their society well into old age (Crews 2003).

References

Adams, R. D. 1969. "Ageing, Involution, and Senescence." *South African Medical Journal* 43(41): 1239–1244.

Agarwal, S. C. 2019. "Understanding Bone Aging, Loss, and Osteoporosis in the Past." In *Biological Anthropology of the Human Skeleton*, 3rd ed., edited by M. A. Katzenberg and A. L. Grauer, 385–414. Hoboken: John Wiley and Sons.

Anderson, A. S., and R. F. Loeser. 2010. "Why Is Osteoarthritis an Age-Related Disease? *Best Practice and Research*." *Clinical Rheumatology* 24(1): 15–26.

AOTA. 2020. "Occupational Therapy Practice Framework: Domain and Process—Fourth Edition." *American Journal of Occupational Therapy* 74(Supplement 2): 7412410010p7412410011–7412410010p7412410087.

Atchinson, B., and Powers Dirette, D. 2017. *Conditions in Occupational Therapy: Effect on Occupational Performance*. Philadelphia: Wolters Kluwer.

Aufderheide, A. C. 2003. *The Scientific Study of Mummies*. Cambridge: Cambridge University Press.

Babu, N.V.J., P. M. Pragada, and G. N. Rao. 2020. "Ethnomedicinal Plants Used to Treat Osteo Arthritis from Andhra Pradesh, India." *International Journal of Botany and Research* 10(1): 55–68.

Balick, M., and R. Lee. 2005. "Inflammation and Ethnomedicine: Looking to Our Past." *Ethnomedicine* 1(5): 389–392.

Battles, H. 2011. "Toward Engagement: Exploring the Prospects for an Integrated Anthropology of Disability." *Vis-à-vis: Explorations in Anthropology* 11(1): 107–124.

Behrensmeyer, A. K., and A. P. Hill. 1980. *Fossils in the Making: Vertebrate Taphonomy and Paleoecology*. Chicago: University of Chicago Press.

Berenbaum, F., I. Wallace, D. Lieberman, and D. Felson. 2018. "Modern-Day Environmental Factors in the Pathogenesis of Osteoarthritis." *Nature Reviews Rheumatology* 14(11): 674–681.

Biehler-Gomez, L., and C. Cattaneo. 2018. "The Diagnostic Implications of Two Cases of Known Rheumatoid Arthritis from the CAL Milano Cemetery Skeletal Collection." *Journal of Forensic Sciences* 63(6): 1880–1887.

Blake, A. J., K. Morgan, J. Bendall, H. Dallosso, B. J. Ebrahim, T. H. Arie, P. H. Fentem, and E. J. Bassey. 1988. "Falls by Elderly People at Home: Prevalence and Associated Factors." *Age and Aging* 17(6): 365–372.

Bonder, B. R., and G. D. Goodman. 2019. "Providing Occupational Therapy for Older Adults with Changing Needs." In *Willard and Spackman's Occupational Therapy*, 13th ed., edited by B.A.B. Schell and G. Gillen, 1055–1064. Philadelphia: Wolters Kluwer.

Brance, M. L., S. Di Gregorio, B. A. Pons-Estel, N. J. Quagliato, M. Jorfen, G. Berbotto, N. J. Quagliato, M. Jorfen, G. Berbotto, N. Cortese, J. C. Raggio, M. Palatnik, I. Chavero, J. Soldano, R. Wong, L. Del Rio, A. Sánchez, and L. R. Brun. 2021. "Prevalence of Sarcopenia and Whole-Body Composition in Rheumatoid Arthritis." *JCR: Journal of Clinical Rheumatology* 27(6S): S153–S160.

Brennan Ramirez, L. K., E. A. Baker, and M. Metzler. 2008. *Promoting Health Equity: A Resource to Help Communities Address Social Determinants of Health.* Atlanta: U.S. Department of Health and Human Services, Centers for Disease Control and Prevention.

Bribiescas, R. G. 2020. "Aging, Life History, and Human Evolution." *Annual Review of Anthropology* 49: 101–121.

Brier, B., P. Vinh, M. Schuster, H. Mayforth, and E. J. Chapin. 2015. "A Radiologic Study of an Ancient Egyptian Mummy with a Prosthetic Toe." *The Anatomical Record* 298: 1047–1058.

Brotto, M., and L. Bonewald. 2015. "Bone and Muscle: Interactions beyond Mechanical." *Bone* 80: 109–114.

Burt, N. M., D. Semple, K. Waterhouse, and N. C. Lovell. 2013. *Identification and Interpretation of Joint Disease in Paleopathology and Forensic Anthropology.* Springfield: Charles C. Thomas.

Casado, J.M.R. 2012. "The History of Geriatric Medicine: The Present; Problems and Opportunities." *European Geriatric Medicine* 3(4): 228–232.

Cawley, W. D., and R. R. Paine. 2015. "Skeletal Indicators of Reactive Arthritis: A Case Study Comparison to Other Skeletal Conditions, such as Rheumatoid Arthritis, Ankylosing Spondylitis, Ankylosing Sero-Negative Spa, and DISH." *International Journal of Paleopathology* 11: 70–74.

Chmielewski, P. 2017. "Rethinking Modern Theories of Ageing and Their Classification: The Proximate Mechanisms and the Ultimate Explanations." *Anthropological Review* 80(3): 259–272.

Chung, K. C., and S. V. Spilson. 2001. "The Frequency and Epidemiology of Hand and Forearm Fractures in the United States." *Journal of Hand Surgery* 26(5): 908–915.

Cohn, E. G., and E. B. Crepeau. 2019. Narrative as a Key to Understanding. In *Willard and Spackman's Occupational Therapy*, 13th ed., edited by B.A.B. Schell and G. Gillen, 142–149. Philadelphia: Wolters Kluwer.

Crews, D. E. 2003. *Human Senescence: Evolutionary and Biocultural Perspectives.* Cambridge: Cambridge University Press.

———. 2005. "Evolutionary Perspectives on Human Longevity and Frailty." In *Longevity and Frailty*, edited by J.-M. Robine, J. R. Carey, Y. Christen, and J.-P. Michel, 57–65. Paris: Springer.

———. 2007. "Senescence, Aging, and Disease." *Journal of Physiological Anthropology* 26(3): 365–372.

Cruz-Jentoft, A. J., F. Landi, E. Topinková, and J.-P. Michel. 2010. "Understanding Sarcopenia as a Geriatric Syndrome." *Current Opinion in Clinical Nutrition and Metabolic Care* 13(1): 1–7.

Cunha, E. 2016. "Compassion between Humans Since When? What the Fossils Tell Us." *Etnográfica* 20(3): 653–657.

Dean, G. E., C. Weiss, J. L. Morris, and E. R. Chasens. 2017. "Impaired Sleep: A Multifaceted Geriatric Syndrome." *Nursing Clinics* 52(3): 387–404.

DeWitte, S. N., and C. M. Stojanowski. 2015. "The Osteological Paradox 20 Years Later: Past Perspectives, Future Directions." *Journal of Archaeological Research* 23(4): 397–450.

Dodig, S., I. Čepelak, and I. Pavić. 2019. "Hallmarks of Senescence and Aging." *Biochemia Medica* 29(3): 483–497.

Domett, K., C. Evans, N. Chang, N. Tayles, and J. Newton. 2017. "Interpreting Osteoarthritis in Bioarchaeology: Highlighting the Importance of a Clinical Approach through Case Studies from Prehistoric Thailand." *Journal of Archaeological Science: Reports* 11: 762–773.

Dufour, D. L. 2006. "Biocultural Approaches in Human Biology." *American Journal of Human Biology* 18(1): 1–9.

Fedarko, N. S. 2011. "The Biology of Aging and Frailty." *Clinics in Geriatric Medicine* 27(1): 27–37.

Fisher, A. G. 2013. "Occupation-Centered, Occupation-Based, Occupation-Focused: Same, Same or Different?" *Scandinavian Journal of Occupational Therapy* 26(3): 162–173.

Flacker, J. M. 2003. "What Is a Geriatric Syndrome Anyway?" *Journal of the American Geriatrics Society* 51(4): 574–576.

Franceschi, C., P. Garagnani, C. Morsiani, M. Conte, A. Santoro, A. Grignolio, D. Monti, M. Capri, and S. Salvioli. 2018. "The Continuum of Aging and Age-Related Diseases: Common Mechanisms but Different Rates." *Frontiers in Medicine* 5(61). doi.org/10.3389/fmed.2018.00061.

Franse, C. B., A. van Grieken, L. Qin, R.J.F. Melis, J.A.C. Rietjens, and H. Raat. 2017. "Socioeconomic Inequalities in Frailty and Frailty Components Among Community-Dwelling Older Citizens." *PLoS One* 12(11): e0187946.

Freire Junior, R. C., J. M. Porto, N. R. Marques, P. E. Magnani, and D. C. Abreu. 2017. "The Effects of a Simultaneous Cognitive or Motor Task on the Kinematics of Walking in Older Fallers and Non-Fallers." *Human Movement Science* 51: 146–152.

Fried, L. P., C. M. Tangen, J. Walston, A. B. Newman, C. Hirsch, J. Gottdiener, T. Seeman, R. Tracy, W. J. Kop, G. Burke, M. A. McBurnie, and Cardiovascular Health Study Collaborative Research Group. 2001. "Frailty in Older Adults: Evidence for a Phenotype." *Journals of Gerontology Series A: Biological Sciences and Medical Sciences* 56(3): M146-M157.

Fulop, T., A. Larbi, J. M. Witkowski, J. McElhaney, M. Loeb, A. Mitnitski, and G. Pawelec. 2010. "Aging, Frailty and Age-Related Diseases." *Biogerontology* 11: 547–563.

Ghosh, P., and M. Smith. 2002. "Osteoarthritis, Genetic and Molecular Mechanisms." *Biogerontology* 3(1–2): 85–88.

Gomes, A., A. Alam, and S. Bhattacharya. 2011. "Ethno Biological Usage of Zoo Products in Rheumatoid Arthritis." *Indian Journal of Experimental Biology* 49: 565–573.

Goodman, A. H., and T. L. Leatherman. (Eds.). 1998. *Building a New Biocultural Synthesis: Political-Economic Perspectives on Human Biology*. Ann Arbor: University of Michigan Press.

Grajo, L., A. Boisselle, and E. DaLomba. 2018. "Occupational Adaptation as a Construct: A Scooping Review of the Literature." *Open Journal of Occupational Therapy* 6(1): Article 2.

Grajo, L. C. 2019. "Theory of Occupational Adaptation." In *Willard and Spackman's Occupational Therapy*, 13th ed., edited by B.A.B. Schell and G. Gillen, 633–642. Philadelphia: Wolters Kluwer.

Greco, E. A., P. Pietschmann, and S. Migliaccio. 2019. "Osteoporosis and Sarcopenia Increase Frailty Syndrome in the Elderly." *Frontiers in Endocrinology* 10: Article 255.

Gutiérrez Robledo, L. M., and M. U. Pérez-Zepeda. 2018. "Sarcopenia: Assessment, Management, and Outcomes." In *Oxford Textbook of Geriatric Medicine*, edited by J.-P. Michel, B. L. Beattie, F. C. Martin, and J. D. Walston, 421–435. Oxford: Oxford University Press.

Haglund, W. D., and M. H. Sorg. 1997. *Forensic Taphonomy: The Postmortem Fate of Human Remains*. Boca Raton: CRC Press.

Hammond, A. 2014. "Rheumatoid Arthritis, Osteoarthritis, and Fibromyalgia." In *Occupational Therapy for Physical Dysfunction*, 7th ed., edited by M. V. Radomski and C. A. Trombly, 1215–1243. Philadelphia: Wolters Kluwer.

Hartl, F. U. 2016. "Cellular Homeostasis and Aging." *Annual Review of Biochemistry* 85: 1–4.

Havelková, P., S. Villotte, P. Velemínský, L. Poláček, and M. Dobisíková. 2011. "Enthesopathies and Activity Patterns in the Early Medieval Great Moravian Population: Evidence of Division of Labour." *International Journal of Osteoarchaeology* 21: 487–504.

Hawkey, D. E., and C. F. Merbs. 1995. "Activity-Induced Musculoskeletal Stress Markers (MSM) and Subsistence Strategy Changes among Ancient Hudson Bay Eskimos." *International Journal of Osteoarchaeology* 5: 324–338.

Hayman, K. J., N. Kerse, L. Dyall, M. Kepa, R. Teh, C. Wham, V. Wright-St Clair, J. Wiles, S. Keeling, M. J. Connolly, T. J. Wilkinson, S. Moyes, J. B. Broad, and S. Jatrana. 2012. "Life and Living in Advanced Age: A Cohort Study in New Zealand—e Puāwaitanga o Nga Tapuwae Kia Ora Tonu, LiLACS, NZ: Study Protocol." *BMC Geriatrics* 12: 33.

Herranz, N. S., and J. S. Gil. 2018. "Mechanisms and Functions of Cellular Senescence." *Journal of Clinical Investigation* 128(4): 1238–1246.

Howell, B. M., and S. H. Bardach. 2018. "'It's a Scoial Thing': Sociocultural Experiences with Nutrition and Exercise in Anchorage, Alaska." *Arctic Anthropology* 55(2): 1–16.

Howell, B. M., M. Seater, K. Davis, and D. McLinden. 2020. "Determining the Importance and Feasibility of Various Aspects of Healthy Ageing among Older Adults Using Concept Mapping." *Ageing and Society* 42(6): 1403–1421.

Huang, D. L., D. E. Rosenberg, S. D. Simonovich, and B. Belza. 2012. "Food Access Patterns and Barriers among Midlife and Older Adults with Mobility Disabilities." *Journal of Aging Research* 2012: 231489.

Inoue, K., S. Hukuda, M. Nakai, K. Katayama, and J. Huang. 1999. "Erosive Peripheral Polyarthritis in Ancient Japanese Skeletons: A Possible Case of Rheumatoid Arthritis." *International Journal of Osteoarchaeology* 9(1): 1–7.

Inouye, S. K., S. Studenski, M. E. Tinetti, and G. A. Kuchel. 2007. "Geriatric Syndromes: Clinical, Research, and Policy Implications of a Core Geriatric Concept." *Journal of the American Geriatrics Society* 55(5): 780–791.

Jacobs, J. M., Y. Maaravi, A. Cohen, M. Bursztyn, E. Ein-More, and J. Stressman. 2012. "Changing Profile of Health and Function from Age 70 to 85 Years." *Gerontology* 58: 313–321.

Kane, R. L., T. Shamliyan, K. Talley, and J. Pacala. 2012. "The Association between Geriatric Syndromes and Survival." *Journal of the American Geriatrics Society* 60(5): 896–904.

Karsenty, G. 2012. "The Mutual Dependence between Bone and Gonads." *Journal of Endocrinology* 213(2): 107–114.

Kaufman, S. R. 1994. "Old Age, Disease, and the Discourse on Risk: Geriatric Assessment in U.S. Health Care." *Medical Anthropology Quarterly, New Series* 8(4): 430–447.

Kemmlert, K., and L. Lundholm. 2001. "Slips, Trips and Falls in Different Work Groups—With Reference to Age and from a Preventive Perspective." *Applied Ergonomics* 32(2): 149–153.

Kerr, J., D. Rosenberg, and L. Frank. 2012. "The Role of the Built Environment in Healthy Aging: Community Design, Physical Activity, and Health among Older Adults." *Journal of Planning Literature* 27(1): 43–60.

Laes, C. 2018. *Disabilities and the Disabled in the Roman World: A Social and Cultural History*. Cambridge: Cambridge University Press.

Landi, F., A. M. Martone, R. Calvani, and E. Marzetti. 2018. "Anorexia of Ageing." In *Oxford Textbook of Geriatric Medicine*, edited by J.-P. Michel, B. L. Beattie, F. C. Martin, and J. D. Walston, 445–453. Oxford: Oxford University Press.

Lardjam, A., R. Mazid, A. Sadaoui, S. Bensahaila, A. Khalfa, W. Khitri, A. Azaiz, N. Djebli, and H. Toumi 2018. "Ethnobotanical Survey on the Use of Traditional Medicine for the Treatment of Osteoarthritis in Oran, Algeria." In *Recent Advances in Environmental Science from the Euro-Mediterranean and Surrounding Regions: Proceedings of Euro-Mediterranean Conference for Environmental Integration (EMCEI-1), Tunisia 2017*, edited by A. Kallel, M. Ksibi, B. D. Hamed, and N. Khélifi, 1413–1417. Cham: Springer.

Lauretani, F., G. Bellelli, G. Pelà, S. Morganti, S. Tagliaferri, and M. Maggio. 2020. "Treatment of Delirium in Older Persons: What We Should Not Do!" *International Journal of Molecular Sciences* 21(7): 2397.

Lawhorne, L. W., J. G. Ouslander, P. A. Parmelee, B. Resnick, and B. Calabrese. 2008. "Urinary Incontinence: A Neglected Geriatric Syndrome in Nursing Facilities." *Journal of the American Medical Directors Association* 9(1): 29–35.

Locquet, M., C. Beaudart, J.-Y. Reginster, and O. Bruyère. 2019. "Association between the Decline in Muscle Health and the Decline in Bone Health in Older Individuals from the SarcoPhAge Cohort." *Calcified Tissue International* 104: 273–284.

Loeser, R. F. 2017. "The Role of Aging in the Development of Osteoarthritis." *Transactions of the American Clinical and Climatological Association* 128: 44–54.

Lyman, R. L. 1994. *Vertebrate Taphonomy*. Cambridge: Cambridge University Press.

Maher, C. 2014. "Orthopaedic Conditions." In *Occupational Therapy for Physical Dysfunction*, 7th ed., edited by M. V. Radomski and C. A. Trombly, 1103–1128. Philadelphia: Wolters Kluwer.

Marks, S. C., and D. C. Hermey. 1996. "The Structure and Development of Bone." In *Principles of Bone Biology*, edited by J. P. Bilezikian, L. G. Raisz, and G. A. Rodan, 3–34. New York: Academic Press.

Marks, S. C., and P. R. Odgren. 2002. "Structure and Development of the Skeleton." In *Principles of Bone Biology*, 2nd ed., edited by J. P. Bilezikian, L. G. Raisz, and G. A. Rodan, 3–32. New York: Academic Press.

Matsumoto, T., N. Itoch, S. Inoue, and M. Nakamura. 2016. "An Observation of a Severely Disabled Infant Chimpanzee in the Wild and Her Interactions with Her Mother." *Primates* 57(1): 3–7.

Matuska, K., and K. Barrett. 2019. "Patterns of Occupation." In *Willard and Spackman's Occupational Therapy*, 13th ed., edited by B.A.B. Schell and G. Gillen, 212–222. Philadelphia: Wolters Kluwer.

McFadden, C., and M. F. Oxenham. 2020. "A Paleoepidemiological Approach to the Osteological Paradox: Investigating Stress, Frailty and Resilience through Cribra Orbitalia." *American Journal of Physical Anthropology* 173(2): 205–217.

McGrath, C., D. Laliberte Rudman, M. Spafford, B. Trentham, and J. Polgar. 2017. "The Environmental Production of Disability for Seniors with Age-Related Vision Loss." *Canadian Journal of Aging* 36(1): 55–66.

McHugh, D., and J. S. Gil. 2018. "Senescence and Aging: Causes, Consequences, and Therapeutic Avenues." *Journal of Cell Biology* 217(1): 65–77.

Milte, R., and M. Crotty. 2014. "Musculoskeletal Health, Frailty and Functional Decline." *Best Practice and Research Clinical Rheumatology* 28(3): 395–410.

Morais, J. A. 2018. "Sarcopenia–Definitions and Epidemiology." In *Oxford Textbook of Geriatric Medicine*, edited by J.-P. Michel, B. L. Beattie, F. C. Martin, and J. D. Walston, 409–413. Oxford: Oxford University Press.

Moreland, B., R. Kakara, and A. Henry. 2020. "Trends in Nonfatal Falls and Fall-Related Injuries among Adults Aged ≥65 Years—United States, 2012–2018." *MMWR: Morbidity and Mortality Weekly Report* 69: 875–881.

Morris, E. H. 1924. *Burials in the Aztec Ruin* (Vol. 26), The Archer M. Huntington Survey of the Southwest. New York: Anthropological Papers of the American Museum of Natural History.

Neogi, T. 2013. "The Epidemiology and Impact of Pain in Osteoarthritis." *Osteoarthritis and Cartilage* 21(9): 1145–1153.

NIH. 2006. "Osteoporosis Overview," 1–10. Bethesda: National Institute of Health, Osteoporosis and Related Bone Diseases.

NOF. 2020. "Safe Movement: Preventing Fragility Fractures: Antifracture Medicine, Safe Movement, Exercise, and Fall Prevention." Arlington: National Osteoporosis Foundation.

O'Brien, M. S., and J. J. McDougall. 2019. "Age and Frailty as Risk Factors for the Development of Osteoarthritis." *Mechanisms of Ageing and Development* 180: 21–28.

Ortner, D. J. 1991. "Theoretical and Methodological Issues in Paleopathology." In *Human Paleopathology: Current Syntheses and Future Options*, edited by D. J. Ortner and A. C. Aufderheide, 5–11. Washington, DC: Smithsonian Institution Press.

Ortner, D. J. 2012. "Differential Diagnosis and Issues in Disease Classification." In *A Companion to Paleopathology*, edited by A. L. Grauer, 250–267. Malden: Blackwell Publishing Ltd.

Pandit, D. N., R. R. Singh, and S. P. Srivastava. 2016. "A Review of Theories Regarding Ageing." *Journal of Biological Engineering Research and Review* 3(1): 21–25.

Porčić, M., and S. Stefanović. 2009. "Physical Activity and Social Status in Early Bronze Age Society: The Mokrin Necropolis." *Journal of Anthropological Archaeology* 28(3): 259–273.

Quinlan, M. B. 2011. "Ethnomedicine." In *A Companion to Medical Anthropology*, edited by M. Singer and P. I. Erickson, 381–403. Hoboken: Blackwell Publishing Ltd.

Rausch, C., Y. Liang, U. Bültmann, S. E. de Rooij, K. Johnell, L. Laflamme, and J. Möller. 2019. "Social Position and Geriatric Syndromes among Swedish Older People: A Population-Based Study." *BMC Geriatrics* 19: 267.

Reynolds, J. C., C. P. Bwiza, and C. Lee. 2020. "Mitonuclear Genomics and Aging." *Human Genetics* 139: 381–399.

Rikkert, M. G. M., A.-S. Rigaud, R. J. van Hoeyweghen, and J. de Graaf. 2003. "Geriatric Syndromes: Medical Misnomer or Progress in Geriatrics?" *Netherlands Journal of Medicine* 61(3): 83–87.

Rockstein, M. 1968. "The Biological Aspects of Aging." *Gerontologist* 8(2): 124–125.

Rose, M. R. 1991. *Evolutionary Biology of Aging*. New York: Oxford University Press.

Rosen, C. J., J. Glowacki, and J. P. Bilezikian (Eds.). 1999. *The Aging Skeleton*. San Diego: Academic Press.

Rothschild, B. M., R. J. Woods, C. Rothschild, and J. I. Sebes. 1992. "Geographic Distribution of Rheumatoid Arthritis in Ancient North America: Implications for Pathogenesis." *Seminars in Arthritis and Rheumatism* 22(3): 181–187.

Sands, R. R. 2010. "Anthropology Revisits Sports through Human Movement." In *The Anthropology of Sport and Human Movement: A Biocultural Perspective*, edited by R. R. Sands and L. R. Sands, 5–37. Lanham, MD: Lexington Books.

Santilli, V., A. Bernetti, M. Mangone, and M. Paoloni. 2014. "Clinical Definition of Sarcopenia." *Clinical Cases in Mineral and Bone Metabolism* 11(3): 177–180.

Savinaya, M. S., J. Narayana, V. Krishna, and S. S. Nayaka. 2019. "A Study on Ethnomedicine Floristics for Treating Arthritis in Aneguli-Maradavalli Village of Sharavathi River Basin, Central Western Ghats, Karnataka." *Ethnobotany Research and Applications* 18(41): 1–7.

Schkade, J. K., and S. Schultz. 1992. "Occupational Adaptation: Toward a Holistic Approach for Contemporary Practice, Part 1." *American Journal of Occupational Therapy* 46(9): 829–837.

Schmeer, C., A. Kretz, D. Wengerodt, M. Stojiljkovic, and O. W. Witte. 2019. "Dissecting Aging and Senescence—Current Concepts and Open Lessons." *Cells* 8(11): 1446.

Sneed, D. 2020. "The Architecture of Access: Ramps at Ancient Greek Healing Sanctuaries." *Antiquity* 94(376): 1015–1029.

Son, J. M., and C. Lee. 2019. "Mitochondria: Multifaceted Regulators of Aging." *BMB Reports* 52(1): 13–23.

Spector, T. D., F. M. Cicuttini, J. R. Baker, J. Loughlin, D. Hart, and J. Hopper. 1996. "Genetic Influences on Osteoarthritis in Women: A Twin Study." *BMJ: British Medical Journal* 312(7036): 940–944.

Stenvinkel, P., and P. G. Shiels. 2019. "Long-Lived Animals with Negligible Senescence: Clues for Ageing Research." *Biochemical Society Transactions* 47(4): 1157–1164.

Stubbs, B., T. Binnekade, L. Eggermont, A. A. Sepehry, S. Patchay, and P. Schofield. 2014. "Pain and the Risk for Falls in Community-Dwelling Older Adults: Systematic Review and Meta-analysis." *Archives of Physical Medicine and Rehabilitation* 95(1): 175–187.

Thompson, M. E., A. G. Rosati, and N. Snyder-Mackler. 2020. "Insights from Evolutionary Relevant Models for Human Ageing." *Philosophical Transactions of the Royal Society B* 375: 2019060.

Tilley, L. 2015. *Theory and Practice in the Bioarchaeology of Care*. New York: Springer.

Toledano-González, A., T. Labajos-Manzanares, and D. Romero-Ayuso. 2019. "Well-Being, Self-Efficacy and Independence in Older Adults: A Randomized Trial of Occupational Therapy." *Archives of Gerontology and Geriatrics* 83: 277–284.

Tornberg, A., and L. Jacobsson. 2018. "Care and Consequences of Traumatic Brain Injury in Neolithic Sweden: A Case Study of Ante Mortem Skull Trauma and Brain Injury Addressed through the Bioarchaeology of Care." *International Journal of Osteoarchaeology* 28(2): 188–198.

Torres, S. 2003. "A Preliminary Empirical Test of a Culturally-Relevant Theoretical Framework for the Study of Successful Aging." *Journal of Cross Cultural Gerontology* 18(1): 79–100.

Townsend, E. A., and R. Marval. 2013. "Can Professionals Actually Enable Occupational Justice?" *Cardenos de Terapia Ocupacional da UFSCar* 21(2): 215–228.

Uchitomi, R., M. Oyabu, and Y. Kamei. 2020. "Vitamin D and Sarcopenia: Potential Vitamin D Supplementation in Sarcopenia Prevention and Treatment." *Nutrients* 12(10): 3189.

van der Putten, G.-J., C. de Baat, L. De Visschere, and J. Schols. 2014. "Poor Oral Health, A Potential New Geriatric Syndrome." *Gerodontology* 31(s1): 17–24.

Wagner, W. 2019. "The Link between Epigenetic Clocks for Aging and Senescence." *Frontiers in Genetics* 10(303): 1–6.

Wilcock, A. A., and E. A. Townsend. 2019. "Occupational Justice." In *Willard and Spackman's Occupational Therapy*, 13th ed., edited by B.A.B. Schell and G. Gillen, 643–660. Philadelphia: Wolters Kluwer.

Willett, A. Y., and R. P. Harrod. 2017. "Cared for Outcasts: A Case for Continuous Care in the Precontact U.S. Southwest." In *New Developments in the Bioarchaeology of Care*, edited by L. Tilley and A. A. Schrenk, 65–84. New York: Springer.

Woo, E. J., and P. W. Sciulli. 2011. "Degenerative Joint Disease and Social Status in the Terminal Late Archaic Period (1000–500 b.c.) of Ohio." *International Journal of Osteoarchaeology* 23(5): 529–544.

Wood, J. W., G. R. Milner, H. C. Harpending, K. M. Weiss. 1992. "The Osteological Paradox: Problems of Inferring Prehistoric Health from Skeletal Samples." *Current Anthropology* 33(4): 343–358.

Wright, L. E., and C. J. Yoder. 2003. "Recent Progress in Bioarchaeology: Approaches to the Osteological Paradox." *Journal of Archaeological Research* 11(1): 43–70.

Wright-St Clair, V., M. Kepa, S. Hoenle, K. Hayman, S. Keeling, M. Connolly, J. Broad, L. Dyall, and N. Kerse. 2012. "Doing What's Important: Valued Activities for Older New Zealand Māori and Non-Māori." *Australian Journal on Ageing* 31(4): 241–246.

Yaussy, S. L. 2019. "The Intersections of Industrialization: Variation in Skeletal Indicators of Frailty by Age, Sex, and Socioeconomic Status in 18th- and 19th-Century England." *American Journal of Physical Anthropology* 170(1): 116–130.

Yeung, S. S. Y., E. M. Reijnierse, V. K. Pham, M. C. Trappenburg, W. K. Lim, C.G.M. Meskers, and A. B. Maier. 2019. "Sarcopenia and Its Association with Falls and Fractures in Older Adults: A Systematic Review and Meta-analysis." *Journal of Cachexia, Sarcopenia and Muscle* 10(3): 485–500.

Yoo, S.-Z., M.-H. No, J.-W. Heo, D.-H. Park, J.-H. Kang, S. H. Kim, and H-B. Kwak. 2018. "Role of Exercise in Age-Related Sarcopenia." *Journal of Exercise Rehabilitation* 14(4): 551–558.

Yu, H., R. Zeng, X. Li, H. Song, Y. Wei, R. Li, W. Wang, and X. Cai. 2016. "Tujia Ethnomedicine Xuetong Suppresses Onset and Progression of Adjuvant-Induced Arthritis in Rats." *Chinese Pharmacological Bulletin* 32(10): 1427–1432.

Zandieh, R., J. Martinez, J. Flacke, P. Jones, and M. Van Maarseveen. 2016. "Older Adults' Outdoor Walking: Inequalities in Neighbourhood Safety, Pedestrian Infrastructure and Aesthetics." *International Journal of Environmental Research and Public Health* 13(12): 1179.

4

Biocultural Perspectives on Aging

Importance of the Microbiome

MELISSA K. MELBY, ANKITA KANSAL, AND MARK NICHTER

Humans are holobionts (Simon et al. 2019), hosts containing communities of *microbiota* (bacteria, fungi, protozoa, and viruses) with numbers similar to human cells (Sender, Fuchs, and Milo 2016), that coexist in a symbiotic relationship and state of dynamic homeostasis. These communities of microbiota act as buffers and translators for hosts as they engage biosocial environments in myriad ways. Microbial communities respond to a constant stream of threats and opportunities to expand their reach and range, providing potential adaptation to environmental changes on a faster timescale than host evolution. Human hosts and their microbes are generally commensal or mutualistic. A commensal relationship exists when the host benefits, while the microbes may not be affected measurably. Microbe-microbe relationships can also be commensal or mutualistic when both species benefit from each other. Only a few microbes become pathogenic. Aging is one factor that affects microbiota ecology, which in turn affects the rate and manifestations of aging.

While the dangers of microbes are well known, microbes also benefit human hosts by breaking down complex carbohydrates to provide energy; turning dietary fiber into short-chain fatty acids (SCFAs) to provide energy and control immune function; producing metabolites (compounds that may be substrates for metabolic reactions or act as signaling molecules to regulate other organisms including the host) (Krautkramer, Fan, and Bäckhed 2021); synthesizing vitamins (e.g., B and K); regulating the immune system; influencing the neuroendocrine system through the gut-brain axis; and protecting against colonization by pathogens. When the balance of commensal/mutualistic and pathogenic microbiota is disturbed (e.g., by infection, diet, stress, antibiotics, or even the aging process), microbial dysbiosis may occur. Dysbiosis may impair regulatory and homeostasis functions (Kim and Jazwinski 2018), increasing risk of inflammation and chronic disease associated with aging (van de Guchte, Blottière, and Doré 2018).

Dysbiosis is an important but controversial concept in microbiome research (Olesen and Alm 2016; Petersen and Round 2014; Hooks and O'Malley 2017). Dysbiotic microbiota are often identified as the microbial communities associated with particular disease states, when compared to "normal" controls (who may or may not have other diseases), and thus understanding of dysbiosis is relative to "normal" or "healthy." The concept raises questions about how we define "normal" or "healthy," how much change or disturbance or balance is meaningful and measurable, and on what scale. Notably, aging does not necessarily entail disease, but aging of different organs and the body's attempts to maintain homeostasis by compensating for age-related loss of function may influence the microbiome and be influenced by it (Reza, Finlay, and Pettersson 2019). When dysbiosis occurs, health-promoting functions of the microbiota may be impaired, and signs of aging may result.

In this chapter, we consider how the human microbiome (aggregate genome of all microbiota residing in and on the body) affects, and is affected by, biocultural and physiological aspects of the aging process. We examine how changes in lifestyle, behaviors, and environment affect the microbiome, and in turn morbidity and mortality. As the experience of aging is influenced by cultural and physical environments, the microbiome may provide a mechanism mediating those factors and producing variation in aging and health outcomes, thereby providing a "missing link" in how culture becomes embodied through development to produce emergent embodied phenotypes (Krieger 2013; Lynch and Hsiao 2019) and situated biologies (Niewöhner and Lock 2018). As such, microbiota may be at the interface of human-environment interactions—at times functioning as part of the human body, at others mediating more distal environments. Microbiota communities are found throughout the body from the skin (see Norton, this volume) and lungs to the gastrointestinal tract and genitals (Mehta et al. 2020). These communities of microbiota are interlinked and can affect each other through their impacts on human physiology. We focus on the gut microbiome, as it has received the most attention and has been shown to influence circadian rhythms; responses to nutrition, metabolism, and immunity; and mental health—all of which change with aging.

Aging Seen through the Lenses of the Microbiome and Health Transitions

Environmental exposures across the life course contribute 70 to 85 percent of variation in aging (Murabito, Yuan, and Lunetta 2012). Microbiota play critical roles in mediating environmental signals associated with shifts in diet and environment, chemical exposures including drugs, and social factors such as co-residence. Genes residing within our own cells influence aging, but the individual human genome is established at conception, and the human population only evolves across generations. An individual's microbiome, on the other hand, experiences multiple generations within the human life span on/in which it lives. Species in the microbiome can change and evolve quickly due to rapid growth and mutation rates (Gordo 2019), horizontal gene transfer (Liu et al. 2012), and changes in their environment (e.g., triggered by changes in host diet that shift microbial community structure by changing energy sources). Thus, evolutionary changes in the microbiome may enable humans to adapt to transitions in lifestyle within one lifetime—changes from hunting and gathering to horticulture, agriculture, and industrialization; changes in population density; and challenges from new diseases. Differences in human gut microbial diversity between non-industrialized and industrialized populations suggest that cultural and environmental changes exert considerable influence on our microbiome (Yatsunenko et al. 2012). Some microbiome changes may allow the host to adapt to new environments (e.g., industrialized diets), but some of these changes may also compromise the host's health (e.g., lifestyle diseases) (Sonnenburg and Sonnenburg 2019a).

Over the course of human history, humans have undergone significant health transitions encompassing shifts in demographics, morbidity, and mortality. During the first epidemiologic transition (Omran 1971) accompanying the Neolithic (a shift from hunting and gathering non-domesticated foods to the deliberate cultivation of plants and domestication of animals), human populations experienced higher morbidity, mortality and fertility rates, and grain consumption led to dental decay (suggesting shifts in the oral microbiome and gastrointestinal tract), osteoporosis, and osteoarthritis (Cohen and Armelagos 1984). The second epidemiological transition followed a shift from rural to urban living, industrialization, and higher population densities, which led to increases in infectious disease. A third epidemiological transition saw shifts in mortality from communicable to non-communicable diseases associated with changes in lifestyles related to overnutrition, obesity, and decreased exercise (Harper and Armelagos 2010). Further transitions have followed, marked by infectious and non-communicable diseases that coexist and predispose one another; the proliferation of commerciogenic diseases, which are associated with the consumption of processed foods and increased exposure to toxins (Jelliffe 1977; Lee and Crosbie 2020); inactivity; antibiotic overuse leading to drug-resistant infections; and emerging and resurgent diseases (Barrett et al. 1998; Gaziano 2010; Rogers and Hackenberg 1987; Santosa et al. 2014).

Each transition has affected the microbiome, which in turn has affected morbidity and mortality rates, suggesting that the microbiome may reveal the impact of human activity on the environment (Sonnenburg and Sonnenburg 2019b) that is captured in the term "Anthropocene," referring to the current geological epoch in which human activity is the dominant factor influencing the environment. Globally, the cause of mortality has shifted from infectious to chronic disease, and research on the microbiome suggests that microbes may play a bigger role in chronic disease than previously thought and that a clear dichotomy between infectious versus chronic disease may not exist (Finlay 2020). Epidemiological transition theory now recognizes that infectious and non-communicable disease do not just coexist but affect one another—that is, infectious disease leads to chronic conditions, chronic disease predisposes and affects infectious disease trajectories (as seen with COVID-19), and antibiotic resistance leads to reemerging infectious diseases.

A broad understanding of health transitions over the human lifecycle requires that we look beyond macro-level factors influencing shifts in morbidity and mortality to the micro-ecology of the microbiome. This leads to questions about how shifts in the microbiome contribute to dramatic increases in allergic and autoimmune diseases (Atiim and Elliott 2016), the reemergence of infectious diseases (Zuckerman et al. 2014), and the rise in chronic diseases associated with aging (Reza, Finlay, and Pettersson 2019). It also demands that we examine how modern health-care practices (e.g., widespread use of antibiotics, Cesarean sections, infant formula) and environmental and ecological transitions (e.g., climate change) contribute to microbiome transitions that significantly impact human morbidity and mortality.

Increases in life expectancy and changes in patterns of morbidity and mortality are not uniform within or between populations. Significant health inequities exist, and morbidity and resilience may be mediated by the microbiome. For example, studies of aging have shown that populations with certain diets (e.g., Mediterranean), physical activity patterns, and social connections (the so-called Blue Zones), have a higher proportion of people reaching healthy old age (Buettner 2012). Microbiome changes are more strongly associated with biological aging (epigenetic alteration and decreased physical/physiological functioning, eventually leading to frailty) than with chronological aging (actual time since birth) (Maffei et al. 2017; O'Toole and Jeffery 2015). This suggests that, in addition to genetics and epigenetics of both host and microbes, societal and structural factors that influence health-promoting lifestyle patterns may contribute to individual and population differences in aging.

Lock and Kaufert (2001) propose the concept of "local biologies" to describe how bodies respond and adapt to local environments, producing variation greater than what genetic differences would suggest. For example, a Mediterranean diet intervention in Europe showed changes in the microbiome associated with health (Ghosh et al. 2020). However, the Mediterranean diet may have different effects on Asian populations with different microbiota, which may constitute a different "local biological optimum" producing an alternative path to healthy aging. Niewöhner and Lock's expanded concept of "situated biologies," which encompasses local biologies, pays credence to environmental epigenetics and the microbiome; "our permeable skin-bound selves comprise a collection of ecosystems of miniaturized communities that are products of our evolutionary past, more recent historical events, and of social and political contingencies of many kinds" (2018, 692). The microbiome influences development through bidirectional connections with hosts and thus is intimately involved with producing emergent embodied phenotypes (Krieger 2013), which characterize the health transitions described above.

Below we first describe the role of the microbiome in a key process (inflammation) that influences how tissues, organs, and bodies age. We then provide two examples highlighting the microbiome's role in producing situated biologies that often lead to increased need for assisted care, which in turn leads to profound environmental and social changes as people age: osteoporosis (gut-bone axis) and neurodegenerative diseases and mental health (gut-brain axis). Next, we focus on microbiome-mediated factors involved in healthy aging, and end with a discussion of anthropological questions about aging raised by a focus on the microbiome.

Microbiome-Mediated Mechanisms of Inflammation

Inflammation is an evolutionary process of tissue repair and aging (Franceschi et al. 2018). The microbiome trains hosts' innate (e.g., macrophages) and adaptive (e.g., lymphocytes) immune systems during critical periods in early life, with long-lasting impacts on immune function, homeostasis, and later-life susceptibility to infectious and inflammatory diseases (Zheng, Liwinski, and Elinav 2020). Inflammation, part of the innate immune system, is a complex biological response to harmful stimuli including pathogens, damaged cells, or irritants. Inflammation is a bodily response that can be directed toward unwanted microbes but may also damage tissues and organs when inflammation becomes chronic, characterized by excessive release of proinflammatory cell-signaling molecules called cytokines (e.g., cytokine storms associated with severe COVID-19).

Chronic stress and stimulation of the innate immune system leads to low-grade, aging-associated inflammation (inflammaging), which is both a hallmark of and risk factor for age-associated diseases (Franceschi et al. 2000). Stress can occur as a response to microbes or as a response to age-associated loss of function in organs and the body's efforts to compensate. Stress can lead to hormesis (adaptive response to low-intensity environmental challenges that enhances the ability to cope with intense stressors) or detrimental effects (Calabrese and Mattson 2017). The threshold between those two paths is influenced by genetic variation as well as environmental exposures (Franceschi et al. 2000) modulated by the microbiome through interactions with the immune system and release of anti-inflammatory compounds such as short-chain fatty acids, dependent on the overall functioning of various organs, which are influenced by age.

Inflammaging has several causes, including cell senescence and debris, immunosenescence, environmental chemicals (including reactive oxygen species and nutrient excess), and gut dysbiosis (Sanada et al. 2018), with the latter highlighted in Figure 4.1. Age-related reduced metabolic function of organs may result in compensatory processes that may lead to inflammation. Inflammaging is associated with changes in gut microbiota composition leading to innate immune response activation and may constitute a shared mechanistic pathway influencing development of sarcopenia, osteoporosis, neurodegenerative diseases, and metabolic syndrome–related diseases like diabetes and cardiovascular disease (Livshits and Kalinkovich 2019).

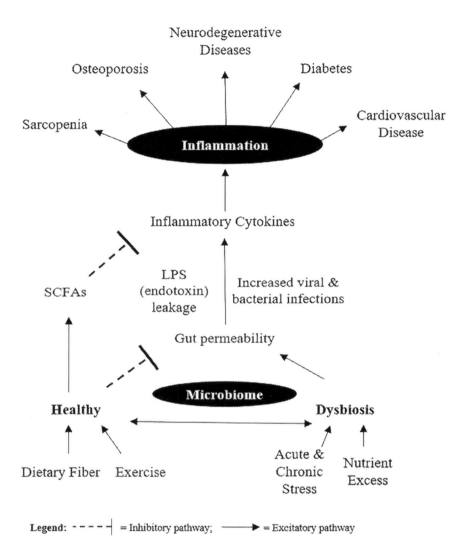

Figure 4.1. Microbiome-Mediated Pathways to Age-Related Inflammation and Disease: Simplified diagram of some key pathways through which factors influencing the microbiome contribute to healthy versus dysbiotic microbiota, with associated changes in gut permeability and inflammatory cytokines, contributing to inflammaging and many age-related diseases. (SCFAs=Short-chain fatty acids such as acetate, propionate, and butyrate; LPS=lipopolysaccharides of Gram-negative bacterial membranes.)

Longevity is inversely correlated with microbiota diversity and positively associated with abundance of bacteria that metabolize fiber into short-chain fatty acids (SCFAs) (Kong et al. 2016), which influence energy metabolism, homeostasis, and immunity (Koh et al. 2016) in ways that promote healthy aging. Thus, the microbiome may play a role in the response to stressors and the degree to which hormetic versus detrimental responses are triggered, in turn impacting aging. While dysbiotic microbiota may drive aging processes, microbiota may also adapt to age-related physiological changes in hosts, contributing to significant individual variation in response to environmental signals (i.e., local biology). One study observed significant variation in glucose levels following consumption of identical meals, but algorithms integrating blood parameters, dietary habits, anthropometrics, physical activity, and gut microbiota (but not host) genetics were able to accurately predict glucose levels (Zeevi et al. 2015). These results support the importance of local biology, including diet, activity, and gut microbiota, in influencing health.

Additionally, social interactions, which may lead to microbial exchange, may also play an important role in aging. For example, studies suggest that transplanting bacteria from young donors into middle-aged individuals extends the life span in animal models (Smith et al. 2017). Such observations raise questions about potential benefits of microbial transfer from young to old individuals, and thus about optimal living arrangements such as multigenerational households versus institutional settings with other older adults, who often have illnesses associated with gut dysbiosis.

The Microbiome's Role in Aging-Related Health Issues

Two conditions that often lead to assisted care and associated changes in living environment and quality of life that appear to have important microbiome connections include: (1) osteoporosis and bone fractures (gut-bone axis); and (2) neurodegenerative diseases and mental health (gut-brain axis). Germ-free mice (used in many microbiome studies) often show impaired development but also show reduced effects of aging, suggesting that microbes are important for normal healthy development but also are involved with deterioration and dysfunction associated with aging. This suggests a "can't live without them (in early life), can't live with them (in later life)" relationship with the microbiome, and highlights how the situated biologies (characterized by which microbes are present and how those shift over time in response to hosts and environments) are key in producing embodied phenotypes across the life course.

Gut-Bone Axis

In Western populations, aging is characterized by increased fracture risk due to osteoporosis, resulting from increased bone resorption relative to bone formation. Bone mineral density peaks around age 25 years, and rates of remodeling are influenced by ethnicity/race, sex, hormonal changes, and metabolic pathways. The microbiota regulates skeletal development, bone homeostasis, pathological bone loss, and bone aging (Hsu and Pacifici 2018) through the gut-bone axis. The gut-bone axis consists of three pathways (Hernandez et al. 2016): (1) nutrient and mineral absorption in the gut; (2) modulation of the mucosal and systemic immune system; and (3) translocation across the intestinal epithelium of microbial metabolites such as vitamins and SCFAs (Zaiss et al. 2019).

High-fiber foods, fructo-oligosaccharides (plant sugars), and inulin-type prebiotics increase beneficial gut bacteria that ferment fiber and release SCFAs, which lower intestinal pH, promoting calcium absorption and leading to bone mineralization (Wallace et al. 2017), as well as modulating intestinal permeability and immune function (Li et al. 2019). In addition to genetic predisposition, osteoporosis is associated with limited physical activity, poor nutritional history, alterations in sex steroid hormones, and inflammatory disorders (Marcus, Dempster, and Bouxsein 2013), all of which influence, and are influenced by, the microbiome. Since microbiota also regulate sex steroid formation (Pace and Watnick 2020), they influence sex differences in inflammatory phenotypes and bone homeostasis. Such factors trigger the formation of osteoclasts, or bone-resorbing cells (Khosla and Pacifici 2013), relevant for the increased bone turnover observed in postmenopausal women.

Not only are antibiotics used to treat infections (Blaser et al. 2021), but subtherapeutic dosages are also used to promote growth in livestock (Cox 2016) by altering gut microbiota associated with bone density increases, although effects vary with developmental stage and sex. Older adults, particularly those in care homes, often have increased antibiotic usage for respiratory illnesses, and are often prescribed antibiotics prophylactically for urinary tract infections (Matthews and Lancaster 2011), leading to chronic low-dose and periodic acute antibiotic exposures, which may impact the microbiome and bone health.

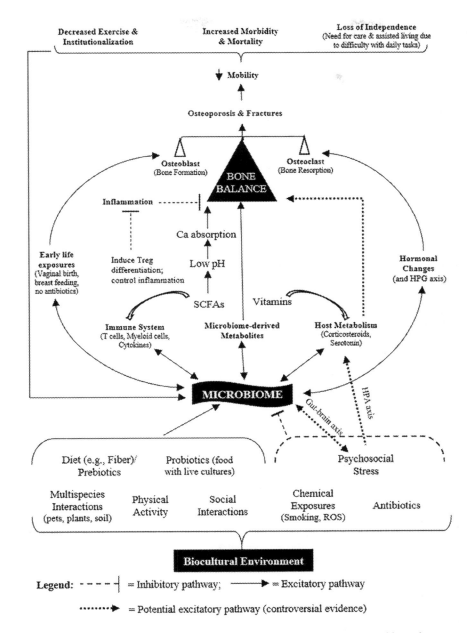

Figure 4.2. Gut Microbiome-Bone Axis: Simplified diagram of some possible pathways through which factors mediated via the microbiome influence bone balance and health (modified from Charles, Ermann, and Aliprantis 2015). (Ca=calcium; HPA=hypothalamic-pituitary-adrenal; HPG=hypothalamic-pituitary-gonadal; ROS=reactive oxygen species.)

While osteoporosis drugs often target osteoclasts to slow bone breakdown, probiotics and/or prebiotics may increase SCFA-producing species, which influence the immune system and signaling that leads to differentiation and proliferation of osteoblasts and increased bone formation. A prebiotic and aerobic exercise intervention prevented knee osteoarthritis in a high fat/sugar (i.e., contemporary industrialized human diet) rat model (Rios et al. 2019), suggesting that microbiome-mediated interventions may be able to counter some of the unhealthy diet-induced effects of bone aging. Diet and exercise impact not only the microbiome and bone but also the brain, with implications for both cognitive and physical frailty.

Gut-Brain Axis and Brain Health

The gut-brain axis regulates and maintains homeostasis, with microbiota playing important roles, particularly in aging (Reza, Finlay, and Pettersson 2019) and neurodevelopmental and neurodegenerative disorders (Cryan et al. 2019). The gut microbiome influences brain health via three primary pathways: (1) neurotransmitters (chemical messengers that transmit messages between neurons or neurons and muscles) and hormones produced by gut microbiota; (2) influences on the immune system and inflammaging; and (3) gut neurons (second numerous after brain neurons), with the vagus nerve conveying signals from internal organs to the brain and vice versa. The gut microbiome also influences the permeability of the intestinal wall and the blood-brain barrier (Braniste et al. 2014), which often show age-related impairment.

Gut microbiota regulate serotonin levels in the intestine, where it is estimated that 90 percent of the serotonin is produced, and microbial metabolites regulate about 50 percent of that production (Fung et al. 2019). Gut bacteria play a role in tryptophan metabolism (Kaur, Bose, and Mande 2019), providing precursors for serotonin and melatonin production, and thus potentially influencing depression and sleep.

The vagus nerve is the main conduit of the parasympathetic nervous system involved in the perception of sensations from inside the body, including sensing and conveying information about microbial metabolites and influencing peripheral inflammation and intestinal permeability (Bonaz, Bazin, and Pellissier 2018). The vagus nerve is involved in mood, immune response, digestion, and heart rate; interventions can affect cytokine production and vagal tone, which correlates with ability to regulate stress responses (Breit et al. 2018). Thus, the vagus nerve provides a direct

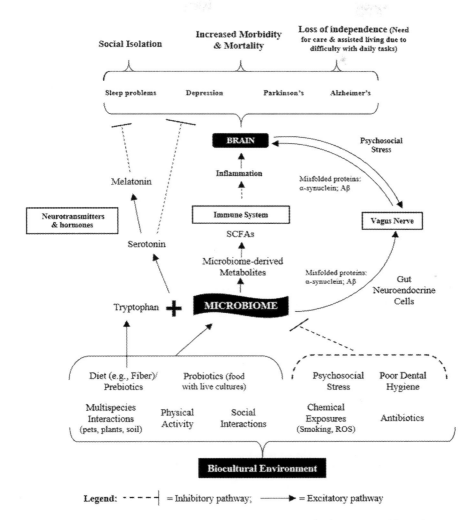

Figure 4.3. Gut Microbiome-Brain Axis: Simplified diagram of some possible pathways through which factors influencing the microbiome contribute to brain health and neurodegenerative diseases. (Aβ=amyloid beta, main component of amyloid plaques in brains of people with Alzheimer's disease; SCFAs=Short-chain fatty acids such as acetate, propionate, and butyrate; Vagus Nerve=bi-directional pathway for neurotransmitters to travel between gut and brain, and for misfolded proteins to travel up to brain to cause damage).

conduit by which gut microbiota can influence brain health; dysbiosis can lead to neurodegenerative diseases; psychosocial stress can affect the microbiome; and biocultural factors can influence aging through stress and the microbiome (Finlay et al. 2019). The gut microbiome influences mental health (Foster and McVey Neufeld 2013), and anxiety, stress, and depression can all be transferred fecally in animal models (Chinna Meyyappan et al. 2020).

The gut microbiome has been identified as a potential driver of neurodegenerative diseases such as Alzheimer's disease (AD) and Parkinson's disease (PD) (Friedland and Chapman 2017; Matheoud et al. 2019), both caused by accumulation of misfolded proteins in the brain. While this is a rapidly evolving field, emerging research suggests that neurodegenerative "diseases of aging" such as AD and PD are associated with much earlier changes in the enteric nervous system, influenced by the gut microbiome (Niesler et al. 2021). In fact, patients with inflammatory bowel disease are twice as likely to develop dementia (Zhang et al. 2021). Signals may travel from gut neuroendocrine cells via the vagus nerve to the brain, bypassing the circulatory system (Willyard 2021). In PD, initial protein misfolding appears to originate in the gut, likely driven by microbiota as evidenced by the following: PD patients show altered gut microflora (Cirstea et al. 2020); α-synuclein deposited early in gut neurons is later found in neuron cell bodies (Kujala et al. 2011); in mouse PD models, intestinal microbiota are required for pathogenesis (Sampson et al. 2016); and cutting the vagus nerve is protective against PD (Liu et al. 2017). Similar observations have been made for AD (Friedland and Chapman 2017). Periodontitis is linked to AD (Dominy et al. 2019), and AD patients have up to three times the circulating levels of bacterial lipopolysaccharide, which triggers neuroinflammation (Batista et al. 2019) and in turn increases brain cell production of amyloid beta that forms the protein tangles characteristic of AD (Zhan, Stamova, and Sharp 2018).

Diet can lower risk of neurodegenerative diseases, suggesting a key role for the microbiome. The Mediterranean diet is associated with lower markers of frailty and inflammation and improved cognitive function (Ghosh et al. 2020). The MIND diet, a combination of the Mediterranean diet and the low-sodium DASH diet consisting of high-fiber plants and limited meat, lowers risk of AD by 53 percent (Morris et al. 2015) and delays PD by up to 10 years, likely through selection for butyrate-producing microbes that dampen inflammation. In addition to diet and exercise, social factors and associated stress may impact an individual's brain, mental health, and aging, via the gut microbiome-brain axis (Finlay et al. 2019; Liu 2017).

How Can the Microbiome Promote Healthy Aging?

To elucidate keys to longevity and healthy aging, researchers have focused on regions where people live longer than average, the aforementioned "Blue Zones" (Poulain et al. 2004). While "good genes" contribute to life expectancy, environmental and lifestyle factors such as diet, physical activity, and social interactions, all mediated by the microbiome, may be what gives these populations an edge on longevity (Dato et al. 2017). While inhabitants of Blue Zones experience age-related decline in organ function, fewer people experience chronic metabolic diseases, suggesting that such diseases are not inevitable outcomes of aging.

Diet

Aging is often accompanied by decreases in fiber-containing foods, leading to shifts in microbiota and contributing to malnutrition. Blue Zones share diets rich in fiber, which promotes growth of microbes that produce SCFAs, which dampen inflammation. For Okinawans, what they eat may be as important as how much they eat, with the phrase "*Hara hachibu*" (eat until your stomach is 80 percent full) being considered a secret to health. In animals, caloric restriction extends life expectancy and may operate through hormesis. The longevity benefits of caloric restriction and diets such as the Mediterranean diet may point to a common microbiome-mediated inflammaging and hormesis mechanism (Martucci et al. 2017), providing a pathway for how diet, physical activity, and other environmental signals influence the microbiome and, in turn, health (Rocca et al. 2019).

Physical Activity

The Blue Zones project found that people who live longer move more frequently during the day (on average, every 20 minutes). Independent of diet, exercise-induced microbial changes in composition and function affect energy homeostasis and decrease pro-inflammatory factors impacting health and aging (Mailing et al. 2019). But even when adults meet total exercise guidelines, "total time spent sitting" and "sitting bout duration" are linked to metabolic disease and mortality (Chang et al. 2020; Patel et al. 2018), with leisure-time sitting more strongly correlated to cardiovascular disease and mortality than occupational sitting (Garcia et al. 2019). Intense exercise also increases stress, pro-inflammatory responses, and consumption of energy-dense foods with less dietary fiber, shifting gut microbiota to less health-promoting species (Clark and Mach 2016), suggesting that exercise may also act through hormesis: high levels may have negative impacts, but low to moderate levels may be good.

Social Connections

Strong social networks are associated with longevity (Smith and Christakis 2008; Roth 2020), but less is known about the biosocial network effect of communal microbiomes. Social networks influence microbial transmission, as evidenced by transmission of pathogens such as SARS-CoV-2. Even non-pathogenic microbes appear associated with social networks, with households sharing microbiota (Lax et al. 2014) and spouses having more similar microbes (Brito et al. 2019). Whether this communal microbiome is due to direct transmission or shared diets, behaviors, and environment remains unclear. But studies among our non-human primate relatives sharing similar diets demonstrate that social behavior is important. The amount of time wild baboons spend with each other strongly influences the microbiome (Tung et al. 2015), and social interaction plays a bigger role than diet as males' gut microbiota changes gradually after dispersal and resembles the new group's microbiota with increasing time in residence (Grieneisen et al. 2017). These primate studies raise questions about the influence of family nuclearization on the microbiome, and housing and living arrangements of older adults (multigenerational families, living alone, or institutionalized settings comprised mostly of other older people and their unrelated caregivers). Among older adults, variation correlated with residence location (community, day-hospital, rehabilitation, to long-term residential care), but similar microbiota groupings were observed when clustering was done by residence or diet (Claesson et al. 2012).

In humans, married couples have greater microbial diversity relative to those living alone (Dill-McFarland et al. 2019). This diversity may partly explain the health benefits of marriage—especially for males, given females' broader social contact due to caregiving across generations and patterns of sociality. This has implications for older adults, who often lose partners as they age and are more likely to live alone. More provocatively, could the microbiome influence sociality in ways that improve health? Animal studies show that microbes can influence social behavior in rodents and fruit flies

(Sharon et al. 2010) and increase the production of the "bonding" hormone oxytocin (Erdman and Poutahidis 2016). Taken together, these results suggest that social interaction may lead to microbial diversity, increasing resilience in the face of environmental stressors, and in turn impact sociality.

Anthropological Queries about Aging through a Microbiome Lens

Questions

Why should anthropologists who study aging pay attention to the microbiome? Microbiota are not simply useful quantitative biomarkers (Gorvitovskaia, Holmes, and Huse 2016) of dietary and environmental exposures. They are shared micro-agents essential to ecosocial interactions (Krieger 2012), agents that signal, buffer, and mediate events to sustain host homeostasis (their environment) in a context of perpetual change. Microbiota also impact all stages of human development, especially during the bookends of (early and later) life.

Our microbiome is shared in myriad biosocial ways through cohabitation, consumption patterns, and even greetings. Recent animal studies provide evidence that social interactions between animals of different ages influence the composition of the microbiome and in turn hosts' abilities to respond to their environments. Human studies demonstrate that interactions with different species (e.g., pets) also impact the microbiome (Azad et al. 2013), thus requiring a multi-species perspective.

Cross-cultural studies of humans are needed to explore how exposure to nature, cohabitation, and contact with those of different age groups at home, during social events, and at work sites influence the microbiome and, in turn, processes like inflammaging. Much remains to be studied about healthy aging. For example, do those who age at home with family members live longer, healthier lives than those who age alone or in nursing homes cared for by staff whose cultural (e.g., diet, socioeconomic status) environments may differ? Are potential differences by residence mediated by the microbiome (Claesson et al. 2012), which may be influenced not only by diet and social interactions but also by the use of disinfectants and medications? How about shifts in environment from a house in the country to an apartment in the city, or vice versa? Do pets impact human microbiota and aging, and do effects differ by type of pet? Viewing residence through a microbiome lens will lead anthropologists to investigate best- and worst-case aging scenarios in new ways. For example, one worst-case scenario might include institutionalized living in built environments that lead to decreased microbial diversity, increased infections, and "need" for antibiotics, which in turn leads to increased dysbiosis, a greater chance of drug-resistant disease, poor treatment response, and increased frailty. In contrast, using a microbiome lens when studying Blue Zones might lead to greater understanding of how social interactions, living in multigenerational families, spending time outdoors gardening, and eating more vegetables and dietary fiber might decrease the risk of chronic diseases commonly associated with aging. Looking beyond personal behavior, anthropologically informed, microbiome-sensitive research might provide insights into cultural and social structural factors that influence behavioral norms in Blue Zones. With aging populations worldwide, anthropologists' research into cultural variation may empower older people and policy makers to provide more paths to healthy aging.

Another avenue of inquiry concerns health inequities and aging as seen through the lens of the microbiome (Amato et al. 2020). We know that social and structural determinants of health lead to stress, and that psychosocial stressors trigger inflammation through stress hormones and the hypothalamic-pituitary-adrenal axis and gut-brain axis. What is the role of the microbiome in both mediating and exacerbating bodily responses to chronic stress associated with poverty, race, racism (Benezra 2020), and other forms of prejudice as well as new stressors associated with ageism? In addition to studying how stress impairs health, are there ways in which resilience is associated with our microbiota through, for example, cultural norms and practices related to routine social interaction at places of worship and socialization, as well as participation in events where one's status as an elder is valued (see Howell et al., this volume)? Krieger (2001, 2012) has argued that epidemiology needs to adopt an ecosocial approach to studying health inequity that acknowledges the ways in which structural vulnerability is embodied. Such an approach to studying how population-based patterns of health are biological expressions of social relations must consider changes in the microbiome, providing a sociopolitical microecology of health that complements the macro-level social determinants of health framework. Anthropological research adopting such a lens has much to contribute to the study of situated biologies, an overarching concept that encompasses but looks beyond local biologies as circumscribed. Situated biologies place emphasis on the epigenetics of body-environment entanglements as our community of microbes (i.e., nested ecosystems) responds to physical, social, and political environments and contingencies (Lock 2017; Niewöhner and Lock 2018).

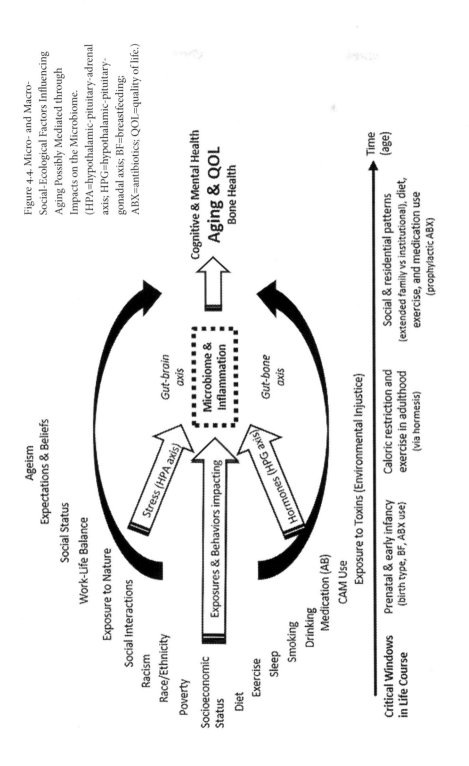

Figure 4.4. Micro- and Macro-Social-Ecological Factors Influencing Aging Possibly Mediated through Impacts on the Microbiome. (HPA=hypothalamic-pituitary-adrenal axis; HPG=hypothalamic-pituitary-gonadal axis; BF=breastfeeding; ABX=antibiotics; QOL=quality of life.)

Implications and Interventions

Cross-cultural variation in lifestyle, social and physical environments, and medication usage impact the microbiome as people age, and potentially mediate differences in life expectancy and healthy aging. Table 4.1 lists some factors, changes associated with aging (particularly in institutionalized settings), effects on the microbiome and health, and recommendations for microbiome-inspired organization and design for elderly (mBIODE) alternatives (see Table 4.1).

Several aging-related changes have synergistic interactions with associated environmental changes, which may set up potential positive feedback loops that lead to poorer health. One potential positive feedback loop involves:

> shifts in diet to softer, processed foods (as teeth decay and swallowing becomes challenging)→decreased dietary fiber→decreased microbiota diversity→more inflammation→more illness→shifts in diet

Fiber supplements, containing only a few types of polysaccharides, may help keep people regular, but cannot support the diversity of microbes sustained by a complex vegetable diet, or the range of physiological functions that diverse microbes carry out.

A second potential positive feedback loop involves the medicalization of aging and use of both prophylactic and curative medications with associated collateral damage to the microbiome that in turn increases risk of disease and need for more medication. While effects of antibiotics on the microbiome are well documented, effects of psychiatric and other drugs on microbiota are less studied. Given high prescription rates and multiple drugs used by older adults (Charlesworth et al. 2015), polypharmacy effects on the microbiome, and the effects of the "microbial pharmacists within us" (Spanogiannopoulos et al. 2016) on xenobiotics including drugs and food (Koppel, Maini Rekdal, and Balskus 2017), need further research. Insights from the microbiome lead to a reconsideration of aging given a health-care transition lens that at once lauds medical advances in keeping people alive longer, but at the same time leads individuals to treatments that can cause their own illnesses and a host of health problems on the rise among older adults.

Diseases such as influenza and COVID-19 exhibit high mortality rates among older adults and may be influenced by cytokine storms associated with inflammaging. Vaccination appears critical to lowering risk, yet vaccination responses are weaker among older adults (CDC 2019). Obesity and metabolic syndrome induce defects in immune cells similar to those observed with aging and result in compromised immune systems that have poor vaccination responses (Frasca 2020). Recognizing that older adults have poor vaccination responses, interventions to promote immune function by supporting the microbiome might decrease risk of disease in the first place, lessen disease sequelae, and support vaccination effectiveness. This support could be done through dietary, exercise, and other lifestyle interventions that likely support health and longevity through multiple pathways.

It is important to distinguish between hygiene and sanitization/disinfection. Hospitals, and by extension nursing homes, rely on heavy disinfectant use to minimize disease spread. But if we understand these environments not as sterile environments defending against pathogens but as ecosystems with most microbial niches already occupied, approaches to preventing pathogens may change (Arnold 2014). Allowing more outdoor air inside care homes might lower relative human-associated microbiota concentrations (including pathogens) and provide health benefits (Meadow et al. 2014).

One of the most interesting anthropological questions is the extent to which care workers bring beneficial or harmful microbial diversity to residents of care homes, and vice versa. Older residents of long-term care facilities show loss of health- and youth-associated microbiota and gain of elderly associated microbiota over time, and less recovery following antibiotics compared to community-dwelling older adults (Jeffery, Lynch, and O'Toole 2016). Thus, care workers may provide an influx of novel microbiota, increasing diversity and youth-associated microbiota among residents' microbiota and perhaps resilience. Do care workers have the necessary contacts with residents (through feeding, bathing, etc.) to facilitate the transfer of diverse and possibly beneficial microbiota? And which behaviors are most effective? What happens when diverse microbiota are introduced into excessively sanitized and medicated environments? These are important research questions to elucidate the ecology of aging in institutional settings.

In summary, the microbiome extends the repertoire of the human genome by extracting dietary energy, fermenting fiber, producing SCFAs, synthesizing vitamins, and modulating the immune system. The microbi-

Table 4.1. Factors and Changes Associated with Aging, Effects on Microbiome and Health, and Alternatives

Factors	Changes commonly associated with aging (particularly in institutionalized care settings)	Effects on MB and potential health impacts	MB-inspired organization and design for elderly (mBIODE) alternatives
Sex	Decreasing sex hormones with age (post-menopause for women)	Possible restructuring of MB	Dietary fiber and phytoestrogens
Diet	Shift to softer and more processed foods as teeth decay and swallowing becomes challenging	Less fiber—> less fermentation and production of SCFAs	High fermentable fiber foods and pre/probiotics
Exercise	Decreased due to impairments	Loss of microbial diversity	Increase exercise, outside to extent possible
Contact with Nature	Less time spent outdoors	Decreased diversity due to environmental exposures	Outdoor or fresh air as much as possible
Pets	Decreased ability to care for pets	Decreased exposure to outdoor MB through pet	Contact with pets (PAWS for people)
Built Environment	Shift from home to highly sanitized institutions (nursing homes, rehab, memory-care facilities)	Decreased diversity profiles; increased human/pathogen MB exposure	More fresh air, windows that open, HVAC systems

Sanitization Practices	Highly sanitized (in facilities)	Decreased diversity; increased AMR; possibly increased pathogens	Less sanitized with antimicrobial products; more fresh air
Generational	Shift from multigenerational homes to solitary living	Less microbial exchange with younger people	Multigenerational (daycare and eldercare in shared spaces)
Social	Multigenerational homes to institutions with other elderly and care workers	MB exchange with other elders; increased AMR; increased dysbiosis; unknown interactions with care workers	Increase interactions with younger people
Antibiotic Use	Collateral damage of curative and prophylactic medications	Loss of MB diversity; increased ABX resistance; increased vulnerability to infections and chronic disease	Avoidance of prophylactic ABX for urinary tract infections by increasing water, pre/probiotics intake
Other Medication	Increased psychiatric medicines	Relatively unknown	Diet, pre/probiotics, exercise, outdoor time, etc.; interventions to support mental health
Vaccination	Weakened vaccination responses	Unknown	Support MB to promote immunity and vaccination response
CAM Use	Possibly decreased/constrained	Unknown	Allow for CAM use if possible
Medical Expenses	Increased costs	Financial stress may negatively impact	Support MB to reduce medical costs at end of life

Notes: ABX=antibiotics; AMR=antimicrobial resistance; CAM=complementary and alternative medicine; MB=microbiome; SCFAs=short-chain fatty acids ome is at the interface of the human genome-environment entanglement, mediating and translating environmental signals into metabolites with physiological and epigenetic effects. Thus, the standard equation of "genotype + environment = phenotype" may need to be revised to "genotype + microbiota genotypes + environment = emergent embodied phenotype."

The microbiome as a lens and pathway holds the potential to illuminate how complex ecosocial interactions and systematic inequities become embodied phenotypes over the life course, producing situated biologies with important implications for healthy aging and well-being in diverse environments.

Acknowledgments

We acknowledge helpful, critical feedback from Kylynda Bauer, Kathy Dettwyler, Brett Finlay, Phillippe Gros, Ryan Harrod, Britteny Howell, Frédéric Keck, Neri de Kramer, Sven Pettersson, Carolina Tropini, Xiaomeng You, and Eglee Zent.

References

Amato, Katherine, Marie-Claire Arrieta, Meghan Azad, Michael Bailey, Josiane Broussard, Carlijn Bruggeling, Erika Claud, et al. "The Human Microbiome and Health Inequities." September 8, 2020. https://www.ipr.northwestern.edu/documents/working-papers/2020/wp-20-44.pdf.

Arnold, Carrie. 2014. "Rethinking Sterile: The Hospital Microbiome." *Environmental Health Perspectives* 122(7): A182–A187. https://doi.org/10.1289/ehp.122-A182.

Atiim, G. A., and S. J. Elliott. 2016. "The Global Epidemiologic Transition: Noncommunicable Diseases and Emerging Health Risk of Allergic Disease in Sub-Saharan Africa." *Health Education & Behavior* 43(1 Suppl): 37s–55s. https://doi.org/10.1177/1090198115606918.

Azad, M. B., T. Konya, H. Maughan, D. S. Guttman, C. J. Field, M. R. Sears, A. B. Becker, J. A. Scott, and A. L. Kozyrskyj. 2013. "Infant Gut Microbiota and the Hygiene Hypothesis of Allergic Disease: Impact of Household Pets and Siblings on Microbiota Composition and Diversity." *Allergy Asthma Clin Immunol* 9(1): 15. https://doi.org/10.1186/1710-1492-9-15.

Barrett, Ronald, Christopher W. Kuzawa, Thomas McDade, and George J. Armelagos. 1998. "Emerging and Re-Emerging Infectious Diseases: The Third Epidemiologic Transition." *Annual Review of Anthropology* 27(1): 247–271. https://doi.org/10.1146/annurev.anthro.27.1.247.

Batista, Carla Ribeiro Alvares, Giovanni Freitas Gomes, Eduardo Candelario-Jalil, Bernd L. Fiebich, and Antonio Carlos Pinheiro de Oliveira. 2019. "Lipopolysaccharide-Induced Neuroinflammation as a Bridge to Understand Neurodegeneration." *International Journal of Molecular Sciences* 20(9): 2293. https://doi.org/10.3390/ijms20092293.

Benezra, Amber. 2020. "Race in the Microbiome." *Science, Technology, & Human Values* 45(5): 877–902. https://doi.org/10.1177/0162243920911998.

Blaser, M. J., M. K. Melby, M. Lock, and M. Nichter. 2021. "Accounting for Variation in and Overuse of Antibiotics among Humans." *Bioessays* 43(2): e2000163. https://doi.org/10.1002/bies.202000163.

Bonaz, B., T. Bazin, and S. Pellissier. 2018. "The Vagus Nerve at the Interface of the Microbiota-Gut-Brain Axis." *Front Neurosci* 12: 49. https://doi.org/10.3389/fnins.2018.00049.

Braniste, V., M. Al-Asmakh, C. Kowal, F. Anuar, A. Abbaspour, M. Tóth, A. Korecka, et al. 2014. "The Gut Microbiota Influences Blood-Brain Barrier Permeability in Mice." *Science Translational Medicine* 6(263): 263ra158. https://doi.org/10.1126/scitranslmed.3009759.

Breit, Sigrid, Aleksandra Kupferberg, Gerhard Rogler, and Gregor Hasler. 2018. "Vagus Nerve as Modulator of the Brain-Gut Axis in Psychiatric and Inflammatory Disorders." *Frontiers in Psychiatry* 9: 1–15. https://doi.org/10.3389/fpsyt.2018.00044.

Brito, Ilana L., Thomas Gurry, Shijie Zhao, Katherine Huang, Sarah K. Young, Terrence P. Shea, Waisea Naisilisili, et al. 2019. "Transmission of Human-Associated Microbiota Along Family and Social Networks." *Nature Microbiology* 4(6): 964–971. https://doi.org/10.1038/s41564-019-0409-6.

Buettner, Dan. 2012. *The Blue Zones: 9 Lessons for Living Longer from the People Who've Lived the Longest*. 2nd ed. Washington, DC: National Geographic.

Calabrese, Edward J., and Mark P. Mattson. 2017. "How Does Hormesis Impact Biology, Toxicology, and Medicine?" *NPJ Aging and Mechanisms of Disease* 3(1): 13. https://doi.org/10.1038/s41514-017-0013-z.

CDC. 2019. *Immunogenicity, Efficacy, and Effectiveness of Influenza Vaccines*. U.S. Centers for Disease Control and Prevention (CDC). https://www.cdc.gov/flu/professionals/acip/immunogenicity.htm.

Chang, Ya-Ju, John Bellettiere, Suneeta Godbole, Samaneh Keshavarz, Joseph P. Maestas, Jonathan T. Unkart, Daniel Ervin, et al. 2020. "Total Sitting Time and Sitting Pattern in Postmenopausal Women Differ by Hispanic Ethnicity and Are Associated with Cardiometabolic Risk Biomarkers." *Journal of the American Heart Association* 9(4): e013403. https://doi.org/doi:10.1161/JAHA.119.013403.

Charlesworth, C. J., E. Smit, D. S. Lee, F. Alramadhan, and M. C. Odden. 2015. "Polypharmacy among Adults Aged 65 Years and Older in the United States: 1988–2010." *Journals of Gerontology. Series A, Biological Sciences and Medical Sciences* 70(8): 989–95. https://doi.org/10.1093/gerona/glv013.

Chinna Meyyappan, Arthi, Evan Forth, Caroline J. K. Wallace, and Roumen Milev. 2020. "Effect of Fecal Microbiota Transplant on Symptoms of Psychiatric Disorders: A Systematic Review." *BMC Psychiatry* 20(1): 1–19. https://doi.org/10.1186/s12888-020-02654-5.

Cirstea, Mihai S., Adam C. Yu, Ella Golz, Kristen Sundvick, Daniel Kliger, Nina Radisavljevic, Liam H. Foulger, et al. 2020. "Microbiota Composition and Metabolism Are Associated with Gut Function in Parkinson's Disease." *Movement Disorders* 35(7): 1208–1217. https://doi.org/https://doi.org/10.1002/mds.28052.

Claesson, M. J., I. B. Jeffery, S. Conde, S. E. Power, E. M. O'Connor, S. Cusack, H. M. Harris, et al. 2012. "Gut Microbiota Composition Correlates with Diet and Health in the Elderly." *Nature* 488(7410): 178–184. https://doi.org/10.1038/nature11319.

Clark, A., and N. Mach. 2016. "Exercise-Induced Stress Behavior, Gut-Microbiota-Brain Axis and Diet: A Systematic Review for Athletes." *Journal of the International Society of Sports Nutrition* 13: 43. https://doi.org/10.1186/s12970-016-0155-6.

Cohen, M. N., and G. J. Armelagos. 1984. *Paleopathology at the Origins of Agriculture*. New York: Academic Press.

Cox, Laura M. 2016. "Antibiotics Shape Microbiota and Weight Gain across the Animal Kingdom." *Animal Frontiers* 6(3): 8–14. https://doi.org/10.2527/af.2016-0028.

Cryan, John F., Kenneth J. O'Riordan, Caitlin S. M. Cowan, Kiran V. Sandhu, Thomaz F. S. Bastiaanssen, Marcus Boehme, Martin G. Codagnone, et al. 2019. "The Microbiota-Gut-Brain Axis." *Physiological Reviews* 99(4): 1877–2013. https://doi.org/10.1152/physrev.00018.2018.

Dato, S., G. Rose, P. Crocco, D. Monti, P. Garagnani, C. Franceschi, and G. Passarino. 2017. "The Genetics of Human Longevity: An Intricacy of Genes, Environment, Culture and Microbiome." *Mechanisms of Ageing* and *Development* 165 (Pt B): 147–155. https://doi.org/10.1016/j.mad.2017.03.011.

Dill-McFarland, Kimberly A., Zheng-Zheng Tang, Julia H. Kemis, Robert L. Kerby, Guanhua Chen, Alberto Palloni, Thomas Sorenson, Federico E. Rey, and Pamela Herd. 2019. "Close Social Relationships Correlate with Human Gut Microbiota Composition." *Scientific Reports* 9(1): 703. https://doi.org/10.1038/s41598-018-37298-9.

Dominy, Stephen S., Casey Lynch, Florian Ermini, Malgorzata Benedyk, Agata Marczyk, Andrei Konradi, Mai Nguyen, et al. 2019. "*Porphyromonas gingivalis* in Alzheimer's Disease Brains: Evidence for Disease Causation and Treatment with Small-Molecule Inhibitors." *Science Advances* 5(1): eaau3333. https://doi.org/10.1126/sciadv.aau3333.

Erdman, S. E., and T. Poutahidis. 2016. "Microbes and Oxytocin: Benefits for Host Physiology and Behavior." *International Review of Neurobiology* 131: 91–126. https://doi.org/10.1016/bs.irn.2016.07.004.

Finlay, B. B. 2020. "Are Noncommunicable Diseases Communicable?" *Science* 367(6475): 250–251. https://doi.org/10.1126/science.aaz3834.

Finlay, Brett B., Sven Pettersson, Melissa K. Melby, and Thomas C. G. Bosch. 2019. "The Microbiome Mediates Environmental Effects on Aging." *BioEssays* 41(10): 1800257. https://doi.org/https://doi.org/10.1002/bies.201800257.

Foster, Jane A., and Karen-Anne McVey Neufeld. 2013. "Gut-Brain Axis: How the Microbiome Influences Anxiety and Depression." *Trends in Neurosciences* 36(5): 305–312. https://doi.org/10.1016/j.tins.2013.01.005.

Franceschi, C., M. Bonafè, S. Valensin, F. Olivieri, M. De Luca, E. Ottaviani, and G. De Benedictis. 2000. "Inflamm-aging. An Evolutionary Perspective on Immunosenescence." *Annals of the New York Academy of Sciences* 908: 244–254. https://doi.org/10.1111/j.1749-6632.2000.tb06651.x.

Franceschi, Claudio, Paolo Garagnani, Paolo Parini, Cristina Giuliani, and Aurelia Santoro. 2018. "Inflammaging: A New Immune-Metabolic Viewpoint for Age-Related Diseases." *Nature Reviews Endocrinology* 14(10): 576–590. https://doi.org/10.1038/s41574-018-0059-4.

Friedland, R. P., and M. R. Chapman. 2017. "The Role of Microbial Amyloid in Neurodegeneration." *PLoS Pathogens* 13(12): e1006654. https://doi.org/10.1371/journal.ppat.1006654.

Fung, Thomas C., Helen E. Vuong, Cristopher D. G. Luna, Geoffrey N. Pronovost, Antoniya A. Aleksandrova, Noah G. Riley, Anastasia Vavilina, et al. 2019. "Intestinal Serotonin and Fluoxetine Exposure Modulate Bacterial Colonization in the Gut." *Nature Microbiology* 4(12): 2064–2073. https://doi.org/10.1038/s41564-019-0540-4.

Garcia, Jeanette M., Andrea T. Duran, Joseph E. Schwartz, John N. Booth, Steven P. Hooker, Joshua Z. Willey, Ying Kuen Cheung, et al. 2019. "Types of Sedentary Behavior and Risk of Cardiovascular Events and Mortality in Blacks: The Jackson Heart Study." *Journal of the American Heart Association* 8(13): e010406. https://doi.org/doi:10.1161/JAHA.118.010406.

Gaziano, J. M. 2010. "Fifth Phase of the Epidemiologic Transition: The Age of Obesity and Inactivity." *Journal of the American Medical Association* 303(3): 275–276. https://doi.org/10.1001/jama.2009.2025.

Ghosh, Tarini Shankar, Simone Rampelli, Ian B. Jeffery, Aurelia Santoro, Marta Neto, Miriam Capri, Enrico Giampieri, et al. 2020. "Mediterranean Diet Intervention Alters the Gut Microbiome in Older People Reducing Frailty and Improving Health Status: The NU-AGE 1-Year Dietary Intervention across Five European Countries." *Gut* 69(7): 1218–1228. https://doi.org/10.1136/gutjnl-2019-319654.

Gordo, Isabel. 2019. "Evolutionary Change in the Human Gut Microbiome: From a Static to a Dynamic View." *PLOS Biology* 17(2): e3000126. https://doi.org/10.1371/journal.pbio.3000126.

Gorvitovskaia, Anastassia, Susan P. Holmes, and Susan M. Huse. 2016. "Interpreting Prevotella and Bacteroides as Biomarkers of Diet and Lifestyle." *Microbiome* 4(1): 15. https://doi.org/10.1186/s40168-016-0160-7.

Grieneisen, Laura E., Josh Livermore, Susan Alberts, Jenny Tung, and Elizabeth A. Archie. 2017. "Group Living and Male Dispersal Predict the Core Gut Microbiome in Wild Baboons." *Integrative and Comparative Biology* 57(4): 770–785. https://doi.org/10.1093/icb/icx046.

Harper, Kristin, and George Armelagos. 2010. "The Changing Disease-Scape in the Third Epidemiological Transition." *International Journal of Environmental Research and Public Health* 7(2): 675–697. https://doi.org/10.3390/ijerph7020675.

Hernandez, C. J., J. D. Guss, M. Luna, and S. R. Goldring. 2016. "Links between the Microbiome and Bone." *Journal of Bone and Mineral Research* 31(9): 1638–46. https://doi.org/10.1002/jbmr.2887.

Hooks, Katarzyna B., and Maureen A. O'Malley. 2017. "Dysbiosis and Its Discontents." *mBio* 8(5): 1–11. https://doi.org/10.1128/mBio.01492-17.

Hsu, E., and R. Pacifici. 2018. "From Osteoimmunology to Osteomicrobiology: How the Microbiota and the Immune System Regulate Bone." *Calcified Tissue International* 102(5): 512–521. https://doi.org/10.1007/s00223-017-0321-0.

Jeffery, Ian B., Denise B. Lynch, and Paul W. O'Toole. 2016. "Composition and Temporal Stability of the Gut Microbiota in Older Persons." *ISME Journal* 10(1): 170–182. https://doi.org/10.1038/ismej.2015.88.

Jelliffe, E. F. Patrice 1977. "Infant Feeding Practices: Associated Iatrogenic and Commerciogenic Diseases." *Pediatric Clinics of North America* 24(1): 49–61. https://doi.org/https://doi.org/10.1016/S0031-3955(16)33386-7.

Kaur, Harrisham, Chandrani Bose, and Sharmila S. Mande. 2019. "Tryptophan Metabolism by Gut Microbiome and Gut-Brain-Axis: An in silico Analysis." *Frontiers in Neuroscience* 13(1365). https://doi.org/10.3389/fnins.2019.01365.

Khosla, Sundeep, and Roberto Pacifici. 2013. "Estrogen Deficiency, Postmenopausal Osteoporosis, and Age-Related Bone Loss." In *Osteoporosis*, 4th ed., edited by Robert Marcus, David Feldman, David W. Dempster, Marjorie Luckey, and Jane A. Cauley, 1113–1136. San Diego: Academic Press.

Kim, Sangkyu, and S. Michal Jazwinski. 2018. "The Gut Microbiota and Healthy Aging: A Mini-Review." *Gerontology* 64(6): 513–520. https://doi.org/10.1159/000490615.

Koh, A., F. De Vadder, P. Kovatcheva-Datchary, and F. Bäckhed. 2016. "From Dietary Fiber to Host Physiology: Short-Chain Fatty Acids as Key Bacterial Metabolites." *Cell* 165(6): 1332–1345. https://doi.org/10.1016/j.cell.2016.05.041.

Kong, F., Y. Hua, B. Zeng, R. Ning, Y. Li, and J. Zhao. 2016. "Gut Microbiota Signatures of Longevity." *Current Biology* 26(18): R832–R833. https://doi.org/10.1016/j.cub.2016.08.015.

Koppel, Nitzan, Vayu Maini Rekdal, and Emily P. Balskus. 2017. "Chemical Transformation of Xenobiotics by the Human Gut Microbiota." *Science* 356(6344): eaag2770. https://doi.org/10.1126/science.aag2770.

Krautkramer, Kimberly A., Jing Fan, and Fredrik Bäckhed. 2021. "Gut Microbial Metabolites as Multi-kingdom Intermediates." *Nature Reviews Microbiology* 19(2): 77–94. https://doi.org/10.1038/s41579-020-0438-4.

Krieger, Nancy. 2001. "Theories for Social Epidemiology in the 21st Century: An Ecosocial Perspective." *International Journal of Epidemiology* 30(4): 668–677. https://doi.org/10.1093/ije/30.4.668.

———. 2012. "Methods for the Scientific Study of Discrimination and Health: An Ecosocial Approach." *American Journal of Public Health* 102(5): 936–944. https://doi.org/10.2105/AJPH.2011.300544.

———. 2013. "History, Biology, and Health Inequities: Emergent Embodied Phenotypes and the Illustrative Case of the Breast Cancer Estrogen Receptor." *American Journal of Public Health* 103(1): 22–27. https://doi.org/10.2105/AJPH.2012.300967.

Kujala, Pekka, Claudine R. Raymond, Martijn Romeijn, Susan F. Godsave, Sander I. van Kasteren, Holger Wille, Stanley B. Prusiner, Neil A. Mabbott, and Peter J. Peters. 2011. "Prion Uptake in the Gut: Identification of the First Uptake and Replication Sites." *PLOS Pathogens* 7(12): e1002449. https://doi.org/10.1371/journal.ppat.1002449.

Lax, Simon, Daniel P. Smith, Jarrad Hampton-Marcell, Sarah M. Owens, Kim M. Handley, Nicole M. Scott, Sean M. Gibbons, et al. 2014. "Longitudinal Analysis of Microbial Interaction between Humans and the Indoor Environment." *Science* 345(6200): 1048–1052. https://doi.org/10.1126/science.1254529.

Lee, Kelley, and Eric Crosbie. 2020. "Understanding Structure and Agency as Commercial Determinants of Health; Comment on 'How Neoliberalism Is Shaping the Supply of Unhealthy Commodities and What This Means for NCD Prevention.'" *International Journal of Health Policy and Management* 9(7): 315–318. https://doi.org/10.15171/ijhpm.2019.127.

Li, L., S. Rao, Y. Cheng, X. Zhuo, C. Deng, N. Xu, H. Zhang, and L. Yang. 2019. "Microbial Osteoporosis: The Interplay between the Gut Microbiota and Bones via Host Metabolism and Immunity." *Microbiologyopen* 8(8): e00810. https://doi.org/10.1002/mbo3.810.

Liu, Bojing, Fang Fang, Nancy L. Pedersen, Annika Tillander, Jonas F. Ludvigsson, Anders Ekbom, Per Svenningsson, Honglei Chen, and Karin Wirdefeldt. 2017. "Vagotomy and Parkinson Disease: A Swedish Register-Based Matched-Cohort Study." *Neurology* 88(21): 1996–2002. https://doi.org/10.1212/WNL.0000000000003961.

Liu, Li, Xiaowei Chen, Geir Skogerbø, Peng Zhang, Runsheng Chen, Shunmin He, and Da-Wei Huang. 2012. "The Human Microbiome: A Hot Spot of Microbial Horizontal Gene Transfer." *Genomics* 100(5): 265–270. https://doi.org/https://doi.org/10.1016/j.ygeno.2012.07.012.

Liu, Richard T. 2017. "The Microbiome as a Novel Paradigm in Studying Stress and Mental Health." *American Psychologist* 72(7): 655–667. https://doi.org/10.1037/amp0000058.

Livshits, G., and A. Kalinkovich. 2019. "Inflammaging as a Common Ground for the Development and Maintenance of Sarcopenia, Obesity, Cardiomyopathy and Dysbiosis." *Ageing Research Reviews* 56: 100980. https://doi.org/10.1016/j.arr.2019.100980.

Lock, Margaret. 2017. "Recovering the Body." *Annual Review of Anthropology* 46(1): 1–14. https://doi.org/10.1146/annurev-anthro-102116-041253.

Lock, Margaret, and Patricia Kaufert. 2001. "Menopause, Local Biologies, and Cultures of Aging." *American Journal of Human Biology* 13(4): 494–504. https://doi.org/https://doi.org/10.1002/ajhb.1081.

Lynch, J. B., and E. Y. Hsiao. 2019. "Microbiomes as Sources of Emergent Host Phenotypes." *Science* 365(6460): 1405–1409. https://doi.org/10.1126/science.aay0240.

Maffei, V. J., S. Kim, E. Blanchard IV, M. Luo, S. M. Jazwinski, C. M. Taylor, and D. A. Welsh. 2017. "Biological Aging and the Human Gut Microbiota." *Journals of Gerontology. Series A, Biological Sciences and Medical Sciences* 72(11): 1474–1482. https://doi.org/10.1093/gerona/glx042.

Mailing, L. J., J. M. Allen, T. W. Buford, C. J. Fields, and J. A. Woods. 2019. "Exercise and the Gut Microbiome: A Review of the Evidence, Potential Mechanisms, and Implications for Human Health." *Exercise and Sport Sciences Reviews* 47(2): 75–85. https://doi.org/10.1249/jes.0000000000000183.

Marcus, Robert, David W. Dempster, and Mary L. Bouxsein. 2013. "The Nature of Osteoporosis." In *Osteoporosis*, 4th ed., edited by Robert Marcus, David Feldman, David W. Dempster, Marjorie Luckey, and Jane A. Cauley, 21–30. San Diego: Academic Press.

Martucci, Morena, Rita Ostan, Fiammetta Biondi, Elena Bellavista, Cristina Fabbri, Claudia Bertarelli, Stefano Salvioli, Miriam Capri, Claudio Franceschi, and Aurelia Santoro. 2017. "Mediterranean Diet and Inflammaging within the Hormesis Paradigm." *Nutrition Reviews* 75(6): 442–455. https://doi.org/10.1093/nutrit/nux013.

Matheoud, D., T. Cannon, A. Voisin, A. M. Penttinen, L. Ramet, A. M. Fahmy, C. Ducrot, et al. 2019. "Intestinal Infection Triggers Parkinson's Disease-Like Symptoms in Pink1(-/-) Mice." *Nature* 571(7766): 565–569. https://doi.org/10.1038/s41586-019-1405-y.

Matthews, S. James, and Jason W. Lancaster. 2011. "Urinary Tract Infections in the Elderly Population." *American Journal of Geriatric Pharmacotherapy* 9(5): 286–309. https://doi.org/10.1016/j.amjopharm.2011.07.002.

Meadow, J. F., A. E. Altrichter, S. W. Kembel, J. Kline, G. Mhuireach, M. Moriyama, D. Northcutt, et al. 2014. "Indoor Airborne Bacterial Communities Are Influenced by Ventilation, Occupancy, and Outdoor Air Source." *Indoor Air* 24(1): 41–48. https://doi.org/10.1111/ina.12047.

Mehta, Supriya D., Dan Zhao, Stefan J. Green, Walter Agingu, Fredrick Otieno, Runa Bhaumik, Dulal Bhaumik, and Robert C. Bailey. 2020. "The Microbiome Composition of a Man's Penis Predicts Incident Bacterial Vaginosis in His Female Sex Partner with High Accuracy." *Frontiers in Cellular and Infection Microbiology* 10(433). https://doi.org/10.3389/fcimb.2020.00433.

Morris, Martha Clare, Christy C. Tangney, Yamin Wang, Frank M. Sacks, David A. Bennett, and Neelum T. Aggarwal. 2015. "MIND Diet Associated with Reduced Incidence of Alzheimer's Disease." *Alzheimer's & Dementia: Journal of the Alzheimer's Association* 11(9): 1007–1014. https://doi.org/10.1016/j.jalz.2014.11.009.

Murabito, Joanne M., Rong Yuan, and Kathryn L. Lunetta. 2012. "The Search for Longevity and Healthy Aging Genes: Insights from Epidemiological Studies and Samples of Long-Lived Individuals." *Journals Of Gerontology. Series A, Biological Sciences and Medical Sciences* 67(5): 470–479. https://doi.org/10.1093/gerona/gls089.

Niesler, Beate, Stefanie Kuerten, I. Ekin Demir, and Karl-Herbert Schäfer. 2021. "Disorders of the Enteric Nervous System—A Holistic View." *Nature Reviews Gastroenterology & Hepatology.* https://doi.org/10.1038/s41575-020-00385-2.

Niewöhner, J., and M. Lock. 2018. "Situating Local Biologies: Anthropological Perspectives on Environment/Human Entanglements." *BioSocieties* 13: 681–697.

O'Toole, Paul W., and Ian B. Jeffery. 2015. "Gut Microbiota and Aging." *Science* 350(6265): 1214–1215. https://doi.org/10.1126/science.aac8469.

Olesen, Scott W., and Eric J. Alm. 2016. "Dysbiosis Is Not an Answer." *Nature Microbiology* 1(12): 16228. https://doi.org/10.1038/nmicrobiol.2016.228.

Omran, Abdel R. 1971. "The Epidemiologic Transition: A Theory of the Epidemiology of Population Change." *The Milbank Memorial Fund Quarterly* 49(4): 509–538. https://doi.org/10.2307/3349375.

Pace, Fernanda, and Paula I. Watnick. 2020. "The Interplay of Sex Steroids, the Immune Response, and the Intestinal Microbiota." *Trends in Microbiology.* https://doi.org/10.1016/j.tim.2020.11.001.

Patel, Alpa V., Maret L. Maliniak, Erika Rees-Punia, Charles E. Matthews, and Susan M. Gapstur. 2018. "Prolonged Leisure Time Spent Sitting in Relation to Cause-Specific Mortality in a Large US Cohort." *American Journal of Epidemiology* 187(10): 2151–2158. https://doi.org/10.1093/aje/kwy125.

Petersen, C., and J. L. Round. 2014. "Defining Dysbiosis and Its Influence on Host Immunity and Disease." *Cellular Microbiology* 16(7): 1024–1033. https://doi.org/10.1111/cmi.12308.

Poulain, Michel, Giovanni Mario Pes, Claude Grasland, Ciriaco Carru, Luigi Ferrucci, Giovannella Baggio, Claudio Franceschi, and Luca Deiana. 2004. "Identification of a Geographic Area Characterized by Extreme Longevity in the Sardinia Island: The AKEA Study." *Experimental Gerontology* 39(9): 1423–1429. https://doi.org/10.1016/j.exger.2004.06.016.

Reza, Musarrat Maisha, B. Brett Finlay, and Sven Pettersson. 2019. "Gut Microbes, Ageing & Organ Function: A Chameleon in Modern Biology?" *EMBO Molecular Medicine* 11(9): e9872. https://doi.org/10.15252/emmm.201809872.

Rios, Jaqueline Lourdes, Marc R. Bomhof, Raylene A. Reimer, David A. Hart, Kelsey H. Collins, and Walter Herzog. 2019. "Protective Effect of Prebiotic and Exercise Intervention on Knee Health in a Rat Model of Diet-Induced Obesity." *Scientific Reports* 9(1): 3893. https://doi.org/10.1038/s41598-019-40601-x.

Rocca, Jennifer D., Marie Simonin, Joanna R. Blaszczak, Jessica G. Ernakovich, Sean M. Gibbons, Firas S. Midani, and Alex D. Washburne. 2019. "The Microbiome Stress Project: Toward a Global Meta-Analysis of Environmental Stressors and Their Effects on Microbial Communities." *Frontiers in Microbiology* 9(3272). https://doi.org/10.3389/fmicb.2018.03272.

Rogers, Richard G., and Robert Hackenberg. 1987. "Extending Epidemiologic Transition Theory: A New Stage." *Social Biology* 34(3–4): 234–243. https://doi.org/10.1080/19485565.1987.9988678.

Roth, A. R. 2020. "Social Networks and Health in Later Life: A State of the Literature." *Sociology of Health & Illness* 42(7): 1642–1656. https://doi.org/10.1111/1467-9566.13155.

Sampson, T. R., J. W. Debelius, T. Thron, S. Janssen, G. G. Shastri, Z. E. Ilhan, C. Challis, et al. 2016. "Gut Microbiota Regulate Motor Deficits and Neuroinflammation in a Model of Parkinson's Disease." *Cell* 167(6): 1469–1480.e12. https://doi.org/10.1016/j.cell.2016.11.018.

Sanada, Fumihiro, Yoshiaki Taniyama, Jun Muratsu, Rei Otsu, Hideo Shimizu, Hiromi Rakugi, and Ryuichi Morishita. 2018. "Source of Chronic Inflammation in Aging." *Frontiers in Cardiovascular Medicine* 5(12). https://doi.org/10.3389/fcvm.2018.00012.

Santosa, Ailiana, Stig Wall, Edward Fottrell, Ulf Högberg, and Peter Byass. 2014. "The Development and Experience of Epidemiological Transition Theory Over Four Decades: A Systematic Review." *Global Health Action* 7: 1–16. https://doi.org/10.3402/gha.v7.23574.

Sender, Ron, Shai Fuchs, and Ron Milo. 2016. "Revised Estimates for the Number of Human and Bacteria Cells in the Body." *PLoS Biology* 14(8): 1–14. https://doi.org/10.1371/journal.pbio.1002533.

Sharon, Gil, Daniel Segal, John M. Ringo, Abraham Hefetz, Ilana Zilber-Rosenberg, and Eugene Rosenberg. 2010. "Commensal Bacteria Play a Role in Mating Preference of *Drosophila Melanogaster*." *Proceedings of the National Academy of Sciences* 107(46): 20051–20056. https://doi.org/10.1073/pnas.1009906107.

Simon, Jean-Christophe, Julian R. Marchesi, Christophe Mougel, and Marc-André Selosse. 2019. "Host-Microbiota Interactions: From Holobiont Theory to Analysis." *Microbiome* 7(1): 5. https://doi.org/10.1186/s40168-019-0619-4.

Smith, Kirsten P., and Nicholas A. Christakis. 2008. "Social Networks and Health." *Annual Review of Sociology* 34(1): 405–429. https://doi.org/10.1146/annurev.soc.34.040507.134601.

Smith, Patrick, David Willemsen, Miriam Lea Popkes, Franziska Metge, Edson Gandiwa, Martin Reichard, and Dario Riccardo Valenzano. 2017. "Regulation of Life Span by the Gut Microbiota in the Short-Lived African Turquoise Killifish." *bioRxiv*: 120980. https://doi.org/10.1101/120980.

Sonnenburg, E. D., and J. L. Sonnenburg. 2019a. "The Ancestral and Industrialized Gut Microbiota and Implications for Human Health." *Nature Reviews Microbiology* 17(6): 383–390. https://doi.org/10.1038/s41579-019-0191-8.

Sonnenburg, Justin L., and Erica D. Sonnenburg. 2019b. "Vulnerability of the Industrialized Microbiota." *Science* 366(6464): eaaw9255. https://doi.org/10.1126/science.aaw9255.

Spanogiannopoulos, Peter, Elizabeth N. Bess, Rachel N. Carmody, and Peter J. Turnbaugh. 2016. "The Microbial Pharmacists within Us: A Metagenomic View of Xenobiotic Metabolism." *Nature Reviews Microbiology* 14(5): 273–287. https://doi.org/10.1038/nrmicro.2016.17.

Tung, Jenny, Luis B. Barreiro, Michael B. Burns, Jean-Christophe Grenier, Josh Lynch, Laura E. Grieneisen, Jeanne Altmann, Susan C. Alberts, Ran Blekhman, and Elizabeth A. Archie. 2015. "Social Networks Predict Gut Microbiome Composition in Wild Baboons." *eLife* 4: e05224. https://doi.org/10.7554/eLife.05224.

van de Guchte, Maarten, Hervé M. Blottière, and Joël Doré. 2018. "Humans as Holobionts: Implications for Prevention and Therapy." *Microbiome* 6(1): 81. https://doi.org/10.1186/s40168-018-0466-8.

Wallace, T. C., M. Marzorati, L. Spence, C. M. Weaver, and P. S. Williamson. 2017. "New Frontiers in Fibers: Innovative and Emerging Research on the Gut Microbiome and Bone Health." *Journal of the American College of Nutrition* 36(3): 218–222. https://doi.org/10.1080/07315724.2016.1257961.

Willyard, Cassandra. 2021. "How Gut Microbes Could Drive Brain Disorders." *Nature* 590: 22–25. https://doi.org/https://doi.org/10.1038/d41586-021-00260-3.

Yatsunenko, T., F. E. Rey, M. J. Manary, I. Trehan, M. G. Dominguez-Bello, M. Contreras, M. Magris, et al. 2012. "Human Gut Microbiome Viewed Across Age and Geography." *Nature* 486(7402): 222–7. https://doi.org/10.1038/nature11053.

Zaiss, M. M., R. M. Jones, G. Schett, and R. Pacifici. 2019. "The Gut-Bone Axis: How Bacterial Metabolites Bridge the Distance." *Journal of Clinical Investigation* 129(8): 3018–3028. https://doi.org/10.1172/JCI128521.

Zeevi, D., T. Korem, N. Zmora, D. Israeli, D. Rothschild, A. Weinberger, O. Ben-Yacov, et al. 2015. "Personalized Nutrition by Prediction of Glycemic Responses." *Cell* 163(5): 1079–1094. https://doi.org/10.1016/j.cell.2015.11.001.

Zhan, Xinhua, Boryana Stamova, and Frank R. Sharp. 2018. "Lipopolysaccharide Associates with Amyloid Plaques, Neurons and Oligodendrocytes in Alzheimer's Disease Brain: A Review." *Frontiers in Aging Neuroscience* 10(42). https://doi.org/10.3389/fnagi.2018.00042.

Zhang, B., H. E. Wang, Y. M. Bai, S. J. Tsai, T. P. Su, T. J. Chen, Y. P. Wang, and M. H. Chen. 2021. "Inflammatory Bowel Disease Is Associated with Higher Dementia Risk: A Nationwide Longitudinal Study." *Gut* 70(1): 85–91. https://doi.org/10.1136/gutjnl-2020-320789.

Zheng, Danping, Timur Liwinski, and Eran Elinav. 2020. "Interaction between Microbiota and Immunity in Health and Disease." *Cell Research* 30(6): 492–506. https://doi.org/10.1038/s41422-020-0332-7.

Zuckerman, Molly Kathleen, Kristin Nicole Harper, Ronald Barrett, and George John Armelagos. 2014. "The Evolution of Disease: Anthropological Perspectives on Epidemiologic Transitions." *Global Health Action* 7: 1–8. https://doi.org/10.3402/gha.v7.23303.

5

Aging and Childcare

A Biocultural Approach to Grandmothering in Ukraine

SOFIYA SHREYER AND JULIE HEMMENT

"Eto samoye strashnoye, ne bit nuzhnoy svoim detyam" (It is the scariest thing, to not be needed by your children), my (Shreyer's) grandmother sighed as I helped her move into an independent living apartment for seniors. This move marked the first time she had lived alone in her whole life. She lived with us since I was born, raising my sister and I as my single mother completed dental school first in Ukraine, then in the United States. During my childhood, my grandmother maintained the whole household—from laundry, to cooking, to my homework—while my mother took on the bread-winner role. This arrangement is very common in Ukraine and other postsocialist states. Families tend to be heavily intergenerational,[1] are frequently single-mother led (Utrata 2008), and grandmothers take on a significant amount of childcare. When my mother remarried and conflicts between my stepfather and grandmother emerged, my grandmother was forced to move into her own apartment nearby. Despite my mother's constant attempts to make her feel loved and needed, my grandmother's sudden isolation left her with a deep sense of dread and confusion. She often laments to me about not knowing what to do or who to be or how to fill her time. After dedicating nearly a quarter of her life completely to raising grandchildren, she now feels betrayed, alone, and "not needed." This chapter is an exploration of grandmotherhood through a critical biocultural lens (Armelagos et al. 1992; Goodman and Leatherman 1998) based on Sofiya Shreyer's research project and a collaboration with Dr. Julie Hemment, a cultural anthropologist with expertise in postsocialist studies. Together, Hemment and Shreyer put these research findings into dialogue with feminist and anthropological scholarship on gender and postsocialism, particularly scholarship on Russia and Ukraine.

At the crossroads of aging and womanhood lies grandmotherhood. Grandmotherhood is a unique trait in the animal kingdom, observed in only a select few, distantly related lineages: a few species of whales, elephants, and, of course, humans. Although every biological being technically has or had a grandmother, intergenerational caretaking of infants is rare because most animals reproduce until very late into their lives, and therefore must raise their own young until they die. Human females have the ability to participate in grandmothering because their reproductive senescence does not match the timeline of senescence in the rest of their bodies. Menopause ends women's reproductive potential long before they reach life expectancy, freeing them up from risky childbearing and instead giving them the ability to invest in their children's children. The grandmother hypothesis, developed in the 1990s by Dr. Kristen Hawkes (2003), places hardworking grandmothers at the center of human evolution and argues that grandmaternal care throughout the human lineage shaped our life histories (Alvarez 2000; Hawkes et al. 1998, 2013; Parga, this volume; Rulu and Sievert, this volume), our sociality (Hawkes and Coxworth 2015), and our biology (Sievert 2006, 2011; Aimé et al. 2017).

However, not all grandmothers contribute equally to their grandchildren. Several studies examining variation in grandmothering found that maternal and paternal grandmothers differ in their effects on families (Gibson and Mace 2005; Jamison et al. 2002; Johow et al. 2011; Perry et al. 2014; Pollet et al. 2007; Sear et al. 2000; Voland and Beise 2002; Zhang et al. 2019). Voland and Beise (2002) utilized historical data from parish registries in Germany to assess whether grandmothers had an impact on the reproductive success of their children. They found children born without a maternal grandmother nearby had a significantly higher risk of mortality. Interestingly, in the first month of an infant's life, living with a paternal grandmother increased the risk of mortality. Similarly, a review of historical families in England found that maternal grandmothers increased the likelihood of a child surviving to age five from 81 to 90 percent (Ragsdale 2004). In a historical sample from Tokugawa, Japan, Jamison et al. (2002) found that the presence of a maternal grandmother in the household decreased the risk of mortality in children by nearly 35 percent, compared with paternal grandmothers who increased the risk of mortality in grandchildren by 10 percent. Among modern day populations, Gibson and Mace (2005) found that maternal grandmothers in Ethiopia improved their grandchildren's height and weight and were more likely to help in their daughter's household than their son's. In rural Gambia, as well, maternal grandmothers were found to be the only grandparent to have significant positive influence on the health of their grandchildren (Sear et al. 2000).

The differential investments of grandmothers have been explained in relation to paternity certainty (Bishop et al. 2009; Chrastil et al. 2006; Euler and Weitzel 1996; Pollet et al. 2007). Maternal grandmothers have near 100 percent certainty that their grandchildren are theirs since they bore their daughters and their daughters bore the grandchildren. Paternal grandmothers have less paternity certainty in their grandchildren because their daughters-in-law may have had children with other men. Another explanation was put forward by Fox et al. (2010), who suggest that grandmothers may have varying investment in grandchildren due to X-chromosome relatedness. While maternal grandmothers are certain to pass their X-chromosome traits to their grandchildren regardless of sex, paternal grandmothers will share X-linked traits only with female grandchildren. Paternal grandmothers' preference for female grandchildren over male may lower their overall positive effect on grandchildren.

While the grandmothering role is greatly diminished in the United States and most late capitalist societies, it remains central in many cultural contexts. In line with the grandmother hypothesis, Shreyer's Ukrainian grandmother stepped in as a primary caretaker while her daughter needed assistance and dedicated herself to caring for Shreyer and her sister, assuming an important and culturally sanctioned role. Grandmotherhood and this perception of being "needed" was central to this grandmother's sense of self, to being seen as a "recognized co-actor, an agent in society" (Hojdestrand 2009, 6). After Shreyer's grandmother had to move away and live on her own, Shreyer saw firsthand the dark side of grandmaternal care so seldom discussed in grandmother studies: a deep sense of loss at this role's conclusion and a sense of dislocation. This realization has prompted Shreyer to shift her focus from the evolutionary impacts of grandmotherhood, to examine grandmothers' own culturally inflected perspectives, health, and well-being. Additionally, Shreyer explores whether the differences between maternal and paternal grandmothers are culturally and socially imbedded. In her research project, Shreyer sets out to explore childcare participation of grandmothers in her home country of Ukraine.

Grandmothers' Health and Childcare Experience

This research project sought to examine how involvement in childcare affects grandmothers' health and well-being, and whether maternal and paternal grandmothers differ in their childcare strategies. Shreyer interviewed sixty-two grandmothers, recruited from both urban and rural communities. The study took place in the city of Kharkiv (population: 1.4 million), a suburban area of Lebedyn (population: 25,000), and a rural village of Sanzhary (population: 1,300). It was designed as a biocultural project that included health questionnaires, anthropometric measurements, and short open-ended questions focused on the grandmother identity and experience. Structured interviews focused on women's symptoms and diagnoses, reproductive history, residence of and access to grandchildren, and childcare. Blood pressure, grip strength, waist and hip circumferences, and height and weight were collected to estimate women's health. To explore the relationship between mental health and caretaking in grandmothers, a series of questions inquired about mental health symptoms, asking whether participants have felt depressed over the past two weeks and how often they feel lonely. A culturally salient mental health measure was added by asking grandmothers about their energy levels (*bodrost*). Although for many women in Ukraine mental health diagnoses terms such as "depression" and "anxiety" remain foreign and unrelatable, mental health is often discussed in terms of how energetic or cheerful, versus how sluggish, one feels. The survey also sought to examine the experience of women who do not perform childcare: do they see their grandchildren as often as they would like, and if not, why not? This was designed to help tease apart the causality between grandmothers' health variables and childcare by exploring whether poor health is the reason for not partaking in childcare duties, rather than the fact that their health variables are worse because they do not perform much childcare. We first present the health indicator data from the project, before going on to present the results of survey data and the insights we gained from them, in dialogue with the ethnographic work in the anthropology of postsocialism, which has uncovered for us a rich context within which grandmotherhood is constructed, embodied, and lived in Ukraine.

Data Analysis and Results

Grandmothers were ranked on a scale of 0 (does not perform childcare) to 5 (performs childcare everyday) to estimate caretaking investment. Intensity of childcare was compared to depression, loneliness, energy levels, grip strength, blood pressure, and a mental health score (a compilation of mental health symptoms and diagnoses that included depression, anxiety, mood swings, irritability, fatigue, and boredom). Grip strength values were transformed into age-adjusted categories of "weak for age," "normal for age," and "strong for age," according to the dynamometer ranking system (Amaral et al. 2019). The lowest blood pressure measure from a participant was scored according to the American Heart Association as having normal blood pressure, elevated blood pressure, hypertension stage 1, hypertension stage 2, and hypertensive crisis. Additionally, we explored whether age is associated with health factors and the reasons for low participation in childcare according to the grandmothers themselves.[2]

The 62 participants ranged in age from 43 to 84 years old, but most were between 60 and 70 years old. In the sample, 35 percent of grandmothers lived in intergenerational households (much higher than the U.S. average and a bit higher than Ukraine's average). We found that women with lower participation in childcare had significantly lower energy (*bodrost*) levels (p=0.01), lower age-adjusted grip strength (p=0.008), higher risk of depression (p=0.02), higher risk of hypertension (p=0.04), and higher loneliness scores (p=0.05). Out of the sample of 62 grandmothers, 18 did not do childcare or see their grandchildren face-to-face on a weekly basis. Fifteen of those women lived far away from their families, either in a different city or in a different country, so weekly face-to-face contact was impossible. For the other three women, although they were close by, their grandchildren lived separately, were older, and were busy with school and university. It therefore seems that low childcare involvement did not stem from poor health or unwillingness to perform childcare in this population. Interestingly, we found that age did not explain the relationships between active grandmothering and health effects. This may be because most of the participants were close in age (between 60 and 70 years old, mean=67.3, median=67).

Maternal and paternal grandmothers had significant differences in how often they perform childcare, as well as the type of childcare they perform. From the 62 interviews conducted, 24 were with maternal grandmothers, 22 were with paternal grandmothers, and 16 were with grandmothers who were both maternal and paternal. There were no significant differences between these groups in age, economic status, health variables, or locale. Grandmothers who were both maternal and paternal had a higher number of children and grandchildren. When comparing maternal and paternal grandmothers in terms of frequency of face-to-face contact, maternal grandmothers saw their grandchildren significantly more often (173.8 days out of the year on average) compared to paternal grandmothers (87.5 days out of the year, p<0.001).[3] Grandmothers who were both maternal and paternal were more likely to see their daughters' children more often. Maternal grandmothers discussed a significantly (p=0.02) wider range of activities that they perform with grandchildren than paternal grandmothers. Additionally, maternal grandmothers were much more likely to perform and encourage education-oriented activities with grandchildren, such as reading, poetry, and visiting museums. Paternal grandmothers, on the other hand, were more likely to encourage sport-oriented activities such as dancing, swimming, and martial arts.

The structured interviews yielded interesting insights into participants' views about grandmothering and its relationship to health. These views did not vary between maternal and paternal grandmothers. Most grandmothers described their role as providing primary assistance for their children and grandchildren. They believed that their main role is to relieve and assist a new family so the young parents can focus on their careers and "living their own lives." One grandmother who lives with her children and grandchildren recounted how when her grandchild was first born, the new parents would quietly open her bedroom door, push the baby carriage inside for her to deal with, and close the door. This was not a frustrating experience for her; she loved raising her grandchildren and sees herself as their primary caregiver. Many other grandmothers shared this feeling of seeing themselves as responsible for their grandchildren's care and wellbeing as not only a tangential babysitter but an essential part of children's upbringing.

As Shreyer jotted their responses to the survey questions, she was struck by the terms they used. Many of the participants described themselves as a kind of sanctuary for grandchildren, using a variety of terms to express this, such as "main pillar," "blanket and pillow," and "source of comfort." Many said that their relationships with grandchildren are special because they provide a relief for the grandchild from a tumultuous, strained, or strict relationship with their parents. Several grandmothers shared that one of their main roles is to spoil grandchildren. According to one grandmother, "their mother doesn't let them do anything"; according to another, "they fear telling their parents things, but not me" and the grandmothers "sympathize" with the grandchildren. Many also focused on the emotional well-being of grandchildren, emphasizing the importance of "being mentors"; teaching morality, intergenerational relationships, and kindness; and showing them how to overcome negativity in life (see also Howell et al. and Agunbiade, this volume, for discussions on generativity).

Significantly, many grandmothers emphasized how different their relationship is with their grandchildren than it was with their own children. Many reflected on how much closer they are with their grandchildren, emphasizing a stronger emotional bond. One of the reasons for the uniqueness of this relationship, according to these participants, is that they have a less hectic lifestyle and more free time to dedicate to childcare. One grandmother explains, "A mom doesn't listen to their child. She doesn't have the time for that, she's busy, but grandma does everything for their grandchildren, shares all her time." Another grandmother further elaborates, "when you're a mom, you don't notice . . . everything passes by itself, we have it differently." When asked about the roles of grandmothers, another participant shared that the most important thing for a grandmother to do is "to give all the attention you weren't able to give to your children to your grandchildren."

Although grandmothers shared that they dedicate more time to childcare now than they did as parents, they also explained that this relationship is not as intense as childcare was for them as mothers. One grandmother explained, "It's very different from motherhood. There's no feeling of strained responsibility." Another grandmother said that it is a different "frame of mind" from parenthood. Another grandmother humorously gave Shreyer advice for when she has grandchildren of her own: "Love your grandchildren. They will avenge you to your children," hinting at strained relationships between parents and children and compared to the relaxed, supportive "camaraderie" between grandchildren and grandmothers. Grandmothers took pride in having a friendship with their grandchildren and being someone grandchildren can trust.

The participants also discussed that they believe grandchildren are good for their mental and physical well-being. A few grandmothers remarked that they noticed having lower blood pressure when they spend time with grandchildren, and that when they are alone, their blood pressure rises. They feel an influx of energy and emotions of joy that they believe are essential to their health. One grandmother noted, "How could I *not* be a grandmother? I sleep better, gives me stamina, some kind of life energy . . ."

while another stated, "They are a retreat from daily life. It's good to have grandchildren when you have depression." A few grandmothers also remarked how much younger they feel with their grandchildren, stating that they "don't allow you to age," and "the more children, the younger the grandmother." It is evident that grandmotherhood is a primary identity for these women, and they believe that their role is to dedicate all of their time to their grandchildren, which in return helps them feel younger and age healthfully. They regard being active in childcare as natural. These answers are in accordance with our health outcome findings, and potentially expand on the stress-buffering effects of active grandmotherhood that result in lower levels of depression, loneliness, and hypertension, as well as higher grip strength and energy.

Nonetheless, some grandmothers also shared some anxieties and concerns about over-involvement. One grandmother warned, "a child's first enemy is their grandmother," and others said that grandmothers must not "meddle," "interfere," or "nag" in childcare. A few grandmothers provided context to these anxieties by voicing that their children explicitly let them know that they will be raising their children differently. Other grandmothers expressed anxiety about change, noting that nowadays, parents know and understand more than they did or are "smarter" than they were when it comes to childcare. These grandmothers felt uncomfortable making decisions regarding their grandchildren without consulting parents and did not offer advice unless they were asked. Resonant with Shreyer's own grandmother's words, these women expressed that they no longer felt needed, and that the terms of grandmotherhood have changed and are at odds with their expectations.

Grandmotherhood through a Critical Biocultural Lens

The term "biocultural" has been applied to countless research projects within anthropology (Hoke and Schell 2020), a field perfectly suited for acknowledging the inseparable and bidirectional connections between biology, culture, and environment in humans. This study design was biocultural in a sense that it acknowledged the cultural institution of grandmotherhood and elicited grandmothers' experiences through short responses and linked it to their health, well-being, and biological outcomes. However, Shreyer was left with more questions than answers. She wanted to probe deeper and to widen her lens to better understand these narratives and the powerful feelings they expressed. She was curious about why Ukrainian grandmothers have such definitive expectations about grandmotherhood, why maternal and paternal grandmothers have such distinct differences in childcare roles, and why it is so common for older women to expect and enjoy being a primary caregiver for grandchildren. This finding is in stark contrast to grandmothers in the United States, who experience a significant amount of caregiver burden when raising grandchildren and suffer negative health consequences as a result of high amounts of caregiving (Baker and Silverstein 2008; Bowers and Myers 1999; Chen et al. 2015; Whitely et al. 2001). Understanding this variation in grandmotherhood experience requires a critical biocultural approach, which recognizes that human experience is shaped by political, economic, and historical forces (Singer 1986). A critical perspective would argue that grandmotherhood cannot be understood without acknowledging the macro-level structures and processes that permeate women's lives, motivations, and expectations (Leatherman and Goodman 2011). It required an engagement with ethnographic works as well, via recent studies within the anthropology of postsocialism.

Grandmotherhood is often written about as a discrete stage in a woman's life, and though this may be true, historically specific sociocultural expectations (gender roles and norms) shape grandmotherhood as an institution as well as women's experience of it. In this sample, this is particularly important because the participants lived through such a turbulent period of history. While they grew up during the Soviet period and were shaped by the gender regime of the socialist state, they became grandmothers during the postsocialist period, when gender norms and ideals shifted radically.[4] By tracking the shifting gender norms and ideals through the participants' life course from socialism to postsocialism, we show that changes in childcare options and household domains, as well as the absence of men, necessitated grandmothers, especially maternal grandmothers, as primary caretakers in postsocialist households and created a culture of dedicated, self-sacrificing grandmothers.

Grandmotherhood in Transition: Shifting Gender Regimes

A rich literature explores the contradictions of the state socialist gender regime. Gender equality was a central claim of the Bolshevik state in the early stages of the Soviet Union. During the Bolshevik era, women were regarded as a necessary part of the workforce, and certain occupations such as agriculture, school-teaching, and medicine were feminized, remaining so throughout the Soviet period (Gal and Kligman 2000). The Bolshevik state also instituted liberal divorce laws (Gal and Kligman 2000), and women gained access to abortion as early as 1920. However, beneath this "façade of liberation" (Utrata 2015, 22) the reality was highly contradictory. Although gender equality was the official position of the socialist state, few policies existed to support women's daily life (Gal and Kligman 2000). Motherhood during the Soviet Union was politicized, and women were supported as "worker-mothers" through honorary titles and verbal encouragement (Utrata 2015, 23). Deeply held essentialist notions surrounding "natural biological differences" between men and women solidified women's role as the sole homemaker, expected to quietly manage both work and domestic responsibilities (Gal and Kligman 2000, 5). A woman's failure to do so reflected poorly on her character. Although the idea of working mothers coming home to work a second shift is not unique to the Soviet context, the conditions of the shortage economy made this labor even more burdensome. The realities of "actually lived socialism" resulted in shortages of domestic goods and appliances that made housework easier and more manageable in the West (Utrata 2015, 24). On top of that, the daycare options provided by the state were inadequate and a last resort for most working women.

Male gender roles in the socialist states were almost as contradictory as female gender roles. In stark comparison to the "mother-hero" archetype carefully built up by the state was the non-existing father archetype. While motherhood was politicized by the socialist state, fatherhood was never emphasized (Utrata 2015, 23), and fathers' responsibilities were not clearly outlined or encouraged. Although women were expected to participate in the workforce, men still dominated leadership positions (Gal and Kligman 2000). Despite the high number of men in leadership roles, in everyday life men's traditional roles were turned upside down by the socialist state. The paternalist policies of the socialist state undermined the traditional provider (bourgeois) male role, and women were consequently dependent on the state rather than men, a unique dynamic in social organization (Gal and Kligman 2000). Thus, throughout the Soviet period, marital ties were fragile. This fact, combined with the demographic shifts of the Second World War, led to the prevalence of households headed by single women. Both Utrata and Gal and Kligman discuss extensively women's low expectations of men in state socialist–era family life, and how men's absence, infidelity, and lack of responsibility became normalized and explained away simply as their nature. This context set the conditions for intergenerational support that continues to be the primary mode of childrearing in postsocialist states. In the context of a strong female presence and the absence of men, grandmothers, and most commonly maternal grandmothers, emerged as stable support systems for working mothers.

Grandmotherhood was also shaped by state socialist economic arrangements. The endemic shortages of the command economy led to the emergence of a vibrant second economy. People relied on family and acquaintance-based networks for survival and access to resources that the state failed to provide. Modes of informal exchange including *blat*, or exchanges of favors, were necessary for a functional life (Ledeneva 1998, 13). The culture of *blat* encouraged "cooperation and mutual support with a long-term perspective" (Ledeneva 1998, 40). Women, including grandmothers, played a key role in this form of provisioning. While grandmothers likely would not consider their efforts as *blat*, their assistance and engagement in informal modes of exchange in times of deficit and struggle was likely central to the maintenance of their family's survival.

Following the collapse of the Soviet Union in 1991, formerly socialist states such as Ukraine and Russia were plunged into a period of massive socioeconomic upheaval and pressured by the West to quickly adapt neoliberal economic reforms. The dislocations of the so-called transition period had major implications for citizens' health and well-being. This sudden end to social cohesion as people knew it, along with dwindling economic stability, gave rise to dramatic changes in the health of populations, marked by various public health indicators. For example, from 1990 to 1994, male life expectancy in Russia fell by 6.2 years (from 63.8 to 57.6) (Leon et al. 1997), fueled by a rise in cardiovascular disease and alcohol consumption. Additionally, infectious diseases, such as tuberculosis, diphtheria, syphilis, and HIV, skyrocketed (Rivkin-Fish 2011). The dismantling of the socialist state meant the erosion of the social safety net and the loss of public institutions including daycares, leaving parents with very few options for childcare. With such, there was a shift in the burden for welfare onto individuals and their families rather than the state. Reduced support from the state resulted in what Harboe (2015) refers to as the "gray zones of welfare," or areas that the state fails to support. This created a system in which people relied increasingly on informal networks and other solutions outside of the state to meet everyday needs.

As scholars of postsocialism have noted, the reforms and democratizing transformations that took place with state socialism's collapse had a markedly gendered character (Einhorn 1993; Gal and Kligman 2000). Democratic and market-oriented reforms hit women doubly hard. They lost both jobs and welfare provision through structural adjustment and faced both gender- and age-based forms of discrimination in the new job market. What is more, since women remained responsible for the bulk of domestic work (cooking, cleaning, shopping, childcare), the burden of coping with the consequences of these policies (increased prices of food, goods, and services) fell largely on their shoulders. In the face of these pressures, as well as increasing labor demands and male absence, grandmothers were forced into ever more time-consuming childcare and homemaker roles (Utrata 2015, 16). The demand for grandmaternal support was therefore already present during state socialism but increased in the postsocialist period. These dynamics explain the high level of participation in childcare in our participants, as well as grandmothers' expectations to be highly involved in childcare.

Anthropologist Jennifer Utrata (2015) examines the implications of this period for family life in Russia. Contemporary Russia has one of the highest rates of divorce in the world and has extraordinarily high rates of single motherhood. Her study, *Women without Men*, reveals how these distinctive gender roles and expectations shape the ways women plan their lives and contextualize their relationships. Cultural expectations and the belief that it is almost impossible to get married after age 25 leads many women to marry young and jump into marriages quickly. This results in tumultuous relationships with unforeseen consequences. For example, many newlyweds end up living with their parents-in-law, which aggravates already existing conflicts and creates new ones. The introduction of market reforms and neoliberal-oriented economic policies led to increased income inequality, undermining close family ties and intergenerational dependencies. Drawing on ethnographic data gathered in 2003–2004, Utrata explores the cultural meaning of single motherhood in Russia, which is not stigmatized as in the United States, but taken for granted. She reports that some attribute high divorce rates and single motherhood to the increasing rates of alcoholism and other "newer capitalist temptations" that men have succumbed to, as a result of being "weak-willed and irresponsible" in the face of new challenges brought about by capitalism (Utrata 2015, 4). Grandmothers, traditionally maternal grandmothers, step in to fill the void of the missing caretaker. Together, gender roles that shape the expectations for hero-mothers, missing the state's and men's resources, and an emphasis on cooperation account for the prevalence of very involved grandmothers.

In Soviet culture, grandmothers were expected to be self-sacrificing for both their children and their grandchildren, with less emphasis on how children pay those efforts back (Utrata 2015). Utrata frames this conflict by discussing the economies of gratitude. Grandmaternal support represents, in Utrata's eyes, an idealized form of care in which older women are expected to "satisfy children's emotional needs for love" while simultaneously easing their children's lives by taking care of the *byt* (household chores) (Utrata 2015, 22). Older women have little choice in the matter, pressured both by the cultural expectations of grandmaternal selflessness and the economic realities of barely existing pensions and nonexistent labor market for older women (Utrata 2015, 145). Ironically, the silent yet gargantuan workload that grandmothers take on encourages the state to further cut family benefits that could ease their burden. The pressure to be self-sacrificing, even if it is welcomed by grandmothers as a necessary part of their identity, often comes at a cost.

Utrata describes in detail the negotiation between mothers and grandmothers regarding responsibilities, the resentment that builds over time when grandmothers don't feel appreciated, and the necessity to develop boundaries in order to retain your own identity outside of being a grandmother. The emotional and physical dedication that grandmothers are often pressured to give to their grandchildren is often not reciprocated due to emerging neoliberal pressures to live in non-intergenerational households, with a growing number of elders in postsocialist states ending up in nursing homes and assisted living facilities. This emerging trend is shocking and new to many elders who grew up in intergenerational homes themselves and expected the same for their own aging process. These radical changes through postsocialist transformations reflect the often-contradictory coexistence of long-standing cultural values, with newer, market-related motives.

Discussion

While maternal and paternal grandmothers differed in how often they saw their grandchildren and the types of activities they did together, they did not differ in health measures or their perspectives on what it means to be a grandmother. Paternal grandmothers did not express less willingness to help their families or to be a safety net for their grandchildren. In this population, the more intensive care from maternal grandmothers was shaped by the postsocialist context of matrilineal bonds and high divorce rates. Due to divorce, absent fathers, and high rates of alcoholism among men, paternal grandmothers have lower or less frequent access to their grandchildren. These findings suggest that less intensive childcare from paternal grandmothers is mitigated by reduced access to grandchildren rather than unwillingness to invest or participate in childcare. Additionally, there were statistically significant differences in health between grandmothers who are heavily involved in childcare and those who are not, but not between maternal and paternal grandmothers (even though paternal grandmothers give less frequent care). This may be explained by the fact that there is a large amount of variation in the childcare that paternal grandmothers provide. In many cases, paternal grandmothers provided as much (and sometimes more) care as maternal grandmothers.

The story of shifting gender regimes through postsocialism and economic transformations brings us back to the idea of being "needed," echoed through Shreyer's grandmother's words and our participants' responses. The desire to be needed is imbedded within the human condition, and as Douglas (1966) theorizes, it is a feeling that embodies belonging to community and being immersed in the social web of mutual responsibility. To be "not needed" is to be deprived of what anthropologists call "social personhood," and not recognized as a "co-actor" in a process one believes as essential to their being (Hojdestrand 2009, 6). The social contract of expecting to be needed is exaggerated by the culture of reciprocity and mutuality in postsocialist countries, where systems of exchanges of favors were (and, to a lesser extent, still are) a way of life. This mutuality, however, is not mutuality of favors but mutuality of relationship (Ledeneva 1998, 148).

As our engagement with postsocialist literature shows, grandmothers were, and still are, a necessary resource for many women raising children by themselves or with limited resources. Soviet families were matrifocal and women depended on "extended mothering" (Rotkirch 2004, 160) to balance the burden of provisioning, childcare, and household chores. This strengthened the dependencies between women, as young mothers depended on their own mothers to be "surrogate wives" (Utrata 2008) to help with childcare and household organization, while older women depended on their children for financial and emotional support. Reciprocal kin support research suggests that within families, women have more dependable and enduring relationships (Rossi and Rossi 1990). Both cultural and political influences in the former Soviet Union have strengthened relationships between mothers and daughters and created a contract of mutual reciprocity. This research shows that as a result of this contract, maternal grandmothers gain increased access to grandchildren and support from their families that has measurable health benefits. When this contract is broken, grandmothers not only lose these benefits, but they additionally begin to feel "not needed," a culturally salient term that represents social disenfranchisement and isolation.

Conclusion

Our quantitative and qualitative data reveals a window into grandmotherhood in Ukraine. Most grandmothers believe that their identity as grandmother is central to who they are, and that their role is to selflessly dedicate themselves to childcare and "ensuring comfort" of their families. They believe that a high level of childcare is good for their health, and indeed this study's health data confirms this, showing that higher levels of childcare results in lower blood pressure, higher grip strength, lower risk of depression and loneliness, and higher energy levels. In this sample, women who reported no involvement in childcare, or a low level of participation, had grandchildren who lived far away, suggesting that within these data the relationship between low childcare and low health is not due to grandmothers' poor health and is outside of their control. Grandmothers' relationships with their grandchildren are viewed as special and unique from other family relationships, highlighting the importance of the culturally sanctioned grandmother/grandchild dyad. We found that the grandmother role and grandmothers' relationships with their grandchildren are vital to their health, well-being, and the aging process. Simultaneously we found that grandmothers who are not able to fulfill this role feel left behind and have increased risk of depression and loneliness, which consequently leads to poor health outcomes.

Our engagement with the postsocialist scholarship contextualizes these findings within a critical biocultural lens and helps us better understand the significance of grandmotherhood in Ukraine. Grandmaternal contributions to their families are seen as expected by both grandmothers themselves and the society around them. Even though grandmotherhood identity and health did not differ for maternal and paternal grandmothers, maternal grandmothers are more frequently engaged in childcare and more likely to be a primary caretaker for a grandchild. The high investment from maternal grandmothers can be explained by the context of postsocialist family dynamics, in which men are often absent and women turn to their mothers for assistance.

The grandmothering identity is so ingrained that when we asked participants how they feel about being a grandmother, they weren't sure how to answer; they would ask, "What else would I be doing?" When this expected role is unfulfilled, grandmothers in Ukraine suffer disproportionately because grandmotherhood is viewed as a natural and vital life stage in the aging of women. Grandmotherhood in Ukraine, as well as anywhere else, is shaped by profound political, economic, and cultural shifts. Investigating the underpinnings and foundations of grandmothering behaviors in a critical and cultural context highlights grandmotherhood as a fluid and complex life stage with biocultural consequences on older women's health and well-being.

Notes

1. More than 30 percent of Ukrainian families are intergenerational, compared to less than 16 percent in the U.S. (U.N. 2017).

2. All analyses were run as chi-square models in R (R Core Team 2017).

3. Frequency of contact and range of activities for maternal and paternal grandmothers were compared using analysis of variance in R (R Core Team 2017).

4. After a tumultuous period of war and conflict, Ukraine was one of the first countries to join the U.S.S.R. in 1922, and remained a communist state until the collapse of the Union in 1991.

References

Aimé, Carla, Jean-Baptiste André, and Michel Raymond. 2017. "Grandmothering and Cognitive Resources Are Required for the Emergence of Menopause and Extensive Post-Reproductive Lifespan." *PLOS Computational Biology* 13(7): e1005631.

Alvarez, Helen Perich. 2000. "Grandmother Hypothesis and Primate Life Histories." *American Journal of Physical Anthropology* 113(3): 435–450.

Amaral, Cledir Araujo, Thatiana Lameira Maciel Amaral, Gina Torres Rego Monteiro, Mauricio Teixeira Leite Vasconcellos, and Margareth Crisóstomo Portela. 2019. "Hand Grip Strength: Reference Values for Adults and Elderly People of Rio Branco, Acre, Brazil." *PLoS ONE* 14(1).

Armelagos, George J., Thomas Leatherman, Mary Ryan, and Lynn Sibley. 1992. "Biocultural Synthesis in Medical Anthropology." *Medical Anthropology* 14(1): 35–52.

Baker, Lindsey A., and Merril Silverstein. 2008. "Preventive Health Behaviors among Grandmothers Raising Grandchildren." *Journals of Gerontology: Series B* 63(5): S304–S311.

Bishop, David I., Brian C. Meyer, Tiffany M. Schmidt, and Benjamin R. Gray. 2009. "Differential Investment Behavior between Grandparents and Grandchildren: The Role of Paternity Uncertainty." *Evolutionary Psychology* 7(1).

Bowers, Bonita F., and Barbara J. Myers. 1999. "Grandmothers Providing Care for Grandchildren: Consequences of Various Levels of Caregiving." *Family Relations* 48(3): 303–311.

Chen, Meng-Chun, Kuei-Min Chen, and Tsui-Ping Chu. 2015. "Caregiver Burden, Health Status, and Learned Resourcefulness of Older Caregivers." *Western Journal of Nursing Research* 37(6): 767–780.

Chrastil, Elizabeth R., Wayne M. Getz, Harald A. Euler, Philip T. Starks. 2006. "Paternity Uncertainty Overrides Sex Chromosome Selection for Preferential Grandparenting." *Evolution and Human Behavior* 27(3): 206–223.

Douglas, Mary. 1966. *Purity and Danger: An Analysis of the Concepts of Pollution and Taboo.* London: Routledge.

Einhorn, Barbara. 1993. *Cinderella Goes to Market: Citizenship, Gender, and Women's Movements in East Central Europe.* New York: Verso.

Euler, Harald A., and Barbara Weitzel. 1996. "Discriminative Grandparental Solicitude as Reproductive Strategy." *Human Nature* 7: 39–59.

Fox, Molly, Rebecca Sear, Jan Beise, Gillian Ragsdale, Eckart Voland, and Leslie A. Knapp. 2010. "Grandma Plays Favorites: X-chromosome Linked Relatedness and Sex-Specific Childhood Mortality." *Proceedings of the Royal Society B* 277(1681).

Gal, Susan, and Gail Kligman. 2000. *The Politics of Gender after Socialism: A Comparative-Historical Essay.* Princeton, NJ: Princeton University Press.

Gibson, Mhairi A., and Ruth Mace. 2005. "Helpful Grandmothers in Rural Ethiopia: A Study of the Effect of Kin on Child Survival and Growth." *Evolution and Human Behavior* 26(6): 469–482.

Goodman, Alan H., and T. L. Leatherman, eds. 1998. *Building a New Biocultural Synthesis: Political-Economic Perspectives on Human Biology.* Ann Arbor: University of Michigan Press.

Harboe, Ida Knudsen. 2015. "Grey Zones of Welfare: Normative Coping Strategies in Rural Lithuania." *Journal of Eurasian Studies* 6(1): 17–23.

Hawkes, Kristen, J. F. O'Connell, N. G. Blurton Jones, H. Alvarez, and E. L. Charnov. 1998. "Grandmothering, Menopause, and the Evolution of Human Life Histories." *Proceedings of the National Academy of Sciences* 95(3): 1336–1339.

Hawkes, Kristen. 2003. "Grandmothers and the Evolution of Human Longevity." *American Journal of Human Biology* 15(3): 380–400.

Hawkes, Kristen, and James E. Coxworth. 2013. "Grandmothers and the Evolution of Human Longevity: A Review of Findings and Future Directions." *Evolutionary Anthropology: Issues, News, and Reviews* 22(6): 294–302.

———. 2015. "Grandmothers and the Evolution of Human Sociality." In *Emerging Trends in the Social and Behavioral Sciences*, 1–11. American Cancer Society.

Höjdestrand, Tova. 2009. *Needed by Nobody: Homelessness and Humanness in Post-Socialist Russia.* Ithaca, NY: Cornell University Press.

Hoke, Morgan K., and Lawrence M. Schell. 2020. "Doing Biocultural Anthropology: Continuity and Change." *American Journal of Human Biology* 32(4): e23471.

Jamison, Cheryl Sorenson, Laurel L. Cornell, Paul L. Jamison, and Hideki Nakazato. 2002. "Are All Grandmothers Equal? A Review and a Preliminary Test of the 'Grandmother Hypothesis' in Tokugawa Japan." *American Journal of Physical Anthropology* 119(1): 67–76.

Johow, Johannes, Molly Fox, Leslie A. Knapp, and Eckart Voland. 2011. "The Presence of a Paternal Grandmother Lengthens Interbirth Interval Following the Birth of a Granddaughter in Krummhörn (18th and 19th Centuries)." *Evolution and Human Behavior* 32(5): 315–325.

Leatherman, Tom, and Alan H. Goodman. 2011. Critical Biocultural Approaches in Medical Anthropology. In *A Companion to Medical Anthropology*, edited by C. C. Gravlee, M. Singer, and P. I. Erickson, 29–48. Hoboken, NJ: Wiley-Blackwell.

Ledeneva, Alena C. 1998. Russia's Economy of Favours: Blat, Networking and Informal Exchange. Cambridge: Cambridge University Press.

Leon, David A., Laurent Chenet, Vladimir M. Shkolnikov, Sergei Zakharov, Judith Shapiro, Galina Rakhmanova, Sergei Vassin, and Martin McKee. 1997. "Huge Variation in Russian Mortality Rates 1984–94: Artefact, Alcohol, or What?" *The Lancet* 350(9075): 383–388.

Perry, Gretchen, Martin Daly, and Shane Macfarlan. 2014. "Maternal Foster Families Provide More Stable Placements Than Paternal Families." *Children and Youth Services Review* 46: 155–159.

Pollet, Thomas V., Daniel Nettle, and Mark Nelissen. 2007. "Maternal Grandmothers Do Go the Extra Mile: Factoring Distance and Lineage into Differential Contact with Grandchildren." *Evolutionary Psychology* 5(4).

R Core Team. 2017. R: A Language and Environment for Statistical Computing. R Foundation for Statistical Computing, Vienna, Austria. https://www.R-project.org/.

Ragsdale, Gillian. 2004. "Grandmothering in Cambridgeshire, 1770–1861." *Human Nature* 15: 301–317.

Rivkin-Fish, Michele. 2011. "Post-Socialism." In *A Companion to the Anthropology of the Body and Embodiment*, edited by F.E. Mascia-Lees. John Wiley & Sons, Ltd.

Rossi, Alice S., and Peter H. Rossi. 1990. *Of Human Bonding: Parent-Child Relations across the Life Course*. New York: Aldine de Gruyter.

Rotkirch, Anna. 2004. "'Coming to Stand on Firm Ground': The Making of a Soviet Working Mother." In *On Living Through Soviet Russia*, edited by D. Bertaux, P. Thompson, and A. Rotkirch. London: Routledge.

Sear, Rebecca, Ruth Mace, and Ian A. McGregor. 2000. "Maternal Grandmothers Improve Nutritional Status and Survival of Children in Rural Gambia." *Royal Society B*, 267(1453).

Sievert, Lynnette Leidy. 2006. *Menopause: A Biocultural Perspective*. New Brunswick, NJ: Rutgers University Press.

———. 2011. "The Evolution of Post-Reproductive Life: Adaptationist Scenarios." In *Reproduction and Adaptation: Topics in Human Reproductive Ecology*, edited by C. G. Nicholas Mascie-Taylor and Lyliane Rosetta, 149–170. Cambridge Studies in Biological and Evolutionary Anthropology. Cambridge: Cambridge University Press.

Singer, Merrill. 1986. "Developing a Critical Perspective in Medical Anthropology." *Medical Anthropology Quarterly* 17(5): 128–129.

United Nations. 2019. "Patterns and Trends in Household Size and Composition: Evidence from a United Nations Dataset." Department of Economic and Social Affairs, Population Division.

Utrata, Jennifer. 2008. "Babushki as Surrogate Wives: How Single Mothers and Grandmothers Negotiate the Division of Labor in Russia," *Program in Soviet and Post-Soviet Studies, Working Paper Series*. Institute of Slavic, East European, and Eurasian Studies, UC Berkeley.

———. 2015. *Women without Men: Single Mothers and Family Change in the New Russia*. Ithaca, NY: Cornell University Press.

Voland, Eckart, and Jan Beise. 2002. "Opposite Effects of Maternal and Paternal Grandmothers on Infant Survival in Historical Krummhorn." *Behavioral Ecology and Sociobiology* 52: 435–443.

Whitley, Deborah M., Susan J. Kelley, and Theresa Ann Sipe. 2001. "Grandmothers Raising Grandchildren: Are They at Increased Risk of Health Problems?" *Health & Social Work* 26(2): 105–114.

Zhang, Cong, Vanessa L. Fong, Hirokazu Yoshikawa, Niobe Way, Xinyin Chen, and Zuhong Lu. 2019. "The Rise of Maternal Grandmother Child Care in Urban Chinese Families." *Journal of Marriage and Family* 81(5).

6

Menopause

A Lifespan Perspective with a Focus on Stress

PETENEINUO RULU AND LYNNETTE LEIDY SIEVERT

Menopause, Stress, and the Lifespan Perspective

Menopause is an event identified in retrospect; that is, the last menstrual period followed by twelve months of amenorrhea. It is a human universal among all females who live to the age of 60. Within the life course, menopause is the transition from the reproductive to post-reproductive stage. This transition is characterized by hormonal changes that contribute to symptoms[1] such as irregular menstruation, trouble sleeping, emotional irritability or depression, hot flashes, body aches, palpitations, fatigue, and vaginal dryness (Prior and Hitchcock 2011; WHO 1996). These symptoms are related primarily to a decline in levels of estrogen (Bruce and Rymer 2009), although it is difficult to differentiate the consequences of lower estrogen from those of aging, as aging and menopause are inevitably linked.

In addition to changes in hormonal levels, there are shifts and stresses in family life during the menopausal years affecting, for example, the onset of depression (Kaufert et al. 1992). Perimenopausal women are twice as likely to develop clinically significant depressive symptoms than women who have not yet undergone the menopausal transition, even in the absence of a history of depression (Cohen et al. 2006). Furthermore, the risk for depression during the menopausal transition appears to increase with the presence of hot flashes (Cohen et al. 2006).

Generally, the menopausal transition happens anywhere from the mid-forties to early fifties, but in some cases, it has been shown to start even earlier (Faubion et al. 2015; WHO 1996). In Western countries, the average age of menopause can vary from 48 to 53 years (Gold et al. 2013;

Morabia et al. 1998; Sievert et al. 2013). Menopausal symptoms can last for up to five years or more (Avis et al. 2015; Freeman et al. 2011), and these symptoms can vary widely across populations, ethnicities, and individuals (Melby et al. 2011; Sievert 2006). Among the most common symptoms reported by women during the menopausal transition are vasomotor symptoms (VMS), which include hot flashes and night sweats. VMS are distinctive symptoms of the menopausal transition and affect women's quality of life (Blümel et al. 2011; López-Alegría and De Lorenzi 2011). About 80 percent of women experience VMS during the menopausal transition (Gold et al. 2006), peaking in frequency around the final menstrual period.

Factors associated with VMS include race/ethnicity as well as lifestyle habits, including smoking, alcohol consumption, exercise, and body mass index (Kakkar et al. 2007; Melby et al. 2011; Sievert et al. 2006). Another factor frequently associated with VMS is level of education, which contributes to increased stress (Gold et al. 2004; Freeman et al. 2011; Sievert et al. 2018). Moreover, perceived stress increased among women with less educational attainment and more financial difficulty (Hedgeman et al. 2018). Stress is also associated with midlife symptoms such as trouble sleeping, headaches, and depressed mood (Cuadros et al. 2012; Martin et al. 2007).

Stress can be defined as the physiological and psychological experience of significant life events, trauma, and chronic strain (Thoits 2010). Early studies on stress (e.g., Selye 1956) focused on physiological stress, and psychological factors were not considered. However, numerous studies have now examined the many factors related to stress, and results indicate that psychological factors play a significant role in stress responses (Cicchetti and Posner 2005; Schneiderman et al. 2005). Lazarus and Folkman (1984) propose that "psychological stress is a particular relationship between the person and the environment that is appraised by the person as taxing or exceeding his or her resources and endangering his or her well-being" (p. 19).

In studies of menopause, stress has been measured in many ways, from recalled exposure to famine (Elias et al. 2003), or abuse during childhood (Thurston et al. 2008), to concurrent levels of cortisol (Gibson et al. 2016). This chapter will apply a lifespan perspective to consider how early life events, as well as concurrent stress, may be associated with age at menopause and symptom experiences at midlife.

Variation in Age at Menopause

As anthropologists, we study age at menopause as an aspect of human variation. Age at menopause is also of interest from an evolutionary perspective because it occurs in the middle of the maximum potential life span. In low- and middle-income countries, median ages at menopause are in the late forties; in high-income countries, median ages at menopause are in the early fifties (Morabia et al. 1998; Sievert 2014). Within countries, an earlier age at menopause is consistently associated with smoking, nulliparity (having no children), lower levels of education, and lower socioeconomic status (SES) (Costanian et al. 2018; Gold et al. 2013; InterLACE Study Team 2019; Lawlor et al. 2003; Mishra et al. 2017). Variation in age at menopause has also been related to intra-uterine and childhood stressors (Hardy and Kuh 2005).

Intra-Uterine Stressors and Age at Menopause

Age at menopause is determined by the number of oocytes (undeveloped eggs) made from germ cells in the fetal ovary and the rate of decline in the number of oocytes through the process of atresia (degeneration) across the life span (Depmann et al. 2015; Richardson et al. 1987). The process of atresia varies by stage of follicle development, but, in general, atresia involves the breakdown of the ovarian follicle. Although age at menopause has a genetic component (Stolk et al. 2012), variation in age at menopause also reflects exposures and development in utero, during childhood, and across adulthood. In utero exposures may have an effect on age at menopause by reducing the number of oocytes or altering the rate of follicular atresia. For example, an earlier age at menopause has been associated with diethylstilbestrol (a type of synthetic estrogen) exposure while in utero (Langton et al. 2022; Steiner et al. 2010). Women who were a part of multiple births, having experienced intra-uterine growth restriction, are also likely to have an early menopause (Ruth et al. 2016).

More akin to our concept of stress, the developmental origins of health and disease (DOHaD) hypothesis suggests that detrimental conditions early in life have late-life consequences, that is, that undernutrition or developmental changes in utero set the stage for chronic diseases in adult life (Barker 1994; Gluckman et al. 2005). For example, during the Dutch famine (1944–1945), individuals who were in utero had a 24 percent increased risk of natural menopause at any age compared with controls, supporting the hypothesis that prenatal nutritional stress can influence the reproductive life span in later life (Yarde et al. 2013).

Several investigators have hypothesized that growth restriction during fetal life, estimated by birth weight, results in a smaller number of primordial follicles in the fetal ovary and an earlier age at menopause (Bjelland et al. 2020; Steiner et al. 2010). This hypothesis has not been supported by physiological measures of ovarian development (de Bruin et al. 2001); however, from a life history perspective, a poor fetal environment may signal to the body that it is better to carry out earlier reproduction in association with an earlier menopause (Tom et al. 2010).

Many studies have found lower birth weight to be associated with an earlier age at menopause (Bjelland et al. 2020; Goldberg et al. 2020; Ruth et al. 2016; Steiner et al. 2010; Tom et al. 2010), suggesting that poor nutrition or developmental constraints in utero may contribute to both a lower birth weight and compromised follicular reserves. Using the large prospective Nurses' Health Study II, Langton et al. (2022) showed that the risk of an early menopause (prior to the age of 45) decreased 7 percent with each one-pound increase in birth weight (HR = 0.93, 95 percent CI: 0.90–0.97). In other words, women who were heavier as babies were more likely to stop menstruating after the age of 45. However, other studies have not found evidence of a correlation between birth weight and age at menopause (Cresswell et al. 1997; Hardy and Kuh 2002; Treloar et al. 2000).

Childhood Stressors and Age at Menopause

The DOHaD hypothesis is not specific to the fetal period. Developmental challenges during infancy and childhood may have later-life effects as well (Murphy et al. 2013; Núñez-de la Mora et al. 2007). With regard to age at menopause, the rate of follicular loss is highest very early in life (Rothchild 2003), therefore nutritional and other stressors may have the most effect on age at menopause during an abbreviated window of early childhood. Hardy and Kuh (2002) used prospective data to show that low weight at two years of age was associated with an earlier menopause, and those who were breastfed had a later age at menopause compared to women who were not breastfed as infants. In the same cohort, there was no association between age at menopause and body size measures at seven years, indicating a critical window in earlier childhood. Cresswell et al. (1997) found that weight at one year of age was associated with an earlier age at menopause, regardless of whether the infants were breastfed or bottle-fed. The relationship between breastfeeding and age at menopause is inconsistent (Ruth et al. 2016; Steiner et al. 2010).

In perhaps the most convincing evidence for an early critical window of development related to age at menopause, Elias et al. (2003) showed that age at menopause was earlier among women in the Netherlands who had been exposed as children to severe famine conditions during the aforementioned 1944–1945 Dutch famine. Women who were severely exposed to famine conditions, based on memories of hunger, cold, and weight loss, experienced menopause earlier than women who were not exposed. Furthermore, exposure during early childhood had the strongest effect, so that women who were severely exposed from ages two to six years demonstrated a 1.83 year decrease in age at menopause compared to the unexposed group.

To further understand the effect of stressors in childhood, we examined age at menopause among Bangladeshi migrants to London and Bangladeshis living in the community of origin in Sylhet, Bangladesh. Women with low and medium levels of education had significantly earlier ages at menopause compared to those with the highest level of education. With regard to stress, an earlier age at menopause was more likely among women who had a history of 3–4 and 5 or more infectious diseases compared to those with a history of 0–2 infectious diseases (Murphy et al. 2013). As with the findings from Elias et al. (2003), our results showed the importance of early life effects in relation to age at menopause, even after adjusting for factors that occur later in the life course.

Many studies have examined age at menopause in relation to measures of socioeconomic adversity, finding that low SES is consistently associated with an earlier age at menopause (Lawlor et al. 2003; Vélez et al. 2010). Specific to childhood, Lawlor et al. (2003) used the British Women's Heart and Health Study to show that women from manual labor social classes who shared a bedroom and grew up in a house without a bathroom or car were more likely to have an earlier age at menopause. In summary, nutritional, immunological, and other types of stress during intra-uterine life and early childhood may contribute to variation in age at menopause. To understand this, we benefit from applying a lifespan perspective.

Variation in Symptom Experience

Anthropologists are also interested in symptom experience as an aspect of human variation. Menopausal symptoms vary across cultures, ethnicity, and geographic regions. It is estimated that hot flashes affect 75–80 percent of women during the menopausal transition (Gold et al. 2006). In the United States, the prevalence of hot flashes and night sweats varies with ethnicity and was found to be lowest among women of Japanese ethnicity (18 percent), with the prevalence increasing among Chinese (21 percent), White (31 percent), Hispanic (35 percent), and Black women (46 percent) (Gold et al. 2000). Other studies among Japanese women also found a lower prevalence of VMS compared to women of European descent (Ishizuka et al. 2008; Lock 1994; Melby 2005). However, results from a study using ambulatory hot flash monitors suggested that Japanese women have the same physiological changes indicative of hot flashes, but do not notice, label, or report the hot flashes to the same extent as women of European descent (Brown et al. 2009).

Studies from India suggest a higher prevalence of hot flashes and night sweats among postmenopausal women as compared to premenopausal women (Aaron et al. 2002; Thakur et al. 2019). That said, the frequency of hot flashes among women in the Indian subcontinent varies by region (see Table 6.1).

The wide variation in symptom experience prompts researchers to explore factors beyond hormones (e.g., social and psychological factors) that might influence symptom experience. As such, studies have indicated that a woman's perception or attitude toward menopause may affect her symptom experience and ability to cope with the menopause transition (George 1996; Hafiz et al. 2007; Sievert and Espinosa-Hernandez 2003). For instance, Bloch (2002) reported that one's attitude toward oneself as well as one's personal style of coping has a great influence on the severity of complaints during menopause.

Menopause is a change of social significance. Cultural beliefs, values, women's role in society, and attitudes toward menopause and aging influence women's experience (Beyene 1986; Flint and Samil 1990; Lock 1994; Ray 2010). For example, in a study of Bengali-speaking Hindu women of West Bengal, India, the majority of women agreed with the positive statement, "The older a woman is, the more valued she is." More than half of the women, irrespective of their menopausal status, described menopause as either a process of aging or a "natural event" in the course of life (Dasgupta and Ray 2017). On the other hand, Bauld and Brown (2009) indicate that high stress coupled with anxiety and depression, low social support, and a negative attitude toward menopause were all associated with higher menopause symptoms and poorer physical health outcomes.

Table 6.1. Prevalence of Hot Flashes in India

Study	Study population	Hot flashes	Risk factors
Borker et al. (2013)	106 women; Kerala	None reported	N/A
Dasgupta and Ray (2009)	Urban (n=70) and rural (110) areas; West Bengal	57.1% (urban) 78.2% (rural)	Low educational status
Gupta et al. (2006)	50 women; Delhi	32%	Poor overall quality of life; current use of antidepressants
Joshi and Nair (2015)	1,000 women: Vadodara, Gujarat	22% Subcategories: Mild (76.8%) Moderate (20.9%) Severe (2.3%)	N/A
Kalhan et al. (2020)	400 women: Haryana	36.7%	Perimenopausal
Khatoon et al. (2018)	300 women; Lucknow	53.3% Subcategories: Mild (45.6%) Moderate (29.3%) Severe (25%)	Low SES; low education (for overall menopause symptoms)
Rulu et al. (2020)	325 women: Nagaland	55.4%	Peri- and postmenopausal status
Sharma and Mahajan (2015)	urban (n=490) and rural (n=380) areas; Jammu	79.4% (urban) 77.4% (rural)	N/A
Thakur et al. (2019)	379 women; Kanpur	28%	Low SES; being perimenopausal; overweight

Hot Flashes and Stress

Hot flashes are anecdotally associated with stress. In one laboratory study of 21 women with at least six hot flashes per day, participants were 47 percent more likely to demonstrate biometrically measured hot flashes and 57 percent more likely to subjectively report hot flashes during stress sessions (e.g., loud noises and arithmetic problems) compared to non-stress sessions (Swartzman et al. 1990). However, results from larger studies have been inconsistent. Self-reported stress has been identified as a determinant of hot flashes in some studies (Avis et al. 2015; Freeman et al. 2011; Gold et al. 2004; Thurston et al. 2008) but not in others (Binfa et al. 2004; Sievert et al. 2007; Thurston et al. 2005). Stress is culture-specific in nature. For example, we found that midlife symptoms were associated with household change in Spain, but with job change in the United States (Sievert et al. 2007).

The Perceived Stress Scale (PSS) is a commonly used measure of stress in studies of hot flashes and other symptoms at midlife (Cohen et al. 1989). The PSS measures the degree to which situations in one's life are considered stressful. For instance, there are questions such as: How often [during the past month] have you felt nervous and stressed? And how often have you felt that things were not going your way? Each question is answered on a Likert scale ranging from 0 to 4, with higher final scores indicating higher perceived stress.

It is important to note that perceived stress varies with age, generally with a significant decrease in negative mood over the years following menopause (Avis et al. 2004; Cohen and Williamson 1988; Warttig et al. 2013). For instance, data from the multi-ethnic Study of Women's Health Across the Nation (SWAN) showed that perceived stress decreased for Black, White, Japanese, and Chinese women, whereas it increased for Hispanic women.

In the longitudinal Penn Ovarian Aging Study, women who experienced moderate or severe hot flashes during the study period had a higher baseline PSS score (21.9) compared to women with mild hot flashes (19.5) or no hot flashes (18.2; $p<0.01$) (Freeman et al. 2011). In a cross-sectional analysis of data from SWAN, the PSS score was significantly associated with VMS after adjusting for ethnicity, lifestyle, and other confounding variables (Gold et al. 2004).

In Campeche, Mexico, we also found PSS scores to be positively associated with the frequency of hot flashes (OR 1.07, 95 percent CI: 1.02–1.12) (Sievert et al. 2018). On the other hand, another recent study from Minnesota, using the PSS-4, reported that somato-vegetative symptoms (hot flashes, heart racing, insomnia, and joint pains) were not associated with the PSS score (Sood et al. 2019).

Cortisol is another biomarker of stress that has been used in studies of hot flashes. Cortisol is produced by the adrenal cortex in response to stress-induced activation of the hypothalamic-pituitary-adrenal (HPA) axis (Dickerson and Kemeny 2004). In the laboratory, among postmenopausal women with frequent severe hot flashes, mean serum cortisol levels peaked 15 minutes after the start of the hot flash (Meldrum et al. 1984). A different laboratory study showed non-significant increases in plasma cortisol levels during hot flashes (Cignarelli et al. 1989).

In the Seattle Women's Health Study, women with increased urinary cortisol had significantly greater hot flash and cold sweat symptom severity compared to women without increased cortisol (Woods et al. 2006). A subsequent analysis grouped women based on the severity of hot flashes, mood changes, awakening at night, joint ache, and problem concentrating. The likelihood of being included in the "high hot flashes, joint ache, awakening at night" group was significantly increased in relation to higher cortisol levels (Cray et al. 2010).

A recent analysis from New York City did not find any association between hot flashes and measures of salivary cortisol (Gerber et al. 2017). In contrast, among 44 women in Pittsburgh, increasing hot flash severity and bother were significantly associated with a diminished change in cortisol levels across the day (Gibson et al. 2016). Similarly, results in Saskatchewan, Canada, showed an association between blunted cortisol awakening response (CAR) and VMS frequency and severity, independent of reproductive hormone levels or sleep disruption (Sauer et al. 2020). In another study from the MsFlash Network in the United States, subtle abnormalities in free cortisol levels and chronic sleep disturbances were associated with greater frequencies of moderate to severe hot flashes (Reed et al. 2016). This literature demonstrates that salivary cortisol results have been inconsistent across studies of varying sample sizes.

Hot flashes have also been examined in relation to Epstein-Barr virus antibodies and levels of C-reactive protein as measures of stress (Sievert et al. 2018) and in relation to neighborhood stress and discrimination as measures of stress (Gerber and Sievert 2018). In the former study, Epstein-Barr virus antibodies and levels of C-reactive protein were not significantly associated with hot flashes. The study on neighborhood stress, however, indicated that increases in neighborhood disorder were significantly associated with the likelihood of hot flashes (OR 1.08, 95 percent CI: 1.01–1.17).

Symptoms at Midlife: A Lifespan Perspective

The previous studies looked at self-reported stress and biomarkers of stress concurrent with hot flashes in a laboratory or in relation to hot flashes during the past two or four weeks. Other studies have considered stressors that occurred earlier in the life span. One such study is the SWAN Mental Health Study where childhood abuse and neglect were assessed using the 28-item short form of the Child Trauma Questionnaire (CTQ). White and Black women who retrospectively reported a history of childhood abuse or neglect had a greater likelihood of hot flashes (OR 1.55, 95 percent CI: 1.10–2.19) and night sweats (OR 1.73, 95 percent CI: 1.24–2.43) in models adjusted for age, smoking, BMI, depressive symptoms, and other variables (Thurston et al. 2008). Similarly, in the MsHeart Study, childhood history of physical or sexual abuse was associated with more frequent physiologically detected VMS during sleep, after controlling for covariates (Carson and Thurston 2019). Furthermore, physical abuse and more frequent physiologic VMS during sleep were higher among non-White women compared to White women ($p=0.007$).

A recent study from the Data Registry on Experiences of Aging, Menopause, and Sexuality examined adverse childhood experiences (ACEs) with overall menopausal symptom burden among midlife women and demonstrated a significant association between the severity of menopausal symptoms and the odds of reporting childhood adversity. The investigators reported that as menopausal symptoms increased from the first to fourth quartile, the odds ratio of reporting 1–3 ACEs increased from 1 to 1.84 ($p < 0.01$), and the odds ratio of reporting ≥ 4 ACEs increased from 1 to 4.51 ($p < 0.01$), compared to no reported ACEs, after adjusting for age, partner status, education, employment status, and hormone therapy (Kapoor et al. 2021).

In summary, there is growing evidence that deleterious experiences during childhood are associated with a greater likelihood of hot flashes during the menopausal transition. This may be because of changes in central nervous functioning related to exposure to childhood abuse. An altered hypothalamic-pituitary-adrenal (HPA) axis may be associated with impaired hypothalamic-pituitary-gonadal functioning, resulting in an increased vulnerability to hot flashes (Thurston et al. 2008).

The Impact of Menopause on Health-Related Quality of Life

Health-Related Quality of Life (HRQoL) is a multidimensional aspect of health and illness that incorporates a range of variables related to health such as physical health and functioning, mental health, emotional well-being, role limitations, and social functioning (e.g., Hays 1998). Menopause, in many cases, is associated with reduced physical activity and the onset, or increased incidence, of other conditions such as diabetes, osteoporosis, or cardiovascular diseases due to aging. Additionally, a shift in social roles or status can be observed. For example, in India, Hindu and Muslim postmenopausal women can participate in rituals from which they were previously excluded (Ray 2010). All these changes (social and biological) can affect the quality of life (QOL) among women.

Some of the changes in QOL can be explained by an increasingly sedentary lifestyle (El Hajj et al. 2020). For instance, a population-based study in Finland reported that physically inactive women had an increased probability of anxiety/depressed mood, somatic symptoms, memory/concentration problems, VMS, and decreased well-being as compared to physically active women (Mansikkamäki et al. 2015). Furthermore, some studies have indicated that women who navigate through the menopausal transition negatively experience poorer HRQoL (Dennerstein et al. 2002; Mishra et al. 2003).

In a longitudinal study from STRIDE, late perimenopausal and early- and late postmenopausal women reported lower HRQoL compared to premenopausal women (Hess et al. 2012). Moreover, women who report hot flashes but are not bothered by them did not experience declines in HRQoL, while those who report both hot flashes and associated bother indicated a decline in all aspects of HRQoL, compared to women who did not report hot flashes. A study among Korean women demonstrated that menopausal women who had worse neuropsychological performance experienced lower levels of HRQoL. Furthermore, cognitive function, especially attention and working memory, was an important factor associated with HRQoL in menopausal women (Lee et al. 2020). Looking ahead to chronic concerns, an earlier age at menopause lowers the risk of breast cancer but increases the risk of osteoporosis and cardiovascular disease (Gallagher 2007; Shuster et al. 2010). In addition, hot flashes appear to be a marker for increased risk of cardiovascular disease (Brown et al. 2011; Thurston et al. 2017).

Conclusion

In summary, menopause is a female human universal. It is a natural physiological transition in a women's life when fluctuating hormones and changing life roles potentially impact one's overall health and sense of well-being. This chapter applies a lifespan perspective to the literature in order to consider how early life events may be associated with later health-related outcomes. From this perspective, intrauterine nutritional stress and early childhood nutritional, immunological, and physical/emotional stress appear to contribute to variation in the timing of menopause and symptom experience at midlife. In addition, self-reported stress and biomarkers of stress during midlife appear to be associated with symptom frequency and severity. Stress is culture-specific, and not all women experience stress or symptoms at the time of menopause. However, future anthropological work on midlife and beyond should consider the role of stress in explaining human variation. Variation in age at menopause and symptom experience have later-life consequences in terms of cardiovascular disease, osteoporosis, and other health concerns. Menopause is both a cumulative point in the life span, showing the effects of early life stress, and a determinant of later health.

Note

1. Following the convention of the literature about menopause, we use the word "symptom." It is not our intent to medicalize the transition.

References

Aaron, Rita, Jayaprakash Muliyil, and Sulochana Abraham. 2002. "Medico-Social Dimensions of Menopause: A Cross-Sectional Study from Rural South India." *National Medical Journal of India* 15(1): 14–17.

Avis, Nancy E., S. F. Assmann, H. M. Kravitz, P. A. Ganz, and M. Ory. 2004. "Quality of Life in Diverse Groups of Midlife Women: Assessing the Influence of Menopause, Health Status and Psychosocial and Demographic Factors." *Quality of Life Research* 13(5): 933–946.

Avis, Nancy E., Sybil L. Crawford, Gail Greendale, Joyce T. Bromberger, Susan A Everson-Rose, Ellen B. Gold, Rachel Hess et al. 2015. "Duration of Menopausal Vasomotor Symptoms over the Menopause Transition." *JAMA Internal Medicine* 175(4): 531–539.

Barker, David J. P. 1994. "The Fetal Origins of Adult Disease." *Fetal and Maternal Medicine Review* 6(2): 71–80.

Bauld, Rosie, and Rhonda F. Brown. 2009. "Stress, Psychological Distress, Psychosocial Factors, Menopause Symptoms and Physical Health in Women." *Maturitas* 62(2): 160–165.

Beyene, Yewoubdar. 1986. "Cultural Significance and Physiological Manifestations of Menopause: A Biocultural Analysis." *Culture Medicine and Psychiatry* 10(1): 47–71.

Binfa, Lorena, Camil Castelo-Branco, Juan Enrique Blümel, María J. Cancelo, Hilda Bonilla, Ingrid Muñoz, Vivian Vergara, et al. 2004. "Influence of Psycho-Social Factors on Climacteric Symptoms." *Maturitas* 48(4): 425–431.

Bjelland, Elisabeth K., Jon M. Gran, Solveig Hofvind, and Anne Eskild. 2020. "The Association of Birthweight with Age at Natural Menopause: A Population Study of Women in Norway." *International Journal of Epidemiology* 49(2): 528–536.

Bloch, A. 2002. "Self-Awareness during the Menopause." *Maturitas* 41(1): 61–68.

Blümel, Juan E., Peter Chedraui, German Baron, Emma Belzares, Ascanio Bencosme, Andres Calle, Luis Danckers, et al. 2011. "A Large Multinational Study of Vasomotor Symptom Prevalence, Duration, and Impact on Quality of Life in Middle-Aged Women." *Menopause* 18(7): 778–785.

Borker, Sagar A., P. P. Venugopalan, and Shruthi N. Bhat. 2013. "Study of Menopausal Symptoms, and Perceptions About Menopause among Women at a Rural Community in Kerala." *Journal of Mid-Life Health* 4(3): 182–187.

Brown, Daniel E., Lynnette Leidy Sievert, Lynn A. Morrison, Angela M. Reza, and Phoebe S. Mills. 2009. "Do Japanese American Women Really Have Fewer Hot Flashes Than European Americans? The Hilo Women's Health Study." *Menopause* 16(5): 870–876.

Brown, Daniel E., Lynnette L. Sievert, Lynn A. Morrison, Nichole Rahberg, and Angela Reza. 2011. "The Relation between Hot Flashes and Ambulatory Blood Pressure: The Hilo Women's Health Study." *Psychosomatic Medicine* 73(2): 166–172.

Bruce, Deborah, and Janice Rymer. 2009. "Symptoms of the Menopause." *Best Practice & Research Clinical Obstetrics & Gynaecology* 23(1): 25–32.

Carson, Mary Y., and Rebecca C. Thurston. 2019. "Childhood Abuse and Vasomotor Symptoms among Midlife Women." *Menopause* 26(10): 1093–1099.

Cicchetti, Dante, and Michael I. Posner. 2005. "Cognitive and Affective Neuroscience and Developmental Psychopathology." *Development and Psychopathology* 17(3): 569–575.

Cignarelli, M., E. Cicinelli, M. Corso, M. R. Cospite, G. Garruti, E. Tafaro, R. Giorgino, and S. Schonauer. 1989. "Biophysical and Endocrine-Metabolic Changes during Menopausal Hot Flashes: Increase in Plasma Free Fatty Acid and Norepinephrine Levels." *Gynecologic and Obstetric Investigation* 27(1): 34–37.

Cohen, Lee S., Claudio N. Soares, Allison F. Vitonis, Michael W. Otto, and Bernard L. Harlow. 2006. "Risk for New Onset of Depression during the Menopausal Transition: The Harvard Study of Moods and Cycles." *Archives of General Psychiatry* 63(4): 385–390.

Cohen, Sheldon, and Gail M. Williamson. 1988. "Perceived Stress in a Probability Sample of the United States." In *The Social Psychology of Health*, edited by S. Spacapan and S. Oskamp, 31–67. Newbury Park, CA: Sage Publications.

Cohen, Sheldon, Tom Kamarck, and Robin Mermelstein. 1989. "A Global Measure of Perceived Stress." *Journal of Health and Social Behavior* 24(4): 385–396.

Costanian, Christy, Hugh McCague, and Hala Tamim. 2018. "Age at Natural Menopause and Its Associated Factors in Canada: Cross-Sectional Analyses from the Canadian Longitudinal Study on Aging." *Menopause* 25(3): 265–272.

Cray, Lori, Nancy Fugate Woods, and Ellen Sullivan Mitchell. 2010. "Symptom Clusters during the Late Menopausal Transition Stage: Observations from the Seattle Midlife Women's Health Study." *Menopause* 17(5): 972–977.

Cresswell, J. L., P. Egger, C.H.D. Fall, C. Osmond, R. B. Fraser, and D.J.P. Barker. 1997. "Is the Age of Menopause Determined In-Utero?" *Early Human Development* 49(2): 143–148.

Cuadros, José L., Ana M. Fernández-Alonso, Ángela M. Cuadros-Celorrio, Nuria Fernández-Luzón, María J. Guadix-Peinado, Nadia del Cid-Martín, Peter Chedraui, et al. 2012. "Perceived Stress, Insomnia and Related Factors in Women Around the Menopause." *Maturitas* 72(4): 367–372.

Dasgupta, Doyel, and Subha Ray. 2009. "Menopausal Problems among Rural and Urban Women from Eastern India." *Journal of Social, Behavioral, and Health Sciences* 3(1): 20–33.

———. 2017. "Is Menopausal Status Related to Women's Attitude toward Menopause and Aging?" *Journal of Women's Health* 57(3): 311–328.

De Bruin, J. P., P.G.J. Nikkels, H. W. Bruinse, M. Van Haaften, C.W.N. Looman, and E. R. Te Velde. 2001. "Morphometry of Human Ovaries in Normal and Growth-Restricted Fetuses." *Early Human Development* 60(3): 179–192.

Dennerstein, Lorraine, Philippe Lehert, and Janet Guthrie. 2002. "The Effects of the Menopausal Transition and Biopsychosocial Factors on Well-Being." *Archives of Women's Mental Health* 5(1): 15–22.

Depmann, Martine, M. J. Faddy, Y. T. Van Der Schouw, P.H.M. Peeters, S. L. Broer, T. W. Kelsey, S. M. Nelson, and F.J.M. Broekmans. 2015. "The Relationship between Variation in Size of the Primordial Follicle Pool and Age at Natural Menopause." *Journal of Clinical Endocrinology & Metabolism* 100(6): E845–E851.

Dickerson, Sally S., and Margaret E. Kemeny. 2004. "Acute Stressors and Cortisol Responses: A Theoretical Integration and Synthesis of Laboratory Research." *Psychological Bulletin* 130(3): 355–391.

El Hajj, Aya, Nina Wardy, Sahar Haidar, Dana Bourgi, Mounia El Haddad, Daisy El Chammas, Nada El Osta, et al. 2020. "Menopausal Symptoms, Physical Activity Level and Quality of Life of Women Living in the Mediterranean Region." *PloS One* 15(3): e0230515.

Elias, Sjoerd G., Paulus AH van Noord, Petra HM Peeters, Isolde den Tonkelaar, and Diederick E. Grobbee. 2003. "Caloric Restriction Reduces Age at Menopause: The Effect of the 1944–1945 Dutch Famine." *Menopause* 10(5): 399–405.

Faubion, Stephanie S., Carol L. Kuhle, Lynne T. Shuster, and Walter A. Rocca. 2015. "Long-Term Health Consequences of Premature or Early Menopause and Considerations for Management." *Climacteric* 18(4): 483–491.

Flint Marcha, Samil RS. 1990. "Cultural and Subcultural Meanings of the Menopause." *Annals of NY Academy of Sciences* 592: 134–148.

Freeman, Ellen W., Mary D. Sammel, Hui Lin, Ziyue Liu, and Clarisa R. Gracia. 2011. "Duration of Menopausal Hot Flushes and Associated Risk Factors." *Obstetrics and Gynecology* 117(5): 1095–1104.

Gallagher J. C. 2007. Effect of Early Menopause on Bone Mineral Density and Fractures. *Menopause* 14(3): 567–571.

George, Theresa. 1996. "Women in a South Indian Fishing Village: Role Identity, Continuity, and the Experience of Menopause." *Health Care for Women International* 17(4): 271–279.

Gerber, Linda M., and Lynnette Leidy Sievert. 2018. "Neighborhood Disorder, Exposure to Violence, and Perceived Discrimination in Relation to Symptoms in Midlife Women." *Women's Midlife Health* 4: 14.

Gerber, Linda M., Lynnette L. Sievert, and Joseph E. Schwartz. 2017. "Hot Flashes and Midlife Symptoms in Relation to Levels of Salivary Cortisol." *Maturitas* 96: 26–32.

Gibson, Carolyn J., Rebecca C. Thurston, and Karen A. Matthews. 2016. "Cortisol Dysregulation Is Associated with Daily Diary-Reported Hot Flashes among Midlife Women." *Clinical Endocrinology* 85(4): 645–651.

Gluckman, Peter D., Mark A. Hanson, and Catherine Pinal. 2005. "The Developmental Origins of Adult Disease." *Maternal & Child Nutrition* 1(3): 130–141.

Gold, Ellen B., Alicia Colvin, Nancy Avis, Joyce Bromberger, Gail A. Greendale, Lynda Powell, Barbara Sternfeld, and Karen Matthews. 2006. "Longitudinal Analysis of the Association between Vasomotor Symptoms and Race/Ethnicity across the Menopausal Transition: Study of Women's Health across the Nation." *American Journal of Public Health* 96(7): 1226–1235.

Gold, Ellen B., Barbara Sternfeld, Jennifer L. Kelsey, Charlotte Brown, Charles Mouton, Nancy Reame, Loran Salamone, and Rebecca Stellato. 2000. "Relation of Demographic and Lifestyle Factors to Symptoms in a Multi-Racial/Ethnic Population of Women 40–55 Years of Age." *American Journal of Epidemiology* 152(5): 463–473.

Gold, Ellen B., Gladys Block, Sybil Crawford, Laurie Lachance, Gordon FitzGerald, Heidi Miracle, and Sheryl Sherman. 2004. "Lifestyle and Demographic Factors in Relation to Vasomotor Symptoms: Baseline Results from the Study of Women's Health Across the Nation." *American Journal of Epidemiology* 159(12): 1189–1199.

Gold, Ellen B., Sybil L. Crawford, Nancy E. Avis, Carolyn J. Crandall, Karen A. Matthews, L. Elaine Waetjen, Jennifer S. Lee, et al. 2013. "Factors Related to Age at Natural Menopause: Longitudinal Analyses from SWAN." *American Journal of Epidemiology* 178(1): 70–83.

Goldberg, Mandy, Heba Tawfik, Jennie Kline, Karin B. Michels, Ying Wei, Piera Cirillo, Barbara A. Cohn, and Mary Beth Terry. 2020. "Body Size at Birth, Early-Life Growth and the Timing of the Menopausal Transition and Natural Menopause." *Reproductive Toxicology* 92: 91–97.

Gupta, P., D. W. Sturdee, and M. S. Hunter. 2006. "Mid-Age Health in Women from the Indian Subcontinent (MAHWIS): General Health and the Experience of Menopause in Women." *Climacteric* 9(1): 13–22.

Hafiz, Israt, Jinzhu Liu, and John Eden. 2007. "A Quantitative Analysis of the Menopause Experience of Indian Women Living in Sydney." *Australian and New Zealand Journal of Obstetrics and Gynaecology* 47(4): 329–334.

Hardy, Rebecca, and Diana Kuh. 2002. "Does Early Growth Influence Timing of the Menopause? Evidence from a British Birth Cohort." *Human Reproduction* 17(9): 2474–2479.

———. 2005. "Social and Environmental Conditions across the Life Course and Age at Menopause in a British Birth Cohort Study." *BJOG: An International Journal of Obstetrics & Gynaecology* 112(3): 346–354.

Hays, Ron D., S. Prince-Embury, and H. Chen. 1998. *RAND-36 Health Status Inventory*. San Antonio, TX: Psychological Corporation.

Hedgeman, Elizabeth, Rebecca E. Hasson, Carrie A. Karvonen-Gutierrez, William H. Herman, and Siobán D. Harlow. 2018. "Perceived Stress across the Midlife: Longitudinal Changes among a Diverse Sample of Women, the Study of Women's Health Across the Nation (SWAN)." *Women's Midlife Health* 4(1): 2.

Hess, Rachel, Rebecca C. Thurston, Ron D. Hays, Chung-Chou H. Chang, Stacey N. Dillon, Roberta B. Ness, Cindy L. Bryce, et al. 2012. "The Impact of Menopause on Health-Related Quality of Life: Results from the STRIDE Longitudinal Study." *Quality of Life Research* 21(3): 535–544.

InterLACE Study Team. 2019. "Variations in Reproductive Events across Life: A Pooled Analysis of Data from 505 147 Women across 10 Countries." *Human Reproduction* 34(5): 881–893.

Ishizuka, Bunpei, Yoshiko Kudo, and Toshiro Tango. 2008. "Cross-Sectional Community Survey of Menopause Symptoms among Japanese Women." *Maturitas* 61(3): 260–267.

Joshi, Mital, and Sirimavo Nair. 2015. "Epidemiological Study to Assess the Menopausal

Problems during Menopausal Transition in Middle Age Women of Vadodara, Gujarat, India." *Indian Journal of Obstetrics and Gynaecology Research* 2(3): 163–168.

Kakkar, V., D. Kaur, K. Chopra, A. Kaur, and I. P. Kaur. 2007. "Assessment of the Variation in Menopausal Symptoms with Age, Education and Working/Non-Working Status in North-Indian Sub Population Using Menopause Rating Scale (MRS)." *Maturitas* 57(3): 306–314.

Kalhan, Meenakshi, Komal Singhania, Priyanka Choudhary, Seema Verma, Pankaj Kaushal, and Tarun Singh. 2020. "Prevalence of Menopausal Symptoms and Its Effect on Quality of Life among Rural Middle-Aged Women (40–60 Years) of Haryana, India." *International Journal of Applied and Basic Medical Research* 10(3): 183–188.

Kapoor, Ekta, Madison Okuno, Virginia M. Miller, Liliana Gazzuola Rocca, Walter A. Rocca, Juliana M. Kling, Carol L. Kuhle, et al. 2021. "Association of Adverse Childhood Experiences with Menopausal Symptoms: Results from the Data Registry on Experiences of Aging, Menopause and Sexuality (DREAMS)." *Maturitas* 143: 209–215.

Kaufert, Patricia A., Penny Gilbert, and Robert Tate. 1992. "The Manitoba Project: A Re-examination of the Link between Menopause and Depression." *Maturitas* 14(2): 143–155.

Khatoon, Fareha, Parul Sinha, Sana Shahid, and Uma Gupta. 2018. "Assessment of Menopausal Symptoms Using Modified Menopause Rating Scale (MRS) in Women of Northern India." *International Journal of Reproduction, Contraception, Obstetrics, and Gynecology* 7(3): 947–951.

Langton, Christine R., Brian W. Whitcomb, Alexandra C. Purdue-Smithe, Lynnette L. Sievert, Susan E. Hankinson, JoAnn E. Manson, Bernard A. Rosner, and Elizabeth R. Bertone-Johnson. 2022. "Association of In Utero Exposures with Risk of Early Natural Menopause." *American Journal of Epidemiology* 191(5): 775–786.

Lawlor, D. A., S. Ebrahim, G. D. Smith. 2003. "The Association of Socio-economic Position across the Life Course and Age at Menopause: The British Women's Heart and Health Study." *BJOG: An International Journal of Obstetrics and Gynaecology* 110(12): 1078–1087.

Lazarus, Richard S. 2000. "Evolution of a Model of Stress, Coping, and Discrete Emotions." In *Handbook of Stress, Coping, and Health: Implications for Nursing Research, Theory, and Practice*, edited by V. H. Rice, 195–222. Thousand Oaks, CA: Sage Publications.

Lazarus, Richard S., and Susan Folkman. 1984. *Stress, Appraisal, and Coping*. New York: Springer Publishing Company.

Lee, Kyoung Suk, Mi Sook Jung, Mijung Kim, Kyeongin Cha, and Eunyoung Chung. 2020. "Impact of Cognitive Aging on Health-Related Quality of Life in Menopausal Women." *Osong Public Health and Research Perspectives* 11(4): 185–193.

Lock, Margaret. 1994. "Menopause in Cultural Context." *Experimental Gerontology* 29(3–4): 307–317.

López-Alegria, Fanny, and D. R. Lorenzi De. 2011. "Lifestyles and Quality of Life of Post-Menopausal Women." *Revista Medica de Chile* 139(5): 618–624.

Mansikkamäki, Kirsi, Jani Raitanen, Nea Malila, Tytti Sarkeala, Satu Männistö, Jonna Fredman, Sirpa Heinävaara, and Riitta Luoto. 2015. "Physical Activity and Menopause-Related Quality of Life – A Population-Based Cross-Sectional Study." *Maturitas* 80(1): 69–74.

Martin, Paul R., Lidia Lae, and John Reece. 2007. "Stress as a Trigger for Headaches: Relationship between Exposure and Sensitivity." *Anxiety, Stress, and Coping* 20(4): 393–407.

Melby, Melissa K. 2005. "Vasomotor Symptom Prevalence and Language of Menopause in Japan." *Menopause* 12(3): 250–257.

Melby, Melissa K., Debra Anderson, Lynnette Leidy Sievert, and Carla Makhlouf Obermeyer. 2011. "Methods used in Cross-Cultural Comparisons of Vasomotor Symptoms and Their Determinants." *Maturitas* 70(2): 110–119.

Meldrum D. R., J. D. Defazio, Y. Erlik, et al. 1984. "Pituitary Hormones during the Menopausal Hot Flash." *Obstetrics and Gynecology* 64: 752–756.

Mishra, Gita D., Nirmala Pandeya, Annette J. Dobson, Hsin-Fang Chung, Debra Anderson, Diana Kuh, Sven Sandin, et al. 2017. "Early Menarche, Nulliparity and the Risk for Premature and Early Natural Menopause." *Human Reproduction* 3(3): 679–686.

Mishra, Gita D., Wendy J. Brown, and Annette J. Dobson. 2003. "Physical and Mental Health: Changes during Menopause Transition." *Quality of Life Research* 12(4): 405–412.

Morabia, Alfredo, Michael C. Costanza, and World Health Organization Collaborative Study of Neoplasia and Steroid Contraceptives. 1998. "International Variability in Ages at Menarche, First Livebirth, and Menopause." *American Journal of Epidemiology* 148(12): 1195–1205.

Murphy, Lorna, Lynnette Sievert, Khurshida Begum, Taniya Sharmeen, Elaine Puleo, Osul Chowdhury, Shanthi Muttukrishna, and Gillian Bentley. 2013. "Life Course Effects on Age at Menopause among Bangladeshi Sedentees and Migrants to the UK." *American Journal of Human Biology* 25(1): 83–93.

Núñez-de la Mora, Alejandra, Robert T. Chatterton, Osul A. Choudhury, Dora A. Napolitano, and Gillian R. Bentley. 2007. "Childhood Conditions Influence Adult Progesterone Levels." *PLoS Med* 4(5): e167.

Prior, Jerilynn C., and Christine L. Hitchcock. 2011. "The Endocrinology of Perimenopause: Need for a Paradigm Shift." *Frontiers in Bioscience* 3: 474–486.

Ray, Subha. 2010. "Is Menopause a Health Risk for Bengali Women?" *Open Anthropology Journal* 3: 161–167.

Reed, Susan D., Katherine M. Newton, Joseph C. Larson, C. Booth-LaForce, N. F. Woods, C. A. Landis, E. Tolentino, et al. 2016. "Daily Salivary Cortisol Patterns in Midlife Women with Hot Flashes." *Clinical Endocrinology* 84(5): 672–679.

Richardson, Sandra J., Vyta Senikas, and James F. Nelson. 1987. "Follicular Depletion during the Menopausal Transition: Evidence for Accelerated Loss and Ultimate Exhaustion." *Journal of Clinical Endocrinology & Metabolism* 65(6): 1231–1237.

Rothchild, Irving. 2003. "The Yolkless Egg and the Evolution of Eutherian Viviparity." *Biology of Reproduction* 68(2): 337–357.

Rulu, Peteneinuo, Lynnette Leidy Sievert, Meenal Dhall, and Elizabeth R. Bertone-Johnson. 2020. "Symptoms at Midlife among Women in Nagaland, India." *American Journal of Human Biology* e23456.

Ruth, Katherine S., John R. B. Perry, William E. Henley, David Melzer, Michael N. Weedon, and Anna Murray. 2016. "Events in Early Life Are Associated with Female Reproductive Ageing: A UK Biobank Study." *Scientific Reports* 6(1): 1–9.

Sauer, Tianna, Laurie Sykes Tottenham, Ashley Ethier, and Jennifer L. Gordon. 2020. "Perimenopausal Vasomotor Symptoms and The Cortisol Awakening Response." *Menopause* 27(11): 1322–1327.

Schneiderman, Neil, Gail Ironson, and Scott D. Siegel. 2005. "Stress and Health: Psychological, Behavioral, and Biological Determinants." *Annual Review of Clinical Psychology* 1: 607–628.

Selye, Hans. 1956. *The Stress of Life*. New York: McGraw-Hill.

Sharma, Sudhaa, and Neha Mahajan. "Menopausal Symptoms and Its Effect on Quality of Life in Urban versus Rural Women: A Cross-Sectional Study." *Journal of Mid-Life Health* 6(1): 16.

Shuster, L. T., D. J. Rhodes, B. S. Gostout, B. R. Grossardt, W. A. Rocca. 2010. "Premature Menopause or Early Menopause: Long-Term Health Consequences." *Maturitas* 65(2): 161–166.

Sievert, Lynnette Leidy. 2006. *Menopause: A Biocultural Perspective*. New Brunswick, NJ: Rutgers University Press.

———. "Anthropology and the Study of Menopause: Evolutionary, Developmental, and Comparative Perspectives." *Menopause* 21(10): 1151–1159.

Sievert, Lynnette Leidy, and Graciela Espinosa-Hernandez. 2003. "Attitudes toward Menopause in Relation to Symptom Experience in Puebla, Mexico." *Women & Health* 38(2): 93–106.

Sievert, Lynnette Leidy, Carla Makhlouf Obermeyer, and Kim Price. 2006. "Determinants of Hot Flashes and Night Sweats." *Annals of Human Biology* 33(1): 4–16.

Sievert, Lynnette Leidy, Carla Makhlouf Obermeyer, and Matilda Saliba. 2007. "Symptom Groupings at Midlife: Cross-Cultural Variation and Association with Job, Home, and Life Change." *Menopause* 14(4): 798–807.

Sievert, Lynnette Leidy, Laura Huicochea-Gómez, Diana Cahuich-Campos, Dana-Lynn Ko'omoa-Lange, and Daniel E. Brown. 2018. "Stress and the Menopausal Transition in Campeche, Mexico." *Women's Midlife Health* 4: 9.

Sievert, Lynnette Leidy, Lorna Murphy, Lynn A. Morrison, Angela M. Reza, and Daniel E. Brown. 2013. "Age at Menopause and Determinants of Hysterectomy and Menopause in a Multi-ethnic Community: The Hilo Women's Health Study." *Maturitas* 76(4): 334–341.

Sood, R., C. L. Kuhle, Ekta Kapoor, J. M. Thielen, K. S. Frohmader, K. C. Mara, and S. S. Faubion. 2019. "Association of Mindfulness and Stress with Menopausal Symptoms in Midlife Women." *Climacteric* 22(4): 377–382.

Steiner, Anne Z., Aimee A. D'Aloisio, Lisa A. DeRoo, Dale P. Sandler, and Donna D. Baird. 2010. "Association of Intrauterine and Early-Life Exposures with Age at Menopause in the Sister Study." *American Journal of Epidemiology* 172(2): 140–148.

Stolk, Lisette, John R. B. Perry, Daniel I. Chasman, Chunyan He, Massimo Mangino, Patrick Sulem, Maja Barbalic, et al. 2012. "Meta-Analyses Identify 13 Loci Associated with Age at Menopause." *Nature Genetics* 44: 260–268.

Swartzman, Leora C., Robert Edelberg, and Ekkehard Kemmann. 1990. "Impact of Stress on Objectively Recorded Menopausal Hot Flushes and on Flush Report Bias." *Health Psychology* 9(5): 529–545.

Thakur, Monika, Maninder Kaur, and Anil Kishore Sinha. 2019. "Assessment of Menopausal Symptoms in Different Transition Phases Using the Greene Climacteric Scale among Rural Women of North India." *Annals of Human Biology* 46(1): 46–55.

Thoits, Peggy A. 2010. "Stress and Health: Major Findings and Policy Implications." *Journal of Health and Social Behavior* 51(1): S41–S53.

Thurston, Rebecca C., James A. Blumenthal, Michael A. Babyak, and Andrew Sherwood. 2005. "Emotional Antecedents of Hot Flashes during Daily Life." *Psychosomatic Medicine* 67(1): 137–146.

Thurston, Rebecca C., Joyce Bromberger, Yuefang Chang, Edie Goldbacher, Charlotte Brown, Jill M. Cyranowski, and Karen A. Matthews. 2008. "Childhood Abuse or Neglect

Is Associated with Increased Vasomotor Symptom Reporting among Midlife Women." *Menopause* 15(1): 16–22.

Thurston Rebecca C., Y. Chang, E. Barinas-Mitchell, J. R. Jennings, R. von Känel, D. P. Landsittel, and K. A. Matthews. 2017. "Physiologically Assessed Hot Flashes and Endothelial Function among Midlife Women. *Menopause* 24(8): 886–893.

Tom, Sarah E., Rachel Cooper, Diana Kuh, Jack M. Guralnik, Rebecca Hardy, and Chris Power. 2010. "Fetal Environment and Early Age at Natural Menopause in a British Birth Cohort Study." *Human Reproduction* 25(3): 791–798.

Treloar, Susan A., Sheda Sadrzadeh, Kim-Anh Do, Nicholas G. Martin, and Cornelis B. Lambalk. 2000. "Birth Weight and Age at Menopause in Australian Female Twin Pairs: Exploration of the Fetal Origin Hypothesis." *Human Reproduction* 15(1): 55–59.

Vélez, Maria P., Beatriz E. Alvarado, Catherine Lord, and Maria-Victoria Zunzunegui. 2010. "Life Course Socioeconomic Adversity and Age at Natural Menopause in Women from Latin America and the Caribbean." *Menopause* 17(3): 552–559.

Warttig, Sheryl L., Mark J. Forshaw, Jane South, and Alan K. White. 2013. "New, Normative, English-Sample Data for the Short Form Perceived Stress Scale (PSS-4)." *Journal of Health Psychology* 18(12): 1617–1628.

Woods, Nancy F., Molly C. Carr, Eunice Y. Tao, Heather J. Taylor, and Ellen S. Mitchell. 2006. "Increased Urinary Cortisol Levels during the Menopause Transition." *Menopause* 13(2): 212–221.

World Health Organization. 1996. *Research on the Menopause in the 1990s: Report of a WHO Scientific Group*. World Health Organization.

Yarde, F., F.J.M. Broekmans, K. M. Van der Pal-de Bruin, Y. Schönbeck, E. R. Te Velde, A. D. Stein, and L. H. Lumey. 2013. "Prenatal Famine, Birthweight, Reproductive Performance and Age at Menopause: The Dutch Hunger Winter Families Study." *Human Reproduction* 28(12): 3328–3336.

II

Medical and Cultural Perspectives on Aging

7

Age-Related Changes in Human Skin

Impacts on Health and Perceptions of Attractiveness

HEATHER L. NORTON

Skin is the primary barrier between the human body and its environment. As our largest organ, it plays a key role in thermoregulation; can prevent and minimize damage from chemical or radiation-induced insults; facilitates the sensation of mechanical stimuli; and provides protection from bacterial, fungal, and viral infections while also supporting a commensal microbial community (see Melby et al., this volume). While the skin's function as a barrier provides protection from the outside world, it also provides others with insight into our own condition, serving as a signal of both age and health status (Fink and Matts 2008; Matts et al. 2007; Fink et al. 2012; Gunn et al. 2009; Christensen et al. 2004). As skin ages, it undergoes a number of changes in structure, function, and appearance, becoming thinner, declining in elasticity, weakening in its ability to fight infection, and suffering from slower rates of epithelial turnover that impair its wound-healing capabilities (Callaghan and Wilhelm 2008b, 2008a; Zouboulis and Makrantonaki 2011; Russell-Goldman and Murphy 2020). These age-related changes to skin begin at birth and accelerate at older ages, compromising the skin's ability to perform its key functions, leading Russell-Goldman and Murphy (2020) to argue that skin aging should be recognized as a disease.

The notion that aged skin is an actual disease, and not just a symptom of the general aging process, places aged skin in a category of conditions that can and should be targeted by biomedical interventions (Mykytyn 2006). By characterizing older individuals as being "at-risk" of developing age-related skin changes, these transformations become things to be surveilled and ultimately "fixed" (Smirnova 2012; Fishman, Settersten Jr., and Flatt 2010). To this end, the consumer market for products or procedures that claim to reverse or correct the perceived negative effects of skin aging continues to grow. Cosmeceuticals, so-called because they go beyond the cosmetic utility of covering up or masking flaws and instead bring about a pharmaceutical, measurable benefit, are a significant part of the anti-aging toolkit (Draelos 2019). Cosmetic medical procedures, sometimes described as "facial rejuvenation," are more extreme measures to correct the perceived flaws of aging skin. In 2019, approximately 80 percent of cosmetic procedures in the United States (including both surgeries and minimally invasive procedures) addressed issues related to facial aging (American Society of Plastic Surgeons 2019). Not surprisingly, given the strong emphasis placed on youth in Western norms of female beauty, the majority of these products and procedures are marketed to women.

In this chapter, I briefly review the basic anatomy of the skin, focusing on components most significantly impacted by aging. I then discuss the intrinsic and extrinsic effects of aging on skin, and how these can directly impact health concerns in older populations. I review different factors related to age perception and the practices used to influence these perceptions. Finally, I explore the still nascent field of skin-aging genetics, which may provide insights into the biological mechanisms of aging as well as the development of new products to counteract signs of aging.

Anatomy of the Skin

The skin is comprised of three primary layers: the epidermis, the dermis, and hypodermis. The exterior epidermis, which is the primary barrier between our bodies and the environment, is composed of four layers of densely packed cells. The most superficial layer, the stratum corneum, consists of 15–30 layers of dried corneocytes and serves as a barrier against dehydration and penetration by foreign microbes. These cells are organized in what is sometimes described as a "brick and mortar" arrangement, embedded in a lipid matrix. The stratum corneum is followed by a layer of flattened keratinocyte cells, making up the stratum granulosum. Immediately below this is the stratum spinosum, consisting of 8–10 layers of keratinocyte cells that produce keratin and water-repelling particles that help make the skin barrier waterproof. The stratum spinosum is also home to Langerhans cells, part of the cutaneous immune defense system, that ingest bacteria and other foreign matter. The deepest epidermal layer, the stratum basale, is connected to the dermis below by the collagen fibers that make up the basement membrane. There are three primary cell types in this layer: keratinocytes, melanocytes, and Merkel cells. Basal keratinocytes in this layer are constantly dividing; as they age, they are pushed upward into more superficial layers of the epidermis.

The stratum basale is also home to melanocyte cells, which are responsible for the production of melanin. Melanin is produced in two primary forms: darker melanin, known as eumelanin, and red-yellow pheomelanin. Skin pigment is largely determined by the total amount of melanin and the ratio of these two types; darker skin will have greater amounts of eumelanin relative to pheomelanin. Eumelanin's ability to quench reactive oxygen species (ROS) provides greater protection than pheomelanin from cellular and DNA damage induced by ultraviolet A and ultraviolet B radiation (Fried and Arbiser 2008; Swope and Abdel-Malek 2018). This has significant impacts for reducing risks of certain skin cancers. Finally, Merkel cells found in this layer stimulate sensory neurons and facilitate our sense of touch.

The dermis itself, located between the epidermis and hypodermis, consists of blood and lymph vessels, sweat glands, hair follicles, and nerves. Fibroblasts, which are the primary component of this dermal layer, secrete collagen and elastin, both of which play a key role in the shape, firmness, and elasticity of skin and form the extracellular matrix (ECM). Small projections of the epidermis down into the dermis, known as rete ridges, help bond the two layers together and promote the ability of the skin to resist shearing forces. The final layer of the skin, the hypodermis, is composed of subcutaneous fat, blood vessels, and nerve cells. This layer of fatty tissue helps anchor the dermis to underlying skeletal tissues. Age-related changes in all three layers can contribute to changes in physical appearance commonly associated with age, but this chapter will primarily focus on changes in the epidermis and dermis.

Age-Related Changes to the Skin

Properties of aging skin can be divided into two categories: those that characterize either intrinsic or extrinsic aging processes. Intrinsic aging factors include chronological age, endogenous hormone levels (Makrantonaki et al. 2010), skin pigmentation (Alexis et al. 2019), and genetic predisposition (Liu et al. 2016; Kanaki, Makrantonaki, and Zouboulis 2016; Makrantonaki and Zouboulis 2007). Two of the most prominent extrinsic aging factors are exposure to ultraviolet radiation (UVR) (Gilchrest 2013; Han, Chien, and Kang 2014) and smoking (Ortiz and Grando 2012; Morita 2007), although others—including exposure to pollution, repetitive muscle movements (like squinting or smiling), and activities related to lifestyle habits—may also play a role (Farage et al. 2008).

Both intrinsic and extrinsic changes to skin can be caused by cellular damage from ROS (Hensley and Floyd 2002; Sohal and Weindruch 2010; Kimball et al. 2018; Poljšak and Dahmane 2012) and a degradation of the collagen found in the extracellular matrix (ECM) (Griffiths et al. 1993; Varani et al. 2000). However, there are also distinct differences between intrinsically and extrinsically aged skin. Intrinsically aged skin is thinner and flatter than the skin of younger individuals due to an attenuation of rete ridges and a decrease in the number of fibroblasts (Callaghan and Wilhelm 2008a). Intrinsically aged skin is also characterized by both reduced amounts of collagen and elastin and an increase in collagen structural abnormalities in the ECM of the dermis (Callaghan and Wilhelm 2008a). This loss and disorganization of collagen leads to the appearance of fine lines or wrinkles and may contribute to skin sagging. More pronounced sagging may also result from the hypodermis pulling away from the underlying skeletal components (Callaghan and Wilhelm 2008a), an aging feature that may be particularly noticeable in the face.

The most well-studied extrinsic factor contributing to skin aging is UV exposure. Relatively to intrinsically aged skin, photoaged skin appears rougher (Callaghan and Wilhelm 2008a) and is more likely to display coarser wrinkles (Vierkötter et al. 2009) instead of the fine lines that characterize intrinsically aged skin. UV damage can also lead to the degradation of the collagen and elastin fibers of the dermis, resulting in thickened and less flexible regions of skin (Gilchrest 2013) known as solar elastoses. Other changes related to photoaging include the development of darkly pigmented spots, known as solar lentigines (or more commonly "age spots" or "liver spots") (Han, Chien, and Kang 2014; Callaghan and Wilhelm 2008a; Yaar and Gilchrest 2001). These regions of hyperpigmentation are characterized by a localized increase in melanogenic activity. Typically, the impacts of photoaging are more severe in lightly pigmented skin compared to darker skin tones with greater amounts of eumelanin. This is attributed to the fact that the higher eumelanin levels of darker skin provide some degree of protection from UV damage (Alexis et al. 2019). These photoprotective effects of eumelanin are also related to the lower rates of skin cancers in individuals with darker skin colors (Agbai et al. 2014; Cestari and Buster 2017).

Skin Appearance and Age Perception

Perceptions of an individual's age may provide clues about their attractiveness and overall health (Fink and Matts 2008; Christensen et al. 2004; Matts et al. 2007; Fink et al. 2012). In certain cultural contexts, age perception based on facial appearance may even provide cues about how to conduct social interactions depending on whether the person is older or younger than oneself (Anzures et al. 2010). While both facial skin and skin from other body sites (i.e., arm and chest) can be utilized to make inferences about age (Fink et al. 2011), the majority of research on age perception as well as cosmetic products and procedures to reduce signs of aging has focused on the facial skin.

Facial age perception seems to be primarily driven by skin topography (wrinkles) (Fink et al. 2011; Fink and Matts 2008; Alexis et al. 2019), pigmentation heterogeneity (e.g., solar lentigines) (Fink et al. 2011; Matts et al. 2007; Fink and Matts 2008; Alexis et al. 2019), and a loss of facial volume (Alexis et al. 2019; Rohrich and Pessa 2007). In a sample of European women, skin topography is a strong cue for perceived age, explaining 80 percent of variation in perceived age estimates (Gunn et al. 2009; Samson et al. 2010; Fink et al. 2011), while localized pigmentation variation serves as a stronger cue for health status (Matts et al. 2007; Fink and Matts 2008). Similar results were obtained in studies that assessed the impact of topography and pigmentation cues on age and health in European men (Fink et al. 2012, 2018). Although more difficult to study (Gunn et al. 2009), changes to both the position and volume of subcutaneous fat in the face (Rohrich and Pessa 2007) may also affect perceptions of age in both men and women.

While all humans will experience signs of facial skin aging if they live long enough, the onset of these signs of aging varies among populations. In a large study of over 3,000 women who self-identified as Black, Hispanic/Latino, Asian, and White, participants were asked to rate 10 signs of facial aging (including severity of wrinkles in specific regions of the face, puffiness under eyes, mid-face volume loss, and lip-volume loss) (Alexis et al. 2019). Women who self-identified as White displayed these signs of aging the earliest (between 40 and 59 years) while women who self-identified as Black did not report these signs until 60–79 years of age (Alexis et al. 2019). The authors noted that severity of these self-assessed aging signs was greatest in women with lighter skin, presumably because low levels of melanin offered little in the way of photoprotection (Alexis et al. 2019). This finding is consistent with previous work reporting that facial skin aging appears later and is less pronounced in darker skin (Alexis and Obioha 2017).

Differences in the timing and prevalence of distinct signs of facial skin aging can also affect facial age perception in different populations. For example, a study of age perception in Chinese women found that heterogeneous pigmentation, rather than skin topography, was used as the primary signal of aging when viewing a panel of Chinese faces (Porcheron et al. 2014). However, when these study participants examined a panel of European faces, skin topography was the primary cue used to infer age (Porcheron et al. 2014). These differences in the factors used to assess age in European and Chinese faces correlates with the age of onset of these features in each group; wrinkling typically occurs earlier in Europeans while age spots are one of the first markers of aging observed in many East Asian populations (Nouveau-Richard et al. 2005; Tsukahara et al. 2004).

Given that these three areas (skin topography, pigmentation heterogeneity, and fat-volume loss) all contribute to perceptions of age, it is not surprising that all are targeted by anti-aging cosmeceuticals and cosmetic plastic surgery procedures. The majority of these over-the-counter cosmeceutical products are marketed specifically to women not only as a way to restore or reclaim youth but also as a way to fulfill one's civic duty of "aging well" (Smirnova 2012), a key feature of the neoliberal approach to health (Rose 2001; Fishman, Settersten Jr., and Flatt 2010). In 2019, two of the top five major cosmetic surgeries in the United States were blepharoplasties (eyelid lifts) and rhytidectomies (face lifts). By far the most common minimally invasive cosmetic procedure was the injection of Botulinum Toxin Type A (Botox©) to treat facial wrinkles; over 7.7 million of these procedures were performed (American Society of Plastic Surgeons 2019). While many of these products and procedures are heavily marketed to women, there is evidence that men are becoming increasingly interested in products and procedures that can help minimize signs of aging (Montes and Santos 2018). Procedures like Botulinum Toxin Type A and soft tissue filler injections increased by 403 percent and 99 percent, respectively, among men over the past twenty years (American Society of Plastic Surgeons 2019).

Health-Related Implications of Aged Skin

While age-related changes to skin are often thought of in terms of their impact on personal appearance, these changes can have significant impacts on human health that go beyond perceptions of youthfulness. Major changes associated with aging skin include reduced skin barrier function, impaired capacity for wound healing, altered immune function, decreased lipogenesis, and reduced sweat production by eccrine glands. In many cases, these alterations may interact with each other or with other existing conditions (e.g., diabetes) to further complicate the care of aging skin.

The lipid content of the stratum corneum declines with age, disrupting the brick-and-mortar structure of this epidermal layer (Al-Nuaimi, Sherratt, and Griffiths 2014). This decline is linked in part to a decline in sebum production related to shifts in sex hormones, such as the decline in estrogen production in post-menopausal women (Zouboulis and Makrantonaki 2011). Age-related changes to the stratum corneum also include changes in skin pH, which can lead to skin dryness (xerosis). Xerosis is one of the most frequent skin conditions reported in older patients worldwide (Hahnel et al. 2017). It is associated with a reduced skin barrier function that allows for the increased penetration of irritants and antigens, potentially increasing contact dermatitis (Seyfarth et al. 2011). Xerosis may also be associated with pruritis, or constant itch, another common complaint in elderly individuals (Hahnel et al. 2017). The frequent scratching of pruritic skin in the context of an already impaired skin barrier is more likely to lead to inflammatory responses and possible infections, two reasons why this condition can be challenging to manage (Chang et al. 2013).

The wound healing process in older skin differs from younger skin in that it is both delayed and altered (Sgonc and Gruber 2013). This impaired healing process has been attributed to a combination of factors, including a decreased inflammatory response, reduced rate of fibroblast replication, and slower keratinocyte proliferation (Al-Nuaimi, Sherratt, and Griffiths 2014). The turnover time, or time that it takes for keratinocytes to migrate from the basal layer of the epidermis to the stratum corneum, is increased by as much as 50 percent in older individuals (Sgonc and Gruber 2013). This longer turnover time leads to a delay in re-epithelialization and a longer time to wound closure. Further complicating healing is the reduced vascularity of the dermis and an increase in the disorganization of collagen in the ECM (Sgonc and Gruber 2013).

Delays and impairment in the wound healing process combined with the reduction in epidermal barrier function are of particular concern for older patients, particularly in the context of skin tears and pressure ulcers. The thinner skin of older adults is more susceptible to shearing and tearing injuries (Hatje et al. 2015; LeBlanc et al. 2018), which are exacerbated by the reduction in elasticity and attenuation of rete ridges that characterizes older skin. Skin tears, which commonly occur on the arms, legs, and back of the hands, can be induced by something as dramatic as sustaining a fall to something as simple as the everyday process of applying and removing adhesives (e.g., from bandages) (Kirkland-Kyhn 2018). Pressure ulcers are localized skin injuries that result from prolonged pressure on the skin, as might be experienced by individuals who are bedridden. These most often develop in skin that covers bony protuberances, including the hips, heels, ankles, and tailbone. Pressure ulcers are rated on a four-point scale, ranging from intact skin with non-blanching erythema (Stage I) to extensive destruction of skin and underlying tissues (Stage IV) (Jaul 2010). More recently, two additional categories, including "unstageable" (characterized by skin covered with a surface of necrotic tissue and a wound of undetermined depth) and "deep-tissue injury" (injury to subcutaneous tissues underneath intact skin), have also been developed by the National Pressure Ulcer Advisory Panel (Ankrom et al. 2005). Pressure ulcers can vary in their impact on an older adult's quality of life; some resolve relatively quickly while others may become chronic and cause intermittent or chronic pain (Jaul 2010). Chronic pressure ulcers, particularly in their latter stages, can lead to death through sepsis or osteomyelitis. Although it can vary by the country and care setting, it is estimated that pressure ulcers can have an incidence of 0.3 to 46 percent in older adult populations worldwide (Hahnel et al. 2017). The wide variation here encompasses differences across countries as well as care settings. In general, there is more data about the prevalence of pressure ulcers in long-term care settings and hospitals than there is about pressure ulcers reported in medical practices, regardless of where the study was conducted (Hahnel et al. 2017). As might be expected, pressure ulcers are reported to occur at higher rates in long-term care settings, but even this can show a wide range of variation within a single nation (Hahnel et al. 2017).

Morphological changes to the Langerhans cells in the dermal layer are associated with impaired cutaneous immune function in older individuals (Zouboulis and Makrantonaki 2011). These cells also experience a decrease in number over time, showing an average decrease of approximately 25 percent between a sample of ten older and ten younger individuals (Bhushan et al. 2004). These changes may be one reason why older individuals are more prone to skin, particularly fungal, infections (Hahnel et al. 2017; Piérard 2001) and viruses like Varicella zoster, responsible for chicken pox and shingles (Chang et al. 2013). A significant number of patients with Varicella zoster also develop persistent neuralgia that can result in inflammation of peripheral neurons even after the zoster rash has resolved (Gilden et al. 2000). The weakened immune function of older skin may be of particular concern when considered along with other age-related skin changes, including the impaired skin barrier function and increased prevalence of xerosis and pruritis, which can facilitate the entry of pathogens into the skin.

Finally, thermoregulatory function shows a decline with age, and elderly individuals are more susceptible to heat-related illness. This has been attributed to both a reduction in cutaneous vascular function as well as a reduction in sweating rate (Rittie and Fisher 2015), and does not appear to be directly linked to hot flushes that occur during menopause, which are associated with a reduction in estrogen levels (Raine-Fenning, Brincat, and Muscat-Baron 2003). Older individuals show a decline in the function of the eccrine sweat glands found in the dermis (Inoue, Kuwahara, and Araki 2004). Thermoregulation is further compromised by a delayed onset of sweating and a reduced capacity to maintain a high sweat rate in response to increased temperatures or exertion (Millyard et al. 2020). Rising global temperatures, combined with the overall shift toward older demographics in populations like the United States and United Kingdom suggest that heat-related illness and death among older individuals are likely to become more frequent (Millyard et al. 2020). Indeed, an increase in heat-related deaths in older populations is already evident in cities like Las Vegas, Nevada, where 76 percent of heat-related deaths from the period of 2007–2016 occurred in individuals over the age of 50 (Bandala et al. 2019).

Genetics of Skin Aging

With an increased desire to understand the molecular processes associated with skin aging, recent studies have begun to explore genetic factors associated with youthful skin appearance. While these investigations will contribute to a broader understanding of the aging process, they may also contribute to the development of novel anti-aging treatments. One challenge of such studies is the way that the particular aging phenotype is defined. For example, is the relevant phenotype *perceived age* (something that would be of consumer interest, but may be difficult to quantitatively assess), or is it instead a more quantitative measurement of some aspect of facial skin aging (wrinkle area, number and size of solar lentigines, skin sagging, etc.)? The development of high-resolution clinical photography methods that can be used to quantitatively assess the degree of age-related traits like wrinkling (Patwardhan et al. 2016) will likely increase the use of such techniques in clinical assessments of facial skin aging and its causes (Hamer et al. 2017). However, to date, different studies have utilized multiple ways to assess facial aging, which can make comparisons across studies difficult. A second key challenge is that several non-genetic factors also influence skin aging, including exposure to UV, smoking, pollution, and general skincare habits and practices (Hamer et al. 2017; Gilchrest 2013; Ortiz and Grando 2012; Ernster et al. 1995; Farage et al. 2008) that may be difficult to assess and control in large-scale genetic studies. It is also possible that genetic factors may interact with these environmental and behavioral factors, further complicating the interpretation of results. The following is a brief summary of the genes believed to impact facial skin aging.

The first genome-wide association study (GWAS) that sought to identify genes associated with skin-aging features focused on three aging-related phenotypes assessed by dermatologists (lentigines, sagging, and wrinkling). This study identified an association between a relatively unknown gene, *STXB5L*, and the severity of photoaging, as well as with sagging and wrinkling phenotypes that were independent of photoaging in a large sample of European women (Le Clerc et al. 2013). The associated variant in this gene was also noted to be linked to the *FBXO40* locus. However, neither *STXB5L* or *FBXO40* had been previously associated with skin or aging, suggesting that additional work to confirm the biological mechanism of the association is necessary. One hypothesis is that one or both may influence skin aging through known roles in inflammation and cancer (Le Clerc et al. 2013). As GWAS are able to detect genetic mutations that are *correlated* with a particular trait, but not necessarily *causative*, it is possible that other loci in genetic linkage with *STXB5L* or *FBXO40* may also be involved. A subsequent study focused on a unique population of Ashkenazi centenarians to identify genes associated with youthful-looking skin as well as any genes generally associated with longevity (Chang et al. 2014). This work identified three genes that may play a role in facial skin appearance, namely *KCND2*, *DIAPH1*, and *EDEM1*. Although no functional studies were performed to determine the mechanism for how these genes influenced facial skin aging, the authors developed several hypotheses based on known gene function.

Of these three loci, the *EDEM1* gene appears to be a strong candidate. It is associated with elongated life span in fruit fly and roundworm models (Liu et al. 2009) and *EDEM1* levels are reduced in the fibroblast cells of mouse aging models (Sadighi Akha et al. 2011). These fibroblasts are also more resistant to cell death induced by external stressors such as UV light. Given this connection, the authors speculate that youthful-looking individuals may have more collagen fibers in their dermis than non-youthful-looking individuals (Chang et al. 2014).

A GWAS of over 2,700 European individuals from the Rotterdam Study (a prospective cohort study in the Netherlands that focuses on various conditions related to age and disease) identified the *MC1R* gene as a candidate associated with perceived age as well as quantitative wrinkle assessments (Liu et al. 2016). The *MC1R* gene is well studied in the field of skin pigmentation because of its strong association with a red-haired and pale-skin phenotype (Flanagan 2000; Rees 2000; Valverde et al. 1995). However, it has also been linked with melanoma risk, independent of pigmentation levels (Valverde 1996; van der Velden et al. 2001), presumably due to reduced DNA-repair capacity (Kadekaro et al. 2010; Hauser et al. 2006). While these associations with lighter pigmentation suggest that certain *MC1R* mutations might make an individual more susceptible to photoaging, the study by Liu and colleagues demonstrated that *MC1R* affected aging phenotypes independent of pigmentation (Liu et al. 2016). Even more interestingly, they found that *MC1R* was associated with perceptions of age that did not depend on skin wrinkling, suggesting that further work is needed to elucidate the cellular pathways through which *MC1R* is mediating age-related skin changes. Associations between *MC1R* and aging phenotype (measured as a microtopography score) were also reported by Law and colleagues in a meta-GWAS analysis of three European cohorts (Law et al. 2017). This same study also reported associations with two other pigmentation-related genes, *SLC45A2* and *IRF4*. Unlike the work of Liu et al. (2016), this work argues that variants at these loci may contribute specifically to photoaged phenotypes, including wrinkling as well as solar lentigines (aged spots) due to their association with lighter skin pigmentation (Law et al. 2017).

While GWAS are one way of identifying genes that are associated with a particular age-related trait, gene expression studies can also provide valuable information by characterizing how gene expression patterns change with age. A study of 158 women of European ancestry examined differences in gene expression profiles across three body sites: the buttocks, the volar forearm, and the cheek in women between the ages of 20 and 74 to assess age-related changes in photo-exposed (forearm and cheek) and photo-protected skin (buttocks) (Kimball et al. 2018). Age-related changes were reported in gene pathways associated with oxidative stress, energy metabolism, senescence, and epidermal barrier function. In addition, the authors reported that the expression profiles of older women who were rated as "exceptional agers" (meaning they looked significantly younger than their chronological age) appeared more similar to the expression profiles of younger women than women in their own age cohort (Kimball et al. 2018). Notably, these differences in expression profiles included higher expression of genes related to mitochondrial function and structure, epidermal structure, and skin barrier function, suggesting that genes beyond just those affecting pigmentation and DNA repair (as reported in the GWAS described above) can influence aging processes in facial skin.

Conclusions

The human skin serves as both a barrier, protecting us from the world around us, and a window into our internal condition. Because our skin is literally the face that we present to the world, we pay particular attention to its appearance and to the signals that it sends to others about us. In many cultures that equate youthfulness with attractiveness and health, anti-aging approaches to skin care have been developed that claim to restore aging skin, rescuing it from a presumed pathological state. These approaches are often heavily gendered, with a strong focus on the need to correct age-related skin "deficiencies" in women (although more recently there have been increasing appeals made to men to address these same issues).

This biomedicalization of skin (Smirnova 2012) casts aging skin as a disease that can be healed, if only we are committed to utilizing the right products to reverse the progress of that disease. It is perhaps ironic, then, that much of what we have learned about the ways that intrinsic and extrinsic aging processes can influence skin, while relevant in developing these anti-aging approaches to skin, can also provide real improvements to the way that specific injuries and diseases are treated or prevented in aging individuals. For example, the reduction and disorganization of collagen fibrils in the dermis that contribute to wrinkles and skin sagging also contribute to the delayed wound healing process that can lead the development of chronic pressure ulcers. Changes in sebum and skin pH levels can lead to skin that is dry and rough in appearance, and can also contribute to the xerosis and pruritis commonly seen in older adults. In the future, it will be interesting to see if the knowledge learned in the biomedical treatment of aging skin can also be utilized to treat cutaneous disorders and diseases in older patients. For example, can information about changes in gene expression profiles in old versus young skin be compared to gene expression profiles in pruritic skin to develop topical products that could naturally restore dryness and reduce itching? Could learning about differences in the microbiome of healthy skin from younger individuals help us better assess skin health around skin tears or pressure ulcers and develop novel treatments that would result in faster healing? Harnessing knowledge gained in the development of products designed to satisfy our need to project an outward face of youth and health may one day help us actually improve the health outcomes of common skin disorders that increase morbidity in older populations.

References

Agbai, Oma N., Kesha Buster, Miguel Sanchez, Claudia Hernandez, Roopal V. Kundu, Melvin Chiu, Wendy E. Roberts, et al. 2014. "Skin Cancer and Photoprotection in People of Color: A Review and Recommendations for Physicians and the Public." *Journal of the American Academy of Dermatology* 70(4): 748–762. https://doi.org/10.1016/j.jaad.2013.11.038.

Alexis, Andrew F., and Jasmine O Obioha. 2017. "Ethnicity and Aging Skin." *Journal of Drugs in Dermatology* 16(6): s77–s80.

Alexis, Andrew F., Pearl Grimes, Charles Boyd, Jeanine Downie, Adrienne Drinkwater, Julie K. Garcia, and Conor J. Gallagher. 2019. "Racial and Ethnic Differences in Self-Assessed Facial Aging in Women: Results from a Multinational Study." *Dermatologic Surgery* 45(12): 1635–1648. https://doi.org/10.1097/DSS.0000000000002237.

Al-Nuaimi, Yusur, Michael J. Sherratt, and Christopher E. M. Griffiths. 2014. "Skin Health in Older Age." *Maturitas* 79(3): 256–264. https://doi.org/10.1016/j.maturitas.2014.08.005.

American Society of Plastic Surgeons. 2019. "Plastic Surgery Statistics Report." https://www.plasticsurgery.org/documents/News/Statistics/2019/plastic-surgery-statistics-full-report-2019.pdf.

Ankrom, Michael A., Richard G. Bennett, Stephen Sprigle, Diane Langemo, Joyce M. Black, Dan R. Berlowitz, and Courtney H. Lyder. 2005. "Pressure-Related Deep Tissue Injury under Intact Skin and the Current Pressure Ulcer Staging Systems." *Advances in Skin & Wound Care* 18(1): 35–42. https://doi.org/10.1097/00129334-200501000-00016.

Anzures, Gizelle, Liezhong Ge, Zhe Wang, Shoji Itakura, and Kang Lee. 2010. "Culture Shapes Efficiency of Facial Age Judgments." Edited by Hans P. Op de Beeck. *PLoS ONE* 5(7): e11679. https://doi.org/10.1371/journal.pone.0011679.

Bandala, E. R., K. Kebede, N. Jonsson, R. Murray, D. Green, J. F. Mejia, and P. F. Martinez-

Austria. 2019. "Extreme Heat and Mortality Rates in Las Vegas, Nevada: Inter-Annual Variations and Thresholds." *International Journal of Environmental Science and Technology* 16(11): 7175–7186. https://doi.org/10.1007/s13762-019-02357-9.

Bhushan, M., M. Cumberbatch, R. J. Dearman, I. Kimber, and C.E.M. Griffiths. 2004. "Exogenous Interleukin-1beta Restores Impaired Langerhans Cell Migration in Aged Skin." *British Journal of Dermatology* 150(6): 1217–1218. https://doi.org/10.1111/j.1365-2133.2004.05973.x.

Callaghan, T. M., and K.-P. Wilhelm. 2008a. "A Review of Ageing and an Examination of Clinical Methods in the Assessment of Ageing Skin. Part 2: Clinical Perspectives and Clinical Methods in the Evaluation of Ageing Skin." *International Journal of Cosmetic Science* 30(5): 323–332. https://doi.org/10.1111/j.1468-2494.2008.00455.x.

———. 2008b. "A Review of Ageing and an Examination of Clinical Methods in the Assessment of Ageing Skin. Part I: Cellular and Molecular Perspectives of Skin Ageing." *International Journal of Cosmetic Science* 30(5): 313–322. https://doi.org/10.1111/j.1468-2494.2008.00454.x.

Cestari, Tania, and Kesha Buster. 2017. "Photoprotection in Specific Populations: Children and People of Color." *Journal of the American Academy of Dermatology* 76(3): S110–S121. https://doi.org/10.1016/j.jaad.2016.09.039.

Chang, Anne L. S., Gil Atzmon, Aviv Bergman, Samantha Brugmann, Scott X. Atwood, Howard Y. Chang, and Nir Barzilai. 2014. "Identification of Genes Promoting Skin Youthfulness by Genome-Wide Association Study." *Journal of Investigative Dermatology* 134(3): 651–657. https://doi.org/10.1038/jid.2013.381.

Chang, Anne L. S., Jillian W. Wong, Justin O. Endo, and Robert A. Norman. 2013. "Geriatric Dermatology Review: Major Changes in Skin Function in Older Patients and Their Contribution to Common Clinical Challenges." *Journal of the American Medical Directors Association* 14(10): 724–730. https://doi.org/10.1016/j.jamda.2013.02.014.

Christensen, Kaare, Maria Iachina, Helle Rexbye, Cecilia Tomassini, Henrik Frederiksen, Matt McGue, and James W. Vaupel. 2004. "'Looking Old for Your Age': Genetics and Mortality." *Epidemiology* 15(2): 251–252. https://doi.org/10.1097/01.ede.0000112211.11416.a6.

Draelos, Zoe D. 2019. "Cosmeceuticals." In *Evidence-Based Procedural Dermatology*, edited by M. Alarn, 479–495. Cham: Springer International Publishing.

Ernster, V. L., D. Grady, R. Miike, D. Black, J. Selby, and K. Kerlikowske. 1995. "Facial Wrinkling in Men and Women, by Smoking Status." *American Journal of Public Health* 85(1): 78–82. https://doi.org/10.2105/AJPH.85.1.78.

Farage, M. A., K. W. Miller, P. Elsner, and H. I. Maibach. 2008. "Intrinsic and Extrinsic Factors in Skin Ageing: A Review." *International Journal of Cosmetic Science* 30(2): 87–95. https://doi.org/10.1111/j.1468-2494.2007.00415.x.

Fink, B., P. J. Matts, C. Brauckmann, and S. Gundlach. 2018. "The Effect of Skin Surface Topography and Skin Colouration Cues on Perception of Male Facial Age, Health and Attractiveness." *International Journal of Cosmetic Science* 40(2): 193–198. https://doi.org/10.1111/ics.12451.

Fink, B., P. J. Matts, D. D'Emiliano, L. Bunse, and B. Weege. 2012. "Colour Homogeneity and Visual Perception of Age, Health and Attractiveness of Male Facial Skin." *Journal of the European Academy of Dermatology and Venereology* 7.

Fink, B., and P. J. Matts. 2008. "The Effects of Skin Colour Distribution and Topography Cues on the Perception of Female Facial Age and Health." *Journal of the European*

Academy of Dermatology and Venereology 22(4): 493–498. https://doi.org/10.1111/j.1468-3083.2007.02512.x.

Fink, B., P. J. Matts, S. Röder, R. Johnson, and M. Burquest. 2011. "Differences in Visual Perception of Age and Attractiveness of Female Facial and Body Skin: Perception of Face and Body Skin." *International Journal of Cosmetic Science* 33(2): 126–131. https://doi.org/10.1111/j.1468-2494.2010.00594.x.

Fishman, Jennifer R., Richard A. Settersten Jr., and Michael A. Flatt. 2010. "In the Vanguard of Biomedicine? The Curious and Contradictory Case of Anti-Ageing Medicine." *Sociology of Health & Illness* 32(2): 197–210. https://doi.org/10.1111/j.1467-9566.2009.01212.x.

Flanagan, N. 2000. "Pleiotropic Effects of the Melanocortin 1 Receptor (MC1R) Gene on Human Pigmentation." *Human Molecular Genetics* 9(17): 2531–2537. https://doi.org/10.1093/hmg/9.17.2531.

Fried, Levi, and Jack L. Arbiser. 2008. "The Reactive Oxygen-Driven Tumor: Relevance to Melanoma: Reactive Oxygen-Driven Tumors." *Pigment Cell & Melanoma Research* 21(2): 117–122. https://doi.org/10.1111/j.1755-148X.2008.00451.x.

Gilchrest, Barbara A. 2013. "Photoaging." *Journal of Investigative Dermatology* 133(July): E2–E6. https://doi.org/10.1038/skinbio.2013.176.

Gilden, Donald H., B. K. Kleinschmidt-Demasters, James J. Laguardia, and Randall J. Cohrs. 2000. "Neurologic Complications of the Reactivation of Varicella–Zoster Virus." *New England Journal of Medicine*, 11.

Griffiths, C. E., A. N. Russman, G. Majmudar, R. S. Singer, T. A. Hamilton, and J. J. Voorhees. 1993. "Restoration of Collagen Formation in Photodamaged Human Skin by Tretinoin (Retinoic Acid)." *New England Journal of Medicine* 329: 530–535.

Gunn, David A., Helle Rexbye, Christopher E. M. Griffiths, Peter G. Murray, Amelia Fereday, Sharon D. Catt, Cyrena C. Tomlin, et al. 2009. "Why Some Women Look Young for Their Age." Edited by Tom Tregenza. *PLoS ONE* 4(12): e8021. https://doi.org/10.1371/journal.pone.0008021.

Hahnel, Elisabeth, Andrea Lichterfeld, Ulrike Blume-Peytavi, and Jan Kottner. 2017. "The Epidemiology of Skin Conditions in the Aged: A Systematic Review." *Journal of Tissue Viability* 26(1): 20–28. https://doi.org/10.1016/j.jtv.2016.04.001.

Hamer, Merel A., Luba M. Pardo, Leonie C. Jacobs, M. Arfan Ikram, Joop S. Laven, Manfred Kayser, Loes M. Hollestein, David A. Gunn, and Tamar Nijsten. 2017. "Lifestyle and Physiological Factors Associated with Facial Wrinkling in Men and Women." *Journal of Investigative Dermatology* 137(8): 1692–1699. https://doi.org/10.1016/j.jid.2017.04.002.

Han, Anne, Anna L. Chien, and Sewon Kang. 2014. "Photoaging." *Dermatologic Clinics* 32(3): 291–299. https://doi.org/10.1016/j.det.2014.03.015.

Hatje, L. K., C. Richter, U. Blume-Peytavi, and J. Kottner. 2015. "Blistering Time as a Parameter for the Strength of Dermoepidermal Adhesion: A Systematic Review and Meta-Analysis." *British Journal of Dermatology* 172(2): 323–330. https://doi.org/10.1111/bjd.13298.

Hauser, Jennifer E., Ana Luisa Kadekaro, Renny J. Kavanagh, Kazumasa Wakamatsu, Silva Terzieva, Sandy Schwemberger, George Babcock, M. B. Rao, Shosuke Ito, and Zalfa A. Abdel-Malek. 2006. "Melanin Content and MC1R Function Independently Affect UVR-induced DNA Damage in Cultured Human Melanocytes." *Pigment Cell Research* 19(4): 303–314. https://doi.org/10.1111/j.1600-0749.2006.00315.x.

Hensley, Kenneth, and Robert A. Floyd. 2002. "Reactive Oxygen Species and Protein Oxidation in Aging: A Look Back, A Look Ahead." *Archives of Biochemistry and Biophysics* 397(2): 377–383. https://doi.org/10.1006/abbi.2001.2630.

Inoue, Yoshimitsu, Tomoko Kuwahara, and Tsutomu Araki. 2004. "Maturation- and Aging-Related Changes in Heat Loss Effector Function." *Journal of Physiological Anthropology and Applied Human Science* 23(6): 289–294. https://doi.org/10.2114/jpa.23.289.

Jaul, Efraim. 2010. "Assessment and Management of Pressure Ulcers in the Elderly: Current Strategies." *Drugs & Aging* 27(4): 311–325. https://doi.org/10.2165/11318340-000000000-00000.

Kadekaro, Ana Luisa, Sancy Leachman, Renny J. Kavanagh, Viki Swope, Pamela Cassidy, Dorothy Supp, Maureen Sartor, et al. 2010. "*Melanocortin 1 Receptor* Genotype: An Important Determinant of the Damage Response of Melanocytes to Ultraviolet Radiation." *FASEB Journal* 24(10): 3850–3860. https://doi.org/10.1096/fj.10-158485.

Kanaki, Theodora, Evgenia Makrantonaki, and Christos C. Zouboulis. 2016. "Biomarkers of Skin Aging." *Reviews in Endocrine and Metabolic Disorders* 17(3): 433–442. https://doi.org/10.1007/s11154-016-9392-x.

Kimball, Alexa B., Maria B. Alora-Palli, Makio Tamura, Lisa A. Mullins, Chieko Soh, Robert L. Binder, Neil A. Houston, et al. 2018. "Age-Induced and Photoinduced Changes in Gene Expression Profiles in Facial Skin of Caucasian Females across 6 Decades of Age." *Journal of the American Academy of Dermatology* 78(1): 1–7. https://doi.org/10.1016/j.jaad.2017.09.012.

Kirkland-Kyhn, Holly. 2018. "Caring for Aging Skin." *American Journal of Nursing* 118(2): 60–63.

Law, Matthew H., Sarah E. Medland, Gu Zhu, Seyhan Yazar, Ana Viñuela, Leanne Wallace, Sri Niranjan Shekar, et al. 2017. "Genome-Wide Association Shows That Pigmentation Genes Play a Role in Skin Aging." *Journal of Investigative Dermatology* 137(9): 1887–1894. https://doi.org/10.1016/j.jid.2017.04.026.

Le Clerc, Sigrid, Lieng Taing, Khaled Ezzedine, Julie Latreille, Olivier Delaneau, Toufik Labib, Cédric Coulonges, et al. 2013. "A Genome-Wide Association Study in Caucasian Women Points Out a Putative Role of the STXBP5L Gene in Facial Photoaging." *Journal of Investigative Dermatology* 133(4): 929–935. https://doi.org/10.1038/jid.2012.458.

LeBlanc, Kimberly, Karen E. Campbell, Eleanor Wood, and Dimitri Beeckman. 2018. "Best Practice Recommendations for Prevention and Management of Skin Tears in Aged Skin: An Overview." *Journal of Wound, Ostomy and Continence Nursing* 45(6): 540–542. https://doi.org/10.1097/WON.0000000000000481.

Liu, Fan, Merel A. Hamer, Joris Deelen, Japal S. Lall, Leonie Jacobs, Diana van Heemst, Peter G. Murray, et al. 2016. "The MC1R Gene and Youthful Looks." *Current Biology* 26(9): 1213–1220. https://doi.org/10.1016/j.cub.2016.03.008.

Liu, Ya-Lin, Wan-Chih Lu, Theodore J. Brummel, Chiou-Hwa Yuh, Pei-Ting Lin, Tzu-Yu Kao, Fang-Yi Li, Pin-Chao Liao, Seymour Benzer, and Horng-Dar Wang. 2009. "Reduced Expression of *Alpha-1,2-Mannosidase I* Extends Lifespan in *Drosophila Melanogaster* and *Caenorhabditis Elegans*." *Aging Cell* 8(4): 370–379. https://doi.org/10.1111/j.1474-9726.2009.00471.x.

Makrantonaki, Evgenia, and C. C. Zouboulis. 2007. "Molecular Mechanisms of Skin Aging: State of the Art." *Annals of the New York Academy of Sciences* 1119(1): 40–50. https://doi.org/10.1196/annals.1404.027.

Makrantonaki, Evgenia, Peter Schönknecht, Amir M. Hossini, Elmar Kaiser, Myrto-Maria Katsouli, James Adjaye, Johannes Schröder, and Christos C. Zouboulis. 2010. "Skin and Brain Age Together: The Role of Hormones in the Ageing Process." *Experimental Gerontology* 45(10): 801–813. https://doi.org/10.1016/j.exger.2010.08.005.

Matts, Paul J., Bernhard Fink, Karl Grammer, and Maria Burquest. 2007. "Color Homogeneity and Visual Perception of Age, Health, and Attractiveness of Female Facial Skin." *Journal of the American Academy of Dermatology* 57(6): 977–984. https://doi.org/10.1016/j.jaad.2007.07.040.

Millyard, Alison, Joe D. Layden, David B. Pyne, Andrew M. Edwards, and Saul R. Bloxham. 2020. "Impairments to Thermoregulation in the Elderly During Heat Exposure Events." *Geriatric Medicine*, 9.

Montes, Jose Raúl, and Elizabeth Santos. 2018. "Evaluation of Men's Trends and Experiences in Aesthetic Treatment." *Journal of Drugs in Dermatology* 17(9): 941–946.

Morita, Akimichi. 2007. "Tobacco Smoke Causes Premature Skin Aging." *Journal of Dermatological Science* 48(3): 169–175. https://doi.org/10.1016/j.jdermsci.2007.06.015.

Mykytyn, Courtney Everts. 2006. "Anti-Aging Medicine: Predictions, Moral Obligations, and Biomedical Intervention." *Anthropological Quarterly* 79(1): 5–31. https://doi.org/10.1353/anq.2006.0010.

Nouveau-Richard, S., Z. Yang, S. Mac-Mary, L. Li, P. Bastien, I. Tardy, C. Bouillon, P. Humbert, and O. de Lacharrière. 2005. "Skin Ageing: A Comparison between Chinese and European Populations." *Journal of Dermatological Science* 40(3): 187–193. https://doi.org/10.1016/j.jdermsci.2005.06.006.

Ortiz, Arisa, and Sergei A. Grando. 2012. "Smoking and the Skin: Tobacco Effects on Skin." *International Journal of Dermatology* 51(3): 250–262. https://doi.org/10.1111/j.1365-4632.2011.05205.x.

Patwardhan, S. V., B. D'Alessandro, M. Thomas, S. D. Kastner, and D. DaSilva. 2016. "OLÉ: Facial Imaging System with Overhead Lighting Environment," 4.

Piérard, Gérald. 2001. "Onychomycosis and Other Superficial A Pan-European Survey." *Dermatology* 202: 220–224.

Poljšak, Borut, and Raja Dahmane. 2012. "Free Radicals and Extrinsic Skin Aging." *Dermatology Research and Practice* 2012: 1–4. https://doi.org/10.1155/2012/135206.

Porcheron, A., J. Latreille, R. Jdid, E. Tschachler, and F. Morizot. 2014. "Influence of Skin Ageing Features on Chinese Women's Perception of Facial Age and Attractiveness." *International Journal of Cosmetic Science*, 9.

Raine-Fenning, Nicholas J., Mark P. Brincat, and Yves Muscat-Baron. 2003. "Skin Aging and Menopause: Implications for Treatment." *American Journal of Clinical Dermatology* 4(6): 371–378. https://doi.org/10.2165/00128071-200304060-00001.

Rees, Jonathan L. 2000. "The Melanocortin 1 Receptor (MC1R): More Than Just Red Hair." *Pigment Cell Research* 13(3): 135–140. https://doi.org/10.1034/j.1600-0749.2000.130303.x.

Rittie, L., and G. J. Fisher. 2015. "Natural and Sun-Induced Aging of Human Skin." *Cold Spring Harbor Perspectives in Medicine* 5(1): a015370–a015370. https://doi.org/10.1101/cshperspect.a015370.

Rohrich, Rod J., and Joel E. Pessa. 2007. "The Fat Compartments of the Face: Anatomy and Clinical Implications for Cosmetic Surgery." *Plastic and Reconstructive Surgery* 119(7): 2219–2227. https://doi.org/10.1097/01.prs.0000265403.66886.54.

Rose, Nikolas. 2001. "The Politics of Life Itself." *Culture and Society* 18(6): 1–30.

Russell-Goldman, Eleanor, and George F. Murphy. 2020. "The Pathobiology of Skin Aging." *American Journal of Pathology*, 14.

Sadighi Akha, Amir A., James M. Harper, Adam B. Salmon, Bethany A. Schroeder, Heather M. Tyra, D. Thomas Rutkowski, and Richard A. Miller. 2011. "Heightened Induction of Proapoptotic Signals in Response to Endoplasmic Reticulum Stress in Primary Fibroblasts from a Mouse Model of Longevity." *Journal of Biological Chemistry* 286(35): 30344–30351. https://doi.org/10.1074/jbc.M111.220541.

Samson, Nadine, Bernhard Fink, Paul J. Matts, Nancy C. Dawes, and Shannon Weitz. 2010. "Visible Changes of Female Facial Skin Surface Topography in Relation to Age and Attractiveness Perception: Perception of Facial Skin Surface Topography." *Journal of Cosmetic Dermatology* 9(2): 79–88. https://doi.org/10.1111/j.1473-2165.2010.00489.x.

Seyfarth, Florian, Sibylle Schliemann, Dimitar Antonov, and Peter Elsner. 2011. "Dry Skin, Barrier Function, and Irritant Contact Dermatitis in the Elderly." *Clinics in Dermatology* 29(1): 31–36. https://doi.org/10.1016/j.clindermatol.2010.07.004.

Sgonc, Roswitha, and Johann Gruber. 2013. "Age-Related Aspects of Cutaneous Wound Healing: A Mini-Review." *Gerontology* 59(2): 159–164. https://doi.org/10.1159/000342344.

Smirnova, Michelle Hannah. 2012. "A Will to Youth: The Woman's Anti-Aging Elixir." *Social Science & Medicine* 75(7): 1236–1243. https://doi.org/10.1016/j.socscimed.2012.02.061.

Sohal, Rajindar S., and Richard Weindruch. 2010. "Oxidative Stress, Caloric Restriction, and Aging," 12.

Swope, Viki, and Zalfa Abdel-Malek. 2018. "MC1R: Front and Center in the Bright Side of Dark Eumelanin and DNA Repair." *International Journal of Molecular Sciences* 19(9): 2667. https://doi.org/10.3390/ijms19092667.

Tsukahara, Kazue, Tsutomu Fujimura, Yasuko Yoshida, Takashi Kitahara, Mitsuyuki Hotta, Shigeru Moriwaki, Pamela S. Witt, F. Anthony Simion, and Yoshinori Takema. 2004. "Comparison of Age-Related Changes in Wrinkling and Sagging of the Skin in Caucasian Females and in Japanese Females." *Journal of Cosmetic Science* 55(4): 351–371.

Valverde, P. 1996. "The Asp84Glu Variant of the Melanocortin 1 Receptor (MC1R) Is Associated with Melanoma." *Human Molecular Genetics* 5(10): 1663–1666. https://doi.org/10.1093/hmg/5.10.1663.

Valverde, P., E. Healy, I. Jackson, J. L. Rees, and A. J. Thody. 1995. "Variants of the Melanocyte-Stimulating Hormone Receptor Gene Are Associated with Red Hair and Fair Skin in Humans." *Nature Genetics* 11: 328–330.

Varani, James, Roscoe L. Warner, Mehrnaz Gharaee-Kermani, Sem H. Phan, Sewon Kang, JinHo Chung, ZengQuan Wang, Subhash C. Datta, Gary J. Fisher, and John J. Voorhees. 2000. "Vitamin A Antagonizes Decreased Cell Growth and Elevated Collagen-Degrading Matrix Metalloproteinases and Stimulates Collagen Accumulation in Naturally Aged Human Skin1." *Journal of Investigative Dermatology* 114(3): 480–486. https://doi.org/10.1046/j.1523-1747.2000.00902.x.

Velden, Pieter A. van der, Lodewijk A. Sandkuijl, Wilma Bergman, Stan Pavel, Leny van Mourik, Rune R. Frants, and Nelleke A. Gruis. 2001. "Melanocortin-1 Receptor Variant R151C Modifies Melanoma Risk in Dutch Families with Melanoma." *American Journal of Human Genetics* 69(4): 774–779. https://doi.org/10.1086/323411.

Vierkötter, Andrea, Ulrich Ranft, Ursula Krämer, Dorothea Sugiri, Verena Reimann, and Jean Krutmann. 2009. "The SCINEXA: A Novel, Validated Score to Simultaneously Assess and Differentiate between Intrinsic and Extrinsic Skin Ageing." *Journal of Dermatological Science* 53(3): 207–211. https://doi.org/10.1016/j.jdermsci.2008.10.001.

Yaar, M., and B. A. Gilchrest. 2001. "Ageing and Photoageing of Keratinocytes and Melanocytes: Ageing and Photoageing of Keratinocytes and Melanocytes." *Clinical and Experimental Dermatology* 26(7): 583–591. https://doi.org/10.1046/j.1365-2230.2001.00895.x.

Zouboulis, Christos C., and Evgenia Makrantonaki. 2011. "Clinical Aspects and Molecular Diagnostics of Skin Aging." *Clinics in Dermatology* 29(1): 3–14. https://doi.org/10.1016/j.clindermatol.2010.07.001.

8

How Old Is Your Patient?

A Medical Anthropological Approach to Age

SUZAN YAZICI AND NILÜFER KORKMAZ YAYLAGÜL

Age refers to the length of time a person has lived, and aging is often defined as the degenerative process of the body with time, associated with decline resulting in death (Bytheway 2011; Appleby 2010; Crews 2007). The fields of gerontology, biology, medicine, and psychology deal with the concept of age and its biologic, chronologic, and social definitions and conceptualization. Yet there are disagreements on defining age and its measurement, stemming from different approaches to studying the aging process (Achenbaum 2005, 23–24).

Definitions of *biological aging* conceptualize aging as the cellular changes during the life span and views the body as an organism. Theories of *social aging* attempt to explain the changes of social roles and lifestyles with advancing age. *Chronological aging* is the numeric representation of a life according to the passage of time, namely in years, while *psycho-social* definitions are focused on the relativity of age (Bytheway 2011, 6–7). Individuals' perceptions about age differ according to social structure, culture, and personal biological features. In this context, perceived age is widely used in academic literature and in daily life (Bordone, Arpino, and Rosina 2020; Scherbov and Sanderson 2016). In contrast, modernity standardizes and institutionalizes age because standards are needed for the management and productivity of institutions (Fry 1999). For example, a certain age is required for the eligibility and enrollment in school, military service, marriage, driver's license, voting privileges, and so on (Baars 1997, Fortes 1984; Appleby 2010). The initialization of age is practiced in four areas: (1) to indicate and document the birth date; (2) to administer bureaucratic procedures; (3) to determine the official intergenerational relations and responsibilities of parenting; and (4) to formulate policies and regulations that restrict access to rights and resources (Bytheway 2011, 9). All these phases clearly take place using birth registration.

Even though birth registration began long ago, it became prominent with industrialization. Records became widespread in Western societies much earlier than in some traditional societies. Birth records in some traditional societies may be disorganized and incomplete, as these societies sometimes do not attach the same degree of importance to birth dates compared to other nations (Saxena, Verma, and Sharma 1986; Helleringer et al. 2019). Therefore, problems related to birth registration have socioeconomic and cultural ramifications.

Having a birth registration is accepted as a human right in the Human Rights Declaration of 1948. Even though the United Nations Convention on the Rights of the Child (UNCRC) indicated that all children must be registered immediately after birth in order to protect their rights (UN 1989), millions of children worldwide live without any birth registrations. Even in Central and Eastern Europe and the Commonwealth of Independent States, in 2005 around 8 percent of children were found to be unregistered. The number of unregistered children varies according to region. Percentages for unregistered children in Latin America and the Caribbean (11 percent), Middle East and Africa (25 percent), East Asia and Pacific (28 percent), Sub-Saharan Africa (63 percent), and South Asia (64 percent) reflect these disparities (UNICEF 2005).

Some countries have been keeping official birth records for centuries. The most accurate records from the past are baptism registers in churches. In Denmark, for example, the first records were kept in churches upon the order of the king in 1645 and became widespread with a law introduced in 1683 (Worsøe 2005). Today, especially in industrialized countries, most births take place in medical facilities where records are made immediately after birth. For individuals who are born at home, the parents' declaration is accepted to process a birth record.

Inaccuracies of birth records are more common among older minority groups, immigrants, and groups with low socioeconomic backgrounds (Rosenwaike and Hill 1996; Hill et al. 1997; Preston et al. 1996; Lauderdale and Kestenbaum 2002). Socioeconomic conditions and late modernization, cultural factors such as religious beliefs, and different traditional perceptions of time are among factors for inaccurate registration (Saxena, Verma, and Sharma 1986; Coale and Li 1991).

Accurate age registrations are important for several reasons. They are an important parameter with effects on social security, health, law, and educational systems (Hill et al. 1997; Rosenwaike and Hill 1996; Hussey and Elo 1997; Jayaraman et al. 2016). The effects of age misreporting on social security, education, death records, asylum claims, and criminal offenses have been discussed widely in literature (Coale and Li 1991; Denic, Saadi, and Khatib 2004; Preston et al. 1996; Hussey and Elo 1997). However, this is not the case for health records and diseases. The importance of age misreporting in health promotion and treatment is vastly under-researched. One exception is Denic, Saadi, and Khatib (2004), who evaluated age records of cancer patients in 72 different countries and reported patients' preferences for age endings with digits 0 and 5. The results on the epidemiology of cancer patients were discussed and the age data quality was found to be low, with higher inaccuracies of age found in populations from the Indian subcontinent and Middle Eastern countries (except UAE men). The authors emphasized that the misreporting of age might bias results, decrease study power, and prevent generalizability of results reporting age-sensitive data. Responding to this gap in the literature, this chapter aims to evaluate cultural aspects of inaccurate birth registration and discuss the effects of age records on health services.

Cultural Aspects of Age Records in Turkey

In the past, birth registration records were not kept widely in Turkey. Modern birth registration started in the Turkish Republic with the first population census in 1927, in which it was found that 7 percent of the population was not registered. Some of this population was unwilling to be registered due to the fear of new taxation and new responsibilities (Tuğluoğlu 2012). Inaccuracies of birth records have been decreasing since the first census; however, they are prevalent among the older population of today. It is important to review the social conditions of that time period to understand the underlying factors. In the past, births took place mainly at home instead of health centers, as it was difficult to travel to city centers where birth registrations were kept. Thus, registrations were done when there was a need to travel to the health center. Birth certificates were not considered necessary documents and were obtained later in life, if needed, for official procedures such as school registrations, hospital treatments, and marriage.

Parallel to this, the birth rate and the infant death rate were high due to epidemics and insufficiency of health services (Tuğluoğlu 2012). Parents were hesitant to register their children until they reached a certain age because of the high possibility of infant and early childhood death. For the same reasons, in case a child with a birth registration (probably not accurately dated) died, a death registration was not requested, and the same birth registration was kept for the next child to be born. In this case, the next child had a birth record that was years older than their chronological age.

Inaccuracy of birth registration is still a familiar phenomenon in daily life in Turkey. This issue is reflected in Turkish literature and has been expressed in a Turkish novel, *Fikrimin İnce Gülü*, as such:

"You were born at 49, right?"
"I am actually 34 years old."
"How come you are born at 49 and are 34 years old?"
"They did it this way back then. They register you late. They have registered me late as well. Why? Ask me why? First, you go late to school . . . Second: you go late to military service . . . Third: you go to *hammam*[1] with your mother even when you are an adult." (Ağaoğlu 1977, 38).

Low literacy in rural areas resulted in a delay to comprehend the modern concept of time. It has taken a long time for the Western concept of years, seasons, months, and days to be accepted in Turkey. Time continues to be perceived by older generations according to the rhythm of nature, agricultural necessities, religious festivals, or important political events in the past. It is not rare to indicate a date of birth as "a week before harvest," "two days after Ramadan," or "the same age as our neighbor."

The perception of childhood and adulthood differs cross-culturally. In traditional societies, children were accepted as mature for marriage once they reached puberty, hence childbearing age. Marriage took place at an earlier age and even child marriage was common among women in Turkey. The age to start university was accepted as "too late for marriage" and, similarly, as "too late for motherhood." One related struggle was that the legal age for marriage was 18. It was a common practice to change the birth date to be over 18 before digitalization; thus, marriages are a common reason for inaccurate birth certificates, especially among women. Unofficial partnerships (*imam* marriage) were common, and children born in such families could not be registered due to the lack of formal requirements.

The illiteracy rate at the second census in 1935 was 91.19 percent among women and 70.65 percent among men (Tuğluoğlu 2012, 75). Most of the women were illiterate or had only a primary education. Illiterate women were not actively participating in the workforce; instead, they were engaged in agricultural and domestic work and married at earlier ages, resulting in the high incidence of age misreporting among women. Today, Turkish women participate more in the workplace and their education level is higher. The literacy level among women has increased to 94.8 percent. This has gradually increased the average age of marriage in Turkey. The mean age for marriage in 2019 was 25 for women and 27.9 for men (TUİK 2019a, b).

Military service is mandatory in Turkey for men over the age of 20. The average length of military service was around 4 years in the 1920s, during the early years of the Turkish Republic. It was shortened to 2 years (Bilgiç, Akyürek, and Koydemir 2015, 111) and is currently 6 months of service. Time spent in military service was considered as a loss of workforce, a reason for late marriages, and—in case of individuals already married—for late childbearing in rural regions. Parents wanted their sons to attend military duties as mature as possible and after their marriage and childbearing responsibilities were fulfilled. In order to go into the military at an older age, men registered their birthdates some years late. For these reasons, age estimation is difficult among older adults in Turkey. This issue is demonstrated in further detail in the analysis presented in the following section, which is based on research findings carried out with Turkish immigrants living in Denmark and Turkish citizens living in Turkey.

Medical Anthropology, Age, and Health Services

Medical anthropology applies anthropological methods and theories to the medical field, which is functional for both practice and theory. Medical anthropology deals with theories of health and illness, its practical meanings, its relations with economy and politics, its biological and cultural interactions, and the individual experiences of health and illness (Pelto and Pelto 1997; Singer and Erickson 2015). The biomedical system posits health and illness within the biological existence of humans, as opposed to the cultural and the social. This system has standardized health and illness in many societies and dominates the field of medicine (Trostle 2005). The biomedical approach has initially ignored the social and cultural processes of health and aging. However, anthropologists have long understood that meanings and attitudes of health and illness are related to social and cultural conditions. Human beings are social and cultural beings just as they are biological creatures. A cultural perspective enables an understanding of illness and medical issues where the biomedical perspective is not able to do so (Kleinman 1978). Medical anthropology tries to understand the biocultural characteristics of health and illness, as well as the conditions of wellness and illness from a cultural perspective, and uses the ethnography and techniques of qualitative method (Korkmaz-Yaylagül and Baş 2016).

Scientific developments and the improvement in medical treatment methods have extended human life. Demographic aging is drawing attention worldwide and especially in developed countries since the end of the twentieth century. A longer life expectancy and lower birth and death rates have resulted in an increase of older individuals among the total population (Kinsella 2000; Preston, Himes, and Eggers 1989). Aging is often associated with illness due to the biomedical domination of discourse. Higher incidence of illness among older individuals, higher risk of age-related diseases such as Alzheimer's disease, and the phenomenon of aging has shifted aging from a natural process into a pathological one worldwide. The subjects of medical anthropology intersect with aging research because medical anthropology enriches the aging experience beyond the pathological biomedical perspective. The treatment and care of chronic health conditions, doctor-patient relations, and the processes of care are related to cultural processes within the medical field (Buch 2015; Leibing and Cohen 2006). Similarly, marginalization or stereotyping of older individuals is common within the larger biomedical worldview (Ory 1995).

Empirical Findings of Inaccurate Age Records

Study 1: The Health Care Use of First-Generation Immigrants Living in Denmark

This qualitative study, titled "Health Care Use of Older Immigrants," was carried out with first-generation Turkish migrants living in Denmark. Mass migration to Western European countries from Turkey had started around the 1960s with bilaterally signed labor force agreements. Migrants from Turkey were mainly from rural regions, were largely illiterate and unskilled, and worked physically in heavy industrial labor. Migration was to countries in need of workforce, such as Germany, France, Holland, Denmark, and other West European countries. Those first-generation migrants are currently over 65 years of age with limited host-country language skills and higher rates of illness compared to the native population (Kristiansen et al. 2016).

This research was designed in order to reveal Turkish migrants' access to health services, health-care utilization, and the social and cultural backgrounds for the health-care use practices of these first-generation immigrants (Korkmaz-Yaylagul and Yazici 2018; Blaakilde et al. 2020). As part of the interviews, their age was asked and the answers directed us to evaluate the accuracy of birth registrations as a distinct subject. Even though the sample of the study consisted of individuals born in Turkey, it is likely that other countries with similar cultural and social backgrounds may face a similar issue.

Methods

This cross-sectional and qualitative research was conducted in Copenhagen in 2011–2012, with the collaboration of Copenhagen University Center of Healthy Aging and Akdeniz University Department of Gerontology. Interviews were conducted with 27 migrants from Turkey and utilized semi-structured questions. All participants signed an informed consent form that had been approved by the University of Copenhagen Ethics Committee. The participants' responses to the question of age exposed a widespread problem of inaccurate birth registrations. Even though age was mainly asked for demographic recording, a new question arose: "Is there any difference between your chronological and official birth date?" This question was asked of participants, and in case of a difference, the degree (years) and the reasons behind it were also questioned. All interviews were tape recorded, transcribed, and analyzed using descriptive thematic analysis method (Braun and Clarke 2006). Data was read by both researchers several times for coding. Consensus was achieved for emerging categories and themes according to the data and research questions.

Findings

Out of 27 respondents, 13 indicated a difference between their chronological and official birth dates. The reasons behind it varied, but certain themes emerged as culturally significant: the use of a certificate of a deceased sibling, or the change of official record due to marriage and to practice military service earlier. The difference in age misrepresentation in birth records was between 2 and 16 years from chronological age. Participants were asked about the impacts of this difference, and one female respondent (aged 64) stated:

> My official birth registration is 4 years younger than my real age. They don't believe it here. I begged the authorities to equate my age with my husband's. I was born in 1951, but I was officially registered as born in 1956. I told the authorities to change it to 1951, but my husband changed it to 1955, thus my real chronological age is now four years older than my official age. I couldn't attend school; they had asked for registration. When I got married, I was 18, but was officially 14. I came here around my 20 years but was officially 16. I got paid as a child; I worked like an adult but received less, like a child.

The respondent was asking the authorities to change the birth registration in order to have the same date of birth as her husband's, but was able to change it for a year only. This participant's response clearly shows how inaccurate records can negatively affect education and work life, with reduced earnings potentially affecting people throughout the life course.

Another respondent revealed that inaccurate official registration resulted in others perceiving her as older, and this was difficult to explain regarding official issues. One female participant stated, "I am 80 years old, but I am younger. You can't explain it here [in Denmark]. They check your registration. They raised my age, for marriage, so that I could marry earlier." The statement that the age inaccuracies were not understood is culturally shaped due to precise birth records in Denmark; however, this would be fairly easily comprehended by Turkish individuals. Another female (aged 60) stated that her change of registration was because of the death of her siblings, and for her brother the reason was military purposes: "My father raised our ages officially. My older sister died, and they have made me take her birth certificate. Similarly, with my brother. His age was also raised because my father wanted him to do his military service while he himself was still alive." Even though younger registration practices are more common for military service, the age of this participant's brother was raised. This case shows that the age registration practices depend on subjective conditions and are shaped according to individual preferences. Respondents explained the reasons for and consequences of inaccurate registration of age. Registration on birth records of deceased siblings is among the most common reasons for inaccurate birth registrations. Problems during official procedures were mentioned by many of the participants. However, none of the respondents mentioned any health-related consequences to these age inaccuracies. This issue is not raised at medical checks as they were not asked specifically about any inaccuracies by their health-care provider. Health-care providers prescribe regular age-based investigations (vaginal smear test, colonoscopy, etc.) according to patients' official birth dates. Patients were not aware of age-based investigations, so they could not ask for any time-based changes. Those problems and related results are therefore left unrecognized.

Study 2: Reasons for Inaccurate Birth Registrations among Older Adults in Antalya

The second study was planned in order to evaluate the prevalence of inaccurate birth records among individuals aged 65 and over due to the high number of birth registration inaccuracies found in the first research study. This cross-sectional, quantitative research was carried out in Antalya, Turkey, in 2013. Birth registrations and official IDs became obligatory in 1972 in Turkey, according to Population Law nr 1587.

A registration obligation of 30 days after birth was introduced in 1983 (1083, Law nr 2828). A fine of 81 Turkish *liras* was set for breaking the law. Around half a million individuals have paid the fine between 2009 and 2014 (Republic of Turkey Ministry of Internal Affairs, Department of Population and Citizenship, 2015). Koç and Eryurt (2010) indicate that the rate of unregistered children between 1993–1998 and 2003–2008 decreased from 26 percent to 6 percent according to Population and Health Research data. Around half of unregistered children are born to unmarried parents. The rest is found to be related to low socioeconomic status (Koç and Eryurt 2010, 116–117). Even though the rate of inaccurate birth records is decreasing, it can be assumed that the rate remains higher for older individuals. This is also indicated in the literature (Saxena, Verma, and Sharma 1986; Preston and Elo 1999; Hussey and Elo 1997). In the Turkish literature, there is no research on inaccurate birth records among older individuals. This study was designed with individuals aged 65 years and over to elucidate the rate and reasons of inaccurate birth registrations.

Methods

Convenience sampling was used to recruit 400 participants to address the research question (Etikan, Musa, and Alkassim 2016). The confidence interval for the sample of adults aged 65 years and over was calculated at

95 percent, and power analysis determined that at least 384 older participants should be recruited from Antalya city, based on population estimates. Four hundred individuals who had applied to the Antalya Education and Research Hospital outpatient clinic were recruited. The inclusion criteria were officially being registered as age 65 and over, and being able to answer the questions. Date of birth, place of birth, gender, whether a difference between the chronologic and official age exist, and the reasons behind any discrepancy were asked. Data was transferred to SPSS 26 software for Windows and analyzed with descriptive statistics. All participants signed an informed consent form that had been approved by the Antalya Education and Research Hospital Ethics Committee.

Findings

The age of respondents was between 65 and 91 years (mean=73.08). Twenty percent (n=80) of respondents revealed a difference between their official records and their chronological age. The mean difference was 4.96, with a minimum of one year and a maximum of 13 years. The rate of inaccuracy by gender was 21.5 percent (n=45) among women and 18.3 percent (n=35) among men. The official records were older than the chronological ages for 36 women and 25 men. The most frequent reason for raised registrations among the sample was indicated as using the death of an older sibling. Marriage was the most common reason for such inaccuracies among women (10 cases).

Official registrations of births less than the chronological age were found for 19 individuals (10 male and 9 female). For most participants, the reason for the discrepancy was parents' neglecting to register their children. The most frequently mentioned reason for men was to attend military service at an older age. Participants also mentioned other reasons such as attending school (n=3) and starting to work (n=2). In total, 36 respondents were not able to indicate any reason for birth record discrepancies.

Discussion

Recording of the age of individuals and regulations based on age for services such as schooling, military service, marriage, and retirement have largely been implemented in modern social life. On the other hand, there are many societies in the world with different rates of inaccurate age registrations. The reasons behind these disparities and the possible health outcomes differ. Difficult socioeconomic conditions of countries and underdeveloped regions are indicated in recent research for current age record inaccuracies (Coale and Li 1991; Saxena, Verma, and Sharma 1986). A decrease in inaccurate birth records over time has also been shown in the literature (Helleringer et al. 2019; Rosenwaike and Hill 1996); however, the rate of inaccurate registrations among the older population is found to still be high among very old individuals in developing countries (Hill, Preston, and Rosenwaike 2000; Preston and Elo 1999). Inaccurate birth registration has fundamental consequences for the older population in regard to social security, demography, and health. Age is a prerequisite for retirement and social aid eligibility. Inaccurate birth registration either may lead to abuse of the social security system or victimization of individuals. Plus, age records are important to reveal the population structure of a society and related analyses. Inaccurate birth records can lead to deviations even though demographers can decrease the effects of age registrations using new models.

The effects of inaccurate age registrations can also lead to problems within the health-care system. Studies about inaccurate age records related to health focus on the analysis of illness and death rates (Lauderdale and Kestenbaum 2002; Hussey and Elo 1997). On the other hand, inaccurate age records are also related to the diagnosis and treatment of diseases. In this chapter, age records have been evaluated using a medical anthropological perspective. Furthermore, cultural and social reasons for inaccurate records have been evaluated and their possible effects on health services have been discussed. Forty-eight percent (n=13) of the respondents of the qualitative research (n=27) and twenty percent (n=80) of the quantitative research (n=400) indicated that their chronological age was different from that of their official birth records. High incidence is striking even though the findings cannot be generalized.

Higher rates found in the qualitative research might exist for several reasons. The main reason could be related to regional characteristics of birthplace. Mass migration to European countries from Turkey in the 1960s were mainly from rural regions (Gitmez 1983). Respondents of the research carried out in Denmark were mainly from Middle Anatolian economically disadvantaged rural regions where infant mortality is found to be high. On the other hand, the quantitative research was carried out in Antalya, and most of the respondents were born in the Mediterranean region. It can be expected that the average rate of inaccurate birth records among older individuals would be over 20 percent for Turkey, but further comprehensive research is needed for more accurate rates.

Possible inaccuracies in birth records should be questioned by medical practitioners for their migrant patients; such inaccuracies can affect prophylactics, diagnostics, and treatment modalities, resulting in either delayed or unnecessary investigations. Age on regular health records is accepted by clinicians, and if just the age is asked, the incorrect age listed on official records will be indicated by the patient. The patient's true chronological age will not be indicated if not specifically requested. The effects of inaccuracies on health-related services were not evaluated in the research, and none of the respondents indicated any health-related problems. As patients might not be aware of the early or late prophylactic and treatment modalities, we can assume that they might not feel the indirect effects and their results.

Cancer screenings and several prophylactic medical practices are based on age. For example, the U.S. Preventive Service Task Force (USPSTF) recommends biannual mammography screenings for women between 50 and 74 years (Grade B), and emphasizes that there is not enough evidence for individuals over the age of 75 (Grade I). Colorectal cancer screenings are recommended between the age of 50 and 75 through occult blood in stool, sigmoidoscopy, and colonoscopy (Grade A); screening between 76 and 85 years is recommended (Grade C); and no screens are recommended for individuals over 85 (Grade D) (USPSTF 2020). If we consider those recommendations according to our findings from the quantitative study, 61 respondents whose age on official registrations is older than their chronological age would call for those screenings earlier, which may result in unnecessary testing and an earlier radiation exposure. As those tests are terminated at a certain age, these respondents will have their last tests years earlier than recommended. Among 209 women in our quantitative sample, 36 would terminate the mammography screening before age 70. Similarly, 61 individuals would terminate colonoscopy screening before they reach 75 years old.

The case of official records being younger than chronological age was encountered less in both studies. Those individuals would start receiving important screenings years later than recommended. According to the quantitative findings, 19 respondents have a difference of more than five years. Among them, only one was male, and he was registered seven years younger than his chronological age. The younger registered respondent would start with their cancer screenings seven years too late. Official birth records of older migrants can differ from their chronological age, which can have negative or positive consequences. Except that an early cancer screening may enable early diagnosis in a few cases, inaccuracies of birth registration more often have negative outcomes in medical practice. From an economic standpoint, younger registered individuals would not be eligible for full rates of salaries or retirement benefits even though they would be chronologically qualified for it. On the other hand, those with older official birth registrations would be eligible for retirement even though they would be chronologically younger.

Conclusion

Chronological age is an important but under-researched issue. Age can be an important factor for timing and evaluation of some medical interventions and practices. Inaccurate birth records or incorrect declarations of chronological age can still be encountered, but this happens much less today due to widespread use of official birth records and digitalization. However, even today, such long-standing problems in the birth registration system can cause problems for older adults. The difference between the real and recorded age, and the cultural reasons behind it, are important to study in order to evaluate their effects on individual health and quality of life.

Health systems in developed countries often have strict rules for medical tests, screenings, and other procedures. Information on inaccuracies of birth registrations should be given to authorities to be recorded in case a significant difference at birth records and chronologic age exists, so that some rules could be reevaluated and flexibility in age-based investigations allowed. Individuals with inaccurate age records should be informed about possible health or medical implications arising from age records. Some invasive and radioactive-containing examination methods that provide evidence for protection of individuals can be delayed for patients with birth records older than the chronological age.

Medical anthropologists could play mediator roles in such clinical research because they have the potential to influence the medical community to acknowledge these culturally and socially salient issues among their patients. It is important to question the real chronological age, especially of older migrants from lower socioeconomic backgrounds and ethnic minority groups coming from developing countries. More comprehensive studies could provide representative information on rates of inconsistencies of records. Likewise, health professionals could gain a culturally sensitive perspective from working with medical anthropologists. The chronological age of their patients, especially those with migrant backgrounds, should be questioned before providing a referral to age-based services.

Acknowledgments

The authors wish to thank Sofiya Shreyer for her suggestions and feedback on an earlier version of this chapter.

Note

1. *Hammam* is a traditional Turkish public bath where boys older than a certain age are not allowed to enter with their mothers.

References

Achenbaum, W. Andrew. 2005. "Ageing and Changing: International Historical Perspectives on Ageing." In *The Cambridge Handbook of Age and Ageing*, edited by Malcolm Johnson, Vern Bengston, and Peter Coleman, 21–29. Cambridge: Cambridge University Press.

Ağaoğlu, Adalet. 1977. *Fikrimin İnce Gülü*. İstanbul: Remzi.

Appleby, Joanna E. P. 2010. "Why We Need an Archaeology of Old Age, and a Suggested Approach." *Norwegian Archaeological Review* 43(2): 145–168.

Baars, Jan. 1997. "Concepts of Time and Narrative Temporality in the Study of Aging." *Journal of Aging Studies* 11(4): 283–295.

Bilgiç, M. Sadi, Salih Akyürek, and F. Serap Koydemir. 2015. "Türkiye'de Askerlik Sistemi Nasıl Olmalıdır?" *Bilge Strateji* 7(13): 97–127.

Blaakilde, Anna Leonora, Signe Smith Jervelund, Suzan Yazici, Signe Gronwald Petersen, and Allan Krasnik. 2020. "Use of Cross-Border Healthcare Services by Elderly Turkish Migrants in Denmark: A Qualitative Study and Some Critical Reflections about Public Health 'Concerns.'" *Nordic Journal of Migration Research* 10(3): 56–72.

Bordone, Valeria, Bruno Arpino, and Alessandro Rosina. 2020. "Forever Young? An Analysis of the Factors Influencing Perceptions of Ageing." *Ageing & Society* 40(8):1669–1693.

Braun, Virginia, and Victoria Clarke. 2006. "Using Thematic Analysis in Psychology." *Qualitative Research in Psychology* 3(2): 77–101. doi:10.1191/1478088706qp063oa.

Buch, Elana D. 2015. "Anthropology of Aging and Care." *Annual Review of Anthropology* 44(1): 277–293. doi:10.1146/annurev-anthro-102214-014254.

Byetheway, Bill. 2011. *Unmasking Age: The Significance of Age for Social Research*. Portland, OR: Policy Press.

Coale, Ansley J., and Shaomin Li. 1991. "The Effect of Age Misreporting in China on the Calculation of Mortality Rates at Very High Ages." *Demography* 28(2): 293–301.

Denic, Srdjan, Hussein Saadi, and Falah Khatib. 2004. "Quality of Age Data in Patients from Developing Countries." *Journal of Public Health* 26(2): 168–171.

Etikan, Ilker, Sulaiman Abubakar Musa, and Rukayya Sunusi Alkassim. 2016. "Comparison of Convenience Sampling and Purposive Sampling." *American Journal of Theoretical and Applied Statistics* 5(1): 1–4.

Fortes, Meyer. 1984. "Age, Generation, and Social Structure." *Age and Anthropological Theory*: 99–122.

Fry, Christine L. 1999. "Anthropological Theories of Age and Aging." In *Handbook of Theories of Aging*, edited by Vern Bengston and Warner Schaie, 271–286. New York: Springer.

Gitmez, Ali S. 1983. *Yurtdışına İşçi Göçü ve Geri Dönüşler: "Beklentiler-Gerçekleşenler."* İstanbul: Alan Yayıncılık.

Helleringer, Stéphane, Chong You, Laurence Fleury, Laetitia Douillot, Insa Diouf, Cheikh Tidiane Ndiaye, Valerie Delaunay, and Rene Vidal. 2019. "Improving Age Measurement in Low-and Middle-Income Countries through Computer Vision." *Demographic Research* 40: 219–260.

Hill, Mark E., Samuel H. Preston, and Ira Rosenwaike. 2000. "Age Reporting among White Americans Aged 85+: Results of a Record Linkage Study." *Demography* 37(2): 175–186.

Hill, Mark E., Samuel H. Preston, Irma T. Elo, and Ira Rosenwaike. 1997. "Age-Linked Institutions and Age Reporting among Older African Americans." *Social Forces* 75(3): 1007–1030.

Hussey, Jon M., and Irma T. Elo. 1997. "Cause-Specific Mortality among Older African-Americans: Correlates and Consequences of Age Misreporting." *Social Biology* 44(3–4): 227–246.

Jayaraman, Jayakumar, Graham J. Roberts, Hai Ming Wong, Fraser McDonald, and Nigel M. King. 2016. "Ages of Legal Importance: Implications in Relation to Birth Registration and Age Assessment Practices." *Medicine, Science and the Law* 56(1): 77–82.

Kinsella, Kevin. 2000. "Demographic Dimensions of Global Aging." *Journal of Family Issues* 21(5): 541–558.

Kleinman, Arthur. 1978. "Concepts and a Model for the Comparison of Medical Systems as Cultural Systems." *Social Science & Medicine. Part B: Medical Anthropology* 12: 85–93.

Koç, İsmet, and Mehmet Ali Eryurt. 2010. "Türkiye'de Beş Yaş Altındaki Çocukların Nüfusa Kayıt Olma Durumları: 1993–2008." *Cocuk Sagligi ve Hastaliklari Dergisi* 53(2): 114–121.

Korkmaz-Yaylagül, Nilüfer, and Ahmet Melik Baş. 2016. "The Issue of Aging in Medical Anthropology Research (Turkish)." *Çukurova Üniversitesi Sosyal Bilimler Enstitüsü Dergisi* 25(3): 139–154.

Korkmaz-Yaylagul, Nilufer, and Suzan Yazici. 2018. "The Perceptions of Elderly Turkish Immigrants of the Health Care Systems in Their Home and Host Countries: A Field Study Focused on Denmark, Britain and Germany." *Journal of Society & Social Work* 29(2): 34–50.

Kristiansen, Maria, Oliver Razum, Hürrem Tezcan-Güntekin, and Allan Krasnik. 2016. "Aging and Health among Migrants in a European Perspective." *Public Health Reviews* 37(1): 1–14.

Lauderdale, Diane S., and Bert Kestenbaum. 2002. "Mortality Rates of Elderly Asian American Populations Based on Medicare and Social Security Data." *Demography* 39(3): 529–540.

Leibing, Annette, and Lawrence Cohen. 2006. *Thinking about Dementia: Culture, Loss, and the Anthropology of Senility*. New Brunswick, NJ: Rutgers University Press.

Ory, M. G. 1995. "Aging, Health, and Culture: The Contribution of Medical Anthropology." *Medical Anthropology Quarterly* 9(2): 281–283. doi:10.1525/maq.1995.9.2.02a00100.

Pelto, Pertti J., and Gretel H. Pelto. 1997. "Studying Knowledge, Culture, and Behavior in Applied Medical Anthropology." *Medical Anthropology Quarterly* 11(2): 147–163.

Preston, Samuel H., and Irma T. Elo. 1999. "Effects of Age Misreporting on Mortality Estimates at Older Ages." *Population Studies* 53(2): 165–177.

Preston, Samuel H., Irma T. Elo, Ira Rosenwaike, and Mark Hill. 1996. "African-American Mortality at Older Ages: Results of a Matching Study." *Demography* 33(2): 193–209.

Preston, Samuel H., Christine Himes, and Mitchell Eggers. 1989. "Demographic Conditions Responsible for Population Aging." *Demography* 26(4): 691–704.

Republic of Turkey Ministry of Internal Affairs Department of Population and Citizenship. 2015. Nüfus İşlemleri. https://www.nvi.gov.tr/dogum-islemleri, December 10, 2015.

Rosenwaike, Ira, and Mark E. Hill. 1996. "The Accuracy of Age Reporting among Elderly African Americans: Evidence of a Birth Registration Effect." *Research on Aging* 18(3): 310–324.

Saxena, Prem C., K. R. Verma, and K. A. Sharma. 1986. "Errors in Age Reporting in India, a Socio-cultural and Psychological Explanation." *Indian Journal of Social Work* 47(2): 127–135.

Scherbov, Sergei, and Warren C. Sanderson. 2016. "New Approaches to the Conceptualization and Measurement of Age and Aging." *Journal of Aging and Health* 28(7): 1159–1177.

Singer, Merrill, and Pamela I. Erickson. 2015. *A Companion to Medical Anthropology*. New York: Wiley.

Trostle, James A. 2005. *Epidemiology and Culture*. Cambridge: Cambridge University Press.

Tuğluoğlu, Fatih. 2012. "Türkiye Cumhuriyeti'nin İkinci Nüfus Sayımı: 20 İlkteşrin 1935 -Ne Bir Eksik Ne Bir Fazla." *Çağdaş Türkiye Tarihi Araştırmaları Dergisi* 12(25): 55–78.

TUİK. 2019a. Türkiye İstatistikleri. Türkiye İstatistik Kurumu.

———. 2019b. Türkiye Toplumsal Cinsiyet İstatistikleri. Ankara: Türkiye İstatistik Kurumu.

UN. 1989. Convention on the Rights of the Child. In *Treaty Series*.

UNICEF. 2005. *The "Rights" Start to Life: A Statistical Analysis of Birth Registration*. UNICEF.

USPSTF. 2020. U.S. Preventive Services Task Force recommendation statement, edited by U.S. Preventive Services Task Force.

Worsøe, Hans H. 2005. *Politikens Håndbog i Slægtshistorie*: Gyldendals Bogklubber. København V: Politikens Forlaghus.

9

The Importance of Traditional Foods and Subsistence Activities for Healthy Aging in Alaska Native Communities

BRITTENY M. HOWELL, RUBY L. FRIED, AND VANESSA Y. HIRATSUKA

Significant cross-cultural variation exists in how people around the globe define "healthy aging." This variation can influence, and be influenced by, lifestyle choices, social environments, and health outcomes. In many Indigenous Alaskan communities, important components of healthy aging include access to traditional foods and engagement in subsistence activities. Although many Alaska Native peoples currently reside in cities, the importance of subsistence activities and foods remains crucial and meaningful for healthy aging in both rural and urban locations. Research suggests that Alaska Native Elders define healthy aging into such categories as community engagement, spirituality, physical health, as well as access to traditional foods and activities that converge to strongly influence diet, activity patterns, and health outcomes (Graves and Shavings 2005; Hopkins et al. 2007; Lewis 2011).

Although the term "healthy aging" is used frequently in the gerontological literature, there is no universal definition of this concept (Michel and Sadana 2017). The phrase "successful aging" is often used interchangeably with "healthy aging" in terms of three main components: low probability of disease and disease-related disability, high cognitive and physical functional capacity, and active engagement with life (Rowe and Kahn 1987). However, this definition has been criticized for focusing too heavily on individual lifestyle choices and physical functioning rather than acknowledging cultural expectations of the aging process and complex interactions with the environment and social inequalities that contribute to health disparities (Katz and Calasanti 2014). Anthropologist Sarah Lamb (2014) argues that this biomedical definition of successful aging is laden with cultural assumptions of individualism influenced by neoliberal attitudes held largely by North Americans while ignoring the biological realities of mortality and human decline at the end of the life span, contributing to a counterproductive aging discourse that blames people for their "failures" to age successfully. Indeed, values of individualism, autonomy, and self-control coalesce to create a culture focused on maintaining youth for as long as possible, resulting in a definition of aging that is characterized as moving away from youth rather than toward an equally important life stage (Gilleard and Higgs 2014, 2015; Foucault 1978).

Instead, an anthropological perspective on aging in Alaska Native communities may consider integrating the concepts of resilience and human adaptability into a more holistic framework for understanding healthy aging. Human adaptability theory frames health outcomes as an indicator of the ability to navigate social, cultural, environmental, and economic conditions (Brewis and Lee 2010; Huss-Ashmore 2000; Ulijaszek 1997). Therefore, a biocultural perspective on human adaptability theory can help anthropologists understand the relationships between biological outcomes and health behaviors as a response to physical and sociocultural environments (Armelagos et al. 1992). For example, Smith-Morris's work (2004, 2006) among the Pima has shown that obesity on the reservation is linked in complex ways to political, economic, sociocultural, and environmental conditions. This work demonstrates that biological outcomes among some Indigenous populations are often most strongly related to sociocultural and physical environmental stressors rather than genetic differences.

In addition, the gerontological concept of healthy aging, which refers to the retention of social, physical, and mental capacities necessary for the maintenance of well-being through the life course (Iwarsson et al. 2007), also helps us frame the relationship between traditional foods, subsistence activities, and healthy aging in Alaska Native communities. This chapter integrates human adaptability perspectives within a framework of resilience and healthy aging (Boyle and Counts 1988; Lavretsky 2014) by examining traditional diet and subsistence activity patterns among Alaska Native Elders through a biocultural lens. Such a model of human adaptability and healthy aging allows anthropologists to elucidate the important role of adaptive strategies and health behaviors on the continued functioning of mental, physical, social, and economic systems in Alaska Native communities as the body slows down its processes with age (Hansen-Kyle 2005). In Alaska, Indigenous communities are dealing with rapid economic, social, and environmental changes that require unique adaptive strategies in order to maintain valued lifeways. Here we present several ways that Alaska Native Elders have adapted how they obtain important foods and pass on cultural information to the next generation amid such sociocultural and environmental changes.

Defining "Alaska Native": Elderhood, Traditional Food, and Subsistence Activities

Alaska has the highest population of Indigenous peoples of any state in the United States, at more than 148,000 individuals, or 19 percent of the general population (U.S. Census Bureau 2019), comprising 11 distinct cultural groups (Alaska Federation of Natives 2020) and collectively referred to as Alaska Native peoples. These groups are distributed geographically across the entirety of the state and consist of Eyak, Tlingit, Haida, and Tsimshian (southeast); Inupiaq and St. Lawrence Yupik (north and northwest); Yup'ik and Cup'ik (southwest); Athabascan (interior and southcentral); Alutiiq (Sugpiaq); and Unangax peoples (Aleutian Islands). The foods, subsistence activities, and cultural practices vary widely across these multiple cultural groups in the largest state in the United States. However, there is reason to suggest that some commonalities exist in the ways that Indigenous peoples of the Circumpolar North view healthy aging, resilience, and adaptability (Akearok et al. 2019; Howell and Peterson 2020). These commonalities include recognition and respect for the interconnectedness of ecology, seeking harmony in interpersonal relationships, spiritual growth through spending time on the land, and reflection on multigenerational knowledge transmission.

The concept of "Elderhood" is generally not defined strictly by chronological age in Circumpolar Indigenous communities, but instead includes broader components of aging such as physical growth, senescence, increasing responsibility for their actions as individuals and as community members, and willingness to transmit accumulated wisdom to the younger generation (Collings 2000, 2001). Among many Alaska Native peoples, Elderhood is generally an honor that community members bestow upon a person as a result of the knowledge they have gained throughout their lives and demonstrate through their actions (Lewis 2010). Therefore, research on

Circumpolar Indigenous aging often includes perspectives from Elders in their forties and fifties, as well as individuals over 60 years old.

The term "traditional food" used in this chapter refers to all culturally accepted food within a particular population that is available from local natural resources (Kuhnlein and Receveur 1996). Alaska Native traditional foods include locally hunted, harvested, fished, and gathered items such as game meat (moose, caribou, etc.), marine mammals (seal, whale, etc.), wild birds and their eggs, berries, greens, and seafood (Redwood et al. 2019). The phrase "subsistence activities" is defined here as any activity related to traditional food procurement or processing such as berry picking, fishing, hunting, and trapping as well as butchering, cutting, smoking fish or meat, and working animal skins and hides (Kuhnlein and Receveur 1996; Redwood et al. 2019; Wheeler and Thornton 2005). In this chapter, we interrogate how cultural, physical, and psychological health benefits of subsistence activities and consumption of traditional foods for Alaska Native Elders may be situated within a framework of human adaptability, resilience, and healthy aging.

Health Impacts of Traditional Foods and Activities among Alaska Native Elders

Traditional diets and subsistence activities of Alaska Native peoples vary due to ecological availability of resources in the large geographic expanse of Alaska. Such variation contributes to our understanding of cross-cultural diversity in population biologies (Ice 2005). In general, locally acquired foods in Alaska are nutrient-dense with high levels of protein, iron, omega-3 fatty acids, vitamins, and antioxidants coupled with low levels of carbohydrates. Traditional foods contain nutrients that are beneficial for healthy aging, such as higher vitamins A, C, D, and B12, calcium, and total dietary fiber (Bersamin et al. 2007). Consumption of greater amounts of traditional foods has been correlated with lower lipids, blood pressure, glucose, and adiposity among Alaska Native peoples (Bersamin et al. 2008; Ryman et al. 2015). Researchers have also explored the role of tundra greens, fish, and marine animals as important components of the subsistence diet, which may result in a high intake of polyunsaturated fatty acids and have a positive impact on glucose tolerance and insulin sensitivity (Aslibekyan et al. 2014). Human adaptability theory suggests that genetic variance observed in Indigenous Arctic populations may have evolved in response to a need to conserve body stores of nutrients due to environmental limitations on its availability in the traditional diet.

Historical and anthropological accounts of Alaska Native peoples include observations of low rates of obesity, diabetes, and cardiovascular disease, with more recent research indicating that both traditional diet and the processes of food harvesting, storage, and preparation contribute to positive health effects (Bjerregaard et al. 2004; O'Brien et al. 2017). For example, Redwood and colleagues (2008) report that subsistence activities such as fishing, picking berries or greens, and cutting and smoking fish or meat were common sources of physical activity for Alaska Native peoples. Participation in subsistence activity was also found to vary by sex and geographic region, with individuals in southwest Alaska reporting more subsistence activities compared to individuals in southeast and southcentral Alaska (an area that includes the state's largest urban center). Such findings have also been reported among Indigenous peoples in Greenland, where non-urban adults engage in more subsistence activities like fishing and hunting than their city-dwelling counterparts (Dahl-Petersen, Jørgensen, and Bjerregaard 2011).

In Alaska, subsistence activities as a form of exercise are also higher among men than women, but do not differ by age (Redwood et al. 2008). Work among Canadian Inuit Elders demonstrates similar gendered patterns, and that Elders exhibit moderate to high levels of physical activity despite high rates of overweight and obesity (Hopping et al. 2010). Ethnographic work among Elders also indicates that engaging in subsistence activities as a form of exercise is viewed to be a personal responsibility that helps maintain healthy aging as well as fight hegemonic discourses of aging as a process of increasing frailty and deterioration (Brooks-Cleator and Lewis 2020).

Despite the aforementioned health benefits of traditional foods and subsistence activities, public health surveillance and ethnographic research have shown a decline in traditional food consumption and subsistence activities among Alaska Native peoples accompanying the shift toward a more market-based diet (McGrath-Hanna et al. 2003). In a ten-year follow-up of an Alaska Native cohort in southcentral Alaska, Redwood and colleagues (2019) found that there was a significant decline in the mean number of traditional foods eaten as well as reduced consumption of multiple traditional foods. Nevertheless, traditional foods continue to play an important role in the health of Elders. In a large study of Alaska Native peoples in three regions of Alaska, over 92 percent of the study population reported eating at least one traditional food in the past year, with the most common being fish, moose, and *agutaq* (a mixture of berries, fat, and dried fish) (Redwood et al. 2008). In general, the proportion of the Alaska Native population eating a traditional diet differs by age and area of residence. For example, researchers have examined red blood cell stable isotope ratios from two Yup'ik villages in southwest Alaska comparing a group of Elder participants to adolescent participants and found differences consistent with increased intake of marine subsistence in Elders, and of market foods in younger participants (O'Brien et al. 2017; Wilkinson, Yai, and O'Brien 2007). Additionally, individuals residing in rural areas have a higher proportion of their diet consisting of traditional foods than those in urban areas (Ballew et al. 2004, 2006).

The health impacts of a lifelong diet of traditional foods on chronic disease risk are not well studied. However, some research has demonstrated possible protective effects of traditional foods rich in omega-3 fatty acids and lean protein in salmon, seal oil, moose, caribou, seal, and walrus, including reduced weight gain as well as improved glucose tolerance and lipid profiles (Ebbesson et al. 2005; Makhoul et al. 2010, 2011). Traditional diets may be low in fiber and high in fat, and when such diets are coupled with exposure to carcinogens derived from diet or the environment, there may be an increased risk of developing precancerous colon polyps (Ocvirk et al. 2020). Additionally, Beaulieu-Jones and colleagues (2015) describe an inverse association of marine food intake with systolic and diastolic blood pressure. However, obtaining traditional foods and engaging in subsistence activities remain an important part of how Elders define healthy aging, which plays an integral role in their health behaviors and biological outcomes.

Conceptualizing Healthy Aging in Alaska Native Communities

Research among Elders demonstrates that these traditional foods and subsistence activities are not just important for physical health, but also play a significant role in the broader cultural definition of healthy aging. Indeed, research shows that healthy aging is defined differently by older adults and biomedical professionals who tend to disagree on the importance of various physiological, psychological, societal, and personal aspects of aging (Hansen-Kyle 2005). In Alaska, older adults define healthy aging in terms of having a positive attitude, a sense of community, and a purpose in life rather than focusing on physical health parameters from a medical model (Howell, Seater, and McLinden 2020; Peterson, Baumgartner, and Austin 2020). The ways that people define and think about healthy aging have a profound effect on their adaptability, resilience, health behaviors, and resulting biological and health outcomes (Torres 2003).

Lewis (2010, 2011, 2013a, 2013b, 2014) has produced much of the literature on how rural Elders define healthy aging. This body of work demonstrates that Elders define healthy aging in holistic terms, encompassing elements of emotional well-being, community engagement, spirituality, and physical health; however, much of the successful aging literature tends to focus on physical health form a biomedical lens (Lewis 2011). Traditional foods and engagement in subsistence activities crosscut these important aspects of healthy aging, as Elders report that these activities increase emotional and physical health, community engagement, and encompass spiritual components. For example, one rural Elder states:

> In urban communities, food isn't traditional, rural has more traditional food, which is like our medicine. Living off of the land helps people age well; food connects who we are as Native peoples. Living off the land is putting your body to use. Keeping up your health and mental balance. Don't have these opportunities in the cities. Cities have more dictated ways of living. There are no Western stresses in villages. Your body becomes weak and lazy in urban cities; there is no access to traditional food. (Lewis 2010, 390)

Ethnographic research by Hopkins et al. (2007) in rural southwestern Alaska also corroborates that Alaska Native women define healthy aging in terms of engaging in subsistence activities, consuming traditional foods, and respecting their Elders. Participants in this qualitative study stated that subsistence activities, such as berry picking and fish processing, are important sources of physical activity. Consumption of these food items is also known to confer health benefits "and make the body strong" (46), especially when compared to *kass'aq* ("white people") market foods. Participants in the Norton Sound region also indicated that subsistence activities are a way to survive and provide for community members, as well as to preserve their culture (Brooks-Cleator and Lewis 2020). Indigenous Elders throughout Alaska view being able to successfully participate in subsistence activities and to teach these activities to others, also called generativity, as a defining feature of healthy aging.

The Role of Generativity

Ethnographic research shows that important components of generativity for Elders are demonstrated through the lens of food and subsistence activities. Anthropologist Robert Rubenstein (2015) defines "generativity" as having an interest in guiding and teaching the next generation in terms of four main elements: people, groups, things, and activities (see also Agunbiade, this volume, for a discussion on generativity). This framework fits well with the holistic nature of Alaska Native healthy aging, since Elders often describe generativity in terms of teaching individuals and groups of younger people about the important aspects of life in Alaska Native communities, which often revolve around the procurement, processing, and consumption of traditional foods. Lewis's (2014) research demonstrates that Elders view the dissemination of traditional knowledge as an important aspect of social and community engagement, which has a profound effect on Elders' ability to age well. His research among individuals aged 50 years and younger has also shown that many Alaska Native peoples view the inability to age well as primarily due to decreases in access to subsistence foods and activities in urban and rural locations alike (Lewis 2013a).

Lewis's research demonstrates the importance of healthy aging perspectives and optimism in rural Alaska Native communities. Elders expressed hope in the face of Westernizing influences, such as the internet and video games, that they will be able to preserve and transmit their traditional subsistence culture to the next generation (Lewis 2013b). For example, one Elder stated that he thinks "young people would begin to understand their grandparents' way of life. And follow the pathway of getting your food and learn the better food values for themselves. I think this would do them well" (Lewis 2014, 278). Rural Elders view themselves as being well positioned to help shape the health of younger Alaska Native peoples by passing on and strengthening their traditional cultures and values in the face of rapid cultural change.

Alaska Native peoples indicate that intergenerational transmission of subsistence activities and cultural knowledge also helps them manage stressful experiences and increase resilience by providing coping strategies and a sense of hopeful optimism for the future generation (Rivkin et al. 2019; Wexler et al. 2014). Ethnographic work among the Inupiaq in northern Alaska corroborates that transmission of food harvesting customs, knowledge, and skills to others results in Elders feeling valued, which greatly improves their quality of life and valuable functioning (Smith et al. 2009).

Although much of the ethnographic work on healthy aging among Elders has been conducted in the interior, southwest, northern, and south-central regions of the state, research in southeast Alaska also indicates the important role of traditional foods and subsistence activities for Alaska Native peoples. For example, Lunda and Green's (2020) study on teaching traditional harvesting practices to children shows that Elders view their role as teachers as an important component of cultural knowledge transmission and identity formation in the next generation. One respondent indicated, "Subsistence is a huge part of our culture, our identity. Everything we have comes from our land. Being able to understand our surroundings is important in understanding who we are" (99). Human adaptability and healthy aging frameworks help us connect how culture, resilience, identity, and behavioral practices affect biological outcomes, because Indigenous adults engaged in teaching subsistence activities report such positive health outcomes as improved diet, increased exercise, and subjective well-being (Burnette, Clark, and Rodning 2018).

Employing Adaptive Strategies for Obtaining Traditional Foods

Recognizing the importance of traditional foods for physical, mental, and spiritual well-being, Alaska Native older adults employ multiple adaptive strategies to obtain these foods despite occasional yet significant barriers, such as living in an urban area, physical limitations, lack of transportation, and increased vulnerability to food insecurity (Fogel-Chance 1993; Howell and Peterson 2020; Skinner et al. 2013). Adaptive strategies include, but are not limited to, engaging in urban food harvesting, food-sharing networks, and traditions of trade and barter; attending potlatches and cultural events; contributing to hunting, gathering, processing, and food storage; and participating in institutional efforts related to food sovereignty and traditional food access.

Although much of the anthropological literature on Elders focuses on rural residents, many of these subsistence foods and activities also inform definitions of healthy aging among Elders living in urban locations. Elders in urban areas may have different access to subsistence foods compared to their counterparts living in rural Alaska, so there may also be meaningful differences in their modes of adaptation. Urban Alaskan communities contrast in many ways from rural communities including greater access to general and specialized medical care that is often unavailable elsewhere in the state, given the presence of the Alaska Native Medical Center and other higher-capacity medical facilities. Howell and Peterson (2020) report that moving to an urban area can be viewed as a chain reaction that leads to weaker ties with family members and decreased access to traditional foods. Indeed, traditional food access is more limited for most residents of urban Alaska, as evidenced by the significantly lower harvest (Alaska Department of Fish & Game 2015) and consumption of these foods (Nobmann and Lanier 2001; Walch et al. 2019) compared to patterns in rural areas.

However, engaging in urban harvesting and food-sharing networks are two adaptive strategies that allow traditional food access among Elders living in urban Alaska. Picking berries is a harvesting activity that can be done within and just outside of city limits. In addition, dip-netting and other fishing activities can be accessed in the southcentral and southeast regions by car or boat. While these activities can be physically rigorous, older adults can contribute directly or by helping process and store the foods that their family and friends may acquire. Such multigenerational efforts commonly occur in rural communities as well, where Elders characterize experiences of harvesting and processing foods as "working together for the future" (Inuit Circumpolar Council-Alaska 2015). It is also a common practice for individuals living in rural areas to send traditional foods to their family members living in cities (Fogel-Chance 1993; Fried 2019; Walch et al. 2019). For example, one Elder living in Anchorage revealed getting her "fish, caribou, moose, ptarmigan, you know, a lot of berries: salmonberries, blueberries, raspberries" from her family members who live in rural areas, "like my cousin's husband works as a foreman in a crab plant and so he can get us crab where we couldn't otherwise afford it" (Howell 2017). Her family in the northwest gets her seal oil and her family in interior Alaska sends her watermelon berries in exchange for fresh fruit from the markets in Anchorage that they cannot obtain in rural Alaska. "It's a bartering system," she reports (150–151). While specific data on the participation of Elders in rural-to-urban food sharing is lacking, it can be assumed that Elders living in Anchorage and other urban centers who receive traditional foods have acquired them in this manner of sharing (Lee 2002).

Looking beyond the urban-rural differences, the value of sharing with Elders in one's community is common among Indigenous populations in the Circumpolar North (Berkes and Jolly 2002; Griffin 2020; Ready 2018).

The Inuit Circumpolar Council's recent publication on Food Sovereignty and Self Governance (2020), which includes many interviews with Elders, reports that sharing and cooperation is apparent in nearly every element of dialogue, and that these values are foundational to Inuit culture. Furthermore, food sharing, especially within families, has been identified as one of the most important ways of adapting to food shortages (Skinner et al. 2013). In a particularly salient demonstration of the importance of sharing, a man from Kivalina, Alaska, spoke about harvesting caribou and sharing with his older parents:

> They can't hunt, they get too old, [so] they're always excited. It's a good feeling to know that my parents are waiting for that [caribou] meat. It's a really good feeling when you give it to them. (Griffin 2020, 338)

From a Canadian Elder's perspective, Collings (2001, 136) also presented the view that one of the best aspects of being an Elder "must be that when they get food brought to them by the younger generation because granny likes it when we bring her food, country food." These accounts, along with millennia of traditional practices and culture, demonstrate the importance of food sharing for continued access to traditional foods among Indigenous Elders in Alaska and the Circumpolar North.

Elders' access to traditional foods can also be achieved through participation at cultural and community events, as well as through organization-based efforts. In 2014, the Traditional Foods Nourishment Act was passed, which allowed traditional foods to be served in facilities including hospitals and eldercare facilities. Following this, the Alaska Native Medical Center has included traditional foods in their cafeteria and to current patients, including berries, salmon, halibut, and reindeer (Rogers 2015; ANTHC 2016; Hillman 2018). In addition, the Hunter Support Program is one example of a formal initiative that provides fish and game to Elders living at *Utuqqanaat Inaat* ("A Place for Elders," a long-term care facility), as well as other community social events (Maniilaq Association 2020). While these are examples of formalized programs, many other Alaska Native villages, community-level entities, and individuals provide traditional foods to Elders consistent with the Alaska Native cultural tradition of sharing foods with community members, and Elders in particular (see, for example, Fienup-Riordan 2000).

While serving as a cornerstone of cultural values, Elder involvement in traditional food sharing is not limited to receiving food from younger family and community members. In fact, it was found that Elders often serve as focal points for the collection and sharing of traditional foods, as demonstrated by the fact that households with Elders provided more meals to other households compared to households without (Ready 2018). The expert knowledge of traditional food harvesting, processing, storage, and preparation is also often held among Elders who are commonly deferred to by other family and community members (Berkes and Jolly 2002; Collings 2011). Traditional knowledge gained over a lifetime can also be applied in response to changes to food availability. For example, traditional knowledge of how to diversify hunting and gathering activities, as well as how to distribute and store traditional foods in times of scarcity, can be used to overcome altered migration and seasonal patterns of harvest species due to climate change (Berkes and Jolly 2002; Griffin 2020). Guo and colleagues (2015) also found that older respondents experienced lower levels of food insecurity compared to younger respondents when they were in charge of food preparation, supporting the idea that knowledge and willingness to contribute in this way can buffer Elders from food shortages.

Food sovereignty is an increasingly important issue among Alaska Native and Indigenous Circumpolar communities (Griffin 2020; Inuit Circumpolar Council-Alaska 2020). Contributing knowledge in service to the maintenance of traditional activities and food harvesting is not necessarily limited to an Elder's family, community, or even geographic region. Equitable co-management and the ability of communities and Tribal governments to determine restrictions on season and amounts of species harvested is seen by many as foundational for increased and enduring access to traditional foods and ways of life. Elders are often involved in efforts to establish and promote food sovereignty through Tribal governments, providing traditional knowledge to Western scientific studies, and through participation in other regulatory and advocacy groups and organizations. Perhaps one of the most prominent examples is the involvement of many Elders across multiple communities in the Inuit Circumpolar Council's Inuit Food Security Project (2015, 2020).

This multi-year, Inuit-led project was conducted across Alaska and the Inuvialuit Settlement Region of Canada, and addressed multiple aspects of traditional food security including food sovereignty, access, knowledge sources, stability, health and wellness, as well as decision-making power and management. Traditional Indigenous knowledge holders were not only involved and interviewed for the project, but they were also among the leaders of the project, which ultimately led to a Traditional Food Security Conceptual Framework and recommendations to strengthen traditional food security (Inuit Circumpolar Council-Alaska 2015). On a community level, many Elders are also involved in Hunters and Trappers Committees (e.g., Aklavik and Inuvik HTCs) that work with other wildlife management bodies, including the State of Alaska. This participation in regional efforts and institutions is an example of an adaptive response to protecting, maintaining, and expanding access to traditional foods that are also evident in Indigenous populations across the Arctic (e.g., Berkes and Jolly 2002).

Discussion

As the Circumpolar North continues to experience rapid and extreme climate change, there are accompanying changes such as thinning of sea ice, thawing of permafrost, and changes in migration patterns of subsistence animals, which have immediate impacts on traditional subsistence activities. Elders advise subsistence hunters and policy makers on adaptive strategies to monitor climate change impacts and maintain subsistence activities (Berner et al. 2016; Inuit Circumpolar Council-Alaska 2015, 2020; Wheeler and Thornton 2005) as well as lead and support resilient responses to disruptive climate-mediated impacts on subsistence food and activities. Elders also draw upon past social and environmental changes; have lived experience in developing and enacting past adaptations; and use these ideas and experiences to address present vulnerabilities in a resilient framework such that subsistence practices continue to support and strengthen social and cultural ideologies of Alaska Native peoples (Wilson 2014).

Anthropologists utilizing biocultural approaches to human adaptability and healthy aging are able to situate Elders' adaptations to a changing sociocultural and physical environment within a perspective of the variation in health that is expressed across and within populations (Leonard 2018; Pike and Williams 2006). Human adaptability theory elucidates the pathways through which sociocultural and environmental conditions affect population biologies and health outcomes (Brewis and Lee 2010; Dufour 2006). In this chapter, we have reviewed the literature on the physical health benefits of traditional foods and subsistence activities as well as demonstrated the ways these activities serve as the conduit through which Indigenous identities are forged and maintained in Alaska Native communities.

Elders contribute to important engagement with, and knowledge transmission of, local food procurement in their communities. This central role of Elders serves the dual effect of increasing their healthy aging outcomes and improving the health of the people around them. While traditional foods and subsistence activities incur positive health benefits for older adults, these activities are also integral to the concept of Elderhood and generativity.

Indigenous peoples across the state of Alaska define healthy aging in terms of their continued community engagement, spirituality, and physical health, as well as their access to traditional foods and activities. The anthropological lens allows us to view traditional foods and subsistence activities as the pathways through which the sociocultural and physical environment comes to affect diet, activity patterns, and health outcomes for Elders. This chapter has also demonstrated the resilience of Elders as they face rapidly changing cultural, economic, and physical environments. Despite challenges, Alaska Native Elders continue to define healthy aging in terms of continued performance of subsistence activities and consumption of traditional foods.

Acknowledgments

The authors wish to thank Sofiya Shreyer for her suggestions and feedback on an earlier version of this chapter.

References

Akearok, Gwen H., Katie Cueva, Jon Petter A. Stoor, Christina V. L. Larsen, Elizabeth Rink, Nicole Kanayurak, Anastasia Emelyanova, and Vanessa Y. Hiratsuka. 2019. "Exploring the Term 'Resilience' in Arctic Health and Well-Being Using a Sharing Circle as a Community-Centered Approach: Insights from a Conference Workshop." *Social Sciences* 8(2): 45.

Alaska Department of Fish & Game. 2015. "Subsistence in Alaska: A Year 2014 Update." Accessed November 10, 2020. https://www.adfg.alaska.gov/static/home/subsistence/pdfs/subsistence_update_2014.pdf.

Alaska Federation of Natives. 2020. "Alaska Native Peoples." Accessed October 19, 2020. https://www.nativefederation.org/alaska-native-peoples/.

Alaska Native Tribal Health Consortium. 2016. "ANMC Serves Healing, Traditional Foods to Our People." Accessed November 4, 2020. https://anthc.org/news/anmc-serves-healing-traditional-foods-to-our-people/.

Armelagos, George J., Thomas Leatherman, Mary Ryan, and Lynn Sibley. 1992. "Biocultural Synthesis in Medical Anthropology." *Medical Anthropology* 14(1): 35–52. http://www.informaworld.com/10.1080/01459740.1992.9966065.

Aslibekyan, Stella, Howard W. Wiener, Peter J. Havel, Kimber L. Stanhope, Diane M. O'Brien, Scarlett E. Hopkins, Devin M. Absher, Hemant K. Tiwari, and Bert B. Boyer. 2014. "DNA

Methylation Patterns Are Associated with n–3 Fatty Acid Intake in Yup'ik People." *Journal of Nutrition* 144(4): 425–430.

Ballew, Carol, Angela Ross Tzilkowski, Kari Hamrick, and Elizabeth D. Nobmann. 2006. "The Contribution of Subsistence Foods to the Total Diet of Alaska Natives in 13 Rural Communities." *Ecology of Food and Nutrition* 45(1): 1–26. https://doi.org/10.1080/03670240500408302.

Ballew, Carol, Angela Ross, Rebecca S. Wells, and Vanessa Hiratsuka. 2004. "Final Report on the Alaska Traditional Diet Survey." Alaska Native Epidemiology Center. Accessed November 20, 2020. http://anthctoday.org/epicenter/publications/Reports_Pubs/traditional_diet.pdf.

Beaulieu-Jones, Brendin R., Diane M. O'Brien, Scarlett E. Hopkins, Jason H. Moore, Bert B. Boyer, and Diane Gilbert-Diamond. 2015. "Sex, Adiposity, and Hypertension Status Modify the Inverse Effect of Marine Food Intake on Blood Pressure in Alaska Native (Yup'ik) People." *Journal of Nutrition* 145(5): 931–938.

Berkes, Fikret, and Dyanna Jolly. 2002. "Adapting to Climate Change: Social-Ecological Resilience in a Canadian Western Arctic Community." *Conservation Ecology* 5(2).

Berner, James, Michael Brubaker, Boris Revitch, Eva Kreummel, Moses Tcheripanoff, and Jake Bell. 2016. "Adaptation in Arctic Circumpolar Communities: Food and Water Security in a Changing Climate." *International Journal of Circumpolar Health* 75(1): 33820.

Bersamin, Andrea, Bret R. Luick, Irena B. King, Judith S. Stern, and Sheri Zidenberg-Cherr. 2008. "Westernizing Diets Influence Fat Intake, Red Blood Cell Fatty Acid Composition, and Health in Remote Alaskan Native Communities in the Center for Alaska Native Health Study." *Journal of the American Dietetic Association* 108(2): 266–273.

Bersamin, Andrea, Sheri Zidenberg-Cherr, Judith S. Stern, and Bret R. Luick. 2007. "Nutrient Intakes Are Associated with Adherence to a Traditional Diet among Yupik Eskimos Living in Remote Alaska Native Communities: The CANHR Study." *International Journal of Circumpolar Health* 66(1): 62–70.

Bjerregaard, Peter, T. Kue Young, Eric Dewailly, and Sven O. E. Ebbesson. 2004. "Review Article: Indigenous Health in the Arctic: An Overview of the Circumpolar Inuit Population." *Scandinavian Journal of Public Health* 32(5): 390–395. https://doi.org/10.1080/14034940410028398.

Boyle, J. S., and M. M. Counts. 1988. "Toward Healthy Aging: A Theory for Community Health Nursing." *Public Health Nursing* 5(1): 45–51. https://doi.org/10.1111/j.1525-1446.1988.tb00559.x.

Brewis, Alexandra, and Sarah Lee. 2010. "Children's Work, Earnings, and Nutrition in Urban Mexican Shantytowns." *American Journal of Human Biology* 22(1): 60–68. https://doi.org/10.1002/ajhb.20954.

Brooks-Cleator, Lauren A., and Jordan P. Lewis. 2020. "Alaska Native Elders' Perspectives on Physical Activity and Successful Aging." *Canadian Journal on Aging/La Revue canadienne du vieillissement* 39(2): 294–304.

Burnette, Catherine E., Caro B. Clark, and Christopher B. Rodning. 2018. "'Living Off the Land': How Subsistence Promotes Well-Being and Resilience among Indigenous Peoples of the Southeastern United States." *Social Service Review* 92(3): 369–400.

Collings, Peter. 2000. "Aging and Life Course Development in an Inuit Community." *Arctic Anthropology* 37(2): 111–125.

———. 2001. "'If You Got Everything, It's Good Enough': Perspectives on Successful Aging in a Canadian Inuit Community." *Journal of Cross-Cultural Gerontology* 16(2): 127–155. https://doi.org/10.1023/A:1010698200870.

———. 2011. "Economic Strategies, Community, and Food Networks in Ulukhaktok, Northwest Territories, Canada." *Arctic*: 207–219.

Dahl-Petersen, Inger K., Marit E. Jørgensen, and Peter Bjerregaard. 2011. "Physical Activity Patterns in Greenland: A Country in Transition." *Scandinavian Journal of Public Health* 39(7): 678–686. https://doi.org/10.1177/1403494811420486.

Dufour, Darna L. 2006. "Biocultural Approaches in Human Biology." *American Journal of Human Biology* 18(1): 1–9. https://doi.org/10.1002/ajhb.20463.

Ebbesson, Sven O. E., Patricia M. Risica, Lars O. E. Ebbesson, John M. Kennish, and M. Elizabeth Tejero. 2005. "Omega-3 Fatty Acids Improve Glucose Tolerance and Components of the Metabolic Syndrome in Alaskan Eskimos: The Alaska Siberia Project." *International Journal of Circumpolar Health* 64(4): 396–408.

Fienup-Riordan, Ann. 2000. *Hunting Tradition in a Changing World: Yup'ik Lives in Alaska Today*. Piscataway, NJ: Rutgers University Press.

Fogel-Chance, Nancy. 1993. "Living in Both Worlds: Modernity and Tradition among North Slope Iñupiaq Women in Anchorage." *Arctic Anthropology*: 94–108.

Foucault, Michel. 1978. *The Will to Knowledge, The History of Sexuality*, Volume 1. London: Penguin.

Fried, Ruby Laurel. 2019. "Biological Memories: Examining Early Indicators of Intergenerational Health among Alaska Native Women and Children Living in Anchorage, Alaska." Northwestern University.

Gilleard, Chris, and Paul Higgs. 2014. *Ageing, Corporeality and Embodiment*. New York: Anthem Press.

———. 2015. "Aging, Ambodiment, and the Somatic Turn." *Age, Culture, Humanities: An Interdisciplinary Journal* 2: 17–33.

Graves, K., and L. Shavings. 2005. "Our View of Dignified Aging: Listening to the Voices of Our Elders." *Journal of Native Aging and Health* 1(1): 29–40.

Griffin, P. Joshua. 2020. "Pacing Climate Precarity: Food, Care and Sovereignty in Iñupiaq Alaska." *Medical Anthropology* 39(4): 333–347.

Guo, Yang, Lea Berrang-Ford, James Ford, Marie-Pierre Lardeau, Victoria Edge, Kaitlin Patterson, IHACC Research Team, and Sherilee L. Harper. 2015. "Seasonal Prevalence and Determinants of Food Insecurity in Iqaluit, Nunavut." *International Journal of Circumpolar Health* 74(1): 27284.

Hansen-Kyle, Linda. 2005. "A Concept Analysis of Healthy Aging." *Nursing Forum* 40(2): 45–57. https://doi.org/10.1111/j.1744-6198.2005.00009.x.

Hillman, Anne. 2018. "To Feed Elders, Traditional Foods Take Untraditional Route." *Alaska Public Media*, February 28, 2018, https://www.alaskapublic.org/2018/02/28/to-feed-elders-traditional-foods-take-untraditional-route/.

Hopkins, Scarlett E., Pat Kwachka, Cécile Lardon, and Gerald V. Mohatt. 2007. "Keeping Busy: A Yup'ik/Cup'ik Perspective on Health and Aging." *International Journal of Circumpolar Health* 66(1): 42–50. http://www.ncbi.nlm.nih.gov/pubmed/17451133.

Hopping, B. N., E. Erber, E. Mead, C. Roache, and S. Sharma. 2010. "High Levels of Physical Activity and Obesity Co-Exist Amongst Inuit Adults in Arctic Canada." *Journal of Human Nutrition and Dietetics* 23: 110–114. https://doi.org/10.1111/j.1365-277X.2010.01096.x.

Hopping, B. N., E. Mead, E. Erber, C. Sheehy, C. Roache, and S. Sharma. 2010. "Dietary

Adequacy of Inuit in the Canadian Arctic." *Journal of Human Nutrition and Dietetics* 23(s1): 27–34.

Howell, B. M., M. Seater, and D. McLinden. 2020. "Using Concept Mapping Methods to Define 'Healthy Aging' in Anchorage, Alaska." *Journal of Applied Gerontology* 35(2): 113–131.

Howell, B. M., and J. R. Peterson. 2020. "'With Age Comes Wisdom': A Qualitative Review of Elder Perspectives on Healthy Aging in the Circumpolar North." *Journal of Cross-Cultural Gerontology* 35(2): 113–131.

Howell, Britteny M. 2017. "Healthy Aging in the North: Sociocultural Influences on Diet and Physical Activity among Older Adults in Anchorage, Alaska." University of Kentucky.

Huss-Ashmore, Rebecca. 2000. "Theory in Human Biology: Evolution, Ecology, Adaptability, and Variation." In *Human Biology: An Evolutionary and Biocultural Perspective*, edited by B. Bogin S. Stinson, R. Huss-Ashmore, and D. O'Rourke, 1–25. New York: Wiley-Liss.

Ice, Gillian H. 2005. "Biological Anthropology and Aging." *Journal of Cross Cultural Gerontology* 20(2): 87–90. https://doi.org/10.1007/s10823-005-9084-6.

Inuit Circumpolar Council-Alaska. 2015. "Alaskan Inuit Food Security Conceptual Framework: How to Assess the Arctic from an Inuit Perspective." *Summary Report and Recommendations Report. Anchorage, Alaska.*

———. 2020. "Food Sovereignty and Self-Governancy: Inuit Role in Managing Arctic Marine Resources." Accessed November 16, 2020. https://secureservercdn.net/104.238.71.250/hh3.0e7.myftpupload.com/wp-content/uploads/20200914-FSSG-Report_LR-1.pdf.

Iwarsson, Susanne, Hans-Werner Wahl, Carita Nygren, Frank Oswald, Andrew Sixsmith, Judith Sixsmith, Zsuzsa Széman, and Signe Tomsone. 2007. "Importance of the Home Environment for Healthy Aging: Conceptual and Methodological Background of the European ENABLE-AGE Project." *The Gerontologist* 47(1): 78–84.

Katz, Stephen, and Toni Calasanti. 2014. "Critical Perspectives on Successful Aging: Does It 'Appeal More Than It Illuminates'?" *The Gerontologist* 55(1): 26–33. https://doi.org/10.1093/geront/gnu027.

Kuhnlein, Harriet V., and Olivier Receveur. 1996. "Dietary Change and Traditional Food Systems of Indigenous Peoples." *Annual Review of Nutrition* 16: 417–442.

Lamb, Sarah. 2014. "Permanent Personhood or Meaningful Decline? Toward a Critical Anthropology of Successful Aging." *Journal of Aging Studies* 29: 41–52.

Lavretsky, Helen. 2014. *Resilience and Aging: Research and Practice*. Baltimore: Johns Hopkins University Press.

Lee, Molly. 2002. "The Cooler Ring: Urban Alaska Native Women and the Subsistence Debate." *Arctic Anthropology* 39(1): 3–9.

Leonard, William R. 2018. "Centennial Perspective on Human Adaptability." *American Journal of Physical Anthropology* 165(4): 813–833.

Lewis, Jordan P. 2010. "Successful Aging through the Eyes of Alaska Natives: Exploring Generational Differences among Alaska Natives." *Journal of Cross-Cultural Gerontology* 25(4): 385–396. https://doi.org/10.1007/s10823-010-9124-8.

———. 2011. "Successful Aging through the Eyes of Alaska Native Elders: What It Means to Be an Elder in Bristol Bay, AK." *The Gerontologist* 51(4): 540–549. https://doi.org/10.1093/geront/gnr006.

———. 2013a. "The Future of Successful Aging in Alaska." *International Journal of Circumpolar Health* 72(1): 21186. https://doi.org/10.3402/ijch.v72i0.21186.

———. 2013b. "The Importance of Optimism in Maintaining Healthy Aging in Rural Alaska." *Qualitative Health Research* 23(11): 1521–1527. https://doi.org/10.1177/1049732313508013.

———. 2014. "The Role of Social Engagement in the Definition of Successful Ageing among Alaska Native Elders in Bristol Bay, Alaska." *Psychology & Developing Societies* 26(2): 263–290. https://doi.org/10.1177/0971333614549143.

Lunda, A., and C. Green. 2020. "Harvesting Good Medicine: Internalizing and Crystalizing Core Cultural Values in Young Children." *Ecopsychology* 12(2): 91–100. https://doi.org/10.1089/eco.2019.0066.

Makhoul, Zeina, Alan R. Kristal, Roman Gulati, Bret Luick, Andrea Bersamin, Bert Boyer, and Gerald V. Mohatt. 2010. "Associations of Very High Intakes of Eicosapentaenoic and Docosahexaenoic Acids with Biomarkers of Chronic Disease Risk among Yup'ik Eskimos." *American Journal of Clinical Nutrition* 91(3): 777–785.

Makhoul, Zeina, Alan R. Kristal, Roman Gulati, Bret Luick, Andrea Bersamin, Diane O'Brien, Scarlett E. Hopkins, Charles B. Stephensen, Kimber L. Stanhope, and Peter J. Havel. 2011. "Associations of Obesity with Triglycerides and C-Reactive Protein Are Attenuated in Adults with High Red Blood Cell Eicosapentaenoic and Docosahexaenoic Acids." *European Journal of Clinical Nutrition* 65(7): 808–817.

Maniilaq Association. 2020. "The Siglauq." Accessed December 1, 2020. https://www.maniilaq.org/siglauq/.

McGrath-Hanna, Nancy K., Dana M. Greene, Ronald J. Tavernier, and Abel Bult-Ito. 2003. "Diet and Mental Health in the Arctic: Is Diet an Important Risk Factor for Mental Health in Circumpolar Peoples?-A Review." *International Journal of Circumpolar Health* 62(3): 228–241.

Michel, Jean-Pierre, and Ritu Sadana. 2017. "'Healthy Aging' Concepts and Measures." *Journal of the American Medical Directors Association* 18: 6.

Nobmann, Elizabeth D., and A. P. Lanier. 2001. "Dietary Intake among Alaska Native Women Resident of Anchorage, Alaska." *International Journal of Circumpolar Health* 60(2): 123–137.

O'Brien, Diane M., Kenneth E. Thummel, Lisa R. Bulkow, Zhican Wang, Brittany Corbin, Joseph Klejka, Scarlett E. Hopkins, Bert B. Boyer, Thomas W. Hennessy, and Rosalyn Singleton. 2017. "Declines in Traditional Marine Food Intake and Vitamin D Levels from the 1960s to Present in Young Alaska Native Women." *Public Health Nutrition* 20(10): 1738–1745. https://doi.org/10.1017/S1368980016001853.

Ocvirk, Soeren, Annette S. Wilson, Joram M. Posma, Jia V. Li, Kathryn R. Koller, Gretchen M. Day, Christie A. Flanagan, Jill Evon Otto, Pam E. Sacco, and Frank D. Sacco. 2020. "A Prospective Cohort Analysis of Gut Microbial Co-metabolism in Alaska Native and Rural African People at High and Low Risk of Colorectal Cancer." *American Journal of Clinical Nutrition* 111(2): 406–419.

Peterson, J. R., D. A. Baumgartner, and S. L. Austin. 2020. "Healthy Ageing in the Far North: Perspectives and Prescriptions." *International Journal of Circumpolar Health* 79(1): 1735036. https://doi.org/10.1080/22423982.2020.1735036.

Pike, Ivy L., and Sharon R. Williams. 2006. "Incorporating Psychosocial Health into Biocultural Models: Preliminary Findings from Turkana Women of Kenya." *American Journal of Human Biology* 18(6): 729–740. https://doi.org/10.1002/ajhb.20548.

Ready, Elspeth. 2018. "Sharing-Based Social Capital Associated with Harvest Production and Wealth in the Canadian Arctic." *PloS One* 13(3): e0193759.

Redwood, Diana G., Gretchen M. Day, Julie A. Beans, Vanessa Y. Hiratsuka, Sarah H. Nash, Barbara V. Howard, Jason G. Umans, and Kathryn R. Koller. 2019. "Alaska Native Traditional Food and Harvesting Activity Patterns over 10 Years of Follow-Up." *Current Developments in Nutrition* 3(11). https://doi.org/10.1093/cdn/nzz114.

Redwood, Diana G., Elizabeth D. Ferucci, Mary C. Schumacher, Jennifer S. Johnson, Anne P. Lanier, Laurie J. Helzer, Lillian Tom-Orme, Maureen A. Murtaugh, and Martha L. Slattery. 2008. "Traditional Foods and Physical Activity Patterns and Associations with Cultural Factors in a Diverse Alaska Native Population." *International Journal of Circumpolar Health* 67(4): 335–348. http://www.ncbi.nlm.nih.gov/pmc/articles/PMC2925499/pdf/nihms225797.pdf.

Rivkin, I., E.D.S. Lopez, J. E. Trimble, S. Johnson, E. Orr, and T. Quaintance. 2019. "Cultural Values, Coping, and Hope in Yup'ik Communities Facing Rapid Cultural Change." *Journal of Community Psychology* 47(3): 611–627. https://doi.org/10.1002/jcop.22141.

Rogers, Jillian. 2015. "Traditional Foods on Menu for Kotzebue Elders." *The Arctic Sounder: Voice of the Arctic Inupiat*, March 13, 2015, http://www.thearcticsounder.com/article/1511traditional_foods_on_menu_for_kotzebue_elders.

Rowe, J. W., and R. L. Kahn. 1987. "Human Aging: Usual and Successful." *Science* 237: 143–149.

Rubinstein, Robert L., Laura M. Girling, Kate De Medeiros, Michael Brazda, and Susan Hannum. 2015. "Extending the Framework of Generativity Theory through Research: A Qualitative Study." *The Gerontologist* 55(4): 548–559.

Ryman, T. K., B. B. Boyer, S. Hopkins, J. Philip, S.A.A. Beresford, B. Thompson, P. J. Heagerty, J. J. Pomeroy, K. E. Thummel, and M. A. Austin. 2015. "Associations between Diet and Cardiometabolic Risk among Yup'ik Alaska Native People Using Food Frequency Questionnaire Dietary Patterns." *Nutrition, Metabolism and Cardiovascular Diseases* 25(12): 1140–1145.

Skinner, Kelly, Rhona M. Hanning, Ellen Desjardins, and Leonard J. S. Tsuji. 2013. "Giving Voice to Food Insecurity in a Remote Indigenous Community in Subarctic Ontario, Canada: Traditional Ways, Ways to Cope, Ways Forward." *BMC Public Health* 13(1): 427.

Smith, Janell, Penelope Easton, Brian Saylor, Dennis Wiedman, and Jim LaBelle. 2009. "Harvested Food Customs and Their Influences on Valuable Functioning of Alaska Native Elders." *Alaska Journal of Anthropology* 7(1): 101–121.

Smith-Morris, Carolyn. 2006. "Community Participation in Tribal Diabetes Programs." *American Indian Culture and Research Journal* 30(2): 85–110.

Smith-Morris, Carolyn M. 2004. "Reducing Diabetes in Indian Country: Lessons from the Three Domains Influencing Pima Diabetes." *Human Organization* 63(1): 34–46.

Torres, Sandra. 2003. "A Preliminary Empirical Test of a Culturally-Relevant Theoretical Framework for the Study of Successful Aging." *Journal of Cross Cultural Gerontology* 18(1): 79–100.

U.S. Census Bureau. 2019. "QuickFacts: Alaska." Accessed October 19, 2020. https://www.census.gov/quickfacts/AK.

Ulijaszek, Stanley J. 1997. "Human Adaptation and Adaptability." In *Human Adaptability: Past, Present, and Future*, edited by S. J. Ulijaszek and A. R. Huss-Ashmore, 7–16. Oxford: Oxford University Press.

Walch, Amanda, Philip Loring, Rhonda Johnson, Melissa Tholl, and Andrea Bersamin. 2019. "Traditional Food Practices, Attitudes, and Beliefs in Urban Alaska Native Women Receiving WIC Assistance." *Journal of Nutrition Education and Behavior* 51(3): 318–325.

Wexler, L., L. Joule, J. Garoutte, J. Mazziotti, and K. Hopper. 2014. "'Being Responsible, Respectful, Trying to Keep the Tradition Alive': Cultural Resilience and Growing Up in an Alaska Native Community." *Transcult Psychiatry* 51(5): 693–712. https://doi.org/10.1177/1363461513495085.

Wheeler, Polly, and Tom Thornton. 2005. "Subsistence Research in Alaska: A Thirty Year Retrospective." *Alaska Journal of Anthropology* 3(1): 69–103.

Wilkinson, Michael J., Youlim Yai, and Diane M. O'Brien. 2007. "Age-Related Variation in Red Blood Cell Stable Isotope Ratios (Delta13C and Delta15N) from Two Yupik Villages in Southwest Alaska: A Pilot Study." *International Journal of Circumpolar Health* 66(1): 31–41.

Wilson, Nicole J. 2014. "The Politics of Adaptation: Subsistence Livelihoods and Vulnerability to Climate Change in the Koyukon Athabascan Village of Ruby, Alaska." *Human Ecology* 42(1): 87–101.

10

Caring for Karma

Death, Rebirth, and the Other "Successful Aging" on the Roof of the World

JING WANG

It was chilly and sunny, a typical winter day in the Phenpo valley of Central Tibet.[1] At around ten o'clock in the morning, I headed out of my house and walked toward Budri's for *manitso* (ma ni tshogs),[2] a monthlong gathering of daily prayer recitations that functions like a merit-making drive for its participants. The elders had borrowed Budri's old, vacant house for the occasion. When I arrived at the gate, I could see *po* (grandfather) Tashi, *po* Sonam, and *mo* (grandmother) Lhamo approaching from the opposite direction. Each was spinning a prayer wheel in one hand and counting a rosary in the other, while murmuring prayers to themselves.

Slowly they arrived, and we greeted each other and went inside. Unpacking our backpacks, we quietly settled into our respective tasks. Po Sonam lit a few sticks of incense in front of a *tangka* (Tibetan hanging scroll painting, *thang ka*) of *chenrezi* (*spyan ras gzigs*), the Buddha of Compassion. Po Tashi took out seven golden bowls, filled them with clean water, and placed them, too, before the tangka. Mo Lhamo put the cabbages in a basin and washed them at the water pump in the courtyard. I picked up the broom and started to sweep the floor. Meanwhile, mo Yangjen also arrived. Putting down her things, she quickly went outside and started a fire in the outdoor stove. Soon, sweet milk tea was boiling, and bubbling on the stove was a pot of a meaty stew of cabbage and beef.

In the room, now filled with the fragrant aroma of the incense and the appetizing smell of milk tea, the four elders settled themselves comfortably in their usual seats: the two older men on the Tibetan-style sofa bed, and the women basked in the warm sunshine on the cushions under the window. Before them were a few low tables where they kept their teacups and other belongings. Sipping tea, we exchanged news and discussed who else might be coming to the manitso later. Po Tashi joked that I had not yet grown tired of hanging out with the old folks, which made everyone laugh.

After a while, po Sonam, the oldest man in the village and one of the leaders of manitso, sensed it was time for their main business and began chanting *om mani padme hum*, the ubiquitous *mani* prayer that is the mantra of the Buddha of Compassion, heard in every corner of the Tibetan cultural world. Through chanting, he had thus signaled that the recitation had now begun; and the group, heeding the cue, became serious and started their own renditions of the melodic chant of the mani prayer, their hands all busy with spinning and counting again.

What I have described above is the beginning of a typical manitso day, which I had observed and participated in many times while conducting fieldwork in an agricultural village (hereafter referred to as Dekyi[3]) in Central Tibet. For one month each year, the Dekyi elders (and some middle-aged women) would gather and recite mantras and prayers together from morning to afternoon, as a way to earn merit to help improve their karmic outcome and gain a favorable rebirth. As illustrated above, the intensive praying session also provided an opportunity for the elders to socialize. They cooked and had meals together. They chatted and had fun during the many breaks dotted throughout the day. For the elders, the annual manitso is one of their many religious endeavors—also including pilgrimages and circumambulations (the act of moving around a sacred object)—that aim to influence their karma for a good rebirth; efforts I have come to call "caring for karma."

Ostensibly, caring for karma seems to be all about the future: the next life. However, I argue that by focusing on the future, the elders also gain the power to improve their situation in this life, to shape their experience of what might be considered "successful aging" in the Tibetan context. Aging "successfully" on the roof of the world is more than staying healthy, active, and independent. Unlike the Western definition, it also embraces loss and decline and involves actively preparing for one's death (see also Rinker, this volume, on similarities in Islam). In the rest of the paper, I seek to demonstrate how focusing on death and rebirth could allow aging to be successful.

The Successful Aging Model

Katz and Calasanti (2015, 26) aptly summarize the importance of the successful aging paradigm, stating that "successful aging is one of gerontology's most successful ideas" and is "crystallized in the work of John Rowe and Robert Kahn." Essentially, Rowe and Kahn argue that "through individual choice and effort" (1998, 37), successful aging can be attained by way of "avoidance of disease and disability, maintenance of high physical and cognitive function, and sustained engagement in social and productive activities" (1997, 439).

The idea of a quantifiable framework that could measure successful aging, and the promise of an aging process that is disease-free and physically and mentally active (or better yet, without any significant aging at all) prove to be appealing to both scholars and the general population. Since its introduction, this biomedical model of successful aging has not only become a dominant conceptual framework in gerontology, but has also inspired both popular and public policy discourses on aging. Thousands of books and articles have been published on the topic of successful aging or the related concepts of healthy, productive, or active aging (Lamb 2014; Lamb, Robbins-Ruszkowski, and Corwin 2017). The World Health Organization advocates active aging as a unifying policy framework to enhance the quality of life in old age (WHO 2015). The public policies, however, are more than about keeping elders healthy. They also intend to turn elders into neoliberal subjects who are responsible for their own health to reduce the cost of care expended on them (Lamb 2014; Liang and Luo 2012). In China, for example, governmental policy promoting active aging emphasizes individual responsibility for one's own health, hoping it would "translate into fewer health costs" (Zhang 2009, 212).

Despite its global appeal, the successful aging model has been widely critiqued. One line of criticism concerns the technicalities and feasibility of successful aging, for example, the "busy ethics" reflected in successful aging that overemphasize activity and productivity (Katz 2000; Katz and Calasanti 2015; Lamb 2014; Liang and Luo 2012). Some point out that the high standard of successful aging is inhibiting for most elders (McLaughlin et al. 2010). Others find it problematic to promote an illusion of "agelessness" that disregards the natural process of aging and decline (Andrews 1999; Corwin 2017, 2020; Liang and Luo 2012; McHugh 2000). Yet others argue that such a formulation neglects social inequalities and health disparities that prevent elders from aging successfully (Martinson and Halpern 2011; Wiles and Jayasinha 2013).

Another line of criticism centers on the underlying ideologies of the successful aging movement and their moral implications. Lamb (2014) demonstrates that the ideas of successful aging that emphasize independence, autonomy, and activity are a particular cultural, biopolitical, and individual-centered vision, despite their seemingly universal appeal. She comments that "the North American models of successful aging are so based on certain foundational cultural principles and visions of personhood—for instance, that decline in old age is bad, and that independence is ideal—that it has at times been difficult to recognize successful aging models as particular cultural visions" (2014, 42). In this model, age-related decline, illness, and death are viewed as moral failures (Katz and Calasanti 2015; Lamb 2014).

These criticisms, however, have not contributed to any significant paradigm shift in aging studies. Some alternative models of aging are being proposed, such as the "conscious aging" (Moody 2009) or "harmonious aging" (Liang and Luo 2012), that recognize decline and emphasize the importance of old-age spirituality (see also Agunbiade, this volume). However, they do not offer much insight on how death could figure in a good old age. Therefore, my aim in this study is to show how actively preparing for and reflecting on decline and death can be part of successful aging (Roberts 2018). As I demonstrate shortly, caring for one's karma has social, psychological, and physical benefits beyond its religious functions.

Field Site and Research Methods

Data for this paper stem from 18 months of ethnographic research on aging and care in Dekyi village between 2014 and 2016, and one month of follow-up research in 2017. Dekyi is located in Linzhou County, Tibet Autonomous Region, China. It roughly corresponds to what is traditionally known as Phenpo (*'phan po*), a vast river valley in Central Tibet (*dbus*), just north of Lhasa. Except in the county and township seats, virtually all residents are ethnic Tibetans who call themselves *Phenpowas* (Phenpo people) and follow Tibetan Buddhist practices in their daily lives.

As in many rural areas in the developing world, farming remains crucial for the villagers' daily subsistence needs; however, cash income from migration to work in the towns and cities is of growing importance, as demands for commodities such as electronic appliances and farming machinery, and the needs to pay for college fees, are increasing. April through October, villagers busy themselves in the fields, cultivating barley, wheat, rapeseeds, and potatoes. At the same time, young men and women as well as middle-aged men spend a good part of the year working outside the village for cash income, periodically returning home to help with intensive farm work.

Buddhism is another central component of village life. Although there is no householder lama or village temple in Dekyi, and the majority of the villagers receive little formal education in Buddhism, they are socialized into a deep-rooted Buddhist culture from an early age through the examples of their parents. They also have plenty of chances to learn from religious professionals. For example, villagers routinely seek advice from monks originally from the village or listen to religious teachings on portable MP3 speakers and cell phones. Through such means, the villagers learn about and receive an education in Buddhism.

Villagers are relatively free to practice Buddhism in their everyday lives.[4] They make daily offerings to the buddhas and gods in their shrine rooms. They chant prayers, count rosaries, and spin prayer wheels in their private homes or collectively with others during special events. They invite monks and nuns from nearby monasteries and nunneries to perform rituals (*zhabs brtan*) for various purposes. They frequently visit temples in the region, following a local timetable of ceremonies or simply spontaneously. When time and money allow, villagers go on pilgrimages that take them out of the Phenpo region. Middle-aged women and elders are the most devout in this respect.

There were altogether 65 households with a population of 303 in Dekyi during fieldwork. Among the villagers, there were 24 elders, or *genko* (*rgan gog*), aged between 60 and 84. Before the introduction of a pension scheme (ch. *xin nongbao*) for rural Tibetans over the age of 60 in 2010,[5] the definition of elders in Dekyi relied not so much on chronological age, but on the physical signs of decline, especially when a person stops performing demanding farming work and is bestowed with the title *momo* (*rmo mo*) or *popo* (*po po*), meaning "grandma" and "grandpa." Afterward, they spend most of their time at home and help with household chores during their children's absence, such as boiling water on the solar stove or feeding the cattle. More importantly, their main focus at this life stage shifts to religious activities for reasons I will come to in the next section.

My research focus on aging and care brought me into close contact with these popos and momos. However, my research was not restricted only to them. Instead, all households in the village were studied, with special attention paid to extended families in order to study intergenerational dynamics. Specifically, qualitative research methods of interviews and participant observation were employed. I interviewed an adult member of each of the 65 households and the 24 elders, as well as at least one of their primary caregivers (co-residing daughters, sons, daughters-in-law, or sons-in-law) to understand aging experiences, care practices, intergenerational relations, and how the villagers account for and make sense of their life experiences. In addition to interviews and informal conversations, observations of daily affairs and special events also provided invaluable insight into the daily experiences of the villagers.

Caring for Karma

In Tibet, caring for karma is essential in old age. When the villagers are younger, they often neglect religious activities because of their day-to-day household management obligations, and it is virtually inevitable that they accumulate negative merit through immoral or non-virtuous actions and behavior. Therefore, on becoming older and with death seemingly more imminent, they consider it essential to engage in religious activities to earn positive merit, which may increase the chance of a better rebirth (Childs 2004; Goldstein and Beall 1997).

Karma, or lé (las) in Tibetan, means "action." It is a fundamental Buddhist concept that in general means one's current and subsequent life conditions are determined by one's past and present actions. This often gives the impression that Buddhism is passive, and that, as faithful Buddhists, the Tibetans are also passive people who await their fate to happen to them. This could not be further from the truth. In caring for their karma, the Tibetan elder villagers actively sought to shape the outcome of their future lives. In so doing, they also gained the power to shape their aging experiences in this life.

According to Tibetan Buddhism,[6] there are six realms associated with cyclic existence (*'khor ba*, samsara). The lower realms consist of hells (extremes of heat, cold, and mental and physical pain), existences as hungry ghosts (eternally hungry but unable to ever satiate their hunger due to a biological design of extremely thin necks), and existences as animals. The higher realms include the human realm, the demi-god realm, and the god realm. The ultimate goal in Tibetan Buddhism is enlightenment or awakening (*sangs rgyas*), in order to attain liberation from cyclic existence, which is itself a manifestation of suffering through ignorance. Of the six realms, only the human realm is conducive to religious learning and practices and is therefore the only realm in which one can strive for enlightenment and awakening.

Enlightenment is considered to be extremely unlikely for most human beings in their present lives, including the lay Tibetans and even those following a religious path. However, Tibetans may believe that their best hope lies in having a favorable *gyewa* (*skye ba*), rebirth, in the human realm, with wealth and leisure to pursue religious endeavors freely; this is exactly what my interlocutors hoped for. In addition, women in general wanted to be reborn as male—not only because more men than women are likely to enter religious institutions in Tibet, but because from everyday experience, women intuitively understood that their disproportionate share of household chores left them with little time for religious practice. Even in their old age, when the elders were supposedly "freed" from mundane responsibilities, older women tended to have less free time than their male counterparts because of gender-based division of labor. For example, older women were more likely to assume the time-consuming responsibility of babysitting.

For Buddhists, one's condition in any given lifetime is determined by one's past meritorious and demeritorious karma. Tibetan Buddhism stresses the necessity of gaining merit through a variety of ways: the recitation of mantras and scriptures, the offering of butter lamps and incense, the performance of pilgrimage, prostrations and circumambulations, donations to religious institutions and professionals, and so on. During my fieldwork, with one exception,[7] all elders engaged in these activities to varying degrees depending on their health, financial resources, and family circumstances. The following is a detailed account of these activities as practiced by the Dekyi elders.

Reciting Mantras and Spinning Prayer Wheels

Reciting mantras and spinning hand-held prayer wheels are a particularly easy way to earn merit and purify negative karma. Simply chanting the mani prayer would not only accumulate merit for the person who performs the recitation but would also bring blessings to all sentient beings experiencing cyclic existence. Similarly, spinning prayer wheels represents turning the "wheel of Dharma" and leads to accumulation of merit and relief of suffering for all.

These activities can be performed any time, as long as the elders' mouths or hands are "free." The elders take advantage of this, reciting prayers and spinning the wheels whenever they can. For instance, when I was chatting with or interviewing the elders, their hands were always busy spinning prayer wheels. When they could be seen walking in the village, they were almost always murmuring the mani prayer, spinning their prayer wheels, and counting their rosaries.

In addition to these private practices, there are several occasions during the year for which the elders (and sometimes middle-aged women) gather and devote themselves wholeheartedly to recitations without the distraction of household chores. These occasions also give the elders an opportunity to recite other popular mantras and prayers. Most of the elders—men and women—have received no formal education and are illiterate, barely able to read anything in Tibetan (very few know any Chinese), least of all the obscure religious scriptures that require special training to read and understand. Not surprisingly, the Dekyi elders seldom recite anything other than the ubiquitous mani prayer on their own. During the collective recitation sessions, however, two lay villagers (one older man and one middle-aged woman) who know how to read scriptures will lead the elders to recite some other popular prayers such as "Praises to the Tara" (*sgrol ma bstod pa*), which is believed to be especially powerful in fulfilling wishes.

The manitso I describe at the beginning of this chapter is a case in point. This is a relatively new tradition. A few years earlier, before I started my fieldwork, a well-respected monk from Dekyi suggested that the elders should dedicate a relatively free period during the winter months to prayers. The suggestion was met with enthusiasm. Since then, each year for a month, the elders devote themselves to recitations without worrying about their daily responsibilities. Other villagers also welcomed this new practice as they believed that the piety of the elders would benefit the whole village, and they showed their support by dropping by and bringing snacks, fruits, special food, or sometimes cash contributions.

Another example is the two-day recitation during the annual ritual of *chökor* (*chos skor*), held to solicit help from local deities to protect crops from natural disasters. While younger villagers circumambulate the village fields with scriptures on their back, the elders spend the two days chanting their mantras and prayers alongside the prescribed recitation of the invited monks. My informants explained that the elders' recitations were particularly valued as a result of their increased religious devotion during old age.

Pilgrimages, Circumambulations, and Donations

Pilgrimages, the second type of caring for karma, usually take the elders outside the village and to the sacred sites in the region and beyond.[8] During pilgrimages, the elders visit temples, circumambulate holy sites and objects, and donate small sums to support the monks or nuns.[9] Thanks to Phenpo's one-time prominence in the Buddhist revival in the eleventh century, there are many monasteries and nunneries in the region; several are only a couple of miles away, a walkable distance by village standards. The elders walk and hitchhike to their destination, carrying their own food and drink. Even taking into account the pilgrims' donations to the monasteries they visit, such trips require little significant financial outlay by the elders. The elders therefore go on pilgrimage in the region often, sometimes with friends and sometimes alone. During pleasant summer days, such pilgrimage trips also double as picnic outings.

When the elders go out of the region for pilgrimage, it is always arranged by their children. Lhasa is a popular pilgrimage destination for the elders, because many elders have children or relatives living there, and there are numerous sacred sites to visit, including the holiest of all, the Jokhang temple. The elders enjoy these long journeys, often returning with tales and anecdotes they talk about for days.

The Other Successful Aging

In stark contrast to the normative Western concept of successful aging, the Dekyi elders embrace decline and interdependence. This is not surprising given that not too long ago the very concept of old age hinged on the signs of physical decline and the cultural ideology of co-residence and interdependence. As mentioned above, in the village one becomes old when one is no longer able to perform what is considered the hardest farming work. With their disengagement from productive work, it is natural for the elders to rely on their children to provide and care for them. The concept of old age fits well with the reciprocal rules of Tibetan filial piety; just as children are provided and cared for by their parents while growing up, parents expect their children to provide and care for them when they grow old (Childs 2004; Goldstein and Beall 1997). For the Dekyi elders, aging successfully largely depends on how their decline and interdependence are interpreted and experienced. Ironically, caring for their karma provides the key to this success.

Accepting Decline and Death

The Buddhist teachings on the transience of life facilitate the elders to come to terms with decline and, eventually, death. In the "Four Noble Truths," Buddha's fundamental teaching on the human condition, the first and the second truths state that human lives are characterized by suffering, and that the origin of suffering is our desires, which in turn stem from our ignorance of the true nature of things, such as impermanence (*mi rtag pa*). That is, things are in a constant state of change.

Villagers seem to understand the impermanence of life—in the sense that one can die at any moment—particularly well, and death for them is not a taboo topic, but seems to be on the elders' minds constantly. For instance, whenever I tried to arrange something with the elders, their answers, "only if I could arise that morning," or "only if I have not died yet," never failed to convey an awareness that death is just around the corner. The mental readiness for death motivates the elders not only to discuss it openly but to actively seek to secure a good death through religious devotion. According to Buddhism, it is crucial to train oneself to enter death calmly so that the consciousness can go the right way toward a favorable rebirth (preferably under the spiritual guidance of a monk or lama). As one elder told me, they are not afraid of death because they have religion with them when they die.

When death is openly discussed, physical or mental decline is an easy topic. They may feel nostalgic about their youth and vigor and they may pray for an "easy" death without suffering from long-term debilitating illness. However, the Dekyi elders I know loved to joke about their graying hair and their loss of sexual vitality, while the elder who had dementia was not stigmatized. As an opportunity for increased religious devotion, they accept decline as a natural process of aging that also comes with less responsibility.

Family Harmony and Happiness

"Without harmony, there would be no happiness." This local saying sums up another important aspect of what constitutes a good old age in Dekyi. Invariably, elders cited family harmony as key to their sense of happiness and well-being. The ideology of harmony, or *champo* (*'cham po*), *tünpo* (*thun po*) in Tibetan, is deeply valued. Religiously speaking, the Tibetans believe that disharmony within family and community would offend gods and goddesses and in turn bring misfortune to the family and the community (Lau 2010). At a more personal level, living in a household rife with conflicts is simply unpleasant and can have dire consequences. Poor familial relationships would also lead to poor caring, and even abusive relationships, sadly but convincingly demonstrated by a number of studies carried out in China in the 1990s (Yan 2003; Wu 2009).

Hence, in Tibet, there is a ritual for exorcising "malicious gossip" (*mi kha*) in order to preserve "cooperative and harmonious relationships" in the community (Kapstein 1997, 527). The Dekyi villagers also use a variety of tactics to prevent or reduce disharmony. The matrilocal practice in which a daughter inherits the familial home and land, and provides old age care, is one example. By keeping a daughter and her husband at home, it eliminates the co-residence of mother-in-law and daughter-in-law under the same roof, and in turn eradicates what is viewed as potentially the most acrimonious relationship in a household (Wang 2018). In addition, a vision of personhood that emphasizes both relationalism and individualism plays a key role in helping the elders achieve a harmonious relationship with their co-residing children (Wang 2020). In this chapter, I want to bring attention to how the religious activities aimed at improving one's fate in the future also enable the elders to shape the outcome of their current situation.

As the Dekyi elders busy themselves with religious activities to actively prepare for their death and rebirth, they are less inclined to compete with their children for household authority or to interfere with the daily management of the households. One articulate older woman explained the positive relationship between religious participation and family harmony best:

> For us elders, the most important things are to recite prayers and visit religious sites. Ideally, we should spend all our time doing just these. So, we let our children run the household, and we can then focus on

our prayers. But, since we live with our children and are cared for by them, we also need to help our children [with domestic chores]. What we can do is to do as much [praying] as we can. When we chant prayers, we forget about our worries. We are not afraid when we die.... I have a harmonious relationship with my daughter. But if conflicts arise between us, I am not worried, because I can just chant prayers all the time.

Echoing this, Tashi, an older man who had recently passed household headship to his daughter, told me that after the transition, he steered away from advising his daughter on household management because he believed his daughter and son-in-law were capable. He also added that his preoccupation with religious activities helped him divert his energy away from his family. He said, "I still think about family management out of habit, when should we plant, when should we harvest, should we build a field for growing fodder, things like these. But when these thoughts arise, I think to myself that now I am not the household head anymore, but an old man. What I should do is to chant prayers all the time."

Whereas these examples show how, through caring for their karma, the elders are able to largely avoid intergenerational competition, which is often the source of familial conflict, the protective power of caring for karma for the elders' mental well-being when conflicts arise is even more striking. The most telling is the example of Lhamo, whose long-standing conflict with her daughter-in-law led to her split with her son's family about a decade ago. Because of this, she is the only elder in the village who does not live according to the old-age ideal of co-residence with offspring in an extended household, cared for by her children. Instead, she lives on her own. Her son and daughter-in-law provide her with roasted barley flour, cooking oil, potatoes, and a little butter and meat. For rice, vegetables, as well as clothes, she has to make do with her meager pension and a single-child reward amounting to around RMB 2,500 (around USD 380) annually. She is pitied by villagers for living alone, having no one to make her bed, wash clothes, or cook for her. However, she is admired as the most pious elder in Dekyi.

Unlike the other elders co-residing with their children, Lhamo has few household responsibilities. She only needs to cook for and feed herself on a daily basis, and to occasionally wash her clothes or collect cow dung for fuel. "Liberated" from domestic chores, she is able to devote nearly all her time to religious practices, which diverted her from her less than ideal situation and give her a sense of purpose. She is the only elder in the village who can do *khangkor* (*khang skor*), circumambulation of the houses, three times a day. During my time there, she attended almost all of the manitso sessions, whereas others usually would miss several because of family responsibilities. Moreover, she goes on pilgrimage often. She told me:

> It would be great if I could live with my son's family. However, it was not working because my daughter-in-law and I did not get along. So now I live by myself. It is much better this way because we leave each other alone and we are happier. My grandchildren come to keep me company and sleep in my room when they have holidays from school. I am invited to stay in my son's house for a couple of days during the New Year and they feed me all the good food they cook. I think this is good arrangement, especially as I have a lot of freedom. I can do whatever I want. I do not need to help them boil water or feed cows. I can recite om mani padme hum all the time. Every day, I go out for three khangkors, morning, noon, and afternoon. I recite prayers and spin the prayer wheel. It is very important for old people like us to do this, and I am happy I am doing this all the time and I can accumulate lots of merit. And when I am reciting, I am not worried, and I am happy.

Virtually all the other elders pity Lhamo for having to live alone and voiced that they did not want to end up in this situation. Some of them, however, echoed the sentiments of Lhamo and pointed out that there was also a "bright" side to her bleak situation; she had a lot of time to devote to earning merit. Mo Yangjen, a good friend of Lhamo, told me, "Lhamo's situation is pitiful. It is very hard. She does not have enough good food to eat. But, on the other hand, she can pray all the time and go on pilgrimage often. And she can do three circumambulations every day, which is good for accumulating merit. I wish I could be like this. But I need to help my daughter [with housework]."

Socializing and Mental Health

In aging studies, the positive relation between socializing and mental well-being has been well-established (Hajek et al. 2017). However, for the Dekyi elders, the opportunity to socialize through work or other social occasions with peers decreases as one grows older and shifts one's focus from public to private spheres. Due to concerns of being perceived as overly gossipy, village adults tend to refrain from visiting each other frequently. Against this background, collective caring for karma activities, in particular the manitso and the pilgrimages, provides the elders with an important venue in which to socialize with each other (see Childs, Goldstein, and Wangdui 2011).

Taking the manitso as an example, for a month the elders who managed to attend kept each other company. They drank tea, shared snacks and food, chatted, and joked with each other. They exchanged news about their family members or people they knew. They comforted each other when occasionally the elders talked about their worries and unhappiness. Moreover, their children or other villagers would often drop by and bring snacks to share with the elders as a way to show their support for this merit-making activity. This enabled the elders to engage in an even wider network of socializing. The elders looked genuinely happy during the manitso. Besides their religious accomplishment, they also reveled in spending time with their old friends in this relaxing environment. Pilgrimages provide a similar occasion for the elders to socialize. The elders often go on pilgrimage in the region together. They usually carry their own food and drink. After they finish visiting the main temples in a monastery or nunnery, the elders will sit down outside on the floor (or the grass) to take a break, while sharing food, stories, worries, and laughter.

The benefits of these social functions are best revealed, however, by the remarks of those who cannot participate. One elderly woman in her late seventies seldom attended collective recitation sessions or made pilgrimage trips due to her poor health, a combination of bad legs, high blood pressure, and poor eyesight. She told me that she especially missed the pilgrimage trips, which took the elders outside their daily routine and the familiar village setting. Besides the worshipping that would cleanse her sins and earn her merit, she also missed companionship with her peers during those trips. She explained:

> It was a lot of fun when I was able to go on pilgrimages with friends. We went to many monasteries together. Summer time was the happiest. We walked [to a religious site], then we spent the whole day worshipping and circumambulating. When we sat down to rest, we talked and talked and had fun [*rtsed mo rtse*]. Nowadays, because

my legs are not well, I cannot go on pilgrimage anymore. I go to pray with the popos and momos sometimes when I feel well. It is good to be with them.

Pilgrimages, Circumambulations, and Physical Well-Being

In Phenpo, traditionally there is not such a concept as exercising to keep fit. However, the idea of circumambulation as a form of exercise that promotes physical health is slowly seeping into Dekyi. Po Dorje, for example, said to me, "We Tibetan elders are healthy because we do a lot of circumambulations. When I was in Lhasa, I went to Jokhang [the most sacred temple in Tibet] every morning and I circumambulated it again and again. This is very good for our body."

Po Dorje had perhaps picked up this idea of exercise and physical health during his annual sojourn in Lhasa where he spent a couple of weeks, right before the Tibetan New Year, with one of his sons who lived there. Lhasa is the capital city of the Tibet Autonomous Region and the most cosmopolitan. During my time in Lhasa, when the Tibetans learned that I was doing research on aging in Tibet, they often volunteered that Tibetan Buddhism was beneficial to both mental and physical health. Circumambulation was especially touted as great for accumulating merit; and while at it, one could also improve one's physical health. Therefore, while the Dekyi villagers have little idea of exercising as a way to stay healthy, a key component of their everyday religious practices serves such a function and potentially contributes to the elders' physical well-being.[10]

Death, Rebirth, and Successful Aging

Decline, death, and dependence have seldom been associated with the concept of successful aging. However, as I have shown in this chapter, physical decline can be seen in positive light, reflection on death can be empowering, and interdependence between elders and their children can bring happiness to both through the increased opportunities for caring for one's karma for a better rebirth.

"Caring for karma" challenges the successful aging model dominant in the West and in aging studies. Most importantly, it demonstrates the significance of making "readiness for death"—being mentally prepared for death—an integral part of aging, and is where the current successful aging model, in denying a place for decline and death, falls short. In order for elders (and those connected to them) to enjoy their aging in the face of imminent death, there must be a degree of mental preparedness for it by all concerned, including the elders themselves. Martin et al. (2015, 22) argues that because "successful aging is inevitably followed by death, it behooves us to consider perspectives on success in achieving a good death," and calls for research to explore the "linkage between a good old age and a good death." As shown by the Tibetan elders depicted in this chapter, not only can a good old age devoted to religious practices lead to a good death, but in uncanny ways, considerations for a good death can also lead to a good old age. Aside from its religious functions, the death- and rebirth-oriented caring for karma is also socially and psychologically satisfying, and physically beneficial, for the elders in this life.

Notes

1. Tibet is notoriously difficult to define. The name has often been used to denote a large area that has been influenced by the Tibetan language and Buddhism, spanning China, Nepal, India, Sikkim, and Bhutan. Research in this paper was carried out in Central Tibet, Ü, within the Tibet Autonomous Region in China, which roughly corresponds to the so-called political Tibet (Richardson 1984), traditionally under the direct rule of the Tibetan government from the earliest Kings to the Dalai Lamas. The other two major Tibetan areas in China are Amdo and Kham, now located in the Chinese provinces of Qinghai, Sichuan, Gansu, and Yunnan.

2. In order to facilitate a smooth reading experience, when Tibetan words are used, the romanization reflects how their pronunciations in Lhasa dialect would sound in English. I also provide transliterations following the standard Wylie system immediately afterward in parentheses. The Chinese transliteration follows the *pinyin* system. When used, it is marked by "ch." before the transliteration.

3. The name of the field site and personal names have all been altered to protect the participants in this study, as is customary in anthropological research.

4. Within the Tibet Autonomous Region, following the flight of the Dalai Lama to India in 1959, religious practices were suppressed, particularly during the Cultural Revolution period (1966–1976). From the 1980s, restrictions were loosened and a revival of Buddhism ensued. See Goldstein and Kapstein (1998) for a detailed account of the Buddhist revival in Tibet. Moreover, while several main monasteries in the region (Nalendra, for example) belong to the Sakyapa school (there are four major Buddhist schools in Tibet), Dekyi villagers do not consider themselves as belonging to any specific school, and they receive teachings and visit temples without discrimination.

5. It is called *xin nongbao* in Chinese, the New Rural Pension Scheme.

6. See Kapstein (2014) for a brief introduction to Tibetan Buddhism.

7. The exception is an eccentric older woman. She lived with her youngest son, who was doing business in another region of Tibet. However, she preferred living by herself in Dekyi so she could spend as much time as she liked drinking beer and playing Mahjong. She was fortunate that her oldest son held a prestigious position in the government and regularly gave her money so she could indulge in her hobbies of drinking and gambling. During my stay, I never saw her doing any religious activities like the other elders.

8. I use the term "pilgrimage" to refer to two different activities: *chunje* (*mchod mjal*) and *nekor* (*gnas skor*). *Chunje* usually means a visit to a religious site, such as a nearby temple; whereas *nekor* or *nejel* (*gnas mjal*) connotes long journeys that take one out of the region where one resides. For more information on pilgrimage in Tibet, see Huber (1999).

9. In the TAR, it is popular to donate a very small amount, as little as RMB 10 cents (less than USD 2 cents), to each of the many donation plates and boxes placed in front of statues and other holy objects in the temples. For one trip, the entire donation usually amounts to less than RMB 10 (USD 2 cents).

10. A strong correlation has been found between mental and physical health (Surtees et al. 2008; Ohrnberger, Fichera, and Sutton 2017).

References

Andrews, Molly. 1999. "The Seductiveness of Agelessness." *Ageing & Society* 19(3): 301–318.

Childs, Geoff. 2004. *Tibetan Diary: From Birth to Death and Beyond in a Himalayan Valley of Nepal*. Berkeley: University of California Press.

Childs, Geoff, Melvyn C. Goldstein, and Puchung Wangdui. 2011. "Externally-Resident Daughters, Social Capital, and Support for the Elderly in Rural Tibet." *Journal of Cross-Cultural Gerontology* 26(1): 1–22.

Corwin, Anna I. 2017. "Grown Old with God: An Alternative Vision of Aging Well." In *Successful Aging as a Contemporary Obsession: Global Perspectives*, edited by Sarah Lamb, 98–111. New Brunswick, NJ: Rutgers University Press.

———. 2020. "Care in Interaction: Aging, Personhood, and Meaningful Decline." *Medical Anthropology* 39(7): 1–15.

Goldstein, Melvyn C., and Cynthia M. Beall. 1997. "Growing Old in Tibet—Tradition, Family, and Changes." In *Aging: Asian Concepts and Experiences Past and Present*, edited by Sussan Formanek and Sepp Linhart, 155–176. Vienna: Austrian Academy of Science Press.

Goldstein, Melvyn C., and Matthew Kapstein, eds. 1998. *Buddhism in Contemporary Tibet: Religious Revival and Cultural Identity*. Berkeley: University of California Press.

Hajek, André, Christian Brettschneider, and Tina Mallon, et al. 2017. "The Impact of Social Engagement on Health-Related Quality of Life and Depressive Symptoms in Old Age–Evidence from a Multicenter Prospective Cohort Study in Germany." *Health Qual Life Outcomes* 15, 140.

Huber, Toni. 1999. *The Cult of the Pure Crystal Mountain: Popular Pilgrimage and Visionary Landscape in Southeast Tibet*. Oxford: Oxford University Press.

Kapstein, Matthew. 1997. "Turning Back Gossip." In *Religions of Tibet in Practice*, edited by Donald S. Lopez, Jr., 527–537. Princeton, NJ: Princeton University Press.
———. 2014. *Tibetan Buddhism*. New York: Oxford University Press.
Katz, Stephen. 2000. "Busy Bodies: Activity, Aging, and the Management of Everyday Life." *Journal of Aging Studies* 14: 135–152.
Katz, Stephen, and Toni Calasanti. 2015. "Critical Perspectives on Successful Aging: Does It 'Appeal More Than It Illuminates'?" *The Gerontologist* 55(1): 26–33.
Lamb, Sarah. 2014. "Permanent Personhood or Meaningful Decline? Toward a Critical Anthropology of Successful Aging." *Journal of Aging Studies* 29: 41–52.
Lamb, Sarah, Jessica Robbins-Ruszkowski, and Anna I. Corwin. 2017. "Introduction: Successful Aging as a Twenty-First-Century Obsession." In *Successful Aging as a Contemporary Obsession: Global Perspectives*, edited by Sarah Lamb, 1–26. New Brunswick, NJ: Rutgers University Press.
Lau, Timm. 2010. "The Hindi Film's Romance and Tibetan Notion of Harmony: Emotional Attachments and Personal Identity in the Tibetan Diaspora in India." *Journal of Ethnic and Migration Studies* 36(6): 967–987.
Liang, Jiayin, and Baozhen Luo. 2012. "Toward A Discourse Shift in Social Gerontology: From Successful Aging to Harmonious Aging." *Journal of Aging Studies* 26: 327–334.
Martin, Peter, Norene Kelly, Boaz Kahana, Eva Kahana, Bradley Wilcox, D. Craig Willcox, and Leonard W. Poon. 2015. "Defining Successful Aging: A Tangible or Elusive Concept?" *The Gerontologist* 55(1): 14–25.
Martinson, Marty, and Jodi Halpern. 2011. "Ethical Implications of the Promotion of Elder Volunteerism: A Critical Perspective." *Journal of Aging Studies* 25(4): 427–435.
McHugh, Kevin E. 2000. "The 'Ageless Self'? Emplacement of Identities in Sun Belt Retirement Communities." *Journal of Aging Studies* 14(1): 103–115.
McLaughlin, Sara J., Cathleen M. Connell, Steven G. Heeringa, Lydia W. Li, and J. Scott Roberts. 2010. "Successful Aging in the United States: Prevalence Estimates from a National Sample of Older Adults." *Journals of Gerontology*: Series B 65B(2): 216–226.
Moody, Harry R. 2009. "From Successful Aging to Conscious Aging." In *The Cultural Context of Aging: Worldwide Perspectives*, 3rd ed., edited by Jay Sokolovsky, 67–76. Westport, CT: Praeger.
Ohrnberger, Julius, Eleonora Fichera, and Matt Sutton. 2017. "The Relationship between Physical and Mental Health: A Mediation Analysis." *Social Science & Medicine* 195: 42–49.
Richardson, Hugh. 1984. *Tibet and Its History*, 2nd ed. Boulder: Shambhala.
Roberts, Scott. 2018. "Successful Aging as Preparation for Successful Dying." *Innovation in Aging* 2(S1): 49.
Rowe, John W., and Robert L. Kahn. 1997. "Successful Aging." *The Gerontologist* 37: 433–440.
———. 1998. *Successful Aging*. New York: Pantheon Books.
Surtees, P. G., N.W.J. Wainwright, R. N. Luben, N. J. Wareham, S. A. Bingham, and K.-T. Khaw. 2008. "Psychological Distress, Major Depressive Disorder, and Risk of Stroke." *Neurology* 70: 788–794.
Wang, Jing. 2018. "Growing Old with Daughters: Aging, Care, and Change in the Matrilocal Family System in Rural Tibet." PhD diss., Case Western Reserve University.
———. 2020. "Keeping Quiet: Aging, Personhood, and Intergenerational Harmony in Rural Central Tibet." *Journal of Aging Studies* 54: 1–9.

Wiles, Janine L., and Ranmalie Jayasinha. 2013. "Care for Place: The Contributions Older People Make to Their Communities." *Journal of Aging Studies* 27(2): 93–101.

World Health Organization (WHO). 2015. World Report on Ageing and Health. Geneva: World Health Organization.

Wu, Fei. 2009. *Suicide and Justice*. London: Routledge.

Yan, Yunxiang. 2003. *Private Life under Socialism: Love, Intimacy, and Family Change in a Chinese Village*. Stanford, CA: Stanford University Press.

Zhang, Hong. 2009. "The New Realities of Aging in Contemporary China: Coping with the Decline in Family Care." In *The Cultural Context of Aging: Worldwide Perspectives*, 3rd ed., edited by Jay Sokolovsky, 196–215. Westport, CT: Praeger.

11

The Aging Body in Islam

Exploring the Experiences of Older,
Dying Muslims in the United States

CORTNEY HUGHES RINKER

> *Whoever does not show mercy to our young ones,*
> *or acknowledge the rights of our elders, is not one of us.*
> Prophet Muhammad

It is no secret that the population of the United States (U.S.) is on average growing older. This trend raises some concern among politicians, health-care providers, administrators, and the public about the future of health care in the country and about how best to ensure the well-being of older adults. The Administration on Aging—the primary agency in the U.S. Department of Health and Human Services to carry out the requirements outlined in the Older Americans Act of 1965, as amended—has stated that between the years of 2009 and 2030, the total number of adults over the age of 65 in the United States will increase from 13 to 19 percent of the population. The age group of 85 and over is estimated to increase by 350 percent within this same time period (Weiner and Tilly 2002). The growth in this segment of the population can place added pressure on publicly funded programs for seniors (such as Social Security and Medicare), the health-care system's resources, and long-term care facilities. Medicare started to fine hospitals that have excessive readmissions in an attempt to pay hospitals based on the quality of care rather than the quantity of care that they offer. This financial deterrence encourages providers to recommend hospice or palliative care when curative treatment may not be the best option for a patient and to make non-critical care options available to keep patients out of the hospital—specifically the Intensive Care Unit (ICU) and the Emergency Department (ED), both of which may be very costly and not always optimal based upon a patient's condition (Rau 2013). Aging is a critical issue in the United States that requires careful coordination among the health-care system, policy makers, local communities, researchers, and scholars in order to make sure the various needs of older adults are met and to avoid provider burnout.

Public health and social work, among other fields and specialties, have demonstrated that enhanced well-being as well as positive health and psychosocial outcomes are associated with different aspects of religious participation (Nelson-Becker 2018; Puchalski and Fernell 2010). As adults age, religion may become a more meaningful part of their everyday lives and personal interactions. For older adults, religious communities could be a source of social interaction and companionship. Furthermore, religion may offer them a way to talk about what happens next, especially if their health is declining or they are unable to engage in desired activities due to the normal effects of aging. For some people, the later stages of life involve a time of self-reflection and greater self-understanding. An older retired gentleman who audited one of my courses on religion spoke up in class when we were talking about the body and aging to state that he is at a point in his life where much of what he hears from media and popular culture is about finding a purpose, something that would make him feel wanted and useful as well as fulfill his time now that he is older. These processes, and the need to find a purpose, create ideal conditions for deeper religious engagement and development. Empirical evidence suggests that religiosity (strong religious beliefs or feelings; orientation toward and involvement in religion) is associated with longer lives and having better physical and mental health; however, there is a need for further research on the ways that religiosity may inform health and the aging experience among different groups of older adults (Bafford 2019, Zimmer et al. 2016). The nuances that surround the intersection of religion and aging is an area that warrants, and can certainly benefit from, further anthropological exploration.

The literature on aging in the United States is vast and comes out of many disciplines (Jensen et al. 2020; Lamb 2019; Rowe, Fulmer, and Fried 2016). However, within this expansive literature, there is relatively little written about the aging experience among Muslim Americans, and in anthropology there are few ethnographic studies of Muslim Americans' lives and experiences (two exceptions are Khabeer 2016 and Mir 2014). Salari (2002) observed that there is little data on older adults in the United States who are

Middle Eastern and/or Muslim (as Islam is practiced worldwide and not all those who are Middle Eastern identify as Muslim, and not all those who are Muslim identify as Middle Eastern), and encouraged more research on family structure, social support, housing, health-care needs, resource utilization, and quality of life so that their needs are not overlooked due to stereotypes and negative connotations. It is important to state upfront that Muslim Americans are diverse in every sense of the word—including race, ethnicity, religiosity, culture, class, immigrant status, and geographic classification (rural vs. urban)—so even though we may be able to make some general statements about Islam and about the Muslim American population, we must also remember that religious beliefs and practices vary and are informed by many factors.

The Pew Research Center (a nonpartisan U.S. think tank) estimates that in 2017, there were approximately 3.45 million Muslims in the United States, which at the time was about 1 percent of the total population. The Muslim population is to double by 2050 to roughly 2.1 percent of the total U.S. population and is anticipated to grow at a faster rate than Hindu and Jewish populations. Between 2010 and 2015, it was estimated that about half of the growth of the Muslim American population was the result of immigration to the United States. Approximately 6 out of 10 Muslim American adults were born abroad and another 18 percent are second-generation Americans born in the United States. With that said, the percentage of foreign-born Muslims will decrease over the next decades as the number of U.S.-born Muslims increases (Grossman 2011). Muslim Americans are overall younger than the U.S. population, but similar to other groups, the number of Muslim Americans who are over the age of 60 is growing (Ajrouch 2016). The projected growth of the Muslim population coupled with the aging trend in the U.S. may mean that more and more adult Muslim children will be seeking medical care and support for their aging parents that is deemed religious, appropriate, and culturally acceptable, and will be making decisions about end-of-life care in the upcoming decades of the twenty-first century.

Aging among Muslims in the United States

I conducted research on the experiences of diverse individuals who identified as Muslim, primarily living in the areas surrounding Washington, D.C., as they or a family member experienced a serious illness and/or end-of-life care between 2013 and 2017. This work mainly focused on their interactions with the U.S. health-care system and the ways that they navigated institutional policies and regulations for care and their own values, religious beliefs, and practices. Upon beginning this research, one of the first things I learned was the difference between how Muslims experience end-of-life care in the United States and in other countries where Islam is the basis of law. Islam has been described as "a way of life" (Barlas 2002, 43) in that it is intended to be an integral part of daily life and to help guide actions. There are multiple schools of jurisprudence and many interpretations of Islam. Scholars of Islam have also poignantly noted that the Qur'an (the words of God) was revealed within a particular context and may need to be reinterpreted in order to apply to the circumstances of today. Sachedina (2009, 145) states, "the solutions that are offered in the Qur'an are culture specific and not normative for a timeless application and, therefore, cannot be used as paradigmatic in delivering judicial decisions that recur throughout human history." Unlike Catholicism, for instance, in which the pope is the worldwide leader, there is not one authority in Islam. Therefore, the processes of debate and reasoning, as well as interpretation, are key within Islam.

Early on I spoke with one Muslim physician who practiced medicine in the United States and in Saudi Arabia over the course of his career. He spoke about the differences in how end-of-life care is practiced in the two countries. He explained to me that in Saudi Arabia it took families much longer to remove unresponsive patients from life support than the families of his Muslim patients in the United States. Because of his specialty, he often saw older patients who had been long suffering from terminal illness and were nearing the end of their lives. This physician attributed this difference to the Islamic principle that the Creator is the one who decides when life starts and when life ends. The physicians and providers are only the facilitators of His will.

There has been much discussion among U.S. policy makers and health-care administrators about how much care is "wasted" in the United States each year, particularly by older adults and those whose conditions are terminal, and about the overutilization of resources and overtreatment by providers (Delaune and Everett 2008; Shaffer and Scherer 2018). This concern of waste and its associated costs has directed the attempts to restructure the U.S. health-care system so that it is not as siloed, meaning that providers and specialties would work together and communicate regularly about patient cases. This siloed nature prevents the exchange of information and can result in the replication of services and tests that may not improve a patient's care. In his practice in the United States, the Muslim physician I interviewed early on in my study found that Muslim families preferred to take dying patients home to pass away in a familiar setting so they could be surrounded by loved ones rather than leave patients in the hospital. He stated the importance of family in Islam as the reason. The practice of removing patients from the hospital as they approach death parallels the push to use less costly and non-critical care options as part of end-of-life care in the United States, which may offer greater comfort and support to dying patients and their families. Even though there is tremendous diversity among Muslim Americans as a religious group, "they all place a high priority on family, particularly parents. Religiously and culturally, many Muslim Americans consider caring for aging parents to be a moral duty" (Ajrouch 2016, 2). We cannot assume that all Muslim Americans hold the same beliefs, and certainly there are various interpretations of religious teachings that depend upon multiple dynamics, but it is worthwhile to think about how religiosity has impacted Muslim Americans' experiences of aging. This is especially timely given the social and political climate in the United States in the decades after the events of September 11, 2001, and under former president Donald Trump (2016–2020), whose administration spouted anti-immigrant rhetoric and privileged White Americans of Northern and Western European descent.

I discovered in my research that an overall consensus among my participants is that Islam encourages the community to take care of all elders. One *hadith* (sayings, practices, and traditions of the Prophet Muhammad) reads, "The Prophet, peace and blessings be upon him, said 'Blessings are with your elders.'" Likewise, the Qur'an reads, "We reverse the growth of those to whom We give long life" (36:68). This passage acknowledges that physical strength and health as well as mental capacity may deteriorate as we become older, a natural part of growing old, and therefore families caring for elders are of the utmost importance. At the same time, I found that the underlying capitalist and neoliberal values of the U.S. health-care system sometimes transformed how this religious principle is interpreted and actually acted upon in everyday life, particularly in decision-making about health and care for ill and/or aging relatives. Al-Heeti (2007) observes that the religion and culture of Muslim Americans and the teachings of religious scholars deter them from placing older family members into nursing homes and other long-term care facilities. Al-Heeti writes, "But this religious tradition comes at a price. Medicaid and Medicare provide funds to cover nursing home stays for many families and elderly individuals, but these programs do not provide the same level of funding to individuals who live at home with family members, or at least not to all families who need care" (2007, 206).

Likewise, I found this to be true in my work in general, though I also found that the use of nursing homes and other long-term care options for elders was viewed as religiously acceptable if the family was not able to provide the complex care that some older adults may require, since not receiving the proper services could increase elders' physical and emotional suffering and place additional burdens on the family. This example about the use of elder care institutions shows how this Islamic principle can be interpreted or followed differently based upon the needs of the patient.

The basis for this chapter comes from my anthropological research on the experiences of Muslim patients, families, physicians, and hospital staff as they interact with the U.S. health-care system during serious or terminal illnesses and end-of-life care. I will delve into some of the themes and patterns that I discovered that may shape the way we write about aging and religion moving forward. I will provide a brief overview of how anthropology has more generally addressed the intersection of aging and religion, then move into a more specific discussion of aging and Islam, specifically within the United States. But first, I will outline my research methods to explain how I came to the conclusion that the physical changes that occur within and to the human body with advanced age and serious illness—such as limited mobility and cognitive decline—coupled with the approach of the American health-care system toward caring for older adults and those who are dying, prompted my participants to reinterpret religious principles and sacred texts, reevaluate their faith and belonging to the broader Muslim community, and complicate or transform their Muslim identities.

Research Methods

When I started this project, I focused on conducting interviews with academics and with imams and leaders at local mosques, as well as connecting with national organizations dedicated to Islam and health care in order to speak with their leaders from around the country. I spoke with academics very early on in my research—those who are in religious studies, aging studies, and bioethics as well as those who are medical doctors (MDs) teaching in a medical school—to give me better context (important issues to explore, particular literature to read) in which I could further develop my questions and study. Using data collected at this broader level, I conducted observations and interviews at a large hospital located about 30 minutes outside of Washington, D.C. There, I attended the morning meeting of the care team I had partnered with for my fieldwork over a period of six months; accompanied physicians from the care team as they cared for older Muslim patients who were nearing the end of life or considered to be "actively dying" (a phrase without a clear definition in the medical literature but used to describe a patient's whose death is imminent; for more, see Hui et al. 2014) and observed their interactions with patients and their families (collecting data on a total of 36 Muslim patient cases); conducted seven semi-structured interviews with patients' family members (one family member from each patient who I followed closely throughout their hospital stays) and six Muslim physicians; conducted five more informal interviews (that took place over a series of interactions) with physicians and staff who did not identify as Muslim but cared for Muslim patients in some capacity; and spoke at length with a volunteer Muslim chaplain at the hospital. I was able to interview three other Muslim chaplains at different hospitals in the United States through one of the national organizations I connected with early on in my project. As part of my research, I also monitored online message boards and forums where people would pose questions to Islamic scholars on topics such as terminal and chronic illness, health care in the United States, caregiving, death, and health insurance and payment.

Drawing from data I collected for my project, my objective in this chapter is to demonstrate that while religion can certainly influence the aging experience and how someone experiences disease—drawing inspiration from Kleinman (1988), making a distinction here between disease (the diagnosis) and illness (the experience)—the bodily changes that come with growing old, particularly when the end of life is near, and caregiving within a medical setting, including navigating payment and procedures, can also inform religious understandings and identities. It is my hope that this chapter, despite being grounded in my specific research, will prompt us to consider new ways of studying and writing about religion and aging, as well as the end of life, in which religious beliefs are conceptualized as informing the aging experience; the aging experience itself is also seen as equally inflecting people's understandings and interpretations of religious teachings.

Overview of Religion and Aging

Idler (2006) suggests that concepts and approaches to studying and theorizing aging can also be applied to the study of religion, and vice versa. Idler states that "any review of religion and aging should begin by underscoring that religion is not one thing, but many—that complex and *distinct* belief systems make religions what they are" (2006, 281). Religion is complex and multidimensional, comprised of beliefs, values, attitudes, and actions. There may be important differences in religious beliefs and engagement over the life course; in how religion contributes to well-being and psychosocial development; in the interactions between religion and politics in society; and in the ways a society's demographic composition influences religious institutions (Idler 2006). Increasingly, scholars have acknowledged the role that religion plays for older adults as they manage physical and social changes that come with later life (such as the death of peers and siblings and having adult children who may have moved away from them) and as they become more attentive to their own mortality (Nelson-Becker 2018). Nelson-Becker reminds us that contemporary aging comes with greater opportunities than in the past, but changes in societies and the world have also brought about a number of new vulnerabilities for older adults and "risks for diminishment, morbidity, and ambiguous dying" (2018, 4). Old age comes with insecurity and ambiguities. Breitholtz and colleagues found in their research that becoming older can come with "living with uncertainty as to how to relate one's own independence and dependence with regard to oneself, and others" (2013, 4). Research has shown that religious beliefs and involvement can be one way that people deal with the various unknowns associated with growing old, both in the empirical sense, in that religious communities can assist in care when needed and provide companionship, and in a more abstract sense, in that belief and faith may be a way to calm anxieties. This can be seen in the work of Corwin (2017), who notes that Catholic nuns have been shown to age successfully as compared to others. Corwin found that care and interactions among nuns in a Franciscan Catholic convent in the United States can be what contributes to their moderate, or slower, decline in old age. Religion may be part of the larger support system that helps older individuals live fulfilling lives in the face of the multitude of challenges that aging brings.

Some of the Muslim physicians in my study noted that religion is a source of hope for dying patients and their families. This was particularly true for the Muslim patients they cared for at the hospital. This has been documented by anthropologists dating back to Malinowski's (1922) influential ethnographic work in the Trobriand Islands in the Pacific around the time of World War I. Malinowski elucidates how the Trobrianders drew on the supernatural to protect them against rough seas and high stress during excursions that were part of the *kula*, an exchange among the elites (mostly men and chiefs) of shell necklaces and armbands that resulted in the gaining of status. One physician at the hospital, who I call Dr. Mir, stated:

> One thing that I found interesting is that regardless of how minute the situation is or how severe the condition or diagnosis are, families usually find religion as, how should I say it, their savior, their support system. Whenever something comes that creates too must stress or difficulty, they want to resort to religion to find out what's going on and what should happen next.

Gamliel (2008) examined the attitudes of adults in elder care facilities in Israel and found that the elderly made explicit references to death and dying, used humor to talk about their deaths, drew on history, and incorporated biblical myths. Gamliel argues it is not the traditional dichotomy of "acceptance" or "denial" of death, but rather "self-transcendence" (2008, 495). Anthropology as well as other disciplines have shown that religion can serve as a coping mechanism in times of stress and emotional turmoil and can be a source of optimism and encouragement (see also Wang and Agunbiade chapters, this volume). At the same time, religion may also be a source of anxiety or even harm; in contexts where religion exists in a complex relationship with the legal, political, and/or social, some people may be excluded from society or have to navigate complicated landscapes in their everyday lives (see Boellstorff 2005 and Shah 2018 for examples).

Scholars have shown that part of how religion is invoked over the life course, and in particular older age, is partially dependent on the link between religious identity and a person's other identities, such as racial, national, or group identity. Mir (2014), in her ethnography based upon her research among Muslim American women at a university in a major city, suggests that their religious identities were informed by how Muslims and Islam have been thought of within American politics and the media. Mir writes, "Their identity goals varied and shifted contextually" (2014, 39). As Mir demonstrates, identities are not static and are created over the life course. At the same time, they are developed and transformed within historical, political, cultural, and social contexts. Identities are multifaceted and can shape the ways that religion impacts the aging experience of a person or a group. Within any society, people create and draw on a wide range of identities as they craft their life stories and attempt to make sense of the world and situate themselves within it (Young 2013). Bornat (2013) found in Eastern and Western Europe that political, economic, and social changes that older adults experienced over an extended period of time influenced the ways that they related to others, society, and religious and secular rituals—including those related to aging and death. Bădică (2013) argues that weaker religiosity in Bulgaria was due to religious and national identity not being as tightly interconnected, as compared to Romania. Bădică (2013) provides evidence gathered through interviews that practicing religious traditions and holding certain religious and moral beliefs were much more integral to the ways people thought of themselves than atheism, socialist ideologies, and repression. Contrary to what was believed, Bădică explains, "socialist secularisation and repression of religion were not as aggressive and successful as the Western side of the Iron Curtain has been led to believe" (2013, 44). Even though some religious ceremonies, such as marriages, funerals, and baptisms, were replaced with secular versions, they still were seen as integral life events. Bădică also notes that there exists the notion of "believing without belonging" (Davie 1994 cited in Bădică 2013, 44), which indicates belief is much more prevalent than actual practice, meaning there is a weaker religious institutionalization.

Scholarship in anthropology and social sciences (e.g., Parvez 2017) illustrates the role that religion plays in identity formation in addition to the multifaceted nature of religious identities; it also highlights that identity creation takes place within and is informed by social, cultural, and political contexts. When it comes to aging, we are prompted to consider the ways in which religion and religious participation inform and transform a person's identity across the life course, as their aging experience can be inflected by their identities; the reverse process can also occur.

I found it productive to understand how the physical and biological changes to the body in later years and as the end of life drew near, and how interactions with the health-care system (itself being socially and culturally constructed) grounded in values stemming from the Enlightenment, such as autonomy and progress, shaped how Muslim patients, families, and providers interpreted Islamic principles about aging and illness and defined themselves as Muslim in the United States. This enabled me to avoid labeling my Muslim participants as being "exceptional," an idea I draw from Mandaville (2017), who, based on his work at the U.S. Department of State, saw how developing programs specifically for Muslims actually clouded their real needs and instead caused them to become a stigmatized or marked group. I acknowledge that religion can influence people's choices when it comes to health care, but I advocate for exercising restraint so as not to overstress the role that Islam plays in Muslim's decisions and behaviors, and instead to look at how religious beliefs and practices become intertwined with concerns about the costs of care for aging and ill relatives; anxieties about caring for a dying parent at home; fear about experiencing physical pain that often accompanies terminal illness such as cancer; daily interactions with providers and the health-care system; and living in a racialized and inegalitarian society. This nexus is what really shapes the aging experience, health decisions, and practices for older Muslims and for their children as they witness their parents aging. The next section details some of my ethnographic data, which highlight the ways religious beliefs held by my participants inform and are informed by individual circumstances and societal contexts to shape the experiences of older Muslims and their children.

Khalid and His Father

Khalid's father was very ill. He was 86 years old and had been in and out of the hospital multiple times. Khalid father's heart was beating with the help of a pacemaker, and he was receiving oxygen. He had congestive heart failure and most of his ailments came naturally from growing older. Khalid appeared to be in his forties. Even though Khalid had siblings who also lived in the local area not too far from him, he was his father's primary decision-maker and caregiver. He remained with his father at all times while he was in the hospital, sleeping on the small couch in the room. His father immigrated to the United States from the Middle East when he was a young adult, and he and his wife raised their children in the D.C. region. I shadowed the physician who took care of his father in the hospital. After I observed their conversation about the next steps in his father's care, the physician left the room and I was able to sit down and talk with Khalid privately.

Khalid expressed to me that culturally and as a Muslim son, he was the one who is to take care of his father. He knew how grave his father's condition really was. This was a difficult situation because Khalid's mother was also very sick. She had been battling cancer, so some of his brothers and sisters were taking care of her at home. Khalid realized his father was declining, but he was also optimistic. On my first visit with the physician, Khalid told me that he would be fine with me returning to observe his father's care and to speak with him but was hoping that he would not actually see me again since his father was supposed to be discharged soon. He was anxious to take his father home and was hopeful that he would be able to leave the hospital later that very afternoon. He wanted his father to receive physical therapy in order to improve his strength. He complained that the physical therapist at the hospital did not make his father do enough exercises during their session. Khalid was working with the case manager to arrange for therapy at home and to make sure they had everything they needed, such as a wheelchair and safety rails for the toilet.

The looming question was how well Khalid's father would do at home. He could be sent to a skilled nursing facility (SNF), but Khalid said that in his culture and as a Muslim, it was unacceptable to send aging and ailing parents to a nursing home because they will become lonely and their health will decline. Khalid thought his father would not be as active and would not be constantly surrounded by his loved ones as he neared death. I followed Khalid's father's care until he was discharged and sent home, which was a few weeks after our initial meeting. His father had experienced respiratory failure and could not breathe well on his own for an extended period of time, which kept him in the hospital. One day after I returned from the Thanksgiving holiday, I noticed he was no longer on the care team's list and so I inquired what happened. I knew Khalid was anxiously waiting to take his father home. The physician said that he had technically been pushed out of the hospital because Medicare would no longer pay for in-patient care. Khalid then filed an appeal with Medicare to extend payment but was denied. The physician said that once Khalid realized how much would be involved in taking care of his father at home, and especially managing his father's pain and taking care of his rapidly declining body, most likely with little help from his siblings, he no longer wanted him to be released from the hospital.

There was a consensus among the imams who I worked with that Islam teaches that when you are sick, you should go to the doctor or another trained professional for care; do not suffer with sickness but seek help. One imam said, "Muslims . . . say . . . go to the doctor. We prefer to go to a Muslim doctor who practices because there are a lot of non-practicing Muslim doctors [in the United States]." Inhorn and Sargent (2006, 1) also observe that Islam is "a religion that can be said to encourage the use of medicine, biotechnology, and therapeutic negotiation and agency in the face of illness and adversity." At the same time, children are to take care of their parents and elders. Kobeisy (2004, 21) writes, "Caring for parents and elders is at the heart of Muslim cultures and traditions and sending one's parents or elder loved ones to nursing homes or hospice facilities is unheard of in most Muslim cultures." However, as one Muslim physician told me, and as Kobeisy says, when aging and ill parents require care that is more than what the family can offer, it is acceptable to send them to an elder care facility or to seek home health care. This is in part because caring for elders carries physical and emotional burdens, and if children cannot provide the care their elders require, it can cause them more distress. Khalid's experience with his father lies at the intersection of these religious principles and demonstrates how they are interpreted and applied in nuanced ways given his and his father's interactions with providers and the health-care system, such as negotiating with insurance. Khalid may have felt more comfortable having his father in the hospital due to the services being readily available to prevent additional burdens on his body, especially if his breathing became troubled or he was in pain. Simultaneously, Khalid became overwhelmed, according to the physician I shadowed who oversaw the case, when caring for his father at home but did not believe that his father should be in an elder care facility. Khalid's father returned to the hospital a few more times over the course of my fieldwork after being discharged and cared for by Khalid at home, and eventually he died there, just a short time after his wife died at a different hospital.

Caring for a Dying Parent

Like Khalid, adult children of aging and dying Muslim parents navigate the U.S. health-care system as well as their parents' religious beliefs during serious illness and end-of-life care. Sometimes they consulted an imam to offer religious guidance on what they should or should not do. Ali, for instance, had to make the decision about removing his father from life support after his father's long battle with a terminal illness. Ali talked about his "Islamic outlook to life" in combination with his experience "growing up a minority" in the United States, and so he grappled with how to bring together recommendations from his father's physicians along with religious teachings. Imam Yousef was called to provide advice to community members, especially adult children, whose relatives were aging and ill. He himself had immigrated to the United States from the Middle East and has been the prayer leader at a vibrant, multicultural mosque near D.C. Imam Yousef explained that end-of-life care was one of the "very prominent" concerns that he addresses in his role. He mentioned "the issue of the cultural clash between Muslims when they are dying or terminally ill and the American culture and what are the parameters, and how to deal with the patient." He said that his role becomes particularly complicated when Muslims do not practice their faith:

> You know many Muslims are not practicing. They come here [to the United States] and they get lost . . . So, these things actually put pressure on the imam because the imam later on will be required by the family to implement the Islamic laws, *Shari'a*, on the deceased unless the deceased has left a will or advance directive stating that "I wouldn't like to be treated as a Muslim."

Imam Yousef brought up the differences he sees between aging parents and their adult children. He stated that the issue he is most often confronted with is when the parents are immigrants to the United States:

> The children grew up to be purely American and they were disconnected completely from the background and the country of their parents. And then, the parent, or one of the parents, die and they come to an imam, me, and say, "We heard that my parent was Muslim. How can we deal with that?" This means that they disconnected their kids completely from Islam.

He noted that "they are Muslims, but they don't know their rights in Islam, or they don't know what they have to do as Muslims." He recalled how those children who had become "disconnected" from their faith were able to reconnect with Islam through care for their ailing parents and the process of dying. Many of them became more engaged with Islam, such as attending the mosque for prayers, because they realized that it was part of their parent's life. Even if the parent was not particularly religious, or what Imam Yousef termed "secular Muslims," the children made the connection that religion was inherently part of their parent's identity.

Ali, who lost his father, expressed to me how his father's illness caused him to reconsider his Muslim identity and religiosity. He connected with the Muslim physician because they had both grown up as Muslims and as part of minority ethnic groups in the United States. Through engaging with his father's care at the hospital, and his interactions with the health-care system, it became apparent that his identity as a Muslim American was in flux and being transformed due to his father's condition and care. The intersection of race, ethnicity, and religion prompted him to navigate the multitude of societal expectations and pressures, which in turn helped shape his Muslim identity. His father's illness had such an impact on his religiosity and how he identified as Muslim that it led him to not bury his father within the 24-hour period, as recommended in Islam. This time period is not mentioned in the Qur'an but is a cultural practice that stems from the desire for cleanliness and to respect the deceased's body (Gray 2011). Ali instead chose to bury his father in the Middle East in his country of birth. Ali did not have his father buried quickly because he himself did not feel the religious or cultural connection to the United States, which partly stems from him growing up as a minority in the country and partly from navigating the health-care system during his father's illness.

Another imam, Imam Mahmoud, stated that sometimes when he visits Muslim patients and families in the hospital, he does not have to talk at all—they just want an ally. "Sometimes it's just about being present. You don't even have to say anything. Sometimes that is more comforting to people, the fact that you have an imam in the room with you." He recognizes that those who immigrated to the United States, including Muslims, face discrimination and even violence because they do not look or act "American," but for him, caring for each other regardless of background and strengthening the community for all are important practices in Islam. Ali's experiences during his father's illness informed what he believes and how he thinks of himself as a Muslim American; in a sense it reified the lack of belonging that he felt in the United States as a religious and ethnic minority.

Discussion

My framing of aging and religion comes partially from my reading of Abu-Lughod (2002). Abu-Lughod recalls being asked by a reporter after the events of September 11, 2001, to offer insight into women and Islam: "The questions were hopelessly general. Do Muslim women believe 'x'? Are Muslim women 'y'? Does Islam allow 'z' for women? I asked her: 'If you were to substitute Christian or Jewish wherever you have Muslim, would these questions make sense?'" (2002, 784). Starting from this premise, I have considered how I can write about illness, aging, and death and not focus solely on Islam or attribute differences in beliefs or behaviors to only religion; religion itself holds various interpretations and definitions, and it must be held in the same frame of other structural forces. Family and caring for elders is important religiously and culturally for Muslims—although, given the globalized world, capitalist logics, and national and international neoliberal policies, this model is changing (Kobeisy 2004). Hussein and Ismail (2017, 276), for instance, write that the Middle East and North Africa may need "a new model of care and new sets of policies for elderly care which moves beyond the over-reliance on women and addresses the new realities posed by changing family and demographic structures in the Arab region." Due to a variety of reasons, it is not possible to only rely on kin to care for older adults, even if it may be more religiously favorable.

In this chapter, I have used my research on the experiences of Muslim Americans with end-of-life care and care during serious illness to show that approaches to the end-of-life can be informed by religion. At the same time, interacting with the U.S. health-care system and changes that occur to the body during illness or normal aging can also inform religious beliefs, practices, and identities. I concur that faith plays a role in health-care decisions, especially regarding serious illnesses and end-of-life care, but I caution us not to overemphasize the role that Islam (or religion more generally) plays in Muslim Americans' choices or actions; it is not always productive and can lead us to miss patients' real health needs and concerns, perhaps even placing them in an even more vulnerable position.

Acknowledgments

This research project was supported by the College of Humanities and Social Sciences and the Ali Vural Ak Center for Global Islamic Studies at George Mason University.

References

Abu-Lughod, Lila. 2002. "Do Muslim Women Really Need Saving? Anthropological Reflections on Cultural Relativism and Its Others." *American Anthropologist* 104(3): 783–790.

Ajrouch, Kristine. 2016. *Community Brief: Muslim Americans and Aging*. Washington, DC: Institute for Social Policy and Understanding.

Al-Heeti, Roaa M. "Why Nursing Homes Will Not Work: Caring for the Needs of the Aging Muslim American Population." *Elder Law Journal* 15(1): 205–232.

Bădică, Simina. 2013. "'I Will Die Orthodox': Religion and Belonging in Life Stories of the Socialist Era in Romania and Bulgaria." In *Ageing, Ritual and Social Change: Comparing the Secular and Religious in Eastern and Western Europe*, edited by Peter Coleman, Daniela Koleva, and Joanna Bornat, 43–66. London: Routledge.

Bafford, Douglas. 2019. "Aging and the End Times: Evangelical Eschatology and Experiences of Elderhood in the U.S. and South Africa." *Anthropology & Aging* 40(1): 32–47.

Barlas, Asma. 2002. *"Believing Women" in Islam: Unreading Patriarchal Interpretations of the Qur'an*. Austin: University of Texas Press.

Boellstorff, Tom. 2005. "Between Religion and Desire: Being Muslim and Gay in Indonesia." *American Anthropologist* 107(4): 575–585.

Bornat, Joanna. 2013. "The Challenge of Difference: Approaching Comparative Oral History." In *Ageing, Ritual and Social Change: Comparing the Secular and Religious in Eastern and Western Europe*, edited by Peter Coleman, Daniela Koleva, and Joanna Bornat, 19–40. Surrey: Ashgate.

Breitholtz, Agneta, Ingrid Snellman, and Ingegerd Fagerberg. 2013. *Nursing Research and Practice* 2013. http://dx.doi.org/10.1155/2013/403717.

Corwin, Anna. 2020. "Care in Interaction: Aging, Personhood, and Meaningful Decline." *Medical Anthropology* 39(7): 638–652.

Davie, Grace. 1994. *Religion in Britain since 1945: Believing without Belonging*. Oxford: Blackwell.

Delaune, Jules, and Wendy Everett. 2008. "Waste and Inefficiency in the U.S. Healthcare System." Cambridge, MA: New England Healthcare Institute.

Gamliel, Tova. 2008. "The Macabre Style: Death Attitudes of Old-Age Home Residents in Israel." *Ethos* 31(4): 495–513.

Grossman, Cathryn Lynn. 2011. "Number of U.S. Muslims to Double." *USA Today*, January 27, 2011. http://usatoday30.usatoday.com/news/religion/2011-01-27-1Amuslim27_ST_N.htm.

Hui, David, Zohra Nooruddin, Neha Didwaniya, Rony Dev, Maxine De La Cruz, Sun Hyun Kim, Jung Hye Kwon, Ronald Hutchins, Christiana Liem, and Eduardo Bruera. 2014. "Concepts and Definitions for 'Actively Dying,' 'End of Life,' 'Terminally Ill,' 'Terminal Care,' and 'Transition of Care': A Systematic Review." *Journal of Pain and Symptom Management* 47(1): 77–89.

Hussein, Shereen, and Mohamed Ismail. 2017. "Ageing and Elderly Care in the Arab Region: Policy Challenges and Opportunities." *Ageing International* 42: 274–289.

Idler, Ellen. 2006. "Religion and Aging." In *Handbook of Aging and the Social Sciences*, edited by Robert H. Brinstock and Linda K. George, 277–300. San Diego: Elsevier.

Inhorn, Marcia C., and Carolyn F. Sargent. "2006 Introduction to Medical Anthropology within the Muslim World." *Medical Anthropology Quarterly* 20(1): 1–11.

Jensen, Leif. Shannon M. Monnat, John J. Green, Lori M. Hunter, and Martin J. Sliwinski. 2020. "Rural Population Health and Aging: Toward a Multilevel and Multidimensional Research Agenda for the 2020s." *American Journal of Public Health* 100: 1328–1331.

Khabeer, Su'ad Abdul. 2016. *Muslim Cool: Race, Religion, and Hip Hop in the U.S.* New York: New York University Press.

Kleinman, Arthur. 1988. *The Illness Narratives: Suffering, Healing, and the Human Condition*. New York: Basic Books.

Kobeisy, Ahmed Nezar. 2004. "Care for Muslim Seniors." *Islamic Horizons* (January/February): 18–21.

Lamb, Sarah. 2019. "On Being (Not) Old: Agency, Self-Care, and Life-Course Aspirations in the U.S." *Medical Anthropology Quarterly* 33(2): 263–281.

Malinowski, Bronislaw. 1922. *Argonauts of the Western Pacific: An Account of Native Enterprise and Adventure in the Archipelagoes of Melanesia New Guinea*. London: Routledge.

Mandaville, Peter. 2017. "The Ambivalence of Islam in U.S. Foreign Policy." Ali Vural Ak Center for Global Islamic Studies Lecture Series. Fairfax, VA, March 7, 2017.

Mir, Shabana. 2014. *Muslim American Women on Campus: Undergraduate Social Life and Identity*. Chapel Hill: University of North Carolina Press.

Nelson-Becker, Holly. 2018. *Spirituality, Religion and Aging: Illuminations for Therapeutic Practice*. Thousand Oaks, CA: Sage.

Puchalski, Christina, and Betty Ferrell. *Making Healthcare Whole: Integrating Spirituality into Patient Care*. West Conshohocken, PA: Templeton Press.

Rau, Jordan. 2013. "Armed with Bigger Fines, Medicare to Punish 2,225 Hospitals for Excess Readmissions." *Kaiser Health News*, August 2, 2013.

Rowe, John W., Terry Fulmer, and Linda Fried. 2016. "Preparing for Better Health and Healthcare for an Aging Population." *Journal of the American Medical Association* 316(16): 1643–1644.

Sachedna, Abdulaziz. 2009. *Islamic Biomedical Ethics*. New York: Oxford University Press.

Salari, Sonia. 2002. "Invisible in Aging Research: Arab Americans, Middle Eastern Immigrants, and Muslims in the U.S." *The Gerontologist* 42(5): 580–588.

Shaffer, Victoria A., and Laura D. Scherer. 2018. "Too Much Medicine: Behavioral Science: Insights on Overutilization, Overdiagnosis, and Overtreatment in Healthcare." *Policy Insights from the Behavioral and Brain Sciences* 5(2): 155–162.

Shah, Shannon. 2018. *The Making of a Gay Muslim: Religion, Sexuality, and Identity in Malaysia and Britain*. Cham: Palgrave Macmillan.

Wiener, Joshua M., and Jane Tilly. 2002. "Population Ageing in the U.S. of America: Implications for Public Programmes." *International Journal of Epidemiology* 31(4): 776–781.

Young, Hilary. 2013. "'God Can Wait': Composing Non-Religious Narratives in Secular and Post-Communist Societies." In *Ageing, Ritual and Social Change: Comparing the Secular and Religious in Eastern and Western Europe*, edited by Peter Coleman, Daniela Koleva, and Joanna Bornat, 67–88. Surrey: Ashgate.

12

Dementia and the Divided Personhood in China

YAN ZHANG

> *My mother's dementia is wu [aggressive]. She hits*
> *people around and throws everything outside of window.*
> *No matter how I much energy and time I've devote*
> *to taking care of her, her conditions do not get better.*
> *Now, no one in my family wants to keep her at home.*
> Mr. Xu

> *Although my mother was diagnosed with dementia,*
> *her conditions are wen [amenable]. She is like a child now.*
> *When you talk to her, she will look at you and seems very*
> *adorable. I don't want to send her to a nursing home.*
> Mrs. Wang

The above two cases demonstrate two different folk understandings of dementia in China. The two mothers were both diagnosed with dementia around 2010. Following the diagnosis, Mr. Xu requested an early retirement so that he could fully devote time to taking care of his mother. Unfortunately, his mother's dementia symptoms were aggression-centered, and according to Mr. Xu, most drugs and non-pharmaceutical strategies were useless in controlling these symptoms. Consequently, Mr. Xu had an enormous burden to take care of his mother. Yet Mrs. Wang, who had taken care of her mother for almost five years when I conducted my fieldwork, held a different understanding of dementia. According to Mrs. Wang, her mother's cognitive ability was equivalent to that of a five-year-old child. She had poor memory and could not tell her family members. What made Mrs. Wang so grateful, however, was that her mother's condition was *wen* dementia without violent tendencies. Therefore, she was "easygoing as long as you take care of everything for her."

While clinical diagnosis for dementia has to follow the biomedical criteria, the biomedical construction does not equal folk understandings of dementia in China. Clearly, the two distinctive constructions—*wen* and *wu*, or amenable and aggressive dementia—demonstrate a distinctive approach to this illness. That is, Shanghainese attribute two subtypes of personhood (i.e., the status or quality of being a person) to people with dementia.[1] This chapter examines the relationship between dementia and personhood and the associated meaning with the divided personhood in Shanghai. I am not going to address what constitutes personhood, when personhood starts, or whether people with dementia are legal rightsholders. Instead, I merely plan to question the traditional cognition-centered personhood. I argue that personhood is dynamic and behaviorally contingent in Chinese culture, and it has the potential to evolve and devolve into a moral state between person and nonperson.

The relationship between personhood and dementia has long been debated among ethicists, medical practitioners, and social scientists of medicine. Affecting the cognitive functions that are considered the basic structure to support the individual's agency, awareness, communication, judgment and reasoning, dementia threatens the identity and personhood of the individual at risk. This biomedical approach to understanding dementia has drawn a lot of critiques. Early scholars have documented dementia as "the loss of self" (Cohen and Eisdorfer 2001; Herskovits 1995), a "social death" (Sweeting and Gilhooly 1997), and a terrible condition that turns people into "zombies" (Behuniak 2011). Kaufman (2006, 23) criticizes the biomedical construction of dementia as "a condition both of death-in-life and of life-in-death." Smith (1992, 51) underlines dementia as the destruction of the human moral agent and "the greatest evil to be avoided." The emphasis on cognitive competence and the associated biomedical construction of personhood exacerbates the extent of impairments experienced by people living with dementia, which causes severe stigma associated with this illness.

Subsequently, some scholars challenge this biomedical approach by shifting the attention to the sociopsychological dimension of personhood (Downs 1997; Kitwood 1993, 1997). Among many of those grappling with the issue of personhood and dementia, the work of Kitwood (1997) has been a touchstone. Advocating the concern for "others," he argues that personhood should be conceptualized more broadly to include relationships and moral solidarity (Kitwood 1990, 1997). Building upon Kitwood's work, Sabat (2001, 2003) develops a theory of "malignant social positioning." This theory underlines the mutual influence between the way individuals with dementia are socially positioned and how we conceptualize dementia. Post (2006) further suggests that the fundamental social determinant of positioning persons with dementia as different and of less value lies a cultural belief that cognitive capacity constitutes the core of personhood.

The hypercognitive culture (Post 2013) is closely related to industrialization, which emphasizes economic productivity. Anthropologists have documented local constructions of personhood and dementia in societies before and during modernization. For example, in India, dementia was traditionally considered an illness with "bad" families, and dementia symptoms were absorbed into cultural categories such as "gone sixtyish" (Cohen 1998). Similarly, in China, senile dementia conditions such as memory loss and childish behavior were considered signs of normal aging (Ikels 1998). These cultural constructions of dementia, however, have been quickly transformed during the process of industrialization. Thanks to advanced biomedical technologies, dementia is now considered a "brain" disease in India (Brijnath and Manderson 2011). The identification of dementia as a stigmatized mental illness in China further challenges the previous cultural construction (Zhang 2018). In a post-industrialized Asian society such as Japan, dementia is also a stigmatized illness yet is the outcome of social disintegration (Traphagan 2000). These various constructions demonstrate that the conceptualization of dementia is both historically and culturally contingent.

While much has been written surrounding the various constructions of dementia and the importance of maintaining personhood for people with dementia, little attention has been paid to the meanings attached to personhood and why personhood is such a difficult status for people with dementia to achieve. This chapter advances our understanding of personhood by examining two different local constructions of dementia in China. As with the two cases in the opening vignette, these two constructions of dementia highlight folk understandings of autonomy, cognitive capacity, and moral or behavioral status, which vary from context to context. Building upon the aforementioned scholars' work, I call attention to the moral dimension of personhood, which lays the foundation for some people with dementia to transform the traditional cognition-based personhood. While acknowledging the variable nature of personhood, I argue that moral status—that is, what matters most for an individual to maintain his/her personhood (Kleinman 2009)—instead of cognitive capacity, plays a significant role in differentiating the two subtypes of dementia in Shanghai. These two constructions of personhood, which are employed by formal or informal caregivers, will also generate different narratives and care practices for people with dementia.

Methods

My exploration of the personhood of people with dementia took place in Shanghai, China. As the "oldest" city in terms of the ratio of the older population in China, Shanghai has a relatively large number of people with dementia (SRCA 2019; Xu et al. 2017; Zhang et al. 1990). However, social services for this group of people are not well developed, and thus dementia care is primarily a family responsibility.

The over 20 months I spent in Shanghai included the entire year of 2017 and annual short visits, mostly in the summer, between 2014 and 2016. During my annual visits to this community, I stayed with two host families who had people with dementia in W community, the primary field site. Between 2010 and 2013, I served as a project manager for a local non-governmental organization (NGO). During my fieldwork and work experience, I was able to participate in community life and conduct interviews with family caregivers, volunteers, local government officials, social service providers, and other stakeholders. In addition to my experience in W community, I conducted in-depth interviews in a nearby memory clinic. Data presented in this chapter consist of 144 interviews with family dementia caregivers that were mainly collected in these two settings. Among these 144 family caregivers, 38 were from W community who were randomly chosen from a community-based dementia care program that had about 200 participants, and the remaining 106 were randomly chosen from the list of regular 500 visitors in the memory clinic. While most people with dementia in my sample had received an official diagnosis, I did not use the diagnosis of a specific type of dementia as a variable given the severe stigma associated with this condition in China. Regarding the three cases without an official diagnosis, however, their family caregivers and other neighborhood residents all acknowledged that there were typical dementia symptoms of their kin (e.g., memory decline, wandering, repetitive questions, and body maintenance care work).

Ages of care recipients ranged from 52 to 101 years old, with a median age of 79. Similarly, there was a broad age range of family caregivers, from 28 to 91 years old (median age 69). About three quarters of family caregivers aged 60 and above, and those under 60 years old were either retired,[2] (temporarily) unemployed, or working part-time jobs. Approximately 46.1 percent were male caregivers and 53.9 percent were female caregivers. All caregivers and care recipients had their household registration in Shanghai.

Due to the comprehensive pension and health-care insurance systems in Shanghai, there were no distinct differences in terms of economic circumstances between family caregivers from W community and those from the memory clinic. Most family caregivers were born in or before the 1960s. Because of the Cultural Revolution and other social movements during the Mao era, education levels of family caregivers were similar and relatively lower compared to those of individuals born after the 1960s. Most caregivers had only about ten years of schooling. Thus, education cannot be a reliable factor to distinguish one subject from the other. Since most family caregivers are seniors or retired, I turn to pension/monthly income as a primary indicator of economic circumstances.

Based on the pensions/monthly income, the majority of families were middle class (n=131); the remaining were relatively poor (n=13). The highest pension reported from one caregiver and one care recipient was about 15,000–20,000 RMB [USD 2,100–2,800] due to the fact that they participated in the Civil War and significantly contributed to the liberation of the country. The majority of family caregivers and care recipients had their monthly pension ranging from 3,000 to 7,000 RMB [USD 420–980].[3] The exact pension varied from case to case due to the years of work history, regional differences, and types of employment. Among the 144 family caregivers, only 13 reported that their monthly income was less than 3,000 RMB [USD 420] per month. Similar statistics were found among care recipients. Regarding the 144 care recipients, only two care recipients had no pension, but relied on government subsidies (790 RMB [USD 110.6] per month in 2017 and 880 RMB [USD 123.2] per month in 2018) because of their advanced age and lack of formal work experience. Simply relying upon government subsidies or monthly pensions is not enough. Many adult children in Shanghai provide various degrees of financial support for their parents, especially those in disadvantaged conditions. In some conditions, such as hospitalization for surgery, adult children often pay the out-of-pocket portion for their parents.

Thus, ascertaining a monthly income for this group of people was not possible, as their monthly incomes fluctuated considerably.

The narratives and experiences I record in the following section were collected primarily in 2017. To preserve confidentiality, I did not provide full names for my informants. Through this ethnographic approach, I aim to reveal the two constructions of dementia and how these folk understandings affect the conceptualization of personhood.

Chinese Perspectives on Persons and Nonpersons

The word "person" in the Chinese cultural context represents more about a moral agent than a biological species. It is the moral personhood that distinguishes human beings from animal beings (Tsai 2009; Yan 2017). Because of the emphasis on morality, not all human beings can attain or maintain the status of being a person. From the Chinese perspective, no one is born a full person, which means that one's biological membership is insufficient to be a full person. An individual has to be socialized to be a person. In order to obtain full personhood, one has to go through continuing cycles of personal development, such as socialization and education. Chinese socialization places heavy emphasis on the learning of moral rules, on explicit emotional manipulation, and on adherence to internalized universalistic codes for behavior (Wilson 1981; Xu 2017). This whole process is called *xue zuo ren* (literally "learning to be a person"), which enables the person to internalize moral standards. After one achieves full personhood such as being an adult, maintaining one's moral status (i.e., *zuo ren*, or "acting as a person") becomes the key to sustain full personhood. Acting as a person means that one has an obligation to engage appropriately in interpersonal relationships, build social networks, and maintain a moral status (Fei 1992; Tu 1996; Yan 2017). After one fulfills one's obligation, one's personhood and rights of being treated as a person are obtained and maintained. Therefore, without manifesting appropriate behavior and fulfilling moral obligation, an individual will not be able to establish social relationships and thus will not receive acknowledgment as a moral agent.

This socialization process that encourages a uniform and idealized personhood seems also to be the one that makes deviance from social rules obvious and frightening. In this sense, an individual who is unable to fulfill his or her social obligation will be seen as a nonperson. Nonpersons do not receive social recognition nor are they acknowledged to be moral agents.

Hence, no social support or social protection will reach this group of people. These nonpersons traditionally include those with mental illnesses (Chiang 2014), HIV/AIDs (Guo and Kleinman 2011), prisoners (Ikels 1997), and even homosexuals (Wang et al. 2019). Because their behavior does not follow social norms, these people are often marginalized, ignored, humiliated, and even treated as nonpersons.

The public's attitude toward dementia is complex. Although seniors with memory decline in imperial China could be culturally protected (Ikels 1998), dementia conditions such as aggression and inappropriate social behavior among young adults were stigmatized (Zhang 2018). As with other mental disorders, such individuals would damage their family "face" [moral status] and were often treated as nonpersons. Some early psychiatry training textbooks even labeled this group of people as "living dead" or "walking dead" (Su and Tao 1951, 236). Medicalization of senile dementia in China has further amplified this stigmatized condition. Without an age distinction, senile dementia, like other mental disorders, is considered problematic and needs biomedical intervention to maintain personal life and social order. Moreover, ancient Chinese people seemed to have long recognized the hereditary component to mental disorders. Medicalization of dementia as a mental disorder reinforces this public notion, which unfortunately correlates dementia and genetic deficiency. Because of the behavioral, moral, and biological undesirability, dementia, as other mental disorders, is a severely stigmatized condition.

While acknowledging that stigma of mental disorders in China is to some degree related to personhood, we do not know what exactly makes those living with dementia assume the status of nonpersons in the eyes of their communities. Also, with an increasing number of elders living with dementia, we do not know what happens when they take on a narrowly defined personhood. The two different constructions of personhood in Shanghai illustrate these answers and the significance of the dynamic nature of personhood in China.

Two Constructions of Personhood in Shanghai

Wu, or Aggressive Dementia

Mrs. Bai's mother was a widow who suffered from dementia in her nineties. She lived in W community throughout her whole life. She had six daughters and one son. The son estranged himself from the large family due to a conflict about 20 years ago. Among the six daughters, one had died, and one lived in a faraway city. The four daughters, ranging from 55 to 70 years old, took turns to care for their mother. However, none of them expressed gratitude to their mother due to her *wu*, or aggressive behavior. On an early morning when I visited Mrs. Bai and her mother, Mrs. Bai complained about her mother's aggressive behavior, which caused them to be sleepless all day long. According to Mrs. Bai, her mother constantly made noises or knocked everything around her—the bed, the chair, the desk, and even the TV—even at night. Moreover, the mother had lost most of her physical functions and became incontinent. If Mrs. Bai did not notice, the mother would throw feces around the room. In order to clean her mother immediately, Mrs. Bai used a blanket, instead of pants, to cover her mother's bottom. Because the mother could not understand people's intentions, she often hit or slapped her daughters when they moved close to her such as in an attempt to clean her body. When I stayed in their home and talked to Mrs. Bai, her mother was unsettled and kept yelling. The family's limited financial resources could not afford them institutional care or a helper, and all care tasks fell on the four daughters. At the age of 55, Mrs. Bai's health condition was poor. When she walked me out one day, Mrs. Bai said, "We hate doing this [*zuo de hen yuan*], day after day for almost eighteen years. Now we are almost dying."

The aggressive dementia condition challenges one's moral personhood. The nearby residents all knew about this aggressive grandma. Surprisingly, no one wanted to help or show any sympathy. Mrs. Ye, a community volunteer who lived nearby, said, "It's a family issue. The quality of her [Bai's mother] life is too low from any aspects. Then, what should I say?" Previously when Mrs. Ye was a member of the neighborhood committee, she often invited Mrs. Bai's mother to attend community events; however, after she became "crazy," no one invited her anymore. "She has already been cut off from our community life," said Mrs. Ye. The rejection of attending community events indicates the social death of people with aggressive dementia. What makes things even worse is that the family also deprives the symbolic position of people with dementia within domestic settings. When I asked Mrs. Bai about opportunities for her mother to interact with other family members, she said frankly:

> We daughters are tired of having this mother, not to say for our relatives. She hasn't been out of this room for almost 10 years. We four sis-

ters are the ones who come in and out. Other family members rarely show up ... Her dementia conditions will not allow her to attend my son's wedding ... Everyone was enjoying the time, [but] suddenly she broke everything. Too embarrassed for us.

It appears that Mrs. Bai acknowledged the appropriate social behavior to maintain one's moral status, which her mother with aggressive dementia had failed to maintain.

Although Chinese elders enjoy a high level of respect from both family members and society, they are equally subjected to the moral responsibility for maintaining their personhood. One famous ancient saying in China goes, "If a senior does not respect oneself or others, a younger person has the right not to show respect" (*wei lao buzun, wei you bujing*). A senior should behave appropriately in line with one's age and social position. By doing so, he or she not only achieves one's moral status but also maintains a harmonious relationship with other people. If not, the individual loses his or her moral status, which further damages one's personhood. People living with aggressive dementia, like Mrs. Bai's mother, challenge these behavioral codes; therefore, their moral personhood is damaged. Even though aggression has been medicalized to underpin one's changes with dementia, the lay public, including family caregivers, still employ behavioral codes to evaluate one's personhood. To some extent, the biomedical understanding supports and even reinforces the cultural and psychological reasoning that dementia threatens one's continuity of moral personhood. The public generally call this group of people "madmen," "madwomen," or "crazy people." Family caregivers, who also value harmonious relationships, often accept this interpretation of aggressive dementia.

Family caregivers' endorsement of the public understanding of *wu* or aggressive dementia further testifies to this moral orientation of personhood. Because of aggressive behavior and the associated overwhelming burden, taking care of people with dementia is more about fulfilling one's moral responsibility than an expression of love or filial piety. The construction of *wu* dementia also legitimizes the suffering of family caregivers. According to local residents, these caregivers, especially adult-child caregivers, were in many aspects good people to their kin. However, living with a family member with aggressive dementia was, according to one caregiver, "so challenging that no one can enjoy the time at home." An adult-child caregiver even said, "There is no affection between us. They [people with dementia] are the parents who drive filial children away!" Many family caregivers lamented that they could not bear the care burden, and some even expressed their resentment toward their parents. Two adult-child caregivers even swore that they would not shed a tear after their parents died. Although Chinese family expect adult children to show respect to elders, this respect is built upon harmonious social order. Aggressive behavior, regardless of senility, threatens the order, which further undermines one's personhood and family relationships. Therefore, those with *wu* dementia often "create more suffering for their family members than for themselves," said Mrs. Bai.

Because of aggressive behavior, some family caregivers tend to institutionalize people with dementia. Mr. Cai eventually decided to send his wife to a nursing home after he witnessed these challenges. According to Mr. Cai, his wife screamed all the time, complained about ghosts at home, and sometimes threw things out of the window. Mr. Cai could not sleep well and eventually had a heart attack. After that, their two daughters, who had work duties, suggested Mr. Cai should hire a nursing aide. However, after several trials, the Cai family gave up because no nursing aide wanted to take care of an individual with aggressive dementia who often physically hit strangers. "We have no choice now, and my mother has driven everyone crazy in our family," said Mrs. Cai, the daughter caregiver, in our conversations.

The aggressive behavior of people with dementia further challenges the capacity of institutional care. Although many nursing homes acknowledged that they offered dementia care, when I conducted my fieldwork, in operation some nursing homes set a high standard to minimize their risk of enrolling elders with aggressive dementia. Mrs. Pu had planned to send her husband to a nursing home because of his aggressive behavior. However, the nursing home rejected her husband because "he can still walk," which meant there was a high risk for him to get lost. Employees of the nursing home Mrs. Pu visited, together with several other nursing homes I visited, expressed that, to minimize their administration risks, they would rather admit those who had completely lost walking abilities than those who had a high likelihood of getting lost. "If an aggressive dementia patient can walk, they will charge more than 10,000 RMB [USD 1,400] per month. If he/she cannot walk, they increase nursing fees, but administration fees will be less. Nursing homes do not want to enroll someone unreliable. I will definitely send him to a nursing home when he cannot walk," said Mrs. Pu.

Due to the folk understanding of aggressive dementia and limited public education on how to manage the aggression, there is a lack of public empathy toward people with aggressive dementia. Because of the lack of moral accountability, such an individual is reduced to a nonperson or less of a person, which is an instance of the extreme stigma in Chinese culture. The division between aggressive dementia and amenable dementia is not only an effort to differentiate subgroups but also a reverse mirror for better understanding what a person should be in Chinese culture.

Wen, or Amenable Dementia

In contrast to the deprived personhood of people with aggressive dementia, members of the public, family caregivers in particular, attribute different degrees of personhood to those with amenable dementia. This personhood, ranging from a full one to an adjusted one, depends not so much on the degree of cognitive capacity but on the moral status of people with dementia. A "full personhood" is often used to describe those with early stage of dementia when they can maintain most social interactions. Along with the progression of disease, family caregivers assign an adjusted personhood to those seniors with childish behavior. Compared to the full personhood that is stable, continuous, and opting for a moral status, the personhood of a childlike senior is dynamic, contingent, and relational. Even though there is a differentiation of behavioral capacities, the amenable tendency of these patients not only enables them to maintain a certain degree of personhood but also mobilizes resources to maintain family-based care rather than institutionalization.

People with amenable dementia achieve full personhood, according to family caregivers, through maintaining appropriate social relationships. Patients in the early stage of dementia preserve their social capacities, such as showing gratitude to other people, which is a key component of personhood in Chinese culture. They might not catch fast conversations or perform well in tasks that require intensive mental labor; however, they can express "sorry" and "thanks" to show their basic social etiquette to people. As such, the ability to maintain one's relational self plays a key role in protecting the moral personhood of people with dementia. For example, Mr. Ding took care of his wife, who was diagnosed with early stage of dementia. Each morning this couple went to the food market for shopping. When Mr. Ding tried to buy some expensive meat or fruits, Mrs. Ding would persuade him not to do so. When Mr. Ding intended to buy expensive things to treat her, she would say "Thank you for being so nice to me." During the interview, Mrs. Ding, even though she had memory problems, constantly appreciated her husband's good deeds simply because "he cooks meat for me every day." Mr. Ding said, "She has been thrifty for her whole life. She never bought herself fancy clothes and was never jealous of other people's lives. Because she is the person who can share weal and woe in life, I will take care of her." Rather than emphasizing autonomy or rationality, a full personhood is attributed to an individual who can maintain basic social relationships, which further justifies one's moral status.

One important behavioral change during the course of dementia is that people become more childish. To solve this conundrum, family caregivers assign an adjusted personhood to those childlike seniors given their sustaining relationships. In Chinese language, "old child" and "childish behavior" are often used to describe seniors returning to a childlike status. Childish behaviors of people with dementia include reduced ability to make judgment, limited speech or word choice in conversations, and being naïve to various conditions, among others. Although there might be an overlap with aggressive dementia in terms of cognitive ability, the peaceful mind, beautiful faces, and the simple affection of people with amenable dementia often remind family caregivers how innocent their kin are. In contrast to aggressive behavior, their amenable behavior establishes an adjusted personhood that not only justifies their needs but also catalyzes the empathy from family caregivers and people around. For example, Mrs. Wang took care of her mother for almost five years. She had poor memory and often repeated the same question. According to Mrs. Wang, her mother was different from those with aggressive dementia:

> She becomes a child now and often calls me "Mom" when she needs something. When I told her that "you are my mom and I am your daughter," she looked at me with her eyes wide open. Her face at that moment was just adorable. Today when I told her that I would go to hospital for her medicine, my mom said "Thank you." I asked her, "Do you want to go out with me?" She said no. You see, she can communicate with you, which makes me feel grateful.

Although her cognitive abilities had diminished along with dementia, Wang's mother was easygoing and could maintain basic social conversation. The amenable tendency enabled her to exercise her agency to maintain the sustainability of her family relationship and to achieve the moral personhood. Therefore, family-based care continued. For some spousal caregivers, this dependent relationship can revert to one in which caregivers are in need of the presence of their spouses with dementia. The reverse relationship of caregiving and care receiving further contextualizes the personhood of people with amenable dementia. Because of their amenable behavior, people with dementia often become more dependent on family caregivers and constantly follow them like a "shadow." For instance, Mr. Huang had taken care of his wife for more than ten years. Many people suggested that he should send her to a nursing home considering the increasing care burden. Mr. Huang said he did not want to because he would "feel lonely if she is absent." Mr. Huang also treated his wife like a "spoiled child":

> I cannot understand what she says, and she may not understand what I say. But she feels great when I applaud her. She cannot recognize many family members, but she knows me and calls me "Dad." She is quiet when I am around. If not, she will cry. It's really hard for me to send her to a nursing home.

Mrs. Huang's amenable behavior was a powerful testimony to her moral personhood. Although she had poor cognitive abilities, she expressed her needs of love through watching and shadowing her husband. Mrs. Huang's childish behaviors, such as crying, liking praise, and calling her husband "Dad," might reduce her full personhood from outsiders' perspective. However, these behaviors catalyzed the empathy from her husband. Moreover, Mrs. Huang became quiet when this couple was together, which made Mr. Huang feel needed. Thus, the presence of his wife formed their dependent relationship (i.e., being mutually needed).

Because of the mutually dependent relationship, many family caregivers feel that their endeavor is worthwhile when they receive positive feedback from people with dementia. Mr. Zheng took care of his wife who was diagnosed with dementia five years ago. Compared to the caregivers who often complained about the burden of dementia care, Mr. Zheng, however, expressed that he felt rewarded when his wife had a smile on her face. Even though she could not speak, the smile represented appreciation for his caregiving. "She cannot express, but I know what she wants to say. It's not about she needs me. Rather, I need her more than she needs me. If she is absent, I will feel lonely," said Mr. Zheng. People living with amenable dementia do not threaten their personhood too much since their relationships with family caregivers are well maintained. Sometimes their relationships are strengthened because of the mutual need. Clearly, the mutual dependency protects people with amenable dementia from being institutionalized.

The transformed caregiving and care receiving relationship is also captured by Kleinman (2009) and Brijnath (2014). Brijnath (2014) argues that caregiving has transformed the forgotten condition of people with dementia into a loving and caring relationship between caregivers and care receivers. Accordingly, caregiving becomes a moral practice that makes caregivers "more present and fully human" (Kleinman 2009, 293). The moral personhood narratives of family caregivers persist in my research findings. While both Brijnath and Kleinman have recognized caregiving as a moral practice of family caregivers, the context of the personhood of people with dementia and its impact on family caregiving is not fully explained. The divided personhood of people with dementia in Shanghai calls for the attention to moral accountability in the construction of personhood and how moral agency can transform one's personhood to maintain or challenge family caregiving.

Discussion and Conclusion

This chapter demonstrates the divided personhood of people with dementia in Shanghai. In contrast to the idea that personhood is hypercognition-oriented in industrialized societies, there is a strong emphasis on the moral dimension in China. The two different constructions of personhood are built upon the moral status of people with dementia, with one group demonstrating the continuity of moral agency and the other demonstrating the lack of it. Moral agency confers a "higher" social order of personhood than the mere biological human membership in Chinese culture. People living with amenable dementia can retain a sense of their moral agency and identity, and thus they can be the person they are. However, due to lack of moral accountability, people with dementia with aggressive behavior distinguish themselves from those with amenable dementia, which further makes them less of a person, or nonperson. It is more about moral status than cognitive capacity that underlies the two constructions of dementia.

The meanings of such a division of the personhood of dementia sufferers are at least twofold. First, family caregivers use this division to negotiate a health identity. Because people living with dementia are interpreted as unable to carry out their social roles, there is a fear of dementia among their relatives. Because of this fear, individuals in the United States who have memory problems try to differentiate their conditions, such as mild cognitive impairment, from dementia (Beard and Neary 2013). Traphagan (2000) also documents the fear of dementia among Japanese elders because elders who fail to maintain mental capabilities are often deemed incapable and unworthy of contributing to the social discourse. Family caregivers in Shanghai who actively endorse the two constructions of dementia intend to question the universal understanding of dementia by differentiating the moral status between two subgroups of people with dementia. By doing so, dementia is no longer a simple biomedical issue; rather, it becomes a moral issue. It is the moral dimension of personhood that people living with aggressive dementia find hard to achieve.

Second, even though there are distinctions between the two subtypes of dementia, both point to the fact that personhood is dynamic and contingent (Tsai 2009; Yan 2017). If there is a process for an individual to achieve a full status of personhood and eventually learn to exercise moral agency, then, changes in the person, such as consciousness and mental capacity or other cognitive abilities, imply a diminution of the personhood (Higgs and Gilleard 2016). While acknowledging this developmental approach is important to understanding the dynamics of personhood over the life course, the dynamics is bounded within the neurocognitive discourse. It overlooks the possibility that cognitive attributes of personhood and moral agency are likely to compromise. In other words, the contingent nature of personhood cannot be fully explained if it is reduced to biomedical attributes. To some extent, moral agency plays a more critical role than biomedical attributes—people with amenable dementia are living proof of such instances in which moral agency overrides biomedical attributes in deciding one's personhood. These individuals retain their moral personhood, even with cognitive impairment.

The two constructions of dementia also make explicit the notion that personhood is a matter of degree. If so, dementia care becomes contingent and relational. People with aggressive dementia lose their personhood because their aggression threatens harmonious relationships with people. Given that accountability is not achieved to maintain one's moral status, family caregivers are reluctant to take care of people with aggressive dementia. Some caregivers even generate resentment toward their aggressive kin. Correspondingly, there is a high tendency for people with aggressive dementia to be institutionalized. Not only domestic settings but also nursing homes do not tolerate interruptive behavior. Some nursing homes set strict criteria to minimize the risk of enrolling people with aggressive dementia. By contrast, people with amenable dementia are attributed to a full or an adjusted personhood due to their ability to maintain harmonious relationships with family caregivers. Even though they have lost their cognitive abilities, their amenable behavior is easier to deal with and is more controllable. Their ability to preserve harmonious relationships with nearby people also attracts more love, care, and respect. As a result, family caregivers continue the family-based care arrangement and try not to institutionalize their kin.

Personhood clearly has a powerful presence in contemporary Chinese society. It is not easy to dismiss the term outright, or even replace it with Western concepts such as "autonomy," "rationality," or "judgment," which have a strong association with neuroscientific bases for personhood. In China, the two constructions of dementia imply that personhood is more of a moral philosophy than a metaphysical concept. Because it requires moral accountability to lay the foundation, people with aggressive dementia can easily lose their moral status and moral personhood. People with amenable dementia, however, are moral agents, capable of maintaining basic social interaction. Consequently, the experiences of family caregivers are contingent. Overall, the division of attributing different types of personhood to people with dementia captures how personhood is locally constructed and how care is influenced by these constructions.

Acknowledgments

This research was funded by the Wenner Gren Foundation for Anthropological Research (#9361), the Luce/American Council of Learned Societies in China Studies, and the College of Arts and Sciences Fellowship at Case Western Reserve University. I am also grateful to Britteny Howell and Ryan Harrod for their suggestions for and edits to this chapter.

Notes

1. The two constructions of personhood for people with dementia in Shanghai can be applied to the broader Chinese society; however, the exact words, such as *wen* or *wu*, used by Shanghainese to describe these two constructions are unique in Shanghai. In other parts of China, people might use different phrases to distinguish between dementia categories.

2. The retirement age in China currently is 60 for men and 55 for female civil servants

and 50 for female workers. By 2038 there will be an equal retirement age for women and men set at 67.

3. The average monthly pension in Shanghai was 4,200 RMB or USD 588 in 2016. See the 2017 report from Shanghai Research Center on Aging. http://www.shrca.org.cn/News/detail.aspx?ID=6892&Page=0.

References

Beard, Renée L., and Tara M. Neary. 2013. "Making Sense of Nonsense: Experiences of Mild Cognitive Impairment." *Sociology of Health & Illness* 35(1): 130–146.

Behuniak, Susan M. 2011. "The Living Dead? The Construction of People with Alzheimer's Disease as Zombies." *Ageing and Society* 31: 70–92.

Brijnath, Bianca. 2014. *Unforgotten: Love and the Culture of Dementia Care in India*. New York: Berghahn Books.

Brijnath, Bianca, and Lenore Manderson. 2011. "Appropriation and Dementia in India." *Culture, Medicine, and Psychiatry* 35(4): 501–518.

Chiang, Howard, ed. 2014. *Psychiatry and Chinese History*. London: Routledge.

Cohen, Donna, and Carl Eisdorfer. 2001. *The Loss of Self–A Family Resource for the Care of Alzheimer's Disease and Related Disorders*. New York: W.W. Norton and Company.

Cohen, Lawrence. 1998. *No Aging in India: Alzheimer's, the Bad Family, and Other Modern Things*. Berkeley: University of California Press.

Corwin, Anna I. 2020. "Care in Interaction: Aging, Personhood, and Meaningful Decline." *Medical Anthropology* 39(7): 638–652.

Downs, Murna. 1997. "The Emergence of the Person in Dementia Research." *Ageing and Society* 17(5): 597–607.

Fei, Xiaotong. 1992. *From the Soil: The Foundations of Chinese Society*. Translated by Gary G. Hamilton and Zheng Wang. Berkeley: University of California Press.

Guo, Jinhua, and Arthur Kleinman. 2011. "Stigma: HIV/AIDS, Mental Illness, and China's Nonpersons." In *Deep China: The Moral Life of the Person (What Anthropology and Psychiatry Tell Us about China Today)*, edited by Arthur Kleinman, Yunxiang Yan, Jing Jun, Sing Lee, Everett Zhang, Pan Tianshu, Wu Fei, and Guo Jinhua, 237–262. Berkeley: University of California Press.

Herskovits, Elizabeth. 1995. "Struggling over Subjectivity: Debates about the 'Self' and Alzheimer's Disease." *Medical Anthropology Quarterly* 9(2): 146–164.

Higgs, Paul, and Chris Gilleard. 2016. "Interrogating Personhood and Dementia." *Aging & Mental Health* 20(8): 773–780.

Ikels, Charlotte. 1997. "Ethical Issues in Organ Procurement in Chinese Societies." *China Journal* 38: 95–119.

———. 1998. "The Experience of Dementia in China." *Culture, Medicine, and Psychiatry* 22: 257–283.

Kaufman, Sharon R. 2006. "Dementia-Near-Death and 'Life Itself.'" In *Thinking about Dementia: Culture, Loss, and the Anthropology of Senility*, edited by Annette Leibing and Lawrence Cohen, 23–42. Piscataway, NJ: Rutgers University Press.

Kitwood, Thomas. 1990. *Concern for "Others": A New Psychology of Conscience and Morality*. London: Routledge.

———. 1993. "Towards a Theory of Dementia Care: The Interpersonal Process." *Ageing and Society* 13(1): 51–67.

———. 1997. *Dementia Reconsidered: The Person Comes First*. Buckingham: Open University Press.

Kleinman, Arthur. 2009. "Caregiving: The Odyssey of Becoming More Human." *The Lancet* 373: 292–294.

Lamb, Sarah. 2014. "Permanent Personhood or Meaningful Decline? Toward a Critical Anthropology of Successful Aging." *Journal of Aging Studies* 29: 41–52.

Leibing, Annette, and Lawrence Cohen. 2006. *Thinking about Dementia: Culture, Loss, and the Anthropology of Senility*. Piscataway, NJ: Rutgers University Press.

Post, Stephen G. 2006. "Respectare: Moral Respect for the Lives of the Deeply Forgetful." In *Dementia: Mind, Meaning, and the Person*, edited by Julian C. Hughes, Stephen J. Louw, and Steven R. Sabat, 223–234. Oxford: Oxford University Press.

———. 2013. "Hope in Caring for the Deeply Forgetful: Enduring Selfhood and Being Open to Surprises." *Bulletin of the Menninger Clinic* 77(4): 349–368.

Sabat, Steven R. 2001. *The Experience of Alzheimer's Disease–Life Through a Tangled Veil*. Oxford: Blackwell Publishers.

———. 2003. "Malignant Positioning and the Predicament of People with Alzheimer's Disease." In *The Self and Others: Positioning Individuals and Groups in Personal, Political, and Cultural Contexts*, edited by Rom Harré and Fathali M. Moghaddam, 85–98. Westport, CT: Praeger Publishers.

Smith, David H. 1992. "Human Dignity, Dementia, and the Moral Basis of Caregiving." In *Dementia and Aging: Ethics, Values, and Policy Choices*, edited by Robert H. Binstock, Stephen G. Post, and Peter J. Whitehouse, 44–54. Baltimore: Johns Hopkins University Press.

Shanghai Research Center on Aging (SRCA). 2019. "Report of the Statistics of Older Population and Social Services Development in 2018." Accessed March 10, 2020. http://www.shrca.org.cn/News/detail.aspx?ID=6892&Page=0.

Su, Zonghua, and Tao Juyin. 1951. *Jingshenbing Xue Gangyao* [Outline of psychiatry]. Shanghai: Chinese Publication Press.

Sweeting, Helen, and Mary Gilhooly. 1997. "Dementia and the Phenomenon of Social Death." *Sociology of Health and Illness* 19(1): 93–117.

Traphagan, John W. 2000. *Taming Oblivion: Aging Bodies and the Fear of Senility in Japan*. Albany: State University of New York Press.

Tsai, Daniel Fu-Chang. 2009. "A Confucian Two-Dimensional Approach to Personhood, Dementia, and Decision-Making." In *Decision-Making, Personhood, and Dementia: Exploring the Interface*, edited by Deborah O'Connor and Barbara Purves, 58–69. London: Jessica Kingsley Publishers.

Tu, Weiming. 1996. "Confucian Traditions in East Asian Modernity." *Bulletin of the American Academy of Arts and Sciences* 50(2): 12–39.

Wang, Yuanyuan, Hu Zhishan, Peng Ke, Xin Ying, Yang Yuan, Jack Drescher, and Chen Runsen. 2019. "Discrimination against LGBT Populations in China." *The Lancet (Public Health)* 4: e440–e441.

Wilson, Richard W. 1981. "Conformity and Deviance Regarding Moral Rules in Chinese Society: A Socialization Perspective." In *Normal and Abnormal Behavior in Chinese Culture*, edited by Arthur Kelinman and Tsung-yi Lin, 117–136. Dordrecht: D. Reidel Publishing Company.

Xu, Jing. 2017. *The Good Child: Moral Development in a Chinese Preschool.* Stanford, CA: Stanford University Press.

Xu, Junfang, Wang Jian, Anders Wimo, Laura Fratiglioni, and Qiu Chengxuan. 2017. "The Economic Burden of Dementia in China, 1990–2030: Implications for Health Policy." *Bulletin of the World Health Organization* 95: 18–26.

Yan, Yunxiang. 2017. "Doing Personhood in Chinese Culture: The Desiring Individual, Moralist Self and Relational Person." *Cambridge Journal of Anthropology* 35(2): 1–17.

Zhang, Mingyuan, Robert Katzman, David Salmon, Jin Hua, Cai Guojun, Wang Zhengyu, Qu Guangya, Igor Grant, Elena Yu, Paul Levy, Melville R. Klauber, and William T. Liu. 1990. "The Prevalence of Dementia and Alzheimer's Disease in Shanghai, China: Impact of Age, Gender, and Education." *Annals of Neurology* 27(4): 428–437.

Zhang, Yan. 2018. "Governing Dementia: A Historical Investigation of the Power of States and Professionals in the Conceptualization of Dementia in China." *Culture, Medicine, and Psychiatry* 42(4): 862–892.

13

Generativity, Gender, and a Good Old Age among Urban-Dwelling Older Yoruba People in Southwest Nigeria

OJO MELVIN AGUNBIADE

Cultural values, beliefs, and practices around old age affect how individuals and social groups make sense of their aging experiences (Torres and Hammarström 2009; Carver and Buchanan 2016). Across the life course, older people are socialized into expectations of growing old as a process that allows individuals to learn and unlearn what expectations are attached to chronological growth, events and relationships that are connected to the process within their sociocultural contexts. These expectations are passed from generation to generation, with some dynamics around changing values, beliefs, and normative ideologies (Fry et al. 1997). As individuals are socialized into dominant cultural expectations, discrepancies exist in conformity, along with the associated rewards and possible punishments attached to those who deviate. Within this social framing, both old and young form networks of relations in interrogating these expectations and acting for personal and collective benefits. Across the life span of individuals, the capacity to attract capital that can enhance socioeconomic status and power is variable due to structural and individual factors. These factors also account for how conformity to sociocultural standards is determined and rewarded or becomes punishable when there is a deviation.

At the superficial level, older people appear socially positioned toward exercising their rights and choices. Such perception appears factual for older people who are among the wealthy, ruling, or social elites. Many cultures in Africa, Nigeria in particular, have such common perceptions of older persons. However, the reality for most older people in Nigeria is the opposite. A few older persons are treated and appreciated with reverence, while many are prone to neglect, physical, emotional, and sexual abuse, and denial of their basic rights. The consequences of such experiences have attracted research attention. However, such research is typically done with little regard to exploring the strategies or measures older people are adopting to mitigate their vulnerability in relationships, and to enhance their aging experiences and well-being.

For example, in low-resource settings, the literature is dominated by evidence on older people's coping with poverty (Barrientos, Gorman, and Heslop 2003; Witham et al. 2019) and engagement in various means to earn a living (Witham et al. 2019; Kwan and Walsh 2018). Such research lacks the dynamic of how older people deploy their agency in structures and networks of relations to conform to societal demands and avoid consequences of noncompliance. Since the capacity to act and negotiate these pressures varies, the implications of conformity will have consequences on aging experiences and well-being.

Among many traditional societies, the challenges of growing older are rapidly increasing, especially in most Nigerian communities (Togonu-Bickersteth and Akinyemi 2014; and Howell et al., this volume). These challenges are primarily connected to socioeconomic problems, such as limited or inadequate income, and lack of formal safety nets (Tanyi, André, and Mbah 2018). Informal support networks in old age are gradually fading away due to high unemployment among adult children, dwindling opportunity to earn a decent income, and the growing spread of poverty among children and relatives who provide financial support for older adults (Togonu-Bickersteth and Akinyemi 2014). As social actors, the average older Yoruba person is beginning to understand the need to reduce their vulnerability to neglect, isolation, and abuse despite competing demands (Agunbiade 2018). Despite the implications of these developments on aging experiences and well-being, there is a scant body of evidence on how older people navigate these challenges in coping with societal expectations around growing old. Thus, this study seeks to generate contextualized evidence on cultural values, beliefs, and practices around old age and how this shapes how older people position themselves to societal expectations within the Yoruba context. The study employs a qualitative methodology to understanding this lived experience and the possible implications for aging-in-place, which entails independence, remaining and living in communities instead of elderly or nursing homes (Wiles et al. 2012).

This chapter adds to the argument on generativity, spirituality, and well-being in old age and how individual agency is deployed differently when negotiating what it means to grow old, minimize neglect, and improve well-being. Erikson (1950) defined generativity as the concern individuals have at some point in their developmental stage in establishing and guiding the next generation. This chapter proceeds with a focus on the literature on societal expectations in old age. It also highlights how the construct of generativity and social practice provides rich frameworks to understand agency and collectivity in sociocultural expectations and interpersonal relationships. The qualitative evidence that emerged was interrogated within these lenses of generativity and social practice in drawing out the possible implications on aging-in-place among the Yoruba people. The chapter concludes with a discussion of findings related to the literature and some of the limitations associated with this study.

Analytical Framework: The Notions of the Good Old Age and Generativity

Cultural expectations and individual experiences dominate what qualifies as successful or the good old age within time and space (Carver and Buchanan 2016; Torres and Hammarström 2009). With the inherent diversity in what is normative, acceptable, or personally satisfying in a good old age, there are calls for more contextual understandings of the complex dynamics of growing older and how to appropriate the dominant and marginal framing within a social setting to improve aging experiences and well-being.

For instance, expectations around old age are captured in religious framings such as the *ifa oral corpus*, daily interactions through proverbs and songs, and images of what old age entails. The aim is to promote good deeds and motivate individuals to act as exemplars as one grows chronologically in age (Abimbola 1975; see also Wang and Hughes Rinker, this volume). Thus, the expectation of this period of the life course is to end one's night in peace and with admirable deeds (Abimbola 1975; Akiwowo 1986). Despite this expectation, there are concerns that the notion of successful aging appears more like an oxymoron (Torres and Hammarström 2009). This assertion captures the complexities around the heterogeneous process of aging while demonstrating the continued need for research that can help improve intervention design to minimize aging challenges.

This study contributes to the debate by adopting generativity as postulated in the theory of human growth and development stages. As such, individuals are socialized into developing the sense to preserve specific values and practices that are considered beneficial and critical to survival for those coming behind (Peterson and Stewart 1996). Erikson postulated that individuals who end up with a sense of generativity are exemplars of progression and have attained a level of consciousness about their mortality as inevitable. Erikson explains further that the concept of generativity has close meaning with popular terms like "productivity" and "creativity," yet both terms cannot substitute for generativity (Erikson 1950, 267).

Generative concerns are acquired through a network of social relations within institutions. These interactions and structures prepare individuals to graduate from early childhood to mid-adulthood (the seventh stage of growth and development). Erikson (1950, 267) argues that individuals become mature at this stage and develop a sense of generativity toward others. He theorized that the thought of becoming generative was not inherent but acquired and dependent on the successful completion of a previous stage in the growth and development process. A core assumption in this theory is that success at performing a generative desire or goal at a previous stage creates motivation for subsequent generative endeavors. An exemplar can be found in the ways social actors sometimes invoke personal satisfaction and approval of parenting to desire and enter grandparenthood. A central thesis in the theory is that social actors intend to commit their experiences, resources, and networks in ensuring that younger or generations coming behind have a better future and more fulfilling life than what they enjoyed. Generativity motivations, goals, and practices could occur in diverse forms, but context plays an important role in shaping what acts, behaviors, activities, and practices are generative (Villar, Serrat, and Pratt 2021). It is in this latter sense that teaching, mentoring, and coaching younger generations to live better are considered common practices of generativity within the study settings. As individuals grow older, their consciousness and a sense of bequeathing critical values and resources that can help others is further nurtured and transmitted as worthy.

In expanding the construct of generativity, Rubinstein and colleagues (2014) emphasize that each social setting and space require some form of generativity from the different social actors depending on their roles and responsibilities. The awareness and variations around these expectations and practices provide rich contextual evidence that could improve our understanding of aging-in-place. Approaching how older people respond to societal pressures on what old age entails, in terms of behavior and practices, can be richly interrogated through the lens of generativity and could bridge the gaps around generativity within cultural settings.

Methods

This chapter's findings emerged from a more extensive study that was guided by a sequential exploratory mixed-method design. Reported here are the results from 12 focus group discussion sessions and 18 semi-structure individual interviews from this larger study. These qualitative components provided the opportunity to explore the notions and experiences of growing older in an urban space in Ibadan, southwest Nigeria. The group and individual interviews were conducted among older Yoruba adults (60+ years) in six communities that are predominantly occupied by older adults of the Yoruba ethnicity (Bodija, Inalende Oke-Bola, Kobiowu, Odo-Oba, Oniyere Aperin, and Sango). The six communities are all located in Ibadan metropolis and are highly congested and populated. All the participants were recruited purposively through male and female gatekeepers who are within the age range of the targeted population. All the participants were briefed on the research objectives and gave their consent before they were involved in the study. Ethical approvals were obtained from the human research ethics committees at the University of the Witwatersrand in South Africa and that of the Obafemi Awolowo University in Ile-Ife, Nigeria. Standards covering the conduct of qualitative research were followed in the recruitment procedure, data collection and analysis. The response rate was high, as most of the eligible participants agreed.

The focus group sessions with men and women were held separately and under the following age categories: 60–69, 70–79, and 80+ years. The separation of participants by gender and age aligned with cultural practices and values among the Yoruba people. Four field-trained and experienced research assistants were involved in the data collection. A total of 12 focus group sessions were held among both genders and across the three age groups in equal proportion. In total, 107 older Yoruba men and women participated in focus groups, averaging 9 males and 8 females per group.

The additional 18 individual interviews were conducted at the end of the 12 FGD sessions. All the 18 interviewees except 6 participated in the FGD sessions. The interviewees were recruited from among the focus groups. The participants who featured in the FGDs were approached to participate in the individual interviews based on their readiness to provide additional insights into their contributions or views during the group discussion. Recruitment of interviewees within the FGD participants provided an opportunity to explore further the positions and experiences that were relayed during the group discussions. It also helped in reaching out to an additional number of individuals that did not participate in the FGDs until saturation was achieved. All these steps produced fruitful responses and contributed toward building good rapport with the participants despite the sensitivity of discussing aging, sexuality, and help-seeking in the study settings. All the group discussions and individual interviews occurred at locations most preferred by the participants, such as in their own homes. Each session was audio-recorded with the consent of the participants and lasted between 57 and 125 minutes.

The qualitative analysis was conducted with a transcription of all the audio-taped discussions and interviews among all 113 participants in Yoruba language and later translated into English. Two experts in both languages did back-to-back translations of the transcripts to ensure minimal loss of expressions and meanings as used in the language of the interviews. Both inductive and deductive coding strategies were used to understand the participants' views and transform the texts into manageable forms for further analysis (Fereday and Muir-Cochrane 2006). The coding commenced with a deductive approach, which involved the development of codes from the thematic issues that were explored in the guides. Each theme consisted of questions that were directed at the participants in facilitating the discussions and interviews. Thereafter, the deductive codes were applied to the transcripts, with many of the codes modified, changed, and categorized based on the views and narratives that were expressed by the participants. The adoption of both methods in the coding enriched the sense that was made from the data. Through this hybrid approach, a thematic strategy was maintained following the suggestions by Fereday and Muir-Cochrane (2006), while the process was aided using NVivo10 for Windows.

Findings

Dimensions and Particularity of "Good Old Age"

The notion of good old age emerged from the discussions as a multidimensional reality in its categories and degrees but binary when a broad classification is applied. In its multidimensional nature, cultural values, beliefs, and individual experiences were domains for assessing whether an older person has a good life or not. For most participants, a good old age can be assessed in objective and subjective ways. Such assessments are based on impressions, experiences, and perceptions of self and the ways others perceive the life an older person is living. The assessment focuses on how the life of an older person has impacted their significant others and their communities, positive events, happenings in their life and that of their significant others, the quality of private and public comportment of such older persons, stability in health, and whether the life of an older person ended well in the form of a peaceful or good death.

The notion of peaceful death or socially preferred death in old age entails the absence of dependence on others and brief or no illness before death. These indicators were mentioned and overtly desired among the participants. For most participants, good old age and good death are interconnected realities. An individual can enjoy self-discipline, live a healthy lifestyle, contentment in life, and divine arrangements. As people who placed an overt emphasis on religious beliefs, values, and practices, it was expected that the participants across the groups shared the view that a good old age and peaceful deaths are achievable by adhering to certain life principles and religious practices. Such practices are also enshrined in wise sayings, proverbs, and myths among the Yoruba, especially those who share such sentiments. For instance, a common Yoruba proverb that was cited in focus groups among older men encapsulates the premium placed on longevity and living a life that could qualify as emulatable:

Pípe láyé lèrè ayé.
"Longevity is the reward for having lived a good life."
(Owomoyela 2005, 289)

In espousing further, the participants ranked and described three interconnected aspects of a good old age. These include healthy aging, material security, and a generative stance around their children's quality of lives and younger relatives.

Generative Traits, Spirituality, and Health in Old Age

Harmonious social relations took center stage in participants' worldview as a sure route to good health and spiritual well-being in old age. In their views, some health challenges, especially those that are medically inexplicable, could be traced to poor relations with others, envy, bitterness, and evil machinations. Therefore, being in good health requires building and sustaining harmonious relationships with others and ancestors. A life full of rancor was described as stressful and as a possible source of chronic illness, what the participants described as *amodi* (ailing, ill, or unwell). The search for solutions for amodi could start at the natural level and then a shift to the preternatural and the supernatural. Such shifts could determine the survival, recovery, and reintegration of the individual with such an experience. In the focus groups among men from the Inalende community, there was a critical focus on how bitterness and rifts among close people could increase vulnerability to inexplicable health conditions. The argument was that generative concerns toward others are an indispensable virtue of ensuring quality social relationships and improving those coming behind and around them for a better future and good health in old age.

While extending the social relevance of good morals and quality interpersonal relations, the participants affirmed that the fear of God could also promote good health in old age. Their explanation of this position rested on religious beliefs and social expectations. According to most Yorubas, some individuals are endowed with the privilege of enjoying good health based on their inner *ore* (head) in predestination (Jegede 2002). The belief is that individuals are made with good inner heads before sojourning to Earth. However, at a point before conception, there is an opportunity to select the type of inner head by choice. Some will select the good one, which is difficult for the enemy to conquer, including ill health as an enemy. For others, their destiny will attract a bad inner head. Upon arrival into this world, steps must be made to investigate the kind of inner head selected at the place of destiny. Whatever the outcome, the belief is that through sacrifice and prayers, the type of inner head selected can be modified. On this, the focus group participants again stated the benefits of seeking the good of others and actively working toward making their lives better now and for the future. For most of the participants, each person must be committed to such virtues and be willing to take responsibility for their health and the associated consequences of deviating.

The participants expressed the view that becoming generative and committed to others' betterment requires some level of adherence to spiritual principles as laid down in their various religious beliefs and practices. Through sacrifice, prayers, and moderation in lifestyle, an individual may become more generative in old age as reverence for God and truthfulness become more straightforward to practice than when they were much younger. Most of the participants indicated that not all older people are generative and concerned about the betterment of those coming behind. Instead, it is through higher spirituality and the inevitability of death where such virtues are cultivated. Part of the process is through religiosity or participation in religious activities:

> It is common to see many elderly people going to church and mosque. They are there to pray for good health and peaceful old age. It is normative to commit yourself to prayers, make sacrifices, enjoy good health in old age [focus group with men aged 80+ years, Oniyere Community].

The emphasis on morality and belief in spirituality was expected, as all participants expressed deep belief in the benefits associated with following spiritual principles. To live in peace with others opens the door for mercy and divine protection from all evils. As observed by some of the focus group participants, such efforts would guarantee a long life for one's children and their protection from everyday evil. Some participants also believed that through living in peace with others, diseases and illnesses that are medically inexplicable or untreatable would not afflict them, as captured below:

> Some individuals have good and strong heads, and such people would enjoy good health and see less evil in life. However, this world's wicked people could make life miserable, except there are interventions through prayers, sacrifice and almsgiving, and good relationship with God. [interview with a male spiritualist aged 74]
>
> Many bad things will happen, including health challenges, when individuals prefer to do things their way. The fear of God protects against strange diseases and untreatable conditions that could drain your income and make your life difficult. [focus group with men aged 70–79, Odo Oba community]

Among this group of participants, the increasing occurrence of medically inexplicable health conditions could be a divine way of forcing humanity to acknowledge God's supremacy and keep spiritual laws. Violations of spiritual laws and flagrant disregard for God bring inexplicable conditions that can make life miserable, especially in old age. As a way out, adherence to religious beliefs and practices, fear of God, and constant prayers are trustworthy measures.

A common prayer that captures one of the critical expectations in old age is to pray against becoming an *agba inira*. Agba inira represents a situation when an individual lives in a socially defined stage and is accepted as old, but with a series of challenges that make the period miserable. Agba inira also includes the occurrence of mysterious or untimely deaths of children or grandchildren, loss of property to natural or human-originated events, and poverty. Thus, old age remains a period to appraise and focus energies on measures that could avert becoming an agba inira, especially for one's children or relatives. The notion of agba inira was tied to generativity and concerns for the well-being of foster and biological children, and other significant others that can reflect societal assessments of a good old age. The more successful and better placed the children around an older person, the higher the chances of earning the label *ojo ale tio dara* (the good old age). More emphasis was placed on this notion, as the participants described the pains of seeing their loved ones in poor condition, which sometimes impacts their well-being and vulnerability to ill health in old age.

Well-Being of Children and Family Members

> *Eetán lelégbè ẹyin; ọmọ bíbí inú ẹni lelégbè ẹni.*
> "Young palm fruits support ripe ones; one's children are one's support." (Owomoyela 2005, 304)

The cultural belief is that children are social investments that should start yielding returns in old age. This social hope for support is normative and cherished. The participants discussed the values and relevance of having successful children. This position was articulated in different ways among the focus group participants:

> A man must live long and not die when his children are young. Once this prayer is answered, he will aspire to bring up his children well, sit back and expect his children to take care of him in old age. [focus group with men aged 70–79 years, Sango Community]

Through socialization and cultural expectations, the exemplary mother and father must exhibit unconditional support and desire for their children and relatives' well-being. However, the core responsibility of being there for one's children belongs more to mothers than fathers. In marriage, Yoruba women are culturally expected to provide diverse forms of care to their husbands, relatives, and children, in particular. These include caring and providing physical, emotional, and spiritual support to ensure the well-being and survival to adulthood. In this generative behavior, parents (especially mothers) have acted responsibly by providing emotional and material support for their children while growing up. Thus, the notion of motherhood among the Yoruba people entails sacrificing personal privileges and rights for the well-being of others, children in particular:

> The focused type of woman would know that she must not just be a mother, but a caring mother (Obinrin ti o ni idojuko yii yoo mọ pe ko gbọdọ jẹ iya nikan, ṣugbọn iya ti o ni abojuto). There is a difference between a mother and a caring mother. *Iya* [a mother] is the woman that can give birth, but *abiyamọ* [motherhood] will not stop at that, she will always be concerned with what children will eat, she will guide them, and she will not only depend on the husband to care/provide for the children but rather be hardworking. You know a wise saying is that only the lazy one can be made to suffer. [focus group with women aged 70–79 years, Sango Community]

Support and generativity of this nature are valued as signs of good motherhood in the Yoruba culture. The provision of such care and support extends to spiritual issues. The consciousness of this social responsibility can be seen in Christianity, Islam, or the traditional Yoruba religion. Prayers and making sacrifices are part of the exemplary forms of support from mothers to their children:

> Mothers are at the center of receiving all the blame when things go wrong with their children. The expectation is that a true mother must go the extra mile to save her child(ren), especially when they are in need, even as grown-up adults. [interview with a 61-year-old woman, Bodija Community]
>
> I, I always pray whatever would happen to my children should happen to me and not them. [focus group with women aged 80+ years, Inalende Community]

Playing the sacrificial role of *abiyamọ* comes with the social expectation of reciprocal care and support from one's children. Such reciprocity is much expected in the advanced period of life, when the physical strength to work and earn a living has dwindled. Through wise sayings, proverbs, and religious teachings (Christianity, Islam, and traditional Yoruba religion), especially in wedding ceremonies and the media, children are reminded of the blessings in reciprocating good motherhood gestures. Across the various focus groups, this expectation was widely shared:

> What is essential is that the children are to be taking care of us, and we will pray for them. A good elderly person will pray for the children, those who are not his or her own, and the neighbors. [focus group with women aged 60–69 years, Bodija Community]

The focus group participants at diverse points lamented the dwindling quality of financial and non-financial support from children. This development was described as disheartening and a likely source of hopelessness for middle-aged adults to live with in older age. In the participants' views, the willingness to fulfill this social obligation still exists, but many adult children are at a disadvantage. Despite the rewards and cultural value of such reciprocity, both parents and children are confronted with different challenges in meeting these obligations and expectations (Adeniyi-Ogunyankin 2012). Larger socioeconomic and political challenges were described as inhibitors and motivators in the sustainability of financially supporting aged parents. Illustrating a demoralizing development, a male focus group participant asked a provocative question about whether becoming old was a reward or a punishment:

> We desire social security for older people. Alternatively, is it a sin to be an elderly person? Why can't the government find social security policies to support the elderly in Nigeria? [focus group with men aged 80+, Oniyere Community]

The rationale for asking the question was clearly understood and expected. The perception might have been influenced by systemic failures in Nigeria and the absence of any concrete strategy for a focused improvement in the quality of life. The average older person that survives the low life expectancy in Nigeria is prone to poor health due to the non-availability of formal support and health insurance for the aged (Adeniyi-Ogunyankin 2012; Togonu-Bickersteth and Akinyemi 2014). This leaves the burden of care and financial responsibilities for accessing health-care services on children and other significant others. What, then, becomes the fate of those without children or with children who are financially incapacitated? The narratives of some participants with supportive children pointed to some possibilities:

> My children have tried, the good Lord will continue to bless them and prosper their ways. I would have been dead by now if not for their support. [interview with a 65-year-old woman, Sango community]
>
> My husband, who was active some years ago, has been dependent on me. I cannot go out for long because he is on medication. No house help; I do almost everything to support him. [interview with a 73-year-old woman, Inalende Oke-Bola community]

Social neglect and marginalization have ripple effects on aging experiences. First, there are possible physical health effects on the older adults themselves. Second, their anxiety over their inability to maintain a healthy aging experience might increase. Some participants lamented the government's unpreparedness and paying lip service to addressing older adults' plight in Nigeria. In the words of an 83-year-old participant, the government has failed them in several ways:

> While I am not waiting for them to eat or drink, I wonder what the sins of the elderly in Nigeria . . . are. There are no plans whatsoever and the art of politics and deceit of the electorate dominate Nigerian politics at different levels. When will there be policies to assist old and older people in coping with health challenges that come with age, feeding, and shelter? When will this come? [focus group with men aged 80+, Oniyere community]

The provision and footing of health bills rest on children, family members, and, in some cases, religious bodies. Total dependence on others, fending for oneself, and poverty are also probable sources of loss of hope for living. Such conditions would only amount to what the participants described earlier as *agba inira*. The emotional challenges of neglect and loneliness in old age could compound individual assessments of their aging as agba inira. This can also increase the likely occurrence of suicidal thoughts and intentions as well as psychological disorders like depression.

Some participants expressed sympathy with their significant others over their daily struggles in supporting them. The increasing difficulty that children, family members, and neighbors experience in providing for their dependents affects the type and quality of support accessible to older adults, depending on such sources. Against this background, some of the focus group participants lamented the increasing difficulty of enjoying old age. These challenges complicate aging for participants who described the difficulties of negotiating an aging experience that is far from agba inira.

The notion of agba inira centers on life events and challenges that make old age a miserable period in an individual's life. Socioeconomic challenges and an inadequate or lack of quality social support can negatively influence aging experiences. Furthermore, the interplay of personal, biological, preternatural, and supernatural forces can also increase the chances of going through a miserable aging experience. Whatever the perceived source(s), reliance on plural and concerted holistic efforts was considered effective in minimizing the possible effects on well-being and anxiety as outcomes in old age.

From the participants' perspectives, the adoption of holistic approaches will produce needed relief and succor when they are confronted with challenges that could make aging a stage of agba inira. In consonance with previous views, a holistic strategy requires moderation, a healthy lifestyle, and harmonious relations with neighbors and God. Good morals before and in old age are seen as fundamental to creating situations that could make life in old age exciting and fulfilling. Possession of such standards provides a social advantage, authority, and boldness to engage in constructive interrogation and appropriation of specific strategies despite challenges and events in life. Such virtues also allow individuals to experience relatively harmonious interactions and relations with humans and the spirit world. Departure from these standards could compromise and expose individuals to events capable of making old age experiences miserable and full of *inira* (pain/misery).

According to the participants, the bottom line is building a network of relations that could provide the needed support in old age. Such networks also increase older people's relevance as they are positioned to provide support, including material support for those around them, especially their children. A burning desire among some participants is the opportunity to leave a material inheritance for their children. The belief is that challenges and events that could make old age miserable and become agba inira are linked to the quality and quantity of social relations in realms of existence. The challenges of surviving independently with frail bodies could create further stress in old age.

To avert these possibilities, the participants emphasized self-reflection and appraisals that would improve personal commitment to the social correctness of a good old age. The gendered responsibility of praying for children and other family members was expressed more often among the female participants. This is consistent with cultural values and practices that position women as caregivers by providing support, especially in emotional terms, for their households and relatives. The well-being of women often suffers as they struggle to fulfill these social obligations (Courtenay 2000). Nevertheless, the aim is to increase the cultural and social capital that comes with old age and capitalize on increasing social support and acceptance. Through this process, rights and privileges are sacrificed despite the possible effects on personal well-being and self-esteem in old age.

Discussion

Aging experiences are shaped by contexts, prevailing beliefs, values, and practices. There are debates on what informs how older people negotiate and interpret the aging process as well as the possible implications for their willingness to maintain social relevance (Breheny and Griffiths 2017; Cruikshank 2013). This study affirms that older people have the capacity to maintain social relevance within their social settings. The consciousness to remain relevant was high especially through conformity and concerns toward younger or upcoming generations. The acceptance and conformity to the social dictates that come with old age and aging would differ within and across social settings as well as among social categories (Cruikshank 2013). In this direction, the findings revealed how age-grade expectations create exemplars for elderly men and women to measure their moral correctness to a good old age. Their interpretations showed that old age could be desirable or miserable, depending on a variety of factors. To avoid the possibility of going through miserable aging, the findings revealed that efforts are needed to measure up to cultural exemplars cumulatively that could ensure the avoidance of agba inira. Against this backdrop, the participants described an exemplary elder from a three-dimensional position that prescribes moral correctness as a requisite to good old age.

From an age-grade lens, an exemplary elder would first be someone with the social consciousness of what is culturally required and expected within a given time. As a mortal being, an older adult is fallible amid life challenges. Nonetheless, such challenges are fluid and should be handled dynamically and reflect the lessons learned in their relations with others. Individuals possess different abilities to navigate life challenges, and no consensus on conformity was presumed. Individuals conform differently to the moral correctness of an elder within their network of relations in a given social setting. Failure and inability to attain moral correctness is excusable when individuals can distill the challenges and draw out some lessons throughout their life spans. Older adults that have successfully learned through the process would likely enjoy quality interpersonal relations with others. In the Yoruba belief system, it is crucial to have harmonious interactions with others, including neighbors, relatives, and ancestors. These are social markers of a good old age in addition to having successful children and grandchildren (Togunu-Bickersteth 1988).

As a continuum, these experiences and processes have a cumulative effect on health, whether physical, mental, emotional, or spiritual. The findings support a holistic view of health and its social dimensionality, especially in interpersonal relations. The participants noted that health challenges are inevitable in old age. However, certain health conditions, especially those that are inexplicable from a traditional medical framework, are viewed as punishment for living outside the exemplary framework. This mode of explanation is consistent with the Yoruba etiological belief in preternatural sources, which include evil machinations and envy (Jegede 2002). Furthermore, the belief that old age also improves spiritual knowledge and possession of strange powers resonates the cultural interpretations of disease etiology and health. The possession of spiritual powers in old age differs among individuals; nonetheless, the social expectation is that the exemplary elders must engage in spiritual activities by seeking help from those who have the powers, making sacrifices and praying for their children's well-being and peace in the community.

Despite the variations in cultural beliefs and practices around aging and exemplary behaviors, studies among Alaska Native Elders in the United States. Studies have revealed how the cultural value of measuring up to the moral correctness of being an "Elder" brings psychosocial satisfaction and social capital in old age (Lewis and Allen 2017; see Howell et al., this volume). The literature demonstrates such common cultural beliefs across various traditional societies regarding the importance of generativity as well as the rewards associated with the provision of care and support for elders. Studies have shown how family members have continued to provide such supports despite the growing burden of providing informal care for older adults (Gupta 2009; del-Pino-Casado, Frías-Osuna, and Palomino-Moral 2011; Brinda et al. 2014; Uwakwe et al. 2009). Among the Yoruba people, the acceptability of this belief revolves around the presumed blessings, which might outweigh the cost (Adeniyi-Ogunyankin 2012). The sanctity of this belief is enshrined in all three main religions (Christianity, Islam, and traditional Yoruba religion) among the Yoruba people (Balogun 2011; Togunu-Bickersteth 1988).

Overall, the presumption was that conformity to the moral correctness that is expected of older adults would minimize the possibility of experiencing agba inira, which includes peaceful death and the well-being of significant others. There are close similarities with the emphasis placed on health by the participants in the study by Fry and colleagues (1997). In this study, the participants portrayed health as a continuum; therefore, individuals play vital roles in their subjective and objective well-being across their life span. A sense of responsibility of the impact of lifestyle and choices on health outcomes aligns with gerontology's life course approach. The literature in this direction affirms a consensus that the intersection of factors across individuals' life span and social categories jointly accounts for the variations in individuals' quality and health status from one stage of growth and development to another (Marengoni et al. 2011).

References

Abimbola, W. 1975. "Iwapele: The Concept of Good Character in Ifa Literary Corpus." In *Yoruba Oral Tradition*, edited by W. Abimbola, 389–420. Ile-Ife: Department of African Languages and Literature University of Ife.

Adeniyi-Ogunyankin, Grace. 2012. "'When Will I Get My Rest?' Neo-liberalism, Women, Class and Ageing in Ibadan, Nigeria." *Agenda* 26(4): 29–36.

Agunbiade, O. M. 2018. "Explanations around Physical Abuse, Neglect and Preventive Strategies among Older Yoruba People (60+) in Urban Ibadan Southwest Nigeria." MSc, Faculty of Social Sciences, Gerontology Unit, University of Southampton.

Akiwowo, A. A. 1986. "Contributions to the Sociology of Knowledge from an African Oral Poetry." *International Sociology* 1(4): 343–358.

Balogun, Muhsin Adekunle. 2011. "Syncretic Beliefs and Practices amongst Muslims in Lagos State Nigeria; With Special Reference to the Yoruba Speaking People of Epe." PhD diss., University of Birmingham.

Breheny, Mary, and Zoë Griffiths. 2017. "'I Had a Good Time When I Was Young': Interpreting Descriptions of Continuity among Older People." *Journal of Aging Studies* 41: 36–43.

Brinda, Ethel M., Anto P. Rajkumar, Ulrika Enemark, Jørn Attermann, and K. S. Jacob. 2014. "Cost and Burden of Informal Caregiving of Dependent Older People in a Rural Indian Community." *BMC Health Services Research* 14(1): 207.

Carver, Lisa F., and Diane Buchanan. 2016. "Successful Aging: Considering Non-Biomedical Constructs." *Clinical Interventions in Aging* 11: 1623.

Courtenay, Will H. 2000. "Constructions of Masculinity and Their Influence on Men's Well-Being: A Theory of Gender and Health." *Social Science & Medicine* 50(10): 1385–1401.

Cruikshank, Margaret. 2013. *Learning to Be Old: Gender, Culture, and Aging*. New York: Rowman & Littlefield Publishers.

del-Pino-Casado, Rafael, Antonio Frías-Osuna, and Pedro A. Palomino-Moral. 2011. "Subjective Burden and Cultural Motives for Caregiving in Informal Caregivers of Older People." *Journal of Nursing Scholarship* 43(3): 282–291.

Erikson, Erik H. 1950. *Childhood and Society*. New York: W.W. Norton & Company.

Fereday, Jennifer, and Eimear Muir-Cochrane. 2006. "Demonstrating Rigor Using Thematic Analysis: A Hybrid Approach of Inductive and Deductive Coding and Theme Development." *International Journal of Qualitative Methods* 5(1): 80–92.

Gupta, Rashmi. 2009. "Systems Perspective: Understanding Care Giving of the Elderly in India." *Health Care for Women International* 30(12): 1040–1054.

Jegede, Ayodele Samuel. 2002. "The Yoruba Cultural Construction of Health and Illness." *Nordic Journal of African Studies* 11(3): 14.

Lewis, J. P., and J. Allen. 2017. "Alaska Native Elders in Recovery: Linkages between Indigenous Cultural Generativity and Sobriety to Promote Successful Aging." *Journal of Cross-Cultural Gerontology* 32(2): 209–222. https://doi.org/10.1007/s10823-017-9314-8.

Marengoni, Alessandra, Sara Angleman, René Melis, Francesca Mangialasche, Anita Karp, Annika Garmen, Bettina Meinow, and Laura Fratiglioni. 2011. "Aging with Multimorbidity: A Systematic Review of the Literature." *Ageing Research Reviews* 10(4): 430–439.

Owomoyela, Oyekan. 2005. *Yoruba Proverbs*. Lincoln: University of Nebraska Press.

Peterson, Bill E., and Abigail J. Stewart. 1996. "Antecedents and Contexts of Generativity Motivation at Midlife." *Psychology and Aging* 11(1): 21.

Rubinstein, Robert L., Laura M. Girling, Kate De Medeiros, Michael Brazda, and Susan Hannum. 2014. "Extending the Framework of Generativity Theory through Research: A Qualitative Study." *The Gerontologist* 55(4): 548–559.

Tanyi, Perpetua Lum, Pelser André, and Peter Mbah. 2018. "Care of the Elderly in Nigeria: Implications for Policy." *Cogent Social Sciences* 4(1): 1555201. https://doi.org/10.1080/23311886.2018.1555201.

Togunu-Bickersteth, Funmi. 1988. "Perception of Old Age among Yoruba Aged." *Journal of Comparative Family Studies*: 113–122.

Togonu-Bickersteth, Funmi, and Akanni Ibukun Akinyemi. 2014. "Ageing and National Development in Nigeria: Costly Assumptions and Challenges for the Future." *African Population Studies* 27(2): 361–371.

Torres, Sandra, and Gunhild Hammarström. 2009. "Successful Aging as an Oxymoron." *International Journal of Ageing and Later Life* 4(1): 23–54.

Uwakwe, Richard, Christian C. Ibeh, Anne Ifeoma Modebe, Emeka Bo, Nkiru Ezeama, Ifeoma Njelita, Cleusa P. Ferri, and Martin J. Prince. 2009. "The Epidemiology of Dependence in Older People in Nigeria: Prevalence, Determinants, Informal Care, and Health Service Utilization. A 10/66 Dementia Research Group Cross-Sectional Survey." *Journal of the American Geriatrics Society* 57(9): 1620–1627.

Villar, F., R. Serrat, and M. W. Pratt. 2021. "Older Age as a Time to Contribute: A Scoping Review of Generativity in Later Life." *Ageing and Society*: 1–22. doi:10.1017/S0144686x21001379.

Wiles, J. L., A. Leibing, N. Guberman, J. Reeve, and R. E. Allen. 2012. "The Meaning of 'Aging in Place' to Older People." *The Gerontologist* 52(3): 357–366.

Anthropological Theory and Methods for Researching Aging

14

Conceptualizing Frailty in the Quick and the Dead

DOUGLAS E. CREWS AND KATHRYN E. MARKLEIN

Among the living, frailty is identified as a set of observable characteristics (phenotypes) of individual physical limitations and declines in function and capabilities (Fried et al. 2001; Rockwood et al. 2005; Searle et al. 2008; Studenski et al. 2004; Walston and Bandeen-Roche 2015). In medical and congregate residential settings, frailty assessments aid in determining needs for physical care and support, special aid or accommodations, and surgical procedures. In gerontology, geriatrics, and human biology, frailty is assessed using clinical and physical measurements such as assessments of strength, mobility, endurance, and mental state. Among the living, frailty indices assess individual physiological and sociocultural competencies (Rockwood, Mogilner, and Mitnitski 2004; Studenski et al. 2004; Walston et al. 2019). Although these methods do not apply directly to the dead, the concepts do.

Medicine, elder care, and bioarchaeology share conceptualizations of frailty. However, given their populations of interest, each has different disciplinary perspectives, definitions, and techniques for assessing frailty. In gerontology and geriatrics, frailty is a measurable phenotype, reflecting *lifelong* outcomes of an individual's phenotype interacting with stressors in their physical and sociocultural environments promoting declines in physical capabilities. Across populations, assessed frailty increases with age, leading to the highest frequency of frailty occurring in older age groups, particularly those aged 70+ years (Crews 2005, 2022; Crews and Zavotka 2006; Kim and Jazwinski 2015; Rockwood et al. 2005; Walston 2005).

Within bioarchaeology, frailty has been variably defined as less resistance to lifetime stressors and consequent increased risk of mortality (DeWitte and Wood 2008; Usher 2000), and as a physiological state of skeletal debility relative to the rest of the adult population (Marklein and Crews

2017; Marklein, Leahy, and Crews 2016). Despite disparities between definitions in bioarchaeology and among living populations, their conceptualizations address complementary aspects within the paradox of skeletal markers. While skeletal lesions indicate a biological marker (biomarker) of stress and wear and tear on the body, osteological lesions, by virtue of the individual having survived long enough to demonstrate evidence of healing, evoke resilience and survival from a stressor (Wood et al. 1992). This paradox is further complicated by non-representativeness of the samples (i.e., outside of mass fatality episodes, such as the eruption of Mt. Vesuvius [79 CE], most skeletal samples are not fully representative of the living population) and by skeletal preservation and recovery (e.g., burial customs and environmental variables may lead to incomplete, fragmentary, or commingled skeletons).

Thus, bioarchaeologists are limited to comparing true or crude prevalence rates of specific markers on recovered skeletal materials. Consequently, frailty assessments within and between cemeteries, by sex, socioeconomic, or age group, are based on individual skeletal traits (biomarkers) and possibly non-representative samples. This poses an interpretive dilemma, as frailty is a whole-body process assessed in the living using biomarkers of function and capabilities such as muscle and bone loss (e.g., strength), physical abilities (e.g., endurance), mobility (e.g., walking speed), physical activity, and physiological resilience (e.g., retention of body mass) (Crews 2005; Fried et al. 2001, 2005; Rockwood et al. 2005; Walston 2005). Whether in the quick or the dead, individual frailty cannot be assessed by any single physiological biomarker, somatic measurement, or skeletal trait. As a result, bioarchaeologists have developed alternative methods for observing similar declines in the long dead based on skeletal indicators of frailty (Marklein, Leahy, and Crews 2016).

Among the dead, skeletal frailty estimates rely on presence and severity of pathological conditions initiated by stressors (e.g., infections, malnutrition), injuries incurred and survived during life, or degenerative processes. These biomarkers represent stressors sufficiently severe to imprint the skeleton without immediate fatal consequences. Thus, pathological skeletal lesions and conditions, including signs of poor growth, damage, infections, injuries, and trauma, reveal a complex narrative about the decedent's physiological health, frailty, and resilience during life. This narrative is further complicated by hidden heterogeneity, individual susceptibilities and resistances to social, environmental, and epidemiologic insults that are difficult to assess in archaeological samples. Today, those who live longest show greater phenotypic frailty as age increases, while those dying at younger ages may show little frailty. This paradox highlights the complicated interaction between resilience and frailty: phenotypic frailty increases with age, increasing physiological and biological dysfunction, but nevertheless individuals also display resilience to acute and chronic stressors.

Here, we review frailty as applied to modern and past populations, documenting differences in biomedical and bioarchaeological conceptualizations, as well as common ground. Ultimately, this conceptual review proposes a common model for assessing frailty in the quick and the dead; culminating in an application to a medieval London subsample archived and assessed at the Museum of London's Center for Human Bioarchaeology and included in their Wellcome Osteological Research Database (WORD, 2020); and utilizes this multiple-perspective approach to frailty among the dead. First, we explore how frailty among the living is based on declining physiological function that limits individual abilities to interface with the environment, halt accumulating stressor-related damage, and maintain strength and mobility. Next, we review bioarchaeological applications of frailty to skeletons, comparing similarities to and differences in conceptualizing frailty in the living. Indicators of frailty observed among the living likely also hampered past populations. Thus, identifiable skeletal indicators in past populations may be interpreted as reflecting sociocultural, ecological, and epidemiological contexts similar to those observed among present populations. Consequently, we apply a human ecology theoretical framework to evaluating frailty in the past and present, while acknowledging individuals and communities varied in their expression of frailty according to their specific biological backgrounds, social structures, and environmental settings. Gerontological models of frailty state that people adapt to their local settings not through evolutionarily processes alone but also by lifelong accommodations and phenotypic adjustments to their lived environments (Crews 2022). Similarly, bioarchaeological theory and research interpret skeletonized biomarkers as accumulated responses and adaptations to environmental stressors during life.

Frailty in the Living

Over the human life span, one experiences multiple imperceptible everyday annoyances along with frequent mild, severe, and sometimes life-threatening stressor encounters. Even *in utero*, growth and development of our tissues, teeth, and bones respond to stressors experienced by our mothers such as malnutrition, lifestyle and social settings, oxygen intake, trauma, and more (Barker 1992; Barker et al. 2009; Kuzawa 2005). Regardless of how short one's life is, in stressful settings those who survive to early childhood already may show signs of frailty: poor bone and somatic growth, shorter stature, and health issues. Today, worldwide, most people live past their seventh decade, as likely did some proportion of past populations. As people age, indicators of frailty increase in scope, severity, and prevalence. Before entering the seventh decade, everyone experiences multiple stressors and related somatic damages, progressive loss of muscle and bone cells, as well as reduced physiological and sensory function. Some individual aspects of frailty likely were initiated prenatally, during infancy, childhood, and even during one's parents' and grandparents' lives (Kuzawa 2005; Barker 1992). Stressors during early life (e.g., malnutrition, mental/physical abuse, restricted physical activity, congenital conditions, neglect) may impact skeletal growth, development, height, bone density, or organ size. Stressors also may permanently imprint on neurological structures, specifically the amygdala, hippocampus, and hypothalamus. During their second and third decades of life, humans attain maximum phenotypic capabilities and somatic stability. Unfortunately, we maintain this peak function through only four decades or so. With increasing age, cellular senescence and losses reduce function and resilience of our tissues, organs, and sensory systems. As cellular losses and malfunctions progress, our mobility and cognitive, physical, and task-performance abilities are hampered, contributing to frailty (Crews 2005, 2022; Walston 2005).

Among the living, frailty indices were developed in clinical and patient care settings as biomedical inventories documenting physical ability and performance declines (Fried et al. 2001; Searle et al. 2008; Walston et al. 2019). Fried and colleagues (2005) illustrate the physiological basis for human frailty as an example of evolutionary inertia, identifying frailty as a clinical syndrome/phenotype and operationalizing a frailty index. Their original index (Fried et al. 2001), includes recent unintentional weight loss of ten-plus pounds, slow walking speed, and self-reported exhaustion, weakness, and low physical activity. Since this first index, multiple frailty indices, many quite complex, have been developed for medical care, clinical, and community research. These indices determine capabilities among seniors and people with disabilities, along with their needs for housing, support, hospitalization, and long-term care (see Crews 2022).

For example, Studenski and colleagues (2004) introduced an index covering multiple domains: mobility, balance, strength, endurance, nutrition, neuromotor performance, medical complexity, health-care utilization, appearance, self-perceived health, activities of daily living (ADLs), emotional and social statuses. Later, Rockwood and colleagues (2005) reported a seven-level Global Clinical Frailty Scale ranging from robust health to complete functional dependence. Their frailty categorizations were based on physician reviews of medical histories, clinical records, comorbidities, functional capabilities, and a 70-item assessment of frailty. Both predicted risks for death and institutionalization, but the clinical index was a more accurate predictor (Rockwood et al. 2005). Among the living, frailty indices provide clinically recognizable and valid assessments of current functional abilities and risk for institutionalization and mortality. Assessed sequentially, frailty indices document alterations in functional abilities. In aggregate, frailty indices estimate variability by age and sex, across age groups, occupations, workloads, environmental stressors, cultural settings, activity levels, diets, and other experiences. Across populations, frailty is identified as a whole-body, age-related phenotype of limited functional ability affecting all who survive sufficiently long.

As age increases, wear and tear, muscle (sarcopenia) and bone loss (osteoporosis), and injury/trauma compromise human mobility. Among the quick, reduced strength, altered gait, poor posture, falls, and reduced physical activity are observed (Rockwood et al. 2005). Factors underlying frailty are not always obvious nor do they always alter the bones of those afflicted. Among the living, not only seniors but also people with physical limitations as well as those with congenital issues and injuries may show high frailty. Today, frailty is generally attributed to declining physical abilities and increasing injuries and disabilities that limit mobility and abilities to interact with both natural and built environments (Crews 2005, 2022; Kim and Jazwinski 2015; Walston et al. 2019).

Why Study Frailty in the Living?

In the living, multiple composite indicators of functional capabilities and physiological biomarkers are associated with current health and risks for disease, institutionalization, and death: ADLs (Katz 1963), biological age (Damon 1975), the cumulative burden of chronic stress (allostatic load)

(Seeman et al. 1997; Sterling and Eyer 1988), and frailty (Fried et al. 2001, 2004; Rockwood et al. 2005; Studenski et al. 2004). Theoretically, these indices reflect patterns of age-related physiological and functional declines secondary to basic human biology and environmental stressors. They integrate a complex array of biomarkers of systemic and somatic declines, stressor damage, and individual phenotypic variability into a single measure of functional well-being. Practically, they are estimates of preclinical and clinical dysfunction underlying current and future health, frailty, morbidity, and mortality (Arbeev et al. 2019; Fried et al. 2001; Kim and Jazwinski 2015; Rockwood et al. 2005).

In the living, frailty is a specific phenotype: weakness, exhaustion, low resilience, reduced physical activity and mobility. It primarily reflects sarcopenia, osteoporosis, and its pre-condition osteopenia (Fried et al. 2001, 2004; Kim and Jazwinski 2015; Studenski et al. 2004; Walston 2005). As a clinical syndrome, frailty reflects genetic, personal, environmental, and sociocultural variation. This is not an adaptive response. Rather, frailty represents losses accumulated over time reflecting functional declines. For example, muscle loss with age reflects underlying cellular senescence, and grip strength (a biomarker for frailty) decreases significantly with age and is associated with disability across populations (Giampaoli et al. 1999). A variety of frailty indices assess late-life phenotypic losses in the quick. While most indices include both losses and declines (e.g., strength, exhaustion), we cannot determine these among the dead.

Frailty in the Dead

Most bioarchaeological research represents frailty as increasing risk of mortality, predicated on individual health and hidden heterogeneity in response to stress and disease (DeWitte and Wood 2008; Usher 2000; Wood et al. 1992). Operationalizing frailty as increased mortality risk has the advantage of analyzing frailty at population-specific levels while considering the osteological paradox (DeWitte et al. 2008, 2010, 2020; Usher 2000; Vaupel et al. 1979). The osteological paradox complicates skeletal research but must be considered in any research design or data interpretation. Wood and colleagues (1992), expanding upon previously posed paleodemographic concerns (Bocquet-Appel and Masset 1982), outline limitations of using skeletal assemblages when determining population structure and vital statistics. Obviously, most skeletal assemblages do not fully represent their populations of origin, nor do they exactly reflect changing population demographics over time or patterns of chronic, degenerative, parasitic, and infectious diseases among members during their lives. In general, interred individuals represent the least resilient members of society, excepting those who passed under untimely, unexpected circumstances (e.g., mass disaster, accidents, homicide, etc.). Additionally, even within a full and dated cemetery, many skeletal remains are incomplete, and recovery is biased by burial type, age, and susceptibility to decay.

Another dilemma related to paleodemography and paleoepidemiology is the occurrence of skeletal lesions. Although skeletal lesions evoke pathological processes, they also demonstrate an active immunological response. Consequently, the presence of a skeletal lesion suggests greater immunocompetency compared to a counterpart skeleton without lesions, who apparently perished before mounting an adequate immune response to survive. Modern recovery methods, evolving theoretical perspectives, and improved statistical methods for mitigating inconsistencies and data issues when examining ancient, often fragmented, skeletal remains have benefited bioarchaeological research (DeWitte and Stojanowski 2015; DeWitte and Wood 2008).

When examining skeletal materials, bioarchaeologists have favored a mortality-based approach to frailty based on hazard models and survivorship analyses to address the osteological paradox. These approaches evaluate likely impacts of bony lesions on survival, while recognizing presence, absence, or severity of lesions may reflect degrees of frailty (increased risk of mortality) and resilience (longer life spans) (DeWitte 2014). One potential limitation of this operationalization is that estimates of skeletal frailty are not directly related to present-day clinical concepts of frailty. For example, "increased risk of mortality" is not a directly viewable diagnosis, whereas "frailty phenotype" is both observable and measurable in the quick and the dead. Therefore, any frailty phenotype for the dead cannot provide a one-to-one comparison with the living. However, by applying current clinical, biomedical, and human biology theory and methods for assessing frailty in the quick to the skeletonized, an alternative but complementary frailty index may be estimated for bioarchaeology and compared to age-based mortality risk estimates. This research into frailty echoes recent calls in bioarchaeology to integrate and incorporate concepts and models from within and without bioanthropology into skeletal studies (Temple and Goodman 2014).

Regardless of age, proper skeletal function and biomechanical stability promote mobility, which in turn promotes sociality, physical activity, health, and survival. Skeletal and muscle cells are integral to health, immune response, calcium and potassium balance, and mineral storage, so damage to or deterioration of these cells contributes to frailty. Mobility, a biomarker of frailty, depends on neurological, physiological, and functional integration across somatic structures to maintain gait, balance, and agility. Wear and tear, cellular losses, accidents, injuries, and fractures damage our bones, weaken skeletal structural integrity, and limit mobility, increasing frailty and reducing physical activity. By altering gait and posture, bone loss and sarcopenia reduce balance, agility, and physical activity, contributing to knee and back pain, osteoarthritis, and fractured vertebra. Spinal degeneration also impinges balance, gait, and mobility. While these frailty biomarkers are directly evidenced in the skeletal record as fractures, osteoarthritis, and osteoporosis/osteopenia, many other pathological conditions may be gleaned from the skeleton.

Fortunately for bioarchaeologists, unfortunately for decedents, when sufficiently severe or untreated, multiple physical and physiological stressors alter bone and surrounding tissues. For example, pathogens from exposed wounds or cuts or bacteria from the body's own microbiome may generate bone responses when not medically treated (see Melby et al., this volume; Roberts and Buikstra 2019). Malnutrition contributes to risk for frailty, morbidity, and mortality among the living (Meyyazhagan and Palmer 2002), and skeletal tissues may show permanent impressions of caloric, protein, and micronutrient deficiencies in children and adults. Bioarchaeologists have developed multiple accurate methods for assessing markers of stress on skeletons, and today, numerous skeletal biomarkers are available for estimating long-term damage, chronic stress, and lifetime challenges in the past (see, for example, Buikstra 2019; Larsen 2015).

Skeletal Frailty Index (SFI)

Due to the breadth and depth of information that can be gleaned from skeletal lesions in human bioarchaeological research, we (Marklein, Leahy, and Crews 2016) suggested frailty in the dead could be operationalized as a specific phenotype that did not necessarily increase risk of death (Fried et al. 2001, 2005). Using a human biological framework and evidence-based indices of frailty applied in health care, we proposed a skeletal frailty index (SFI) based on data observable in bioarchaeological samples (Marklein,

Leahy, and Crews 2016). As with frailty in the living, skeletal frailty is proposed as a cumulative phenotype that developed during a deceased individual's lifetime. As the skeletal record from early to historical populations shows, humans of the past experienced frailty as a result of muscle and bone loss, as observed today. Other than osteoporosis, such losses may not be directly observable on skeletons. Nor are walking speed, weight loss, activity, strength, or endurance observable. However, multiple skeletal markers reflect outcomes of these processes, which, when observed, oftentimes indicate severity of the condition.

The original SFI, combining 13 skeletal and dental conditions, was conceived as a means for tabulating and quantifying a somatic frailty phenotype in past populations. However, unlike modern frailty indices, the SFI considers cumulative frailty biomarkers over the life span (see Table 14.1). Several biomarkers included in SFI are derived from modern assessments of frailty (e.g., immobility, altered gait, bone loss). For example, osteoarthritis, intervertebral disc disease, and rotator cuff disease lead to reduced mobility in the living, and therefore likely reflect similar losses when observed on skeletal materials, making these conditions skeletal proxies for reduced walking speed and physical activity (Ling and Bathon 1998; Waldron 2009). Additionally, fractures contribute to decreased mobility and prolonged recuperation times from trauma with age due to lower bone density, slower bone regeneration, and sarcopenia (Clark et al. 2017). Pathological conditions like osteopenia and osteoporosis place individuals at heighted risks for non-traumatic and minimally traumatic events (Brickley and Ives 2009), making bone condition a direct marker of phenotypic frailty among the living (Fried et al. 2001) and dead (Agarwal 2019; Brickley and Agarwal 2003).

Other skeletal markers, which do not directly correlate with modern frailty measures of physical impairment and bone and muscle loss, nonetheless convey evidence of lifetime stress, specifically dietary inadequacy, infectious processes, and decreased immune response. Disruptions to childhood growth and development may have long-term impacts on an individual's resilience to adulthood stressors, increasing their risk of later-life chronic conditions and mortality (Barker 1992; Kuzawa 2005; Armelagos et al. 2009; Gowland 2015). Disrupted growth is observable as growth stunting and tooth enamel defects. Stunting of the skeleton, specifically long bones, suggests significant undernourishment during childhood and adolescent growth and correlates with poorer biological health and increased morbidity (Bailey et al. 1984; Cameron 2007). Linear enamel hypoplasia (LEH) is another measure of childhood stress encapsulated in the permanent teeth of adult individuals. As with stunting, LEH demonstrates periods of growth arrest during infancy through early and late childhood, when dental enamel is forming. Often, LEHs are associated with early life mortality and increased adulthood morbidity (Armelagos et al. 2009).

In addition to childhood contributors to frailty, skeletons also testify to ongoing somatic and immunological responses, whether nutritional, infectious, or cancerous. When unresolved, continuing nutritional stress into adulthood may manifest as pathological bone in the skeleton. In the skull, lesions attributable to overactive production of blood cells, called porotic hyperostosis and cribra orbitalia, present along the cranial vault and orbital plates, respectively. These lesions are multifactorial in origin but are generally associated with severe anemia (e.g., iron deficiency), folic acid deficiency, and inherited thalassemia (Walker et al. 2009). Many individuals with these conditions live many years while suffering chronic fatigue, weakness, and neurological consequences (Graham, Arvela, and Wise 1992). In the postcranial skeleton, vitamin D deficiency may compromise structural integrity of long bones, increasing the risk of fracture in weight-bearing limbs. Skeletal manifestation of osteomalacia (rickets, in children) results when bone cannot be mineralized, and "soft" tissue accumulates in cortical and trabecular bone. Untreated, individuals with osteomalacia may suffer bone and muscle pain, muscle weakness, fractures, or a compromised gait (Holick 2006).

Some responses to stressors may only manifest outwardly, for example, those that are skin deep (e.g., psoriasis, allergic responses), while others penetrate to the bones. For example, periosteal new bone (PNB) may present on bones as a response to localized infection/trauma or more severe systemic infection (Larsen 2015; Roberts 2019; Weston 2008, 2012). Presence of PNB suggests an active immune response at time of death. It also indicates allocating available resources away from somatic and cellular maintenance and repair, leaving an individual less resilient to additional insults. While PNB can be found throughout the body, periodontal disease (PD) is a specific inflammatory condition within the alveolar bones of the maxillae and mandible. Although PD occurs more frequently in older individuals, it is not uncommon in young adults and may range in severity from inflamed gingivae to antemortem tooth loss, conditions that may directly affect consumption patterns (Irfan, Dawson, and Bissada 2001;

Larsen 2015). Lastly, neoplastic disorders, ranging from a localized, benign osteoma to a malignant, metastatic cancer, may present on skeletal remains (Waldron 2009). While benign tumors may be asymptomatic, metastatic cancers, which penetrate and impact skeletal tissues, contribute to considerable pain and suffering and may alter functional abilities and mobility in affected individuals (Clines 2013).

Despite the phenotypic frailty associated with this suite of skeletal conditions, those experiencing greater stressors that imprinted their skeletons during life likely were more resilient than those who succumbed earlier in life or with fewer skeletal markers of frailty at the same age. Individuals who survived longer likely experienced increased weakness and reduced physical activity as they aged, but they still lived sufficiently long to be the oldest in their communities, some likely achieving ages into and past their sixties. Multiple pathological processes and stressors occurring during life leave impressions on human skeletons. Therefore, frailty indices, developed among the living (Crews 2005; Fried et al. 2004; Kim and Jazwinski 2015; Rockwood et al. 1994), provide an evidence-based methodology for developing a SFI appropriate for examining the influence of frailty on health and survival in the past (Marklein and Crews 2017; Marklein, Leahy, and Crews 2016).

We designed and operationalized the SFI to measure individual skeletal frailty using a summation of conditions and traits known to permanently mark the skeleton during life (Marklein, Leahy, and Crews 2016). We compared skeletal frailty, based on a suite of characteristics representing entire individual skeletons, across sample subgroupings using their average SFI scores. Incorporating standard skeletal frailty biomarkers, reported previously as indicators of health (Goodman and Martin 2002; Steckel et al. 2005), the SFI includes biomarkers and pathological lesions representing four stressor categories: childhood growth perturbation, nutritional deficiency and infection, physical activity, and trauma, reflecting those used in living samples (Crews 2005; Fried et al. 2004; Walston 2005). All skeletal biomarkers were scored as "0" or "1," according to whether the condition qualified as being indicative of low/no or high frailty, respectively (see Table 14.1; see Marklein, Leahy, and Crews 2016). For most biomarkers, 0 or 1 was assigned to represent absence or presence of a condition. For other biomarkers, scores of 0 or 1 were assigned according to the state of the observed pathological lesion—for example, active versus healing/healed. Once each biomarker was assigned a score, zeros and ones were summed, representing that person's specific SFI score. Thus quantified, SFI scores provide an overall skeletal/dental index of stress-related somatic dysfunction and loss of abilities occurring during an individual's life. Rather than comparing means for each different biomarker (e.g., frequencies of periosteal bone growth, infectious diseases, linear enamel hypoplasia) by age and sex or burial circumstances, we examine differential distributions of frailty (SFI) across and within groups as a continuous variable using normal (means, standard deviations, explained variance) and inferential statistics (t-tests and analyses of variance and covariance).

Although our definition of "skeletal frailty" and interpretation of the SFI varies from other definitions and interpretations in bioarchaeology, it aligns well with a previous definition of skeletal frailty by Wood and colleagues (1992, 345): "individual biological characteristics associated with . . . susceptibility, propensity, or relative risk with respect to disease and death." When applied with risk of mortality data and crude prevalence rates, the SFI provides a more complete picture of individuals in a community susceptible to early life mortality, and an appraisal of how different individuals incurred and acquired their phenotypic frailty through "normal" aging and individually specific circumstances.

Frailty in Medieval London

Exploring the efficacy of dual approaches to frailty, we compared estimates of skeletal frailty (SFI) to mortality risk (hazard analysis) results between monastic and nonmonastic cemetery skeletal samples (adult males) from medieval London (DeWitte, Boulware, and Redfern 2013; Marklein and Crews 2017; Marklein, Leahy, and Crews 2016). Hazard analyses and age-at-death distributions indicated significantly reduced risks of mortality among adult monastic males compared to nonmonastic (lay) males (De-Witte, Boulware, and Redfern 2013). Results foregrounded health and longevity benefits of life in monastic communities during the medieval period. However, this hazard and death narrative does not inform us regarding the general health or phenotypic frailty of individuals in monastic or nonmonastic settings. Did monastic lifeways promote longevity? If so, did longer lives translate into greater frailty, suggesting a morbidity-mortality paradox?

All demographic and paleopathological data analyzed in this case study were collected from the open-access WORD, so differential diagnoses were made by Centre for Human Bioarchaeology (CHB) curators and age es-

Table 14.1. Skeletal Biomarkers and Frailty Score

Stress category	Frailty biomarker	Scores and measurements	Frailty score "1"	Supportive literature
Growth	1) Femoral length	Lengths in quadrants	Shortest lengths (1/4)	(Bogin 2020; Saunders and Hoppa 1993; Steckel 1995)
	2) Femoral head diameter	Diameters in quadrants	Smallest diameters (1/4)	(Ruff, Trinkaus, and Holliday 1997)
	3) Linear enamel hypoplasia (LEH)	Present/absent	Present	(Goodman and Armelagos 1985; Goodman et al. 1987; Goodman and Rose 1990; Hillson 1996)
Nutrition and infection	4) Periosteal new bone (PNB)	Active, healing, absent	Active	(DeWitte 2014; Roberts 2019; Weston 2012)
	5) Periodontal disease	Present/absent	Present	(Hillson 1996; Waldron 2009)
	6) Porotic hyperostosis (PH)/ cribra orbitalia (CO)	Present/absent	Present	(Walker et al. 2009; Stuart-Macadam 1992; Rivera and Mirazón Lahr 2017)
	7) Rickets/osteomalacia	Present/absent	Present	(Mays, Brickley, and Ives 2006; Reginato and Coquia 2003)
	8) Neoplasms	Present/absent	Present	(Marques et al. 2018)
	9) Osteoporosis	Present/absent	Present	(Agarwal 2019)
Activity	10) Osteoarthritis	Present/absent	Present	(Waldron 2009; Anderson and Loeser 2010; Jurmain 1980)
	11) Intervertebral disc disease (IVD)	Present/absent	Present	(Waldron 1991)
	12) Rotator Cuff Disorder (RCD)	Present/absent	Present	(Waldron 2009)
Trauma	13) Fracture	Present/absent	Present	(Lambert 1997; Milner and Smith 1990; Walker 1989)

Note: Skeletal biomarkers are incorporated into each individual's cumulative frailty score (SFI) with diagnostic criteria for high ("1") and low ("0") frailty designations. For this 13-biomarker SFI, individuals may express a frailty phenotype from 0 to 13.

Supportive literature: Publications verifying specific biomarkers indicate frailty (see Marklein and Crews 2017).

Table 14.2. Monastic and Non-Monastic Cemetery Sites

	Cemetery	Dates	Total sample	Excavated adult males (% of sample)	Adult males in present study (% of male sample)
Monastic	Bermondsey Abbey	1117–1538 CE	201	147 (73.1%)	34 (23.1%)
	Merton Priory	1066–1540 CE	676	485 (71.7%)	34 (7.0%)
	Total		877	632 (72.1%)	68 (10.8%)
Nonmonastic	Guildhall Yard	1140–1350 CE	68	18 (26.5%)	10 (55.6%)
	Spital Square	1200–1500 CE	124	43 (34.7%)	9 (20.9%
	St. Mary Graces	1350–1538 CE	389	136 (35%)	23 (16.9%)
	St. Benet Sherehog	1250–1666 CE	39	8 (20.5%)	1 (12.5%)
	Total		620	205 (33.1%)	43 (21.0%)

Note: Chronological dates and cemetery skeletal sample information from which this study's smaller samples were derived.

timates, especially for older individuals, were limited to specific ranges: 18–25 years, 26–35 years, 36–45 years, and over 46 years (Powers, 2012). Estimating 13-biomarker SFI scores (see Table 14.1) for adult individuals (over 18 years) from the same monastic and nonmonastic skeletal collections (see Table 14.2), we observed that monastic males lived longer than nonmonastic males while exhibiting higher average frailty (SFI: 3.12 ± 1.32, range 0–6) than their lay counterparts (SFI: 2.79 ± 1.49, range 0–6) (see Table 14.3). While not statistically significant (p=0.22) for the full sample, within the oldest age group significant differences occurred. Nonmonastic males over 46 years old exhibited significantly lower SFI than their monastic counterparts (p=0.0001). Monastic males showed significantly higher crude prevalence rates (CPR) of osteoarthritis (p=0.043) and intervertebral disc disease (p=0.004) (see Table 14.4). Conditions associated with childhood stress (LEH) and adulthood immunocompetence (PNB and PD) did not differ significantly between monastic and nonmonastic groups, but still were more frequent among long-lived monastic males.

Together, SFI distributions and CPR results add to the original frailty

Table 14.3. Skeletal Frailty by Cemetery Context within Each Age Group

Age categories	Monastic (n=68)			Non-monastic (n=43)			p-value
	Mean SFI	SD	Range	Mean SFI	SD	Range	
18–25 years	2.80	0.45	2–3	2.92	1.38	1–6	0.78
26–35 years	2.47	1.13	0–4	2.50	1.84	1–6	0.96
36–45 years	3.00	1.39	0–6	3.13	1.45	0–5	0.78
>46 years	3.94	1.16	1–5	1.75	0.58	1–2	0.0001**
All ages	*3.12*	*1.32*	*0–6*	*2.77*	*1.51*	*0–6*	*0.22*

Note: Welch's two sample t-test (*p-value<0.05, **p-value<0.001).

Table 14.4. Frequencies of Adult Males with Observed Skeletal Conditions

	Monastic (n=68)		Non-monastic (n=43)		Pearson's χ^2 (p-value)
LEH	52	0.76	26	0.60	3.23 (0.072)
PNB	26	0.38	10	0.23	2.70 (0.101)
PH/CO	6	0.09	6	0.14	0.72 (0.397)
PD	56	0.82	34	0.79	0.19 (0.667)
AM fracture	19	0.28	9	0.21	0.69 (0.407)
OA	21	0.31	6	0.12	4.10 (0.043)*
IVD	38	0.56	12	0.28	8.33 (0.004)**
RCD	6	0.09	2	0.05	0.69 (0.408)
Osteoporosis	0	0.00	1	0.02	1.60 (0.207)
Rickets	0	0.00	0	0.00	(1.00)
Neoplasm	2	0.03	0	0.00	1.29 (0.256)

Notes: Corresponding CPR in monastic or non-monastic subsample, and Pearson's χ^2 results. LEH: linear enamel hypoplasia; PNB: periosteal new bone; PH/CO: porotic hyperostosis/cribra orbitalia; AM: antemortem; OA: osteoarthritis; IVD: intervertebral disc disease; and RCD: rotator cuff disease.

*p-value<0.05, **p-value<0.001

results for medieval London monastic and nonmonastic samples. Jointly, they offer a more nuanced portrayal of lived experiences in these urban/urban-adjacent groups, reaching alternative but complementary conclusions. By virtue of their religious affiliation and living circumstances (e.g., access to higher quality foods, living quarters and amenities, daily activity, etc.), monastic males experienced significantly lower risks of mortality throughout adulthood (Hatcher, Piper, and Stone 2006). However, increased longevity resulted in greater age-related wear and tear on their skeletons, as seen in their higher rates of degenerative joint diseases. Further dissecting SFI distributions, the frailest individuals in each age group were remarkably similar between monastic and nonmonastic males, until later years in life. These results suggest a medieval London adult male likely lived longer under monastic conditions than nonmonastic, although specific ages at death are indeterminable.

However, among nonmonastic men, the few who attained estimated ages of 46+ years enjoyed lower skeletal frailty. These observations reflect mortality and morbidity patterns observed across modern populations; lower proportions of men survive to later ages than women, apparently reflecting selective mortality of frailer males (Kim and Jazwinski 2015). Frailty estimates among nonmonastic males likely reflect aspects of variability in skeletal frailty and mortality risk across medieval London's lay communities. While the medieval London economy supplied sufficient commodities for those with financial means, most of London's populace likely wavered between feast and famine, with the majority of people "teeter[ing] precariously on the brink of hunger" (Rawcliffe 2013, 230). For some, this lack of food resources, atop general lack of domestic amenities and medical interventions, would have resulted in increased risk of death, as observed by DeWitte and colleagues (2013), and the disparity in frailty observed both between monastic and lay males and within the lay male subsample. For monastic individuals, residential settings like Bermondsey Abbey and Merton Priory provided residents more nutritious and diverse diets (Miller and Saxby 2007). Coupled with religious doctrines for physical health and activity, which established expectations for daily productive chores and work (Lawrence 1984), the monastic lifestyles in medieval London created an equation for survival of long-lived individuals with higher skeletal frailty (e.g., osteoarthritis, IVD).

By contrast, most nonmonastic males in these London samples did not experience ready access to economic, nutritional, and medicinal resources as their monastic counterparts did, and thus suffered higher risk of mortality (DeWitte, Boulware, and Redfern 2013). Nevertheless, nonmonastic male adults in the oldest age category (46+ years) presented the lowest skeletal frailty scores relative to not just the oldest monastic age group but all age groups within the medieval sample. Three of the four nonmonastic males derive from the St. Mary Graces cemetery, which accommodated members of both the lay community and high religious and socioeconomic status (WORD, 2020). The burial placements of these individuals—under the church's north nave, beneath a later row of the church, and within St. Anne's Chapel—testify to the high status of these individuals within the parish community (Grainger and Phillpotts 2011). As arguably affluent members of this lay community, these individuals were buffered from many of the nutritional, economic, and epidemic stressors that daily harassed the lower-class members. As a result, skeletons of high-socioeconomic individuals, especially the more resilient who survived to later years, manifested fewer markers of skeletal frailty. Similar patterns in skeletal frailty among socioeconomic groups have been observed throughout bioarchaeological samples (Robb et al. 2001; Watkins 2012). These results highlight the importance of considering social and economic factors in an individual's resilience and expression of skeletal frailty. Further, they speak to the changeability of both resilience and frailty as a person accommodates and adapts to stressors throughout their lifetime. Given living circumstances in medieval London (e.g., poor sanitation, pathogens, food insecurity), selective mortality within and between monastic and nonmonastic males likely was predicated on multiple genetic, socioeconomic, environmental, personal, and sociocultural benefits and stressors.

Concluding Remarks

The definition of "skeletal frailty" proposed by Marklein and colleagues (Marklein and Crews 2017; Marklein, Leahy, and Crews 2016) reflects theoretical developments in human biology, along with substantial research on the frailty phenotype and frailty indices among the living (Searle et al. 2008; Walston et al. 2019), and their integration into bioarchaeology (see Temple and Goodman 2014). The applied 13-biomarker SFI provides individual- and population-level representations of cumulative frailty. Results from this medieval London case study illustrate one tenet of the osteological paradox, namely resilience: individuals more susceptible to life's stressors tend to die before evidence of wear and tear on their bodies skeletonize. Those who survive more years tend to accumulate more skeletal biomarkers of stress and manifest greater phenotypic frailty than their contemporaries who died at earlier ages. While this index operationalizes another conceptualization of frailty in bioarchaeology, we maintain that studies of frailty in the dead may be best served through the complementary approaches of mortality risk and frailty phenotype, which together address and mitigate the osteological paradox. For example, McFadden and Oxenham (2020) demonstrated categorizing skeletal indicators as criteria for resilience and frailty in their paleoepidemiological examination of cribra orbitalia among samples in the Global History of Health Project. They highlighted how such individual conditions impact mean survival across populations. In this way, future applications of the SFI may evaluate high ("1") and low ("0") frailty of individual biomarkers based on their associations with lower or higher average survival in population-specific data. Lastly, as age at death is critical to understanding past frailty patterns, the application of newer methods for aging, especially among the oldest age categories (Cave and Oxenham 2016; McFadden, Cave, and Oxenham 2019), in medieval and other archaeological samples, will provide more nuanced interpretations of frailty during later decades of life.

As with other approaches to assessing associations among health, frailty, and lifeways among past populations, the SFI makes use of data observable from skeletal samples. The suggested approach compiles these related but divergent datapoints to estimate a frailty phenotype based on similar indices among living humans. Considering frailty as an individual phenotypic expression of multiple biological processes, in variable states of function and dysfunction, enables bioarchaeologists to envision past populations and their skeletal assemblages as more than victims (i.e., individuals at risk of death). Using a composite assessment of lifetime frailty, they can view skeletonized individuals as once active members of their communities; people who experienced daily and long-term stressors comparable to those people still face today and survived in what likely were harsher environments.

References

Agarwal, Sabrina C. 2019. "Understanding Bone Aging, Loss, and Osteoporosis in the Past." In *Biological Anthropology of the Human Skeleton*, edited by M. A. Katzenberg and A. L. Grauer, 385–414. Hoboken, NJ: John Wiley and Sons.

Arbeev, Konstantin G., Svetlana V. Ukraintseva, Olivia Bagley, Ilya Y. Zhbannikov, Alan A. Cohen, Alexander M. Kulminski, and Anatoliy I. Yashin. 2019. "'Physiological Dysregulation' as a Promising Measure of Robustness and Resilience in Studies of Aging and a New Indicator of Preclinical Disease." *Journals of Gerontology: Series A* 74(4): 462–468.

Armelagos, George J., Alan H. Goodman, Kristin N. Harper, and Michael L. Blakey. 2009. "Enamel Hypoplasia and Early Mortality: Bioarcheological Support for the Barker Hypothesis." *Evolutionary Anthropology: Issues, News, and Reviews: Issues, News, and Reviews* 18(6): 261–271.

Bailey, Stephen M., Stanley N. Gershoff, Robert B. McGandy, Amorn Nondasuta, Puangtong

Tantiwongse, Dusanee Suttapreyasri, Joy Miller, and Paula McCree. 1984. "A Longitudinal Study of Growth and Maturation in Rural Thailand." *Human Biology*: 539–557.

Barker, David J. P. 1992. "Fetal Origins of Diseases of Old Age." *European Journal of Clinical Nutrition*.

Barker, David J. P., Clive Osmond, Eero Kajantie, and Johan G. Eriksson. 2009. "Growth and Chronic Disease: Findings in the Helsinki Birth Cohort." *Annals of Human Biology* 36(5): 445–458.

Bocquet-Appel, Jean-Pierre, and Claude Masset. 1982. "Farewell to Paleodemography." *Journal of Human Evolution* 11(4): 321–333.

Brickley, Megan B., and Rachel Ives. 2009. *The Bioarchaeology of Metabolic Bone Disease*. Amsterdam: Academic Press.

Brickley, Megan B., and Sabrina C. Agarwal. 2003. "Techniques for the Investigation of Age-Related Bone Loss and Osteoporosis in Archaeological Bone." In *Bone Loss and Osteoporosis*, edited by S. C. Agarwal and S. C. Stout, 157–172. Boston MA: Springer.

Buikstra, Jane E. 2019. *Ortner's Identification of Pathological Conditions in Human Skeletal Remains*. Amsterdam: Academic Press.

Cameron, Noël. 2007. "Growth Patterns in Adverse Environments." *American Journal of Human Biology* 19(5): 615–621.

Cave, Christine, and Marc Oxenham. 2016. "Identification of the Archaeological 'Invisible Elderly': An Approach Illustrated with an Anglo-Saxon Example." *International Journal of Osteoarchaeology* 26.1: 163–175.

Clark, Dan, Mary Nakamura, Ted Miclau, and Ralph Marcucio. 2017. "Effects of Aging on Fracture Healing." *Current Osteoporosis Reports* 15(6): 601–608.

Clines, Gregory A. 2013. "Overview of Mechanisms in Cancer Metastases to Bone." In *Primer on the Metabolic Bone Diseases and Disorders of Mineral Metabolism*, edited by Clifford J. Rosen, 671–676. Hoboken, NJ: Wiley-Blackwell.

Crews, Douglas E. 2005. "Evolutionary Perspectives on Human Longevity and Frailty." In *Longevity and Frailty*, edited by Jean-Marie Robine, James R. Carey, Yeves Christen, and Jean Pierre Michel, 57–65. Paris: Springer.

———. 2022. "Aging, Frailty, and Design of Built Environments." *Journal of Physiological Anthropology* 41(1): 1–16.

Damon, Albert. 1975. *Physiological Anthropology*. Oxford: Oxford University Press.

DeWitte, Sharon N. 2014. "Differential Survival among Individuals with Active and Healed Periosteal New Bone Formation." *International Journal of Paleopathology* 7: 38–44.

DeWitte, Sharon N., and Christopher M. Stojanowski. 2015. "The Osteological Paradox 20 Years Later: Past Perspectives, Future Directions." *Journal of Archaeological Research* 23(4): 397–450.

DeWitte, Sharon N., and James W. Wood. 2008. "Selectivity of Black Death Mortality with Respect to Preexisting Health." *Proceedings of the National Academy of Sciences* 105(5): 1436–1441.

DeWitte, Sharon N., and Jelena Bekvalac. 2010. "Oral Health and Frailty in the Medieval English Cemetery of St Mary Graces." *American Journal of Physical Anthropology* 142(3): 341–354.

DeWitte, Sharon N., Jessica C. Boulware, and Rebecca C. Redfern. 2013. "Medieval Monastic Mortality: Hazard Analysis of Mortality Differences between Monastic and Nonmonastic Cemeteries in England." *American Journal of Physical Anthropology* 152(3): 322–332.

DeWitte, Sharon N., and Samantha L. Yaussy. 2020. "Sex Differences in Adult Famine Mortality in Medieval London." *American Journal of Physical Anthropology* 171(1): 164–169.

Fried, Linda P., Catherine M. Tangen, Jeremy Walston, Anne B. Newman, Calvin Hirsch, John Gottdiener, Teresa Seeman, Russell Tracy, Willem J. Kop, and Gregory Burke. 2001. "Frailty in Older Adults: Evidence for a Phenotype." *Journals of Gerontology Series A: Biological Sciences and Medical Sciences* 56(3): M146–M157.

Fried, Linda P., Evan C. Hadley, Jeremy D. Walston, Anne B. Newman, Jack M. Guralnik, Stephanie Studenski, Tamara B. Harris, William B. Ershler, and Luigi Ferrucci. 2005. "From Bedside to Bench: Research Agenda for Frailty." *Science of Aging Knowledge Environment: SAGE KE* (31): pe24.

Fried, Linda P., Luigi Ferrucci, Jonathan Darer, Jeff D. Williamson, and Gerard Anderson. 2004. "Untangling the Concepts of Disability, Frailty, and Comorbidity: Implications for Improved Targeting and Care." *Journals of Gerontology Series A: Biological Sciences and Medical Sciences* 59(3): M255–M263.

Giampaoli, Simona, Luigi Ferrucci, Francesca Cecchi, C. Lo Noce, Agata Poce, Francesco Dima, Augusto Santaquilani, Maria Fenicia Vescio, and Alessandro Menotti. 1999. "Hand-Grip Strength Predicts Incident Disability in Non-Disabled Older Men." *Age and Ageing* 28(3): 283–288.

Goodman, Alan H., and Debra L. Martin. 2002. "Reconstructing Health Profiles from Skeletal Remains." In *The Backbone of History: Health and Nutrition in the Western Hemisphere*, edited by R. H. Steckel and J. C. Rose, 11–60. Cambridge: Cambridge University Press.

Gowland, Rebecca L. 2015. "Entangled Lives: Implications of the Developmental Origins of Health and Disease Hypothesis for Bioarchaeology and the Life Course." *American Journal of Physical Anthropology* 158(4): 530–540.

Graham, Stephen M., Otto M. Arvela, and Graham A. Wise. 1992. "Long-Term Neurologic Consequences of Nutritional Vitamin B12 Deficiency in Infants." *Journal of Pediatrics* 121(5): 710–714.

Grainger, Ian, and Christopher Phillpotts. 2011. *The Cistercian Abbey of St Mary Graces, East Smithfield, London*. London: Museum of London Archaeology.

Hatcher, John, Alan John Piper, and David Stone. 2006. "Monastic Mortality: Durham Priory, 1395–1529." *Economic History Review* 59(4): 667–687.

Holick, Michael F. 2006. "The Role of Vitamin D for Bone Health and Fracture Prevention." *Current Osteoporosis Reports* 4(3): 96–102.

Irfan, Uma M., Debora V. Dawson, and Nabil F. Bissada. 2001. "Epidemiology of Periodontal Disease: A Review and Clinical Perspectives." *Journal of the International Academy of Periodontology* 3(1): 14.

Katz, T. F. 1963. "ADL Activities of Daily Living." *Journal of the American Medical Association* 185(914.10): 1001.

Kim, Sangkyu, and S. Michal Jazwinski. 2015. "Quantitative Measures of Healthy Aging and Biological Age." *Healthy Aging Research* 4.

Kuzawa, Christopher W. 2005. "Fetal Origins of Developmental Plasticity: Are Fetal Cues Reliable Predictors of Future Nutritional Environments?" *American Journal of Human Biology* 17(1): 5–21.

Larsen, Clark S. 2015. *Bioarchaeology: Interpreting Behavior from the Human Skeleton*. Cambridge: Cambridge University Press.

Lawrence, Clifford Hugh. 1984. *Medieval Monasticism: Forms of Religious Life in Western Europe in the Middle Ages*. London: Routledge.

Ling, Shari Miura, and Joan M. Bathon. 1998. "Osteoarthritis in Older Adults." *Journal of the American Geriatrics Society* 46(2): 216–225.

Marklein, Kathryn E., and Douglas E. Crews. 2017. "Frail or Hale: Skeletal Frailty Indices in Medieval London Skeletons." *PloS ONE* 12(5): e0176025.

Marklein, Kathryn E., Rachael E. Leahy, and Douglas E. Crews. 2016. "In Sickness and in Death: Assessing Frailty in Human Skeletal Remains." *American Journal of Physical Anthropology* 161(2): 208–225.

McFadden, Clare, and Marc F. Oxenham. 2020. "A Paleoepidemiological Approach to the Osteological Paradox: Investigating Stress, Frailty and Resilience through Cribra Orbitalia." *American Journal of Physical Anthropology* 173(2): 205–217.

McFadden, Clare, Christine Cave, and Marc Oxenham. 2019. "Ageing the Elderly: A New Approach to the Estimation of the Age-at-Death Distribution from Skeletal Remains." *International Journal of Osteoarchaeology* 29(6): 1072–1078.

Meyyazhagan, Swarnalatha, and Robert M. Palmer. 2002. "Nutritional Requirements with Aging. Prevention of Disease." *Clinics in Geriatric Medicine* 18(3): 557–576.

Miller, Pat, and David Saxby. 2007. *The Augustinian Priory of St Mary Merton, Surrey: Excavations 1976–90*. London: Museum of London Archaeology.

Powers, Natasha, ed. 2012. *Human Osteology Method Statement*. London: Museum of London Archaeology.

Rawcliffe, Carole. 2013. *Urban Bodies: Communal Health in Late Medieval English Towns and Cities*. Woodbridge, Suffolk: Boydell & Brewer Ltd.

Robb, John, Renzo Bigazzi, Luca Lazzarini, Caterina Scarsini, and Fiorenza Sonego. 2001. "Social 'Status' and Biological 'Status': A Comparison of Grave Goods and Skeletal Indicators from Pontecagnano." *American Journal of Physical Anthropology* 115(3): 213–222.

Roberts, Charlotte A. 2019. "Infectious Disease: Introduction, Periostosis, Periostitis, Osteomyelitis, and Septic Arthritis." In *Ortner's Identification of Pathological Conditions in Human Skeletal Remains*, 3rd ed., edited by J. E. Buikstra, 285–319. Amsterdam: Elsevier.

Roberts, Charlotte A., and Jane E. Buikstra. 2019. "Bacterial Infections." In *Ortner's Identification of Pathological Conditions in Human Skeletal Remains*, 3rd ed., edited by J. E. Buikstra, 321–439. Amsterdam: Elsevier.

Rockwood, Kenneth, Alexander Mogilner, and Arnold Mitnitski. 2004. "Changes with Age in the Distribution of a Frailty Index." *Mechanisms of Ageing and Development* 125(7): 517–519.

Rockwood, Kenneth, Roy A. Fox, Paul Stolee, Duncan Robertson, and B. Lynn Beattie. 1994. "Frailty in Elderly People: An Evolving Concept." *Canadian Medical Association Journal* 150(4): 489–495.

Rockwood, Kenneth, Xiaowei Song, Chris MacKnight, Howard Bergman, David B. Hogan, Ian McDowell, and Arnold Mitnitski. 2005. "A Global Clinical Measure of Fitness and Frailty in Elderly People." *Canadian Medical Association Journal* 173(5): 489–495.

Searle, Samuel D., Arnold Mitnitski, Evelyne A. Gahbauer, Thomas M. Gill, and Kenneth Rockwood. 2008. "A Standard Procedure for Creating a Frailty Index." *BMC Geriatrics* 8: 24.

Seeman, Teresa E., Burton H. Singer, John W. Rowe, Ralph I. Horwitz, and Bruce S. McEwen. 1997. "Price of Adaptation–Allostatic Load and Its Health Consequences: MacArthur Studies of Successful Aging." *Archives of Internal Medicine* 157(19): 2259–2268.

Steckel, R. H., C. S. Larsen, P. W. Sciulli, and P. L. Walker. 2005. The Global History of Health Project: Data Collection Codebook. The Ohio State University, Columbus, OH.

Sterling, P., and J. Eyer. 1988. "Allostasis: A New Paradigm to Explain Arousal Pathology." In *Handbook of Life Stress, Cognition and Health*, edited by S. Fisher and J. Reason, 629–649. New York: J. Wiley and Sons.

Studenski, Stephanie, Risa P. Hayes, Ruth Q. Leibowitz, Rita Bode, Laurie Lavery, Jeremy Walston, Pamela Duncan, and Subashan Perera. 2004. "Clinical Global Impression of Change in Physical Frailty: Development of a Measure Based on Clinical Judgment." *Journal of the American Geriatrics Society* 52(9): 1560–1566.

Temple, Daniel H., and Alan H. Goodman. 2014. "Bioarcheology Has a 'Health' Problem: Conceptualizing 'Stress' and 'Health' in Bioarcheological Research." *American Journal of Physical Anthropology* 155(2): 186–191.

Usher, Bethany M. 2000. "A Multistate Model of Health and Mortality for Paleodemography: Tirup Cemetery." PhD dissertation, The Pennsylvania State University.

Vaupel, James W., Kenneth G. Manton, and Eric Stallard. 1979. "The Impact of Heterogeneity in Individual Frailty on the Dynamics of Mortality." *Demography* 16(3): 439–454.

Waldron, Tony. 2009. *Palaeopathology*. Cambridge: Cambridge University Press.

Walker, Phillip L., Rhonda R. Bathurst, Rebecca Richman, Thor Gjerdrum, and Valerie A. Andrushko. 2009. "The Causes of Porotic Hyperostosis and Cribra Orbitalia: A Reappraisal of the Iron-Deficiency-Anemia Hypothesis." *American Journal of Physical Anthropology* 139(2): 109–125.

Walston, Jeremy D. 2005. "Biological Markers and the Molecular Biology of Frailty." In *Longevity and Frailty*, edited by James R. Carey, Jean-Marie Robine, Jean Pierre Michel, and Yves Christen, 83–90. New York: Springer Publishing.

Walston, Jeremy D., and Karen Bandeen-Roche. 2015. "Frailty: A Tale of Two Concepts." *BMC Medicine* 13(1): 1–3.

Walston, Jeremy D., Karen Bandeen-Roche, Brian Buta, Howard Bergman, Thomas M. Gill, John E. Morley, Linda P. Fried, Thomas N. Robinson, Jonathan Afilalo, and Anne B. Newman. 2019. "Moving Frailty toward Clinical Practice: NIA Intramural Frailty Science Symposium Summary." *Journal of the American Geriatrics Society* 67(8): 1559–1564.

Watkins, R. 2012. "Variation in Health and Socioeconomic Status within the W. Montague Cobb Skeletal Collection: Degenerative Joint Disease, Trauma and Cause of Death." *International Journal of Osteoarchaeology* 22(1): 22–44.

Wellcome Osteological Research Database (WORD). Accessed November 10, 2020. https://www.museumoflondon.org.uk/collections/othercollection-databases-and-libraries/centre-human-bioarchaeology/osteological-database.

Weston, Darlene A. 2008. "Investigating the Specificity of Periosteal Reactions in Pathology Museum Specimens." *American Journal of Physical Anthropology* 137(1): 48–59.

———. 2012. "Nonspecific Infection in Paleopathology: Interpreting Periosteal Reactions." In *A Companion to Paleopathology*, edited by Anne L. Grauer, 492–512. Hoboken, NJ: John Wiley & Sons.

Wood, James W., George R. Milner, Henry C. Harpending, and Kenneth M. Weiss. 1992. "The Osteological Paradox: Problems of Inferring Prehistoric Health from Skeletal Samples." *Current Anthropology* 33(4): 343–370.

15

Methodological Issues in Participatory Research with Older Adults

JEAN J. SCHENSUL

Conceptualizing Older Adulthood

In life course research, the official determination of older adulthood is generally defined as 60 or 65 years of age, depending on the source (CDC 2020). Medically oriented definitions of aging take into consideration general health and functionality (Estes and Binney 1989). Anthropologists recognize that aging is culturally and contextually defined (Ory 1995; Perkinson and Solimeo 2013; Sokolovsky 2020). By taking a hermeneutic or "emic" perspective, anthropologists consider older adults' own understandings of aging (Song and Kong 2015) while interpreting them from a theoretical perspective (Bhasin 2007).

In debating ways of understanding aging, some anthropologists have argued for approaches that recognize and address the physical, functional, and cognitive vulnerabilities of aging (Nicolescu 2019). Others examine resilience, coping, and efforts of older adults to remain relevant in their communities (Carr and Weir 2017; Pines and Giles 2020; Perkinson 1993; Shenk and Sokolovsky 2001). Still others examine service adaptations to support aging adults in the absence of family members and traditional support systems (Iris and Berman 2009). These approaches to the study of aging in context usually draw on qualitative, narrative, and case study methods useful in understanding meaning and reflecting the voices of study participants. While they are invaluable in contributing to our understanding of older adulthood across cultures, their mix of empirical and phenomenological research approaches is primarily driven by the interests of the researcher rather than the concerns and active involvement of the older adults themselves.

Collaborative or participatory research is a realistic, resilience-based approach to applied gerontology that recognizes older adults as resources, with agency. Thus, it can have both sociological, anthropological, mental health, and political implications. Engagement in a participatory research process has multiple benefits, such as supporting group solidarity, promoting critical thinking and problem solving, and illustrating to public audiences the informed opinions of a group of older adults and their caregivers who might otherwise not be heard.

In this chapter, I suggest collaborative research approaches and methods that can be used to position the active involvement of older adults in research that contributes to science, their own welfare, and the well-being of others. These approaches can be organized under community-based participatory action research (CBPR), co-involvement in intervention studies, and participatory action research (PAR). This chapter will define each approach and discuss building research partnerships and collaborative research designs and methods, dissemination approaches, and ethical considerations in participatory and collaborative research with older adults. It draws heavily from the work of the Institute for Community Research (ICR), an independent research center that has conducted participatory forms of research with older adults in the eastern United States for the past three decades, as well as the work of other researchers.

Definitions: Approaches to Participatory Research with Older Adults

While the three approaches mentioned above, CBPR, co-involvement, and participatory action research all involve collaboration between researchers and older adults, each views collaboration somewhat differently and they vary in purpose and degree of older adult involvement and leadership. *Community-based participatory research* forges partnerships between researchers and community organizations or other service settings to conduct research exploring issues that require some form of intervention or action. These studies often involve multiple organizational partners serving older adults and may or may not include older adults themselves (Schensul and LeCompte 2016a; Schensul 2020). Each partner plays a role in research direction, methodology, and results utilization (Blevins, Morton, and McGovern 2008). *Co-involvement* of older adults in collaborative intervention studies emphasizes the direct involvement of older adults in the design and actualization of interventions or actions (Lassen 2019; Bindels et al. 2014). Participatory action research (PAR) with older adults directly involves older adults themselves as leaders in research for action to remedy problems that affect them. Here, researchers are the facilitators but not the drivers of the research questions, implementation, and related action. The action itself can in turn lead to further research or inquiry (Blair and Minkler 2009). These approaches can be interdependent and synergistic; for example, a PAR project may lead to co-involvement in intervention, and a CBPR project may also involve the direct participation of the clients served by an organization or informal community leaders. These three approaches represent a continuum from greater researcher to greater older adult direction.

Common to these approaches is the development of research partnerships between formally trained researchers, housing and social service organizations serving older adults, management and staff of their residential buildings, and older adults themselves. Also shared is the repertoire of mixed methods that anthropologists can draw on, which includes interviews of all kinds, various forms of mapping, consensus and other forms of elicitation analysis, narrative and digital forms of storytelling, participatory audiovisual research, and surveying (Schensul and LeCompte 2016b; Bernard 2018; Gubrium and Sankar 1994). These methods can be tailored to the study team, topic, design, and setting, and the stage and status of development of the study participants. Areas that differ are: 1) the approach to research readiness training and joint learning that occurs in building a collaborative or participatory study; 2) the level of involvement of the partners in the study activities; 3) the role of the researcher in leadership and support for the project; and 4) the ways the data are used.

Crosscutting Methodological Concerns

Building Research Partnerships

Anthropologists work in communities that share identifiable cultural norms, assumptions, rituals, and practices. Examples of communities are townships, neighborhoods, congregate housing, apartment complexes, clinics, and long-term care settings. Regardless of shared identity with any of these communities, intersectionality calls for recognizing and addressing actual or perceived differences in power, status, race/ethnicity, language, age, education, and other factors that can impede or facilitate building and sustaining relationships (Carbado et al. 2013; Holman and Walker

2020; Shaw, Howard, and Franco 2020). Reflection on intersectionality is the responsibility of all the partners, not just the researcher, since each has a different positionality in relation to all the others. To address intersectional differences, support group cohesion, and to avoid possible conflict and build trust among partners, the roles, responsibilities, contributions, and authority of all members in the project should be defined as clearly as possible (Chang, Simon, and Dong 2016).

Identifying the "right" partners is important. Partners are selected because they meet criteria such as commitment, resources, networks, and the reach they bring to the issue (Radda et al. 2003). Identifying potential partners begins with mapping and inventorying the organizations serving older adults, key aging representatives, and places where older adults live, congregate, shop, and work. Partners may include senior centers, community centers and organizations serving older adults, older adult advocacy groups, church groups, residential communities, clinics and hospitals, and long-term care or congregate residences. Building relationships across multiple social boundaries takes time, so researchers should plan to spend at least several months meeting with potential partners and others in settings relevant to their interests.

It is helpful to establish a "living alliance" of researchers, service and government organizations, and informal groups interested in research on and with older adults that can meet on a regular basis to develop a research agenda and advance decisions and funding for research projects (Radda and Schensul 2011). Such alliances can be organized by university departments, schools or centers, or community organizations concerned with the welfare of older adults. The trust and rapport that emerges over time makes it easier to respond to new opportunities when they arise. For example, the Older Adult Oral Health Research Strategic Alliance (OHRSA), formed by the University of Connecticut School of Dental Medicine and the Institute for Community Research, developed a research and policy agenda where members played different supportive roles in several studies before it was integrated into a broader oral health alliance.

Identifying a Researchable Problem

Sometimes a study problem is identified by the researcher, who then negotiates with other partners to recognize it as important to their constituencies. Researchers from the Institute for Community Research (ICR) observed from field studies on HIV risk among drug users that people struggling with substance-use disorder, including women, were entering subsidized senior housing and possibly exposing residents to HIV infection (Schensul, Levy, and Disch 2003). They learned from building residents' concerns about unrecognized female visitors to their building, and evidence of drug use in the stairwells. The ICR ream approached an older adult advocacy organization serving low-income senior housing as well as the management of several buildings to suggest a study of HIV exposure in high-risk buildings (Radda et al. 2003).

On other occasions, a community may approach researchers with a question or issue. Some of the participants in the HIV study were concerned about residents who seemed depressed or suicidal and wanted to understand this problem (see Sidebar 15.1). This observation resulted in a partnership study involving anthropologists, gerontologists, building administrations, mental health providers, and older adults focusing on definitions of depression, access to culturally appropriate mental health care, and a mental health mobile clinic in buildings following the completion of data collection (Schensul et al. 2006).

Establishing Agreements with Partners

Agreements about participation in a study can be formal or informal. All formal organizations have administrative and management structures that both set and respond to policies and are subject to legal and insurance considerations. Usually, details of the study must be negotiated and formalized in advance. Often a written agreement is required that may involve obtaining legal advice. For each study with older adults in low-income senior housing residences, the ICR obtained memorandums of agreements that described the time commitments of staff and residents, the involvement of all parties, activities to take place, and any compensation for residents and staff. It also specified responsibilities for any possible legal liabilities. Agreements with voluntary groups and community residents also take time because they are built on trusting relationships. Conducting PAR with these groups involves much less bureaucracy and provides direct access to community residents, but brings with it other challenges, including irregular and inconsistent membership; limited financial, spatial, and staff resources; and little research capacity (Blair and Minkler 2009). At the same time, a well-funded PAR project can, with cost sharing, bring greater stability to such groups.

Negotiating Entry in a Participatory Project

On initiation, researchers will need to navigate the site's social and geographic terrain, communicating with facility gatekeepers, resident committees, and informal leaders. People in these positions can play supportive or obstructive roles, so it is important to identify their concerns and ask their advice about research directions. In low-income public housing, for example, typical roles include the on-site manager, an activities coordinator, tenant associations, and other informal decision-making groups or networks. In institutional settings, they might involve senior management, department heads, floor staff, special services staff, and residents. Learning the socio-spatial geography of a site is important to identify recruitment opportunities where people naturally gather, hold informal interviews, maintain interview privacy, and situate programs or activities to be maximally inclusive (see Sidebar 15.1).

At the same time, research staff developed connections with resident committees and groups of residents to introduce the study, destigmatize mental

---

SIDEBAR 15.1

Case Study

Building a Partnership to Confront Depression in Older Adults

To respond to resident concerns about depression, the lead investigator and author of this chapter, an anthropologist with experience in research design, qualitative methods, and gerontology, formed a partnership to develop a comprehensive approach to understanding and managing depression in older adults. It included research and clinical expertise in aging mental health and quantitative analysis as well as referral opportunities for mental health emergencies through a network of clinics providing services to older adults. The partnership also included an agency advocating for, and funding, older adult services as well as six large subsidized senior housing apartment buildings in central Connecticut, where management was interested in the problem of depression. This team met monthly, reviewed research design and emerging data results, and took on different roles as needed as the study progressed.

health, and introduce referral opportunities for more serious mental health problems. A hospital-based gerontological mental health clinic agreed to introduce a service to address mental health problems into study buildings once the data collection phase had ended. This service was staffed with bilingual mental health professionals and delivered in an empty apartment at times convenient for building residents who could not travel or did not want to be seen at an outside mental health clinic (Schensul et al. 2006).

There are numerous guidelines for building strong, equitable, community-researcher partnerships (Michelle, Baskett, and Bechstein 2011; Schensul and LeCompte 2016a). All of them emphasize transparency; trust-building through recognition of mutual interests and inter-partner differences; researcher commitment to understanding, communities, culture and setting; and population and equitable cost sharing (D'Alonzo 2010). Good partnerships are worth the effort as they generally produce better research and often result in lasting research programs and long-standing relationships.

Research Design and Methods

In an ideal collaboration, all partners should play a part in building and/or selecting the elements of a good research design. The repertoire of methods for working with older adults and the organizations that serve them is broad. Partners should also be able to explain, support, implement, and understand the results of the research. Since most service organizations are not familiar with rigorous research and intervention studies, and researchers are not always familiar with the constraints of service provision, both training and negotiation are needed to evolve a workable joint study.

Once a research topic has been identified, basic elements of a strong research design and methods are as follows.

1. *Identifying research questions.* Good research questions frame the topic, content, and context of the study. Building research questions collaboratively allows all partners to identify their concerns and gaps in knowledge in a facilitated process. Discussions are best facilitated by a researcher and a community partner to model the contributions of both. All partners can then organize and prioritize the questions into a more focused study.
2. *Building a research model.* A research model is a "local theory" that diagrams multiple factors associated with the study topic. Most anthropological research begins with personal experience,

the research questions, and the literature, all of which should be synthesized into a model to guide the study methodology. Building an initial model together allows all partners to identify and unpack the study topic (the dependent domain) and its correlates using their own knowledge base. The model helps a group to identify hypotheses, conscious and unconscious biases, and areas of initial agreement and disagreement. It is a start point, with domains to be explored both qualitatively and quantitatively depending on the study. Children and adults of all ages can create research models with help. Some examples of research models based on ICR studies build by study team members working with older adults are depicted in Figures 15.1 and 15.2.

3. *Deciding on a research design.* Among the most common designs used in research on aging are case studies or ethnographies of institutional settings; cross-sectional qualitative studies, such as observations and interviews with people with dementia; cross-sectional mixed-methods studies combining qualitative work

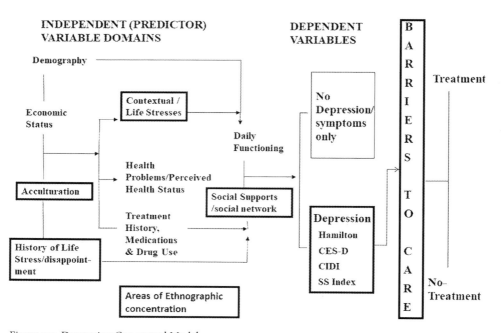

Figure 15.1. Depression Conceptual Model.

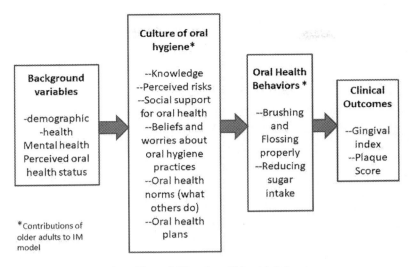

Figure 15.2. Good Oral Health Model Based on Older Adult Input.

and surveys; longitudinal designs following people over time; interactions between older adults and others, especially caregivers; and intervention designs comparing and evaluating one program with another for comparison. All members of the research team should understand, discuss, and critique the study design rationale and implications. The uses of these designs by anthropologists are described in more detail in the *Ethnographer's Toolkit*, books 1 and 7 (LeCompte and Schensul 2010).

4. *Deciding on data collection methods.* In research with older adults, the research methods that anthropologists typically use may be adapted to accommodate the capacities of all the partners, including the older adults themselves. Beginning a study with observations, informal and more structured interviews, and other forms of engaged storytelling helps to tailor any other methods that follow. Data collection options include:

Observation. Participant observation, more systematically structured empirical approaches to observation or a combination of both, provide information on "how things work," key actors, how people interact, managing the study environment, entry to meetings and activities, and the extent to which people are empowered to act on their own. Older adults are very aware of their social surroundings and can share their observations in their own environments with researchers.

In-depth interviews with key informants and older adult community or congregate residents help researchers learn about the topic and its context in greater depth from those directly involved as actors. These interviews are best conducted in person, but during the coronavirus pandemic, researchers are learning how to use phone interviews and other digital technologies to conduct intimate interviews from a distance (Verhage et al. 2020). Older adults can conduct brief interviews with peers and especially during the conduct of interventions in which they interact with others.

Group interviews, including focus groups (Schatz, Seeley, and Zalwango 2018) and "walk along interviews" (Van Cauwenberg et al. 2012), show how people interact with each other and what they think about the topic and help build rapport between researchers, older adults and other partners, and among partnership members themselves. Group interviews are useful during the discovery phase and later on in reacting to research results or planning interventions. They are ideal for drawing older adults into discussions around research topics and interventions of importance to them.

Elicitation techniques are creative ways to obtain responses from people that can be coded or classified later to assess the cultural interpretations of a group. Responses can be elicited from photographs or drawings related to a theme. Older Latinx adults uncomfortable with the idea of dementia were shown drawings of older Latinos with dementia based on a Latino artist's observations and asked about their reactions. This allowed for deeper conversation about the meaning of dementia in their lives and created images for use in a Spanish coloring book for grandchildren about dementia (Wetle and Schensul 1989), as well as a photographic exhibit. Another option is to invite older adults to make films, collages, or other products on a theme and interpret them for researchers and their peers. Older adults working on an influenza vaccine uptake project created a film based on a set of messages they forged to reduce their peers' fears of vaccination and its consequences, which was used in an intervention study, and to promote vaccine uptake through the media (Schensul et al. 2009).

Consensus analysis, another frequently used form of elicitation with older adults, first elicits items in a cultural domain and then asks respondents to group the concepts which are then conceptually designated as cultural subthemes. Consensus analysis is similar to concept mapping (Howell, Seater, and McLinden 2020), in that it provides a group measure of agreement with these subthemes but consensus analysis identifies degree of proximity that allows for further exploration of range of variation in the population in relation to "mainstream" cultural norms, beliefs or values (Aguilera-Velasco et al. 2017). The groupings analyzed with software result in thematic classifications that can be used in interviews and surveys that explore similarities and variations quantitatively, as well as to facilitate more discussion around the themes (Welgama 2016).

Mapping locates key concepts on surfaces, including actual geographic surfaces, and bodies. Maps can be viewed or drawn by older adults as part of life history reconstruction. Older adults can use maps or spatial memory to characterize important locations in their experience. With group-drawn maps (i.e., social maps), members can identify places where people gather, where local historical events occurred, and how places change. Mapping the body enables people to locate emotions and physical sensations enabling them to describe how illness affects them (Coetzee et al. 2019). The literature on group geographic and other forms of mapping for participatory research on aging is relatively sparse. Nonetheless, the approach has great potential especially when combined with observations of contexts where older adults live, shop, and work, providing opportunities to interview them or the people that support them. These observations and interviews can occur during "walking tours," a first step in participant observation, in which researchers walk through neighborhoods and in locations where older adults gather and use the opportunity to meet people as they go, or scheduled visits to mapped sites where seniors participate in activities or wait for services. These engagements act as an introduction to the locations, situations, and lived experiences of residents.

Ecomap, genograms, and networks are all interactive ways of identifying social networks, social supports, and communication networks (Rempel, Neufeld, and Kushner 2007; York Cornwell and Goldman 2020). Ecomaps can also be used to identify resources, sources of power, and obstacles to change. Genograms diagram intergenerational patterns of illness or addiction, and social networks can be used to discuss relationships with family members, friends, peers, and others. These elicitation tools help researchers and older adults, individually and in groups, learn more about their social selves in social settings. They can also provide a good picture of individual variation in responses and group or cultural patterning.

Life narratives elicit older adults' reflections on their lives from which themes, patterns, and sequences can be extracted. Narratives can be organized around timelines, photographs, or other objects that enable respondents to recollect, reflect, and recount their stories. Building a life story creates intimacy between the interviewer and the older adult respondent that can be informative and therapeutic for both. Storytelling in any form serves many purposes from enhancing personal dignity, meaning, and identity, to relationship building, reduction of loneliness and solitude, and even offering culturally rooted life histories to a wider public (Brotman, Ferrer, and Koehn 2019). These stories can be shared in videos and films that older adults produce (Burns, Kwan, and Walsh 2020).

Ethnographic surveys are important in illustrating the range of variation in a population. Ethnographic surveys consist of variables and scales that ideally emerge directly from the field setting and population rather than being borrowed wholesale from other studies (Krause 2002; Schensul and LeCompte 2012). Surveys should be reviewed with a representative sample of members of the study population to make sure the questions are understood before administration to a larger sample. Generally older adults prefer conversation over surveys, so survey administrators including peer surveyors should use their own judgment in relating to respondents but avoid influencing responses or taking up too much survey time with conversation. Survey results can also result in intervention development (see Sidebar 15.2).

> **SIDEBAR 15.2**
>
> **Case Study**
>
> *The "Loneliness Study"*
>
> Loneliness emerged as a central problem among older adults in subsidized senior housing during the first several months of lockdown during the coronavirus pandemic via a brief survey on coping. From these findings, a partnership of principal investigators (PIs), agencies, and a mental health expert obtained a seed grant to survey and interview 80 older, low-income Black, Hispanic, South/SE Asian, and White adults about loneliness. Participants were asked for their ideas about using the internet to reduce loneliness, a chronic problem even in the absence of the coronavirus. The evidence showed that older adults far preferred face-to-face encounters and enjoyed storytelling. The team has now invited a nurse anthropologist who directs an international storytelling center to join the team. The study team is now planning a reminiscence-based storytelling intervention for individuals and groups to reduce loneliness with an advisory group of older adults that can be implemented once elders have been vaccinated for COVID-19.

Co-Development and Co-Conduct of Interventions

An intervention is an intentional introduction of a program, activity, or treatment into the ongoing life of a social community. Communities independently design and implement interventions all the time with and without scientific input. Anthropological public health interventions are those developed in collaboration with the study community based on their needs. Anthropologists have historically shied away from interventions (Rylko-Bauer, Singer, and Willigen 2006), but collaboration with communities and groups of older adults often calls for, even demands, interventions out of need and because any marginalized community, especially communities of color, want to see returns on their investment in research studies. Interventions designed by anthropologists working with providers and users includes the entire research, co-development, co-implementation, and evaluation sequence. With the recognition that individual behavior exists in a cultural context and web of relationships, it is becoming increasingly important to develop multilevel interventions with synergistic effects (Schensul and Trickett 2009; Lewis et al. 2016; Agurs-Collins et al. 2019). One such example mentions conducting reminiscence work with people with dementia and at the same time changing the institutional setting so that staff and administration are able to create a reminiscent environment and use reminiscence tools post intervention (Woods et al. 2018).

Team development of a promising intervention begins with formative work to identify a need for change, at what level the change should occur, and what the content and approach of the change effort will be. Tools for

---

SIDEBAR 15.3

Case Study
Community Decision-Making on Medication Management Interventions

A group of researchers and older adult residents of senior housing apartment buildings, concerned about proper medication management, learned that their peers were using up to 20 medications each day without always knowing why. Researchers in the group wanted to implement a peer-to-peer intervention, with suggestions for medication literacy and management. However, when asked what to do and whether this approach might work, participants said that people in their community would not like to be approached by their peers on anything related to their medications, which they considered a confidential matter. They decided that people in their community would much prefer to come to a community event where they could mingle with their friends and learn from an expert regarding good medication management practice. They also wanted pharmacists to do reviews of medication on-site.

developing ethnographic or culturally specific interventions are available to researchers and can be utilized by teams to develop their own interventions and test them (Schensul and LeCompte 2016c; Okraku et al. 2017). Older adults are critical partners in the process because they can readily identify what would or would not be effective in their setting, what the content of an intervention should be, and how to deliver it effectively (see Sidebar 15.3). Co-design is especially important with new approaches and technology (Mannheim et al. 2019; Wright et al. 2018).

In a multilevel design, older adults can act as peer interventionists at the individual level, and as empowered peer role models and "influencers" of changing norms and policies at the group or community level. The case of Good Oral Health, a bi-level community-based clinical trial to improve oral health of older adults, illustrates these principles (see Sidebar 15.4).

SIDEBAR 15.4

Case Study

Good Oral Health; A Bi-level Intervention to Improve Oral Hygiene of Older Adults

This interdisciplinary, intersectional, collaborative study took place from 2011 to 2020 showing the advantages of a long-term partnership. First, the lead investigators at ICR and the UCONN dental school established partnerships with oral health advocates, dental school faculty, managers and management, and residents of 22 rent-subsidized senior housing residences in central Connecticut to build support for oral hygiene research. Informal discussion groups with residents identified their health concerns and established oral health as a priority. In-depth discussion of issues around dental access resulted in the development of a set of concepts to include in an intervention to improve oral health, including reasons for avoiding dental care, oral health knowledge, fears about contracting oral diseases, and worries about oral health self-management. Residents also were

(continued)

(Sidebar 5.4—*continued*)

interested in playing a role in the planned intervention and the opportunity to get together to discuss oral health with an expert.

The study team created a theoretical framework based on residents' concerns and linked it to an existing theoretical framework, the Integrated Health Behavior Change model adapted for oral health (IM) (see Figure 15.1). This led to a bi-level approach that included face-to-face counseling tailored to individual needs and a community-level oral health campaign with residents as health educators to change oral hygiene norms. The counseling intervention was conducted by older health educators from the same ethnic/racial backgrounds as participants, and addressed concepts in the IM model through participants' narratives about their own oral health and hygiene concerns. For the campaign, older adult peer educators received training to prepare messages, games, and activities pegged to the concepts in the IM model and used them to guide discussions with campaign attendees. A successful pilot study evolved into a full-scale clinical trial in which elders as peer educators played a central role (Schensul et al. 2019).

Participatory Research with Older Adults

Participatory Action Research (PAR) with older adults involves them in learning how to design and implement research on an issue that affects them directly and to use both the process and results to influence behavior, policy, and programmatic practice. PAR is an empowerment approach rooted in the work of activist social scientists of the past 70 years that begins with the premise that older adults should own research on issues affecting them directly. PAR with older adults is a multifaceted group process that reduces isolation, improves communication, enhances reasoning skills, and provides the informational basis to argue for needed structural changes. The successful involvement of older adults as peer educators, advocates, and as producers of information strongly suggests its feasibility and potential effectiveness in enhancing older adult voices. Unlike youth PAR, however, there are few examples of projects in which older adults, especially in marginalized community situations, are involved in full-scale research for action. Notably, PAR approaches have been criticized for their lack of genuine involvement of older adults (Corrado et al. 2019).

The most popular approach to PAR with older adults is Photovoice, an approach that stems from Paulo Freire's use of photos to elicit understandings of discrimination and oppression and can readily engage older adults as full participants (see Sidebar 15.5). Photovoice uses photographs taken by older adults as vehicles for them to tell their story to each other, display the photos, and use the images to mount related action for change (Baker and Wang 2006; Hergenrather et al. 2009; Novek, Morris-Oswald, and Menec 2012).

SIDEBAR 15.5

Case Study
The Recipes for Life Project

Food and family are important themes as people reflect on their lives and remember their parents and family events, often in other countries. Older adults also have important life lessons to share and have the desire to feel useful in their communities. "Recipes for Life," a multimodality Photovoice project with diverse older adults in senior housing, was devised to reduce social isolation and inspire life review and reflection through photographs and text. The project team engaged a retired, bilingual, Puerto Rican communications professor and professional photographer to teach volunteers how to use digital cameras. He took professional photographs of each volunteer free of charge. An anthropologist interviewed volunteers about their lives, their favorite recipes, the memories surrounding food and family events, and their "recipes" or recommendations for others based on their life experiences. Older adult volunteers advised on the curated exhibit that included their mounted professional portraits, recipes for food and life, and their own photographs with descriptions. Many of the contributors spoke about their lives and photos at the many exhibits of the materials in their city (Radda and Schensul 2011).

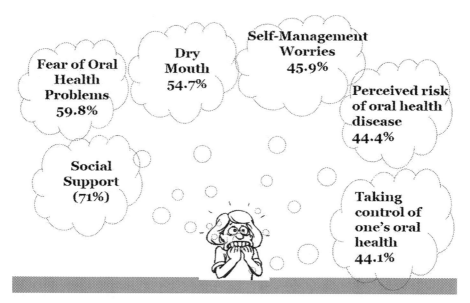

Figure 15.3. The Areas That People Needed the Most Improvement.

Joint Analysis of Data

Each of the data collection methods has an associated approach to analysis. Usually that involves identifying themes and patterns from the qualitative data. Several of the methods like mapping, consensus analysis, and PAR approaches based on photographs or video usually involve the research team and participants in joint analysis while they are actually working on the data. Researchers with quantitative skills usually take the lead in analyzing survey data. Figuring out ways of presenting the data to the rest of the study team involves two key elements: identifying the most salient or the most puzzling results for presentation and discussion; and presenting the data in a form that makes it understandable to the audience, using infographics.

There are few examples of PAR with older adults in which the PAR team members analyze either qualitative or survey data. Qualitative data can be analyzed and interpreted either through ongoing discussions based on interviews, team members' conduct, or by preparing texts that share a common theme, illustrating the texts and discussing them with the PAR group. It is certainly possible for some older adults to analyze survey data either by using basic statistical software like Microsoft Excel or a menu-driven software program like IBM SPSS, especially if they are mathematically literate. Otherwise, researchers can represent results with infographics and other visuals and use them for discussion and interpretation (see Figure 15.3).

Sharing Research Results

Research results should always be shared within the study team and in the communities or other settings where a study takes place. It is easier to share thematic geographic information systems (GIS)–based stories or visual data than survey data with team members. Sharing survey data requires more consideration to arrive at the most salient results for specific audiences. Using simple frequencies, cross tabulations, charts, diagrams, and other visual aids can be helpful in promoting discussion of the results (see Sidebar 15.6). [INSERT FIG 15.4]

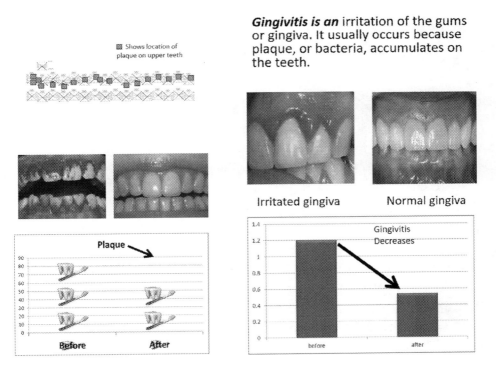

Figure 15.4. Graphs Showing Improvements in Gingival Index and Plaque Scores.

> **SIDEBAR 15.6**
>
> Case Study
> *Sharing Good Oral Health Study Results with the Study Team and Older Adult Participants*
>
> This study, a clinical trial, precluded sharing any results with either the study team or study participants till after data collection was complete. At the study's end, PIs Schensul and Reisine presented a slideshow to the entire study team of twenty people at an afternoon lunch. The slide series showed photographs of all project activities, summarized outcome results, and left room for discussion and review. Each member of the team received a commemorative poster with their photograph and the slide series on a flash drive (see Figure 15.5). To prepare for dissemination to study participants, the study team members decided to host events at each study building with refreshments, a slide presentation, and an oral hygiene "refresher." All residents were welcome to attend. The team decided to present a slide that cartooned the issues addressed most frequently in the face-to-face intervention (see Figure 15.3), and to show examples of improvement in plaque scores and gingival index (see Figure 15.4). These sessions were enjoyable and very well received. Dental hygienists showed each resident their improvement in reducing plaque. When the final results were ready, after the team had dispersed, PIs summarized the main effects of the intervention for them in simple text by email and in a Zoom presentation.

Ethical Considerations in Collaborative or Participatory Work with Older Adults

All studies that collect data from human subjects require review by an authorized Human Subjects Institutional Review Board (IRB) or Ethics Review Committee. These reviews require a study protocol, consent forms, and instruments in advance, making typical qualitative ethnographic research a challenge. Intervention studies that test new approaches to health or quality-of-life issues are an added burden since in many countries they

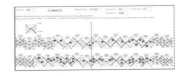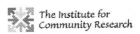

Figure 15.5. Commemorative Poster of GOH Study Staff.

are subject to additional requirements of a clinical trial, modeled after medical and drug trials. The preparation of these materials for review and the length of time required to receive the results of a review can be frustrating especially to partners who are accustomed to moving needed programs ahead without these additional protections. Starting the review process as early as possible is desirable especially when service partners or older adults have to learn the process of application along with the researchers. This chapter has concentrated on collaborative and participatory research with independently living older adults able to decide on participation in a study. Clinical, long-term care, or assisted living residences have their own additional requirements for ensuring resident safety and may even have their own IRBs. For community-based work, elders must be able to give permission to participate in a study. Older adults under legal guardianship or conservatorship for financial, health, or cognitive/mental health reasons require permission from guardians to participate. It is important to ensure that participants are able to evaluate and agree to the requirements of the research when they consent. Consent forms are often written by lawyers and have to be made understandable especially for those with limited formal education. For people who cannot write, IRBs generally require a witness to the consent, in addition to the consenter. Sleeplessness, pain, family responsibilities, or other factors may cause seniors to reschedule their appointments or miss program activities. Often rescheduling may signal reluctance to participate. Defining the boundaries between invitation to participate and harassment requires good judgment, and at times, consultation with others. Older adults may have strong negative opinions about others in their community and prefer to avoid those individuals, offering challenges to group activities. Interviewing or intervening in a private apartment can result in unexpected situations such as observation of potential abuse by caregivers or an undetected illness or injury that requires action. All partners should prepare themselves to understand and address such situations as they occur.

Summary Discussion

In this chapter, I have summarized principles and practices for collaborative and participatory research with older adults that place them in positions central to research and practice. The chapter describes collaborative approaches between researchers and organizations serving older adults, and ways that older adults can be integrated into this research or can do research on their own with assistance from academically trained partners.

The many ways that anthropologists engage in ethnographic mixed-methods research can be readily adapted for group research, data collection, analysis, and interpretation, and many methods are readily adopted by older adults for their own intervention and representation activities. Critical to this approach is rapport-building through researchers' partnerships with organizations serving older adults, and groups of older adults themselves. Partnerships take time to develop but, once established, may endure over long periods of time. It is a short journey from the typical ethnographer's individualized research practices to engaging other key partners in both research and interventions for life-quality improvement of older adults. It is a longer journey to engage older adults in the conduct of their own research to guide their voices to command social change. The chapter poses a challenge to gerontologists and anthropologists involved in gerontological research to take these steps to ensure that the subjects of research become partners in knowledge production and social change to improve their quality of life.

References

Aguilera-Velasco, María de los Ángeles, Martín Acosta-Fernández, Sergio Adalberto Franco-Chávez, and Rubén Soltero-Avelar. 2017. "Cultural Consensus about Happiness among the Elderly." *European Scientific Journal* 13(20): 1–9.

Agurs-Collins, Tanya, Susan Persky, Electra D. Paskett, Shari L Barkin, Helen I. Meissner, Tonja R. Nansel, Sonia S. Arteaga, Xinzhi Zhang, Rina Das, and Tilda Farhat. 2019. "Designing and Assessing Multilevel Interventions to Improve Minority Health and Reduce Health Disparities." *American Journal of Public Health* 109(S1): S86–S93. doi:10.2105/ajph.2018.304730.

Baker, Tamara A., and Caroline C. Wang. 2006. "Photovoice: Use of a Participatory Action Research Method to Explore the Chronic Pain Experience in Older Adults." *Qualitative Health Research* 16(10): 1405–1413. doi:10.1177/1049732306294118.

Bernard, H. Russell. 2018. *Research Methods in Anthropology: Qualitative and Quantitative Approaches*, 6th ed. Lanham, MD: Rowman and Littlefield.

Bhasin, Veena. 2007. "Medical Anthropology: A Review." *Studies on Ethno-Medicine* 1(1): 1–20. doi:10.1080/09735070.2007.11886296.

Bindels, Jill, Vivianne Baur, Karen Cox, Servé Heijing, and Tineke Abma. 2014. "Older People as Co-Researchers: A Collaborative Journey." *Ageing and Society* 34(6): 951–973. doi:10.1017/s0144686x12001298.

Blair, Thomas, and Meredith Minkler. 2009. "Participatory Action Research with Older Adults: Key Principles in Practice." *The Gerontologist* 49(5): 651–662. doi:10.1093/geront/gnp049.

Blevins, Dean, Bridget Morton, and Rene McGovern. 2008. "Evaluating a Community-Based Participatory Research Project for Elderly Mental Healthcare in Rural America." *Clinical Interventions in Aging* 3(3): 535–545. doi:10.2147/cia.s1540.

Brotman, Shari, Ilyan Ferrer, and Sharon Koehn. 2019. "Situating the Life Story Narratives of Aging Immigrants within a Structural Context: The Intersectional Life Course Perspective as Research Praxis." *Qualitative Research* 20(4): 465–484. doi:10.1177/1468794119880746.

Burns, Victoria, Crystal Kwan, and Christine A. Walsh. 2020. "Co-producing Knowledge through Documentary Film: A Community-Based Participatory Study with Older Adults with Homeless Histories." *Journal of Social Work Education* 56(sup1): S119–S130. doi:10.1080/10437797.2020.1723763.

Carbado, Devon W., Kimberlé Williams Crenshaw, Vickie M. Mays, and Barbara Tomlinson. 2013. "Intersectionality: Mapping the Movements of a Theory." *Du Bois Review: Social Science Research on Race* 10(2): 303–312. doi:10.1017/S1742058x13000349.

Carr, Kelly, and Patricia L. Weir. 2017. "A Qualitative Description of Successful Aging through Different Decades of Older Adulthood." *Aging & Mental Health* 21(12): 1317–1325. doi:10.1080/13607863.2016.1226764.

CDC. 2020. "Healthy People: Older Adults." In *Healthy People 2020*, edited by Centers for Disease Control and Prevention (CDC)/HCHS. Atlanta, GA: CDC/NCHC.

Chang, E. Shien, Melissa A. Simon, and XinQi Dong. 2016. "Using Community-Based Participatory Research to Address Chinese Older Women's Health Needs: Toward Sustainability." *Journal of Women & Aging* 28(4): 276–284. doi:10.1080/08952841.2014.950511.

Coetzee, Bronwyne, Rizwana Roomaney, Nicola Willis, and Ashraf Kagee. 2019. "Body Mapping in Research." In *Handbook of Research Methods in Health Social Sciences*, edited by Pranee Liamputtong, 1237–1254. Singapore: Springer.

Corrado, Ann Marie, Tanya Elizabeth Benjamin-Thomas, Colleen McGrath, Carri Hand, and Debbie Laliberte Rudman. 2019. "Participatory Action Research with Older Adults: A Critical Interpretive Synthesis." *The Gerontologist* 60(5): e413–e427. doi:10.1093/geront/gnz080.

D'Alonzo, Karen. 2010. "Getting Started in CBPR: Lessons in Building Community Partnerships for New Researchers." *Nursing Inquiry* 17: 282–288. doi:10.1111/j.1440-1800.2010.00510.x.

Estes, Carroll L., and Elizabeth A. Binney. 1989. "The Biomedicalization of Aging: Dangers and Dilemmas1." *The Gerontologist* 29(5): 587–596. doi:10.1093/geront/29.5.587.

Gubrium, Jabar F., and Andrea Sankar. 1994. *Qualitative Methods in Aging Research*. Thousand Oaks, CA: Sage Publications.

Hergenrather, Kenneth C., Scott D. Rhodes, Chris A. Cowan, Gerta Bardhoshi, and Sara Pula. 2009. "Photovoice as Community-Based Participatory Research: A Qualitative Review." *American Journal of Health Behavior* 33(6): 686–698. doi:10.5993/ajhb.33.6.6.

Holman, Daniel, and Alan Walker. 2020. "Understanding Unequal Ageing: Towards a Synthesis of Intersectionality and Life Course Analyses." *European Journal of Ageing*. doi:10.1007/s10433-020-00582-7.

Howell, B. M., M. Seater, and D. McLinden. 2020. "Using Concept Mapping Methods to Define 'Healthy Aging' in Anchorage, Alaska." *Journal of Applied Gerontology*. doi:10.1177/0733464819898643.

Iris, Madelyn, and Rebecca Berman. 2009. "Aging Research in Service Settings: Ethno-gerontological Work in Practice." *Anthropology News* 50(8): 26. doi:10.1111/j.1556-3502.2009.50826_1.x.

Krause, Neal. 2002. "A Comprehensive Strategy for Developing Closed-Ended Survey Items for Use in Studies of Older Adults." *Journals of Gerontology: Series B* 57(5): S263–S274. doi:10.1093/geronb/57.5.S263.

Lassen, Aske Juul. 2019. "Agencements of Reanimation: Facilitating an Active Old Age through Danish Co-Creation Initiatives." *Anthropology & Aging* 40(2): 14. doi:10.5195/aa.2019.166.

LeCompte, Margaret, and Jean Schensul. 2010. *Designing and Conducting Ethnographic Research: An Introduction*, 2nd ed. Edited by Jean Schensul and Margaret LeCompte. 7 vols. Vol. 1, *Ethnographer's Toolkit*. Lanham, MD: Rowman and Littlefield.

Lewis, Megan A., Tania M. Fitzgerald, Brittany Zulkiewicz, Susana Peinado, and Pamela A. Williams. 2016. "Identifying Synergies in Multilevel Interventions: The Convergence Strategy." *Health Education & Behavior* 44(2): 236–244. doi:10.1177/1090198116673994.

Mannheim, Ittay, Ella Schwartz, Wanyu Xi, Sandra C. Buttigieg, Mary McDonnell-Naughton, Eveline J. M. Wouters, and Yvonne van Zaalen. 2019. "Inclusion of Older Adults in the Research and Design of Digital Technology." *International Journal of Environmental Research and Public Health* 16(19): 3718. doi:10.3390/ijerph16193718.

Michelle, Vazquez Jacobus, Robert Baskett, and Christina Bechstein. 2011. "Building Castles Together: A Sustainable Collaboration as a Perpetual Work-in-Progress." *Gateways: International Journal of Community Research and Engagement* 4: 65–82.

Nicolescu, Gabriela. 2019. "Keeping the Elderly Alive: Global Entanglements and Embodied Practices in Long-Term Care in Southeast Italy." *Anthropology & Aging* 40(1): 77–93. doi:10.5195/aa.2019.202.

Novek, Sheila, Toni Morris-Oswald, and V. Menec. 2012. "Using Photovoice with Older Adults: Some Methodological Strengths and Issues." *Ageing & Society* 32: 451–470.

Okraku, Therese Kennelly, Valerio Leone Sciabolazza, Raffaele Vacca, and Christopher McCarty. 2017. "A Mixed Method Approach for Identifying Emerging Fields and Building Collaborative Teams: Leveraging Network Ethnography to Design Experimental Interventions." *Ethnographic Praxis in Industry Conference Proceedings* 2017(1): 177–196. doi:10.1111/1559-8918.2017.01146.

Ory, Marcia G. 1995. "Aging, Health, and Culture: The Contribution of Medical Anthropology." *Medical Anthropology Quarterly* 9(2): 281–283. doi:10.1525/maq.1995.9.2.02a00100.

Perkinson, Margaret A. 1993. "Maximizing Personal Efficacy in Older Adults." *Physical & Occupational Therapy in Geriatrics* 10(3): 57–72. doi:10.1080/J148v10n03_05.

Perkinson, Margaret A., and Samantha L. Solimeo. 2013. "Aging in Cultural Context and as Narrative Process: Conceptual Foundations of the Anthropology of Aging as Reflected in the Works of Margaret Clark and Sharon Kaufman." *The Gerontologist* 54(1): 101–107. doi:10.1093/geront/gnt128.

Pines, Rachyl, and Howard Giles. 2020. "Dancing While Aging: A Study on Benefits of Ballet for Older Women." *Anthropology and Aging* 1(1). doi:10.5195/aa.2020.209.

Radda, Kim E., Jean Jessica Schensul, William B. Disch, Judith A. Levy, and Carmen Y. Reyes. 2003. "Assessing Human Immunodeficiency Virus (HIV) Risk among Older Urban Adults: A Model for Community-Based Research Partnership." *Family & Community Health* 26(3): 203–213.

Radda, Kim E., and Jean J. Schensul. 2011. "Building Living Alliances: Community Engagement and Community-Based Partnerships to Address the Health of Community Elders." *Annals of Anthropological Practice* 35(2): 154–173. doi:10.1111/j.2153-9588.2011.01087.x.

Rempel, Gwen R., Anne Neufeld, and Kaysi Eastlick Kushner. 2007. "Interactive Use of Genograms and Ecomaps in Family Caregiving Research." *Journal of Family Nursing* 13(4): 403–419. doi:10.1177/1074840707307917.

Rylko-Bauer, Barbara, Merrill Singer, and John Van Willigen. 2006. "Reclaiming Applied Anthropology: Its Past, Present, and Future." *American Anthropologist* 108(1): 178–190. doi:10.1525/aa.2006.108.1.178.

Schatz, Enid, Janet Seeley, and Flavia Zalwango. 2018. "Intergenerational Care For and By Children: Examining Reciprocity through Focus Group Interviews with Older Adults in Rural Uganda." *Demographic Research* 10: 2003–2026.

Schensul, Jean Jessica. 2020. "Community Based Research Partnerships for Co-constructing Participatory Forms of Social Justice Research and Action." *Tracce Urbane* 8: 42–67.

Schensul, Jean Jessica, and Edison Trickett. 2009. "Introduction to Multi-level Community Based Culturally Situated Interventions." *American Journal of Community Psycholology* 43(3–4): 232–240.

Schensul, Jean Jessica. Robison, Julie, Carmen Y. Reyes, K. Radda, S. Gaztambide, and W. B. Disch. 2006. "Building Interdisciplinary/Intersectoral Research Partnerships for Community-Based Mental Health Research with Older Minority Adults." *American Journal of Community Psychology* 38(1/2): 79–93.

Schensul, J., Susan Reisine, James Grady, and Jianghong Li. 2019. "Improving Oral Health in Older Adults and People with Disabilities: Protocol for a Community-Based Clinical Trial (Good Oral Health)." *Journal of Medical Internet Research: Research Protocols* 8(12): e14555. doi:10.2196/14555.

Schensul, Jean Jessica, and Margaret LeCompte. 2016a. "Building Partnerships and Collaborations for Ethnography in Action." In *Ethnography in Action*, edited by Jean Schensul and Margaret LeCompte, 84–129. Lanham, MD: Rowman and Littlefield.

Schensul, Jean Jessica, Judith A. Levy, and William B. Disch. 2003. "Individual, Contextual, and Social Network Factors Affecting Exposure to HIV/AIDS Risk among Older Residents Living in Low-Income Senior Housing Complexes." *JAIDS: Journal of Acquired Immune Deficiency Syndromes* 33(2): S138.

Schensul, Jean Jessica, and Margaret LeCompte, eds. 2012. *Essential Ethnographic Methods: A Mixed Methods Approach.* Lanham, MD: Rowman and Littlefield.

——. 2016. *The Ethnographer's Toolkit.* Lanham, MD: Rowman and Littlefield.

Schensul, Jean Jessica, Kim Radda, Emil Coman, and Elsie Vazquez. 2009. "Multi-level Intervention to Prevent Influenza Infections in Older Low Income and Minority Adults." *American Journal of Community Psychology* 43(3/4): 313–329.

Shaw, Jackie, Jo Howard, and Erika López Franco. 2020. "Building Inclusive Community Activism and Accountable Relations through an Intersecting Inequalities Approach." *Community Development Journal* 55(1): 7–25. doi:10.1093/cdj/bsz033.

Shenk, Dena, and Jay Sokolovsky. 2001. "Introduction: Positive Adaptations to Aging in Cultural Context." *Journal of Cross-Cultural Gerontology* 16(1): 1–3. doi:10.1023/a:1010642813571.

Sokolovsky, Jay. 2020. *Cultural Context of Aging: Global Perspectives.* Santa Barbara, CA: Praeger.

Song, Misoon, and Eun-Hi Kong. 2015. "Older Adults' Definitions of Health: A Metasynthesis." *International Journal of Nursing Studies* 52(6): 1097–1106. https://doi.org/10.1016/j.ijnurstu.2015.02.001.

Van Cauwenberg, Jelle, Veerle Van Holle, Dorien Simons, Riet Deridder, Peter Clarys, Liesbet Goubert, Jack Nasar, Jo Salmon, Ilse De Bourdeaudhuij, and Benedicte Deforche. 2012. "Environmental Factors Influencing Older Adults' Walking for Transportation: A Study Using Walk-Along Interviews." *International Journal of Behavioral Nutrition and Physical Activity* 9(1): 85. doi:10.1186/1479-5868-9-85.

Verhage, Miriam, Lucia Thielman, Lieke de Kock, and Jolanda Lindenberg. 2020. "It Takes Two to Tango." In *Age of Covid Blog Series*, August 14, 2020, edited by Celeste Pang, Cristina Douglas, Janelle Taylor, and Narelle Warren. Anthropology and Aging: University of Pittsburgh. https://anthropologyandgerontology.com/it-takes-two-to-tango/.

Welgama, Jayaprasad. 2016. "The Meaning of Being an Elderly Person among the Sinhalese: An Ethnographic Perspective." *International Journal of Arts and Commerce* 5(5): 27–43.

Wetle, T., and J. Schensul. 1989. "Identifying Symptoms of Alzheimer's Disease among Elderly Puerto Ricans and Their Family Caregivers." Newsletter of the University of Connecticut Center on Aging, Winter.

Woods, B., L. O'Philbin, E. M. Farrell, A. E. Spector, and M. Orrell. 2018. "Reminiscence Therapy for Dementia." *Cochrane Database of Systematic Reviews* 3 (Art. No.: CD001120). doi:10.1002/14651858.CD001120.pub3.

Wright, Kathy D., Carolyn H. Still, Lenette M. Jones, and Karen O. Moss. 2018. "Designing a Cocreated Intervention with African American Older Adults for Hypertension Self-Management." *International Journal of Hypertension* 2018: 7591289. doi:10.1155/2018/7591289.

York Cornwell, Erin, and Alyssa W. Goldman. 2020. "Local Ties in the Social Networks of Older Adults." *Journals of Gerontology: Series B*. doi:10.1093/geronb/gbaa033.

16

Recruiting Participants for Dementia Research without Saying "Dementia"

A Site Study in Central Mexico

ERIC E. GRIFFITH

> *It's important that you not start the conversation by saying "Alzheimer" or "dementia." We have had, at another institution, two lawsuits filed against us [by family members of patients] for "labeling and treating patients as insane" after diagnosing them with dementia. (translated by the author from Spanish)*

I received this text message from the director of an assisted living facility in central Mexico in mid-2018 while trying to recruit participants for my dissertation research on Alzheimer's disease (AD) caregiver experiences. Several days prior, the director had generously agreed to put me in touch with families who participated in the facility's day programs and had expressed a willingness to be interviewed for my project. At first, this seemed like a major breakthrough. Following the advice of local experts, I had spent weeks volunteering at day programs for older adults, hanging up recruitment flyers at churches and grocery stores, and offering regular information sessions and public lectures about AD. Despite this legwork, I had struggled to even identify families who had an AD diagnosis, to say nothing of finding eligible participants who were interested in being interviewed. A collection of possible participants referred to me by an established local business was exactly the recruiting breakthrough I had been seeking. The above text message, however, deflated my optimism and I began to assume this would be another recruiting dead end. After recovering from the initial disappointment, further reflection generated an epiphany; by saying "dementia" in my previous recruitment efforts, I had been alienating a huge percentage of possible participants. That realization left me with an even bigger question: How do you recruit for a dementia study without saying "dementia"? In this chapter I will briefly outline the "recruitment crisis" in Alzheimer's disease and related dementias (ADRD) research, and then explain how I attempted to answer that question at my field site.

Recruitment Crisis

Dementia, defined as abnormal progressive deterioration of memories and other cognitive abilities (Kandel et al. 2013), affected approximately 44 million to 47 million people worldwide, as of 2016 (World Health Organization 2015; Nichols et al. 2019). Examples of specific dementia diagnoses include Alzheimer's disease, frontotemporal dementia, Lewy body dementia, and others; these diseases are grouped together as ADRD. The primary risk factor for ADRD is advanced age (van der Flier and Scheltens 2005); as many high-income countries experience declining birth rates and longer life expectancies, the average age will rise globally and a higher proportion of the population will be at risk for these diseases in the coming years (Prince et al. 2016; Sosa-Ortiz et al. 2012). The increasing prevalence of ADRD diagnoses will have profound public health and sociocultural consequences (Anderson and McConnell 2007; Larson and Langa 2008). For example, the total economic impact of AD alone could approach several trillion dollars by midcentury (Jia et al. 2018). Given the large-scale effect that ADRD will have on the global community, research of all types, from qualitative ethnographic studies to pharmacological trials, will be increasingly important to understanding these debilitating conditions.

Recruitment difficulties and discussions of appropriate sample size in ADRD research have been well documented, dating back to at least 1993 (Cotrell and Schulz 1993; Treves et al. 2000). Recent literature describes a worsening "recruitment crisis" that jeopardizes both the viability and efficiency of ADRD research projects (Fargo et al. 2016).

In many cases, the initial point of contact for people living with ADRD, the primary care physician, indirectly impedes possible research recruitment. Primary care physicians are often unaware of research opportunities for patients even when willing to facilitate recruitment (Jones et al. 2010), or communication barriers (Singh et al. 2008) make it difficult to fully explain available studies. Some primary care physicians also misdiagnose or fail to document ADRD symptoms (van den Dungen et al. 2010; Mitchell, Meader, and Pentzek 2011). Misdiagnosis can occur for several reasons, including a lack of universally utilized diagnostic criteria, lack of recognition of cognitive impairment by patients or family members, and/or a dearth longitudinal patient data to document cognitive decline. (See Yokomizo, Simon, and de Campos Bottino 2014 for a review.) Additionally, diagnostic criteria for ADRD have evolved over time (Lopez et al. 2011), which may make it difficult for physicians in some areas to make up-to-date diagnoses. Some physicians also hesitate to offer a diagnosis if they do not have sufficient time for comprehensive examination or if they do not believe that an ADRD diagnosis will improve a patient's overall quality of life or health (Phillips, Pond, and Goode 2011). The exact number of missed diagnoses is difficult to determine, but one review documented a diagnosis sensitivity for ADRD by primary care physicians ranging from 0.26 to 0.69 (Bradford et al. 2009). In other words, physicians correctly diagnosed ADRD in roughly 26–69 percent of cases. The connection between recruitment and diagnosis has been amplified as many studies have begun to focus on the earliest stages of ADRD, especially in AD (Calamia, Bernstein, and Keller 2016; Reiman et al. 2011; Watson et al. 2014). Thus, delayed diagnosis eliminates possible early-stage participants from these trials. Conversely, the more severe cognitive decline of individuals suffering later stage ADRD can also be an impediment to research recruitment (Cowdell 2008; Bartlett, Milne, and Croucher 2019); this is especially problematic for research purposes because it inhibits the ability to document the full variation in cognitive changes that people experience in later stage ADRD. Regardless of the exact quantified impact, the barrier at the initial point of contact for potential participants likely plays a significant role in impeding recruitment as it eliminates numerous eligible candidates.

From a logistical perspective, many people living with ADRD require significant assistance with activities of daily living (ADLs) and may not be able to consent to research participation. To account for these limitations, protocols often recruit in caregiver/diagnosed person dyads, and the caregiver then either participates in the study or ensures protocol adherence from their partner (Bartlett, Milne, and Croucher 2019; Szabo et al. 2018). Recruiting dyads adds an additional person to the administrative process, which can complicate logistics and has been attributed to at least one failed clinical trial (Mapstone, Elbourne, and Roberts 2007), and can also increase associated research costs (Hunninghake, Darby, and Probstfield 1987; Morrison, Winter, and Gitlin 2016). If the caregiver is an adult child, they are more likely to be working full-time or be otherwise occupied, which can complicate scheduling (Grill et al. 2013; Bartlett, Milne, and Croucher 2019). In some cases, the caregiver and person diagnosed with ADRD live separately, increasing the research travel burden for one or both parties (Grill and Galvin 2014; Kolanowski 2013). Some participants are also intimidated by the invasive or cumbersome requirements of clinical trials. Physically uncomfortable procedures (e.g., brain scans), adverse reaction to medications, and previous negative experiences with clinical trials have all been documented to deter participants from considering taking part in research (Watson et al. 2014).

Bureaucratic and protocol-based difficulties also complicate recruitment. A lack of consensus on ethical standards for ADRD research, especially relating to recruitment (see West et al. 2017 for an overview), has prevented the development of universal standards, or even guidelines, for contacting potential participants. Accordingly, it is possible, if not likely, that the lack of best-practice guidance has left some researchers writing recruitment protocols that are unnecessarily burdensome. A possible solution is to include people who have been recently diagnosed with ADRD in research planning in order to incorporate their experiences and opinions into policies that seek to balance ethical rigor with recruiting feasibility (Holland and Kydd 2015; Howell and Shogren 2019). Overall, restrictions related to study inclusion criteria, such as only accepting individuals at a certain stage of the disease or who are not taking certain medications, means that only 20–25 percent of people diagnosed with AD are eligible for any given research trial (Cooper, Ketley, and Livingston 2014; Fargo et al. 2016). Additional discussion and research on this topic would be beneficial to both researchers and participants.

Interestingly, the COVID-19 pandemic may have pushed investigators to consider alternate research methods that could mitigate logistical barriers for cases where traveling to a research site is burdensome for participants, a frequently reported concern of familial caregivers (Lawrence et al. 2014). Online and phone-based interviews were used to investigate a number of topics in 2020, including the effect of quarantine on social engagement (Wiese et al. 2020); caregiving during "stay-at-home" orders (Savla et al. 2020); the efficacy of television or phone-based health and social support (Goodman-Casanova et al. 2020); and whether or not existing cognitive screeners can be adapted for administration via telephone (Larner 2020). It is unclear whether these remote research methods will continue to proliferate post-pandemic, but the early results from the existing projects are promising and may provide continuing models for involving communities in research who have been excluded in the past (Bartlett, Milne, and Croucher 2019).

Demographic Challenges to ADRD Research Recruitment

People from diverse racial and ethnic backgrounds are often under-recruited in ADRD research despite being at higher risk for ADRDs (see Chin, Negash, and Hamilton 2011 for a review). It is estimated that 90 percent of participants in AD clinical trials identify as non-Hispanic White individuals as of 2007 (Faison et al. 2007). This disparity can be attributed to several factors, including practical effects such as clinical trials that exclude comorbidities that are more common in racial or ethnic minorities (Watson et al. 2014), and cultural effects such as a general distrust of the clinical trial process among Black individuals (Corbie-Smith et al. 1999; Zhou et al. 2017). As another example, in a qualitative study interviewing 25 Chinese American families, Hinton and colleagues (2000) identified four additional key themes that may impede recruitment: 1) the belief that ADRD-related changes are a normal part of aging; 2) participating in research could increase stress; 3) a stigma around AD in the community made formal diagnosis unlikely; and 4) research was unlikely to benefit the participants. Immigration status and language barriers have also been identified as obstacles for the Hispanic community in the United States (Gelman 2010). Overall, after reviewing the literature on recruitment of ethnic minorities in the United Kingdom, Waheed and colleagues (2019) have identified community and patient education, health services, and researchers' training as areas of focus that can alleviate these disparities.

In addition to the concerns with underrepresentation of ethnic and racial minorities in ADRD research, recruitment generally under-samples several other groups relative to the overall population of families living with ADRD. Among caregivers, spouses are more willing than adult children to participate in research (Cary et al. 2015); most ADRD care occurs in the household, and yet most recruitment, especially in multinational projects, happens elsewhere (e.g., assisted living facilities) (Brodaty and Donkin 2009); and the experiences of male caregivers are under-analyzed and under-reported, despite making up about 28 percent of all in-home caregivers (Houde 2002).

These misrepresentations could have significant downstream effects on the accuracy of how ADRDs are understood. Within an ethnographic or social science context, there is significant room for improvement.

Recruitment Barriers in Mexico

With the above context in mind, I began to consider how to answer the question outlined in the introduction of this chapter: Is it possible to recruit for ADRD research without saying "dementia"? At this point, I had several months of experience at my field site in Mexico. The population of the metro area was about three million people with a wide range of socioeconomic variation. The large number of universities in the area created an educated and young pocket of society, contrasted with the overall state population, which is the third most impoverished in Mexico (Carrasco 2018). The relatively large and urban population, many of whom have access to either private or public medical care, ensured that there would be sufficient cases of AD diagnosed in the area to enroll my study. I just had to figure out how to find participants.

Further complicating matters, I was focused on recruiting patient/caregiver dyads living together in the home. Research carried out in institutionalized settings suggests that people living with ADRD can experience significant decline in quality of life (Zimmerman et al. 2003); level of care varies on between different races or ethnicities (Rivera-Hernandez, Kumar, and Epstein-Lubow 2018); and, as mentioned above, the majority of AD care worldwide is given by family members in the household. Thus, to better represent the global reality of AD, I chose to include only participants who still lived at home to mitigate the effects of institutional living. The interview protocol with each family included an open-ended, semi-ethnographic interview style to reflect the primary goal of reproducing the caregiver's perspective within the data (Spradley 2016). I created a custom questionnaire/list of themes to be asked in each interview, drawing on prior reporting that identified crucial topics in ADRD caregiving. Each participating dyad also completed a battery of neuropsychological tests to facilitate comparison of AD symptoms between the United States and Mexico. The battery consisted of tests commonly used to evaluate AD in Mexico (Ramírez Díaz et al. 2013) and the United States (Weiner and Lipton 2009).

The caregiver completed the following questionnaires: Katz Activities of Daily Living Assessment, Lawton and Brody Instrumental Activities of

Daily Living Scale, Neuropsychiatric Inventory, and the Informant Questionnaire on Cognitive Decline in the Elderly Test. These four tests ask the caregiver to assess the behavior, emotional state, and cognitive state of the person diagnosed with AD. The person diagnosed with AD was evaluated with the following instruments: Maze Test, National Sleep Foundation Sleep Diary, and the Consortium to Establish a Registry for Alzheimer's Disease Neuropsychological Battery. These evaluations capture the details of specific neural deficits as well as depressive symptoms, the most common psychiatric comorbidity of AD. Each interview generally lasted two to four hours in the home, and families could choose to split the interview across two visits. In all cases, the interviews were audio recorded with the consent of the participants.

Several past studies have recommended establishing strong community relationships to facilitate recruitment (examples include Dilworth-Anderson, Thaker, and Detry Burke 2005; and Wong et al. 2019). In this spirit, I formalized a collaboration with a local physician. The doctor had private funding to implement AD education and community outreach programs and to provide free or subsidized medical services to families who needed assistance seeking AD care. But she was also struggling to identify families living with AD and enlisted my help in overhauling the community outreach materials. In return, she agreed to endorse my project to community members who were interested in research opportunities.

The next step was to identify the specifics of the recruitment barriers in this region and develop a strategy to mitigate them. The first barrier was stigma of ADRD; the nursing home director who asked me not to mention "dementia" was voicing a larger stigma of the label "dementia" or "Alzheimer's" in the area. For example, "dementia" is synonymous with insanity for many people, hence the lawsuits equating the two words. Evidence of stigmatized attitudes about ADRDs can be seen in the material culture, as well. Here is a translated example from a Mexican university website (emphasis mine):

> *This would explain why some people believe that dementia is synonymous with madness.* Strictly speaking, yes, a person who suffers from dementia loses their mental faculties; however, it is not because of a mental disorder or psychopathy—it is caused by a disease that affects several regions of the brain and therefore affects various functions. (El Colegio de la Frontera Norte 2019)

ADRD stigma takes many forms, including both public stigmas and self-stigmas (for a comprehensive review, see Nguyen and Li 2020). Stigma has real and measurable negative consequences for people living with ADRD. Here are just two examples: the public stigma can delay help-seeking for ADRD-related symptoms, which negatively impacts treatment; and stigma among medical clinicians may exclude people living with ADRD from making decisions about their own care (see Herrmann et al. 2018 for a comprehensive review). These effects, and others, can accumulate and eventually have a negative impact on quality of life for people living with ADRD and for their families (Phillipson et al. 2015). ADRD stigma is believed to be widespread; for example, one study in Brazil documented stigma-associated beliefs in over 40 percent of a five-hundred-person cross-section across multiple sociodemographic groups (Blay and Peluso 2010). Perhaps surprisingly given the global preponderance of ADRD, Herrmann and colleagues (2018) concluded in a review of existing publications that more research is needed on evidence-based methods to reduce ADRD stigma. Nearly all experimental approaches to reducing stigma identified by these researchers did not involve persons living with ADRDs. Instead, the experiments often took the form of exposing the lay public to hypothetical vignettes (Johnson et al. 2015) or a proposed stigma reduction ad campaign (Van Gorp, Vercruysse, and Van den Bulck 2012). Given the widespread presence of stigma, it likely would have been very difficult to fully recruit for my study while trying to ignore the ADRD stigma entirely, and would have biased my sample (i.e., focusing only on families who eschew ADRD stigma would not be representative). Thus, I would need to work around this complication while recruiting.

A general lack of education about ADRD in the community created a second barrier by making it more difficult to explain to possible participants the importance of research. In collaboration with my physician collaborator, I helped organize an AD awareness walk in the city as a public outreach measure. As part of the walk, we administered a survey to gauge general attitudes about ADRD. Included in the survey was a yes/no question asking if the participant had ever had a family member who had been diagnosed with ADRD; a multiple-choice option asking participants to select the ADRD-related topic they would most like to know more about; and two questions asking participants how much they agreed with the statements "Dementia/Alzheimer's disease is a disability," and "There are sufficient resources and support for people diagnosed with dementia and Alzheimer's disease in the community" on a five-point scale ranging from "strongly disagree" (1) to "strongly agree" (5).

In total, 226 people filled out the survey. With regard to topics they would like to learn more about, respondents most often chose "General Information" (34 percent), "Prevention" (20 percent), and "Caregiving" (18 percent). Those who had a family member affected by ADRD were significantly more likely to say the condition is a disability ($M=4.26$) compared to those who did not have an affected family member ($M=3.29, p=.007$). Those who had a family member affected were also less likely to say that there are sufficient ADRD resources in the community ($M=2.03$) when compared to those who did not have a family member affected by the disease ($M=2.54, p=.043$). Taken together, I interpreted the desire for additional basic information about ADRDs, coupled with the differences in perception between those who had experienced the illness firsthand and those who had not, to mean that there was possibly a low level of ADRD awareness in the community. By extension, the lack of information about ADRD in much of the public consciousness complicated my recruitment process—how could I explain the importance of my study if ADRD awareness/knowledge was generally low?

My preliminary data indicated that families in this city were hesitant to seek out an official diagnosis, creating a third barrier. Upon final analysis of the collected data, I found that the families in Mexico waited longer to get an AD diagnosis than families in the United States. The explanations for the delay in Mexico include internal family factors, such as the belief that memory loss is a normal part of aging, and external factors, such as the inability to find a physician willing and able to make the diagnosis, which often overlap (Griffith 2021). The most complete picture of diagnosis seeking in Mexico comes from Valencia-González, Ramírez-Santos and Acosta-Castillo (2017), who found that from a sample of people over 65 in a public hospital in Mexico City ($N=81,900$), only 14.3 percent of the probable cases of dementia were being diagnosed, based on the estimated 6–8 percent prevalence rate nationwide (Sosa-Ortiz 2012). This aligns with research that has shown that ADRDs are underdiagnosed in middle-income countries (Nakamura et al. 2015). Overall, this is a barrier to recruitment as delayed diagnosis reduces the number of families who realize they are experiencing ADRD.

A Model for Overcoming Recruitment Barriers

After identifying stigma, a general lack of information about ADRD in the community, and a hesitancy to seek out diagnosis or treatment for cognitive symptoms as key recruitment barriers, I began working with my collaborator on developing a model that could reach possible participants under these limitations. We ultimately settled on a vignette-based approach combined with a reframing of community outreach materials to focus on "normal vs. abnormal aging" rather than "dementia." In practice, this took the form of beginning public presentations at community events for seniors by reading three vignettes: one depicting early-stage, non-specific dementia; another on mild cognitive impairment; and a final vignette on normal aging. Here is one example of the vignette depicting probable dementia (translated from Spanish by the author):

> At 3 p.m., while waiting for your physician at your doctor's office, John (a 71-year-old man) arrives with his son. You approach them and ask how they are doing and why they are at the doctor's office. You notice that John does not recognize you even though you have been neighbors for a long time and until just last year he shopped at the store where you buy your groceries. John's son apologizes and tells you that John frequently does not recognize even him or his other son. He tells you that they came to the doctor because recently John has been having memory and language problems (he forgets a word or repeats the same word time after time). While you are talking to his son, John starts shouting, "I want to go home, I'm healthy. He just wants to kick me out of my house and sell it."

The vignettes were adapted from a prior study examining social distance from people living with ADRD in Israel (Werner 2005). They were translated to Spanish and my collaborator agreed that they represented the intended diagnoses. A vignette approach has been used with ADRD research in the past but, to my knowledge, has not been operationalized as a recruitment tool in a community setting; rather, vignettes often serve as a prompt in an interview to collect a respondent's impressions or attitudes of ADRDs (see Johnson 2015 as an example). After reading the three vignettes, audience members were asked to identify which, if any, of the stories represented someone who was experiencing abnormal aging. They were then asked if they knew anyone who might fit that description. This opened the door to present additional material explaining when an older adult should be concerned about a cognitive change and may wish to seek out medical advice. To conclude the presentation, we took audience questions and then my collaborator offered to speak privately with anyone who had specific questions or wished to follow up with her for cognitive screening at a later time. She would then forward participants interested in research to me after making an initial diagnosis.

Discussion

Audience members generally responded enthusiastically to this presentation format. By reframing the theme as "aging vs. abnormal aging," my collaborator and I seemed to avoid triggering any stigma-related judgments about the content, creating a space to use the vignettes to introduce the idea of problematic age-related cognitive changes. The follow-up materials provided education about ADRD, helping to satisfy the need for more general information, followed by an offer from a physician to do additional screening. This method rapidly helped identify several families for possible interviews. In total, 11 of the 32 interviews included in my final dataset were made via connections with the collaborating physician after one of these outreach events. No other collaboration or recruitment method netted more than five families, making this the most quantitatively successful use of time.

This experience also revealed possible design improvements in future research. Notably, I only accepted families who had been diagnosed with "probable Alzheimer's disease." That limitation eliminated several possible participants who could not or did not wish to obtain a specific diagnosis. In hindsight, given the difficulty in recruiting familial caregivers, projects based in medical or biocultural anthropology would likely be better served with broader inclusion criteria. A community-based recruitment method results in a sample that is diverse, both in terms of stage of the disease and family composition, allowing for richer descriptions of the cultural realities of AD. Finally, this study did not consider participant retention (i.e., participant follow-through in a multi-contact protocol) because of the single-contact nature of the interview protocol. Retention has been acknowledged in the literature as a related but unique issue relative to recruitment, and it is unclear whether the recruitment strategy described here would create unique retention concerns in a longer study.

In conclusion, it is possible to recruit participants for AD research without using the word "dementia." Crucially, recruitment strategies were most successful when sidestepping language that would trigger a stigmatized reaction. Specifically, redirecting community outreach materials toward aging and away from the term "dementia" while collaborating with a physician mitigated the stigma effect, allowed for face-to-face recruiting, and legitimized the project to the local population. While the specifics of this strategy were designed with central Mexico in mind, it is possible that the broader methods (e.g., vignettes as conversation starters) could be applied to other contexts with culturally appropriate modifications.

References

Alzheimer's Disease International. "Participation in Dementia Trials and Studies: Challenges and Recommendations." (2014).

Anderson, Lynda A., and Stephen R. McConnell. 2007. "Cognitive Health: An Emerging Public Health Issue." *Alzheimer's & Dementia: The Journal of the Alzheimer's Association*: S70–S73.

Bartlett, Ruth, Richard Milne, and Rebecca Croucher. 2019. "Strategies to Improve Recruitment of People with Dementia to Research Studies." *Dementia* 18(7–8): 2494–2504.

Blay, Sergio Luis, and Erica Toledo Pisa Peluso. 2010. "Public Stigma: The Community's Tolerance of Alzheimer Disease." *American Journal of Geriatric Psychiatry* 18(2): 163–171.

Bradford, Andrea, Mark E. Kunik, Paul Schulz, Susan P. Williams, and Hardeep Singh. 2009. "Missed and Delayed Diagnosis of Dementia in Primary Care: Prevalence and Contributing Factors." *Alzheimer Disease and Associated Disorders* 23(4): 306–314.

Brodaty, Henry, and Marika Donkin. 2009. "Family Caregivers of People with Dementia." *Dialogues in Clinical Neuroscience* 11(2): 217–228.

Calamia, Matthew, John P. K. Bernstein, and Jeffrey N. Keller. 2016. "I'd Do Anything for Research, But I Won't Do That: Interest in Pharmacological Interventions in Older Adults Enrolled in a Longitudinal Aging Study." *PLoS One* 11(7): e0159664.

Carrasco, Fernando Pliego. 2014. *Las Familias en Puebla*. Universidad Popular Autonoma del Estado de Pueblac, A. C.

Cary, Mark S., Jonathan D. Rubright, Joshua D. Grill, and Jason Karlawish. 2015. "Why Are Spousal Caregivers More Prevalent Than Nonspousal Caregivers as Study Partners in AD Dementia Clinical Trials?" *Alzheimer Disease and Associated Disorders* 29(1): 70–74.

Chin, Alexander L., Selamawit Negash, and Roy Hamilton. 2011. "Diversity and Disparity in Dementia: The Impact of Ethnoracial Differences in Alzheimer's Disease." *Alzheimer Disease and Associated Disorders* 25(3): 187–195.

Cooper, Claudia, Daniel Ketley, and Gill Livingston. 2014. "Systematic Review and Meta-analysis to Estimate Potential Recruitment to Dementia Intervention Studies." *International Journal of Geriatric Psychiatry* 29(5): 515–525.

Corbie-Smith, Giselle, Stephen B. Thomas, Mark V. Williams, and Sandra Moody-Ayers. 1999. "Attitudes and Beliefs of African Americans toward Participation in Medical Research." *Journal of General Internal Medicine* 14(9): 537–546.

Cotrell, Victoria, and Richard Schulz. 1993. "The Perspective of the Patient with Alzheimer's Disease: A Neglected Dimension of Dementia Research." *The Gerontologist* 33(2): 205–211.

Cowdell, Fiona. 2008. "Engaging Older People with Dementia in Research: Myth or Possibility." *International Journal of Older People Nursing* 3(1): 29–34.

Dilworth-Anderson, Peggye, Samruddhi Thaker, and Joan M. Detry Burke. 2005. "Recruitment Strategies for Studying Dementia in Later Life among Diverse Cultural Groups." *Alzheimer Disease & Associated Disorders* 19(4): 256–260.

El Colegio de la Frontera Norte. "Demencia: Causas Acumuladas que se Manifiestan en la Vejez." El Colegio de la Frontera Norte, March 3, 2019. https://www.colef.mx/estemes/demencia-causas-acumuladas-que-se-manifiestan-en-la-vejez/.

Faison, Warachal E., Susan K. Schultz, Jeroen Aerssens, Jennifer Alvidrez, Ravi Anand, Lindsay A. Farrer, Lissy Jarvik et al. 2007. "Potential Ethnic Modifiers in the Assessment and Treatment of Alzheimer's Disease: Challenges for the Future." *International Psychogeriatrics* 19(3): 539–558.

Fargo, Keith N., Maria C. Carrillo, Michael W. Weiner, William Z. Potter, and Zaven Khachaturian. 2016. "The Crisis in Recruitment for Clinical Trials in Alzheimer's and Dementia: An Action Plan for Solutions." *Alzheimer's & Dementia* 12(11): 1113–1115.

Gelman, Caroline Rosenthal. 2010. "Learning from Recruitment Challenges: Barriers to Diagnosis, Treatment, and Research Participation for Latinos with Symptoms of Alzheimer's Disease." *Journal of Gerontological Social Work* 53(1): 94–113.

Goodman-Casanova, Jessica Marian, Elena Dura-Perez, Jose Guzman-Parra, Antonio Cuesta-Vargas, and Fermin Mayoral-Cleries. 2020. "Telehealth Home Support During COVID-19 Confinement for Community-Dwelling Older Adults with Mild Cognitive Impairment or Mild Dementia: Survey Study." *Journal of Medical Internet Research* 22(5): e19434.

Griffith, Eric. 2021. "A Cross-Cultural Comparison of the Behavioral Variation of Families Living with Alzheimer's Disease." PhD diss., University of Massachusetts Amherst.

Grill, Joshua D., and James E. Galvin. "Facilitating Alzheimer's Disease Research Recruitment." *Alzheimer Disease and Associated Disorders* 28(1): 1–8.

Grill, Joshua D., Rema Raman, Karin Ernstrom, Paul Aisen, and Jason Karlawish. 2013. "Effect of Study Partner on the Conduct of Alzheimer Disease Clinical Trials." *Neurology* 80(3): 282–288.

Herrmann, Lynn K., Elisabeth Welter, James Leverenz, Alan J. Lerner, Nancy Udelson, Cheryl Kanetsky, and Martha Sajatovic. 2018. "A Systematic Review of Dementia-Related Stigma Research: Can We Move the Stigma Dial?" *American Journal of Geriatric Psychiatry* 26(3): 316–331.

Hinton, Ladson, Zibin Guo, Jennifer Hillygus, and Sue Levkoff. 2000. "Working with Culture: A Qualitative Analysis of Barriers to the Recruitment of Chinese-American Family Caregivers for Dementia Research." *Journal of Cross-Cultural Gerontology* 15(2): 119–137.

Holland, Suzanne, and Angela Kydd. 2015. "Ethical Issues When Involving People Newly Diagnosed with Dementia in Research." *Nurse Researcher* 22(4): 25–29.

Houde, Susan Crocker. 2002. "Methodological Issues in Male Caregiver Research: An Integrative Review of the Literature." *Journal of Advanced Nursing* 40(6): 626–640.

Howell, B. M., and Shogren, K. A. 2019. "Differing Understandings of Informed Consent Held by Research Institutions, People with Intellectual Disability, and Guardians: Implications for Inclusive, Ethical Research." In *Research Involving Participants with Cognitive*

Disability and Difference: Ethics, Autonomy, Inclusion, and Innovation, edited by M. A. Cascio and E. Racine, 27–37. Oxford: Oxford University Press.

Hunninghake, Donald B., Charles A. Darby, and Jeffrey L. Probstfield. 1987. "Recruitment Experience in Clinical Trials: Literature Summary and Annotated Bibliography." *Controlled Clinical Trials* 8(4): 6–30.

Jia, Jianping, Cuibai Wei, Shuoqi Chen, Fangyu Li, Yi Tang, Wei Qin, Lina Zhao et al. 2018. "The Cost of Alzheimer's Disease in China and Re-estimation of Costs Worldwide." *Alzheimer's & Dementia* 14(4): 483–491.

Johnson, Rebecca, Kristin Harkins, Mark Cary, Pamela Sankar, and Jason Karlawish. 2015. "The Relative Contributions of Disease Label and Disease Prognosis to Alzheimer's Stigma: A Vignette-Based Experiment." *Social Science & Medicine* 143: 117–127.

Jones, Roy W., S. Andrieu, S. Knox, and J. Mackell. 2010. "Physicians and Caregivers: Ready and Waiting for Increased Participation in Clinical Research." *Journal of Nutrition, Health & Aging* 14(7): 563–568.

Kandel, E. R., J. H. Schwartz, T. M. Jessell, S. A. Siegelbaum, and A. J. Hudspeth. 2013. *Principles of Neural Science*. New York: McGraw-Hill Education.

Kolanowski, Ann, Paula Mulhall, Andrea Yevchak, Nikki Hill, and Donna Fick. 2013. "The Triple Challenge of Recruiting Older Adults with Dementia and High Medical Acuity in Skilled Nursing Facilities." *Journal of Nursing Scholarship* 45(4): 397–404.

Larner, Andrew J. 2020. "Cognitive Testing in the COVID-19 Era: Can Existing Screeners Be Adapted for Telephone Use?" *Neurodegenerative Disease Management* 11(1): 77–82.

Larson, Eric B., and Kenneth M. Langa. 2008. "The Rising Tide of Dementia Worldwide." *The Lancet* 372(9637): 430–432.

Lawrence, Vanessa, James Pickett, Clive Ballard, and Joanna Murray. 2014. "Patient and Carer Views on Participating in Clinical Trials for Prodromal Alzheimer's Disease and Mild Cognitive Impairment." *International Journal of Geriatric Psychiatry* 29(1): 22–31.

Lopez, Oscar L., Eric McDade, Mario Riverol, and James T. Becker. 2011. "Evolution of the Diagnostic Criteria for Degenerative and Cognitive Disorders." *Current Opinion in Neurology* 24(6): 532–541.

Mapstone, J., D. Elbourne, and I. Roberts. 2007. "Strategies to Improve Recruitment to Research Studies [Cochrane Methodology Review]." *Cochrane Database of Systemic Reviews* 2.

Mitchell, Alex J., Nicholas Meader, and Michael Pentzek. 2011. "Clinical Recognition of Dementia and Cognitive Impairment in Primary Care: A Meta-Analysis of Physician Accuracy." *Acta Psychiatrica Scandinavica* 124(3): 165–183.

Morrison, Karen, Laraine Winter, and Laura N. Gitlin. 2016. "Recruiting Community-Based Dementia Patients and Caregivers in a Nonpharmacologic Randomized Trial: What Works and How Much Does It Cost?" *Journal of Applied Gerontology* 35(7): 788–800.

Nakamura, Antonio Eduardo, Davi Opaleye, Giovanni Tani, and Cleusa P. Ferri. 2015. "Dementia Underdiagnosis in Brazil." *The Lancet* 385(9966): 418–419.

Nguyen, Trang, and Xiaoming Li. 2020. "Understanding Public-Stigma and Self-Stigma in the Context of Dementia: A Systematic Review of the Global Literature." *Dementia* 19(2): 148–181.

Nichols, Emma, Cassandra E. I. Szoeke, Stein Emil Vollset, Nooshin Abbasi, Foad Abd-Allah, Jemal Abdela, Miloud Taki Eddine Aichour et al. 2019. "Global, Regional, and National Burden of Alzheimer's Disease and Other Dementias, 1990–2016: A Systematic Analysis for the Global Burden of Disease Study 2016." *The Lancet Neurology* 18(1): 88–106.

Phillips, Jill, Dimity Pond, and S. Goode. 2011. "Timely Diagnosis of Dementia: Can We Do Better." Canberra: Alzheimer's Australia.

Phillipson, Lyn, Christopher Magee, Sandra Jones, Samantha Reis, and Ellen Skaldzien. 2015. "Dementia Attitudes and Help-Seeking Intentions: An Investigation of Responses to Two Scenarios of an Experience of the Early Signs of Dementia." *Aging & Mental Health* 19(11): 968–977.

Prince, Martin, Gemma-Claire Ali, Maëlenn Guerchet, A. Matthew Prina, Emiliano Albanese, and Yu-Tzu Wu. 2016. "Recent Global Trends in the Prevalence and Incidence of Dementia, and Survival with Dementia." *Alzheimer's Research & Therapy* 8(1): 1–13.

Ramírez Díaz, S. P., G. Albert Meza, R. E. Albrecht Junghanns, I. C. Zúñiga Gil, Bedia Reyes, L. A. Barba Valadez, E. Almanza Huante, and Leonardo Eleazar Cruz Alcalá. 2015. "An Overview on Assessment Tests for Alzheimer's Disease in Mexico. The National Dementia Survey: A Study from the Mexican Group of Specialists in Dementias." *Journal of Aging Research & Clinical Practice* 4(1): 44–49.

Reiman, Eric M., Jessica Langbaum, Adam S. Fleisher, Richard J. Caselli, Kewei Chen, Napatkamon Ayutyanont, Yakeel T. Quiroz, Kenneth S. Kosik, Francisco Lopera, and Pierre N. Tariot. 2011. "Alzheimer's Prevention Initiative: A Plan to Accelerate the Evaluation of Presymptomatic Treatments." *Journal of Alzheimer's Disease* 26(S3): 321–329.

Rivera-Hernandez, Maricruz, Amit Kumar, Gary Epstein-Lubow, and Kali S. Thomas. 2019. "Disparities in Nursing Home Use and Quality among African American, Hispanic, and White Medicare Residents with Alzheimer's Disease and Related Dementias." *Journal of Aging and Health* 31(7): 1259–1277.

Savla, Jyoti, Karen A. Roberto, Rosemary Blieszner, Brandy Renee McCann, Emily Hoyt, and Aubrey L. Knight. 2020. "Dementia Caregiving During the 'Stay-at-Home' Phase of COVID-19 Pandemic." *Journals of Gerontology Series B: Psychological Sciences and Social Sciences.*

Singh, Hardeep, Aanand Dinkar Naik, Raghuram Rao, and Laura Ann Petersen. 2008. "Reducing Diagnostic Errors through Effective Communication: Harnessing the Power of Information Technology." *Journal of General Internal Medicine* 23(4): 489–494.

Sosa-Ortiz, Ana Luisa, Isaac Acosta-Castillo, and Martin J. Prince. 2012. "Epidemiology of Dementias and Alzheimer's Disease." *Archives of Medical Research* 43(8): 600–608.

Spradley, James P. 2016. *The Ethnographic Interview*. Long Grove: Waveland Press.

Szabo, Sarah M., Carol J. Whitlatch, Silvia Orsulic-Jeras, and Justin D. Johnson. 2018. "Recruitment Challenges and Strategies: Lessons Learned from an Early-Stage Dyadic Intervention (Innovative Practice)." *Dementia* 17(5): 621–626.

Treves, Therese A., R. Verchovsky, S. Klimovitsky, and A. D. Korczyn. 2000. "Recruitment Rate to Drug Trials for Dementia of the Alzheimer Type." *Alzheimer Disease & Associated Disorders* 14(4): 209–211.

Valencia-González, Damaris, Rocío Ramírez-Santos, and Gilberto Isaac Acosta-Castillo. 2017. "Prevalence of Dementia in a General Hospital in Mexico." *Alzheimer's & Dementia* 13(7): P840.

van den Dungen, Pim, Harm W. M. van Marwijk, Henriëtte E. van der Horst, Eric P. Moll van Charante, Janet MacNeil Vroomen, Peter M. van de Ven, and Hein P. J. van Hout. 2012. "The Accuracy of Family Physicians' Dementia Diagnoses at Different Stages of Dementia: A Systematic Review." *International Journal of Geriatric Psychiatry* 27(4): 342–354.

van der Flier, Wiesje M., and Philip Scheltens. 2005. "Epidemiology and Risk Factors of Dementia." *Journal of Neurology, Neurosurgery & Psychiatry* 76(5): v2–v7.

Van Gorp, Baldwin, Tom Vercruysse, and Jan Van den Bulck. 2012. "Toward a More Nuanced Perception of Alzheimer's Disease: Designing and Testing a Campaign Advertisement." *American Journal of Alzheimer's Disease & Other Dementias* 27(6): 388–396.

Waheed, Waquas, Nadine Mirza, Muhammed Wali Waheed, Amy Blakemore, Cassandra Kenning, Yumna Masood, Fiona Matthews, and Peter Bower. 2020. "Recruitment and Methodological Issues in Conducting Dementia Research in British Ethnic Minorities: A Qualitative Systematic Review." *International Journal of Methods in Psychiatric Research* 29(1): 1–17.

Watson, Jennifer L., Laurie Ryan, Nina Silverberg, Vicky Cahan, and Marie A. Bernard. 2014. "Obstacles and Opportunities in Alzheimer's Clinical Trial Recruitment." *Health Affairs* 33(4): 574–579.

Weiner, Myron F., and Anne M. Lipton, eds. 2009. *The American Psychiatric Publishing Textbook of Alzheimer Disease and Other Dementias*. Washington, DC: American Psychiatric Pub.

Werner, Perla. 2005. "Social Distance towards a Person with Alzheimer's Disease." *International Journal of Geriatric Psychiatry: A Journal of the Psychiatry of Late Life and Allied Sciences* 20(2): 182–188.

West, Emily, Astrid Stuckelberger, Sophie Pautex, Janneke Staaks, and Marjolein Gysels. 2017. "Operationalising Ethical Challenges in Dementia Research–A Systematic Review of Current Evidence." *Age and Ageing* 46(4): 678–687.

Wiese, Lisa Kirk, Jennifer Lingler, Ishan Canty Williams, Nancy E. Schoenberg, and James E. Galvin. 2020. "Engaging Rural Older Minority Adults in Dementia Research during a Pandemic-Associated Quarantine." *Alzheimer's & Dementia* 16: e047225.

Wong, Roger, Takashi Amano, Shih-Yin Lin, Yuanjin Zhou, and Nancy Morrow-Howell. 2019. "Strategies for the Recruitment and Retention of Racial/Ethnic Minorities in Alzheimer Disease and Dementia Clinical Research." *Current Alzheimer Research* 16(5): 458–471.

World Health Organization. 2015. "The Epidemiology and Impact of Dementia: Current State and Future Trends." Geneva: World Health Organization.

Yokomizo, Sharon Sanz Simon, and Cássio Machado de Campos Bottino. 2014. "Cognitive Screening for Dementia in Primary Care: A Systematic Review." *International Psychogeriatrics* 26(11): 1783–1804.

Zhou, Yan, David Elashoff, Sarah Kremen, Edmond Teng, Jason Karlawish, and Joshua D. Grill. 2017. "African Americans Are Less Likely to Enroll in Preclinical Alzheimer's Disease Clinical Trials." *Alzheimer's & Dementia: Translational Research & Clinical Interventions* 3(1): 57–64.

Zimmerman, Sheryl, Philip D. Sloane, Christianna S. Williams, Peter S. Reed, John S. Preisser, J. Kevin Eckert, Malaz Boustani, and Debra Dobbs. 2005. "Dementia Care and Quality of Life in Assisted Living and Nursing Homes." *The Gerontologist* 45(S1): 133–146.

17

Future Directions for an Anthropology of Aging

BRITTENY M. HOWELL AND RYAN P. HARROD

Conclusion

The chapter authors have provided an overview of some anthropological understandings of aging, how it is similar to and different from our primate relatives, and the various ways we experience the process of getting older through time and place. The value of this volume is that it brings together anthropologists specializing in different subfields to provide insight into the development of anthropological research on the aging process. While this book does not cover the entirety of anthropological inquiry on aging, it does provide a holistic overview of some key current and future directions of research on this increasingly important topic. The authors in this volume have contributed unique insights on human aging, including evolutionary and biological perspectives, medical and cultural viewpoints, and the use of anthropological methods and theory for researching aging.

The more we understand the complex biological processes involved with aging and our cultural perceptions of what it means to get older, we can see the value in using a biocultural anthropological approach (Dufour 2006; Armelagos et al. 1992; Goodman and Leatherman 1998) to understand this human universal. With the advent of modern medicine and development of vaccinations and treatments for a variety of conditions that contribute to early mortality, people in our society are living longer. From a purely biological perspective, we might only focus on how aging will affect the body or mind, but from a biocultural perspective we know that the impact of any changes are contingent upon how our society views getting older and the ways people interact with older adults. In many parts of the world, we have to recognize that systemic inequality (e.g., racism, classism, etc.) can greatly affect who lives into old age and how people with age-related changes are cared for and valued. We believe, however, that when anthropologists "tack" across disciplines such as public policy (Park and Littleton 2013), we will continue to see progress toward addressing these issues of discrimination and inequality. As a result, the probability of more people living a healthy life past the age of 65 years of age will (hopefully) increase. With this increase, we need to understand more than ever the biocultural nature of aging and address cultural misunderstandings and biases about the process of getting older.

The intent of this volume is not only to theorize about aging but to shift the narrative of our understanding of aging in society. Outside of academia, people are beginning to challenge the aging discourse and argue that the way we talk about age-related changes has a concrete impact on mainstream society. This is an incredibly salient point right now, since the global coronavirus pandemic has resulted in some egregious examples of ageist public language. Popular media in locations across the globe, from the United States to Belgium and many places in between, provided both paternalistic discourses of protecting older adults to blatantly ageist language about the duty of older adults to put themselves at risk for the good of local economies (Verbruggen, Howell, and Simmons 2020).

In 2021, a social media campaign was launched to update terminology and ideas about how we think and talk about the process of aging in society. In a viral post on the Motherhood app by Chrissy Teigen, there was a challenge to move beyond simplistic descriptions of complex phenomenon by critiquing the use of the term "geriatric pregnancy" by medical professionals (Women's Health 2021). Women are having, or attempting to have, babies at increasingly older ages in the United States and equating these pregnancies with the term "geriatric" is problematic. In fact, the use of the term as applied to older adults has also been critiqued by the medical profession. Slevin (2003) suggests that because of "negative associations of 'oldness.' . . . the term geriatric has attained strong negative connotations. It is even sometimes used as a term of derision to describe an older person (with implications of physical deterioration, lack of mental competence and/or unhygienic habits)" (Slevin 2003, 410). Since older adults are one of the most negatively stereotyped groups in society (Krasil'nikova 2010; Weiss and Kornadt 2018), this is hardly surprising.

However, researchers and scientists are far from immune to these negative connotations of aging. Cohen et al. (2019) point out that much biological and medical work focuses on research questions related to physical and functional age-related declines rather than changes or adaptations. Biomedical research also tends to approach aging as a problem to be solved, to prolong life at all costs, although the wishes of older adults are often centered around very different goals such as maintaining autonomy, social relationships, generativity, and avoiding suffering (Howell, Seater, and McLinden 2020; Van Leeuwen et al. 2019). In this volume, the authors have attempted to simultaneously acknowledge the biological and social changes associated with growing older while deconstructing common misunderstandings and biases that have been perpetuated in the literature for far too long.

Future Directions

The future of anthropological inquiry on aging can take several important possible directions. Primarily, the goal of an anthropology of aging is to deepen our understanding of how humans age, as biological and cultural beings, through time and place. This includes biocultural perspectives comparing human aging with the aging patterns of other primates (Thompson, Rosati, and Snyder-Mackler 2020). For example, Lacreuse and colleagues (2020) compared human and non-human primates to understand the changes in executive function and the role that biology, nutrition, and hormones play, which may provide some insight into dementia. However, we also need to understand the life histories and evolutionary nature of aging. In a review article, Bribiescas (2020) highlights the value of not only comparing human and non-human primates but also including an understanding of the ways that evolution shaped how we age, the role of the ecological setting, and a consideration of how social conditions impact how a person ages in a particular society. Bribiescas (2020) discusses the prevalence of colon cancer in industrial and small-scale societies, but we could examine the presence or absence of any number of age-related changes using this approach. Anthropologists sometimes struggle to define exactly how to assess age-related changes.

Recent work by Ubelaker and Khosrowshahi (2019), studying both human skeletal remains and living individuals, found that there are challenges that make accurate age estimation based on biological changes difficult, and new approaches are being developed to address these limitations. In 2020, two articles were published focused on challenging researchers to reevaluate the accuracy of our aging techniques and critically assess how we might narrow the age-range estimations of older individuals (Clark et al. 2020; Getz 2020). As Getz (2020, 9) notes, "the application of the statistical technique alone cannot overcome the effects of skeletal indicators that are poorly correlated with chronological age in certain parts of the adult lifespan." We need to acknowledge that people age differently and that this is going to be reflected in the bones.

Next, we suggest that anthropologists contribute substantially to the public health research on current demographic and economic trends. Changes in fertility, life expectancy, and population-age structures suggest that anthropologists should focus on the implications of a far greater population of older adults than the world has ever seen (National Academies of Sciences, Engineering, and Medicine 2018). The public health and public policy literature is riddled with language that suggests this "burgeoning" and "rapidly growing" population of seniors is nothing but a burden on resources and local economies. Such a "silver tsunami" of older adults has captured the public imagination as a wave of white-haired people crashing through society, siphoning off resources in their wake faster than they can be replaced. While resources may well be prematurely depleted in some places, such ageist constructions ignore the fact that older adults also contribute substantially to local economies, spending 56 cents of each dollar in the United States. Older adults also contribute substantially to caregiving tasks for grandchildren and provide much of the volunteer base that help make many social service and other nonprofits financially viable. Unfortunately, demographers and epidemiologists have been forecasting these changes in our aging society for years, but public policy has chosen to ignore addressing this growing segment of our population. Additionally, this "silver tsunami" is a relatively short-term problem, one that can be expected to end as any human generation does eventually. There are also many other ways in which older adults are contributing to society that often get left out of the public health and policy literature. However, ethnographic work can help provide examples of such important contributions to society that older adults hold, as well as change the discourse from a deficit-based "drain on resources" to a perspective of asset-based value provided by older adults in society.

These demographic shifts have also resulted in increased health disparities for ethnically and racially diverse elders, as well as lesbian, gay, bisexual, transgender, queer, etc. (LGBTQ+) seniors (Herdt and De Vries 2003). Due to a variety of complex and regionally situated variables, segments of older adults around the world are considered "vulnerable" to worsening socioeconomic conditions, inequalities, and health and quality-of-life outcomes. There is also much work to still be done to understand the health disparities of aging ethnic minorities within and outside of the United States. Anthropologists using biocultural, feminist/queer, life-course perspectives, or political-economic theoretical approaches can elucidate some of the more intractable research areas of such disparities in public health, history, and social policy (Fabbre 2015).

For example, demographers continue to struggle with how to measure health and other disparities because they often do not know who identifies in which race, ethnicity, gender, or other identity categories in such multicultural and diverse societies as the United States. Censuses and surveys often rely on respondent self-identification of these characteristics, but they are subject to shifting definitions and reporting patterns of these categories across time and place (Sandefur, Campbell, and Eggerling-Boeck 2004). Anthropologists have historically contributed substantially to the understanding of how and why definitions of race, ethnicity, and identity shift throughout history and from place to place, and we can continue to strive to identify how these patterns may be conceptualized for older adults.

Briller and Carillo (2020) provide an overview of the anthropology of care, highlighting our field's long history of researching the meaning of care around the world, family and informal caregiving networks, and care provided in policy and biomedical institutions. We join Briller and Carillo in encouraging anthropologists to continue this important work regarding how people are cared for in older adulthood, and to recognize that this area is more than just an academic exercise. An anthropology of aging is also an *applied* anthropology, where we can contribute to geriatrics and medical practice, ethics, health education and promotion, and even engineering and design. Since many questions about human biological and cultural variation can be addressed within older adulthood, we would like to see more anthropologists contributing to this important work and encouraging students to consider careers in gerontology (see Harman 2005).

Since aging occurs both individually and collectively, an anthropological perspective on aging interrogates the political, environmental, social, and economic conditions that are contributing to health and other disparities for older adults around the world (Lynch and Danely 2013). By applying anthropological insights to an aging world, we can reveal the cultural values, norms, and expectations that shape people's life-course experiences. Combining the biological and cultural variation in aging experiences, as demonstrated in this book, anthropology of aging scholars can holistically explore what it means to be human.

References

Armelagos, George J., Thomas Leatherman, Mary Ryan, and Lynn Sibley. 1992. "Biocultural Synthesis in Medical Anthropology." *Medical Anthropology* 14(1): 35–52. http://www.informaworld.com/10.1080/01459740.1992.9966065.

Bribiescas, Richard G. 2020. "Aging, Life History, and Human Evolution." *Annual Review of Anthropology* 49: 101–121.

Briller, Sherylyn, and Erika Carrillo. 2020. "Applying Anthropological Insight in an Aging World." In *Oxford Research Encyclopedia of Anthropology*.

Cohen, Alan A., Mélanie Levasseur, Parminder Raina, Linda P. Fried, and Tamàs Fülöp. 2019. "Is Aging Biology Ageist?" *Journals of Gerontology: Series A* 75(9): 1653–1655. https://doi.org/10.1093/gerona/glz190.

Dufour, Darna L. 2006. "Biocultural Approaches in Human Biology." *American Journal of Human Biology* 18(1): 1–9. https://doi.org/10.1002/ajhb.20463.

Fabbre, Vanessa D. 2015. "Gender Transitions in Later Life: A Queer Perspective on Successful Aging." *Gerontologist* 55(1): 144–153. https://pubmed.ncbi.nlm.nih.gov/25161264/.

Goodman, Alan H., and T. L. Leatherman. 1998. "Traversing the Chasm between Biology and Culture: An Introduction." In *Building a New Biocultural Synthesis: Political-Economic Perspectives on Human Biology*, edited by A. H. Goodman and T. L. Leatherman, 3–41. Ann Arbor: University of Michigan Press.

Harman, Robert. 2005. "Applied Anthropology and the Aged." In *Applied Anthropology: Domains of Application*, edited by Satish Kedia and John Van Willigen, 307–340. Westport, CT: Praeger.

Herdt, Gilbert, and Brian De Vries, eds. 2003. *Gay and Lesbian Aging: Research and Future Directions*. New York: Springer Publishing Company.

Howell, B. M., M. Seater, and D. McLinden. 2020. "Using Concept Mapping Methods to Define 'Healthy Aging' in Anchorage, Alaska." *Journal of Applied Gerontology* 35(2): 113–131.

Krasil'nikova, M. 2010. "Older People: New Opportunities or Just Another Limitation?" *Russian Social Science Review* 51(4): 16–33.

Lacreuse, Agnès, Naftali Raz, Daniel Schmidtke, William D. Hopkins, and James G. Alisha Herndon. 2020. "Age-Related Decline in Executive Function as a Hallmark of Cognitive Ageing in Primates: An Overview of Cognitive and Neurobiological Studies." *Philosophical Transactions of the Royal Society B* 375(1811). doi.org/10.1098/rstb.2019.0618.

Lynch, Caitrin, and Jason Danely. 2013. *Transitions and Transformations: Cultural Perspectives on Aging and the Life Course*. Vol. 1. Berghahn Books.

National Academies of Sciences, Engineering, Medicine, and Committee on Population. 2018. "Future Directions for the Demography of Aging: Proceedings of a Workshop." National Academies Press. Accessed April 21, 2021. https://www.nap.edu/catalog/25064/future-directions-for-the-demography-of-aging-proceedings-of-a.

Park, Julie, and Judith Littleton. 2013. "Tacking between Disciplines: Approaches to Tuberculosis in New Zealand, the Cook Islands, and Tuvalu." In *When Culture Impacts Health*, edited by C. Banwell, S. Ulijaszek, and J. Dixon, 157–166. New York: Elsevier.

Sandefur, G., M. E. Campbell, and J. Eggerling-Boeck. 2004. "Racial and Ethnic Identification, Official Classifications, and Health Disparities." In *Critical Perspectives on Racial and Ethnic Differences in Health in Late Life*, edited by N. B. Anderson, R. A. Bulatao, and B. Cohen, 25–52. Washington, DC: National Academies Press.

Slevin, Oliver. 2003. "A Nursing Perspective on Older People: The Problem of Ageism." In *Theory and Practice of Nursing: An Integrated Approach to Caring Practice*, 2nd ed., edited by Lynn Basford and Oliver Slevin, 409–426. Cheltenham: Nelson Thornes.

Thompson, Melissa E., Alexandra G. Rosati, and Noah Snyder-Mackler. 2020. "Insights from Evolutionary Relevant Models for Human Ageing." *Philosophical Transactions of the Royal Society B* 375(1811): doi.org/10.1098/rstb.2019.0605.

Ubelaker, Douglas H., and Haley Khosrowshahi. 2019. "Estimation of Age in Forensic Anthropology: Historical Perspective and Recent Methodological Advances." *Forensic Sciences Research* 4(1): 1–9.

Van Leeuwen, Karen M., Miriam S. Van Loon, Fenna A. Van Nes, Judith E. Bosmans, Henrica C. W. De Vet, Johannes C. F. Ket, Guy A. M. Widdershoven, and Raymond W.J.G. Ostelo. 2019. "What Does Quality of Life Mean to Older Adults? A Thematic Synthesis." *PloS ONE* 14(3): e0213263.

Verbruggen, Christine, Britteny M. Howell, and Kaylee Simmons. 2020. "How We Talk about Aging during a Global Pandemic Matters: On Ageist Othering and Aging 'Others' Talking Back." *Anthropology & Aging* 41(2): 230–245.

Weiss, David, and Anna E. Kornadt. 2018. "Age-Stereotype Internalization and Dissociation: Contradictory Processes or Two Sides of the Same Coin?" *Current Directions in Psychological Science* 27(6): 477–483. https://doi.org/10.1177/0963721418777743.

Women's Health. 2021. "Chrissy Teigen Is on a Mission to Rid the Stigma of Expectant Mothers over 35." Women's Health. Accessed April 1, 2021. https://www.womenshealth.com.au/chrissy-teigen-is-on-a-mission-to-rid-the-stigma-of-expectant-mothers-over-35.

Contributors

Ojo Melvin Agunbiade, PhD, is senior lecturer in the Department of Sociology and Anthropology at Obafemi Awolowo University, Nigeria. He recently coauthored "'The Night Comes Early for a Woman': Menopause and Sexual Activities among Urban Older Yoruba Men and Women in Ibadan, Nigeria" in the *Journal of Women & Aging*.

Douglas E. Crews, PhD, is professor of anthropology and public health at The Ohio State University. Recent publications have appeared in *PLOS ONE, American Journal of Physical Anthropology, General and Comparative Endocrinology,* and *Stress*. He coedited *Biological Anthropology and Aging: Perspectives on Human Variation over the Life Span* and authored *Human Senescence: Evolutionary and Biocultural Perspectives*.

Ruby L. Fried, PhD, is assistant professor of health sciences in the Institute for Circumpolar Health Studies at the University of Alaska Anchorage. She has authored publications related to traditional food use in Alaska, maternal health, and life span development in the *American Journal of Human Biology, Evolutionary Anthropology,* and *Journal of Developmental Origins of Health and Disease*.

Eric E. Griffith, PhD, is a postdoctoral associate at the Samuel DuBois Cook Center on Social Equity at Duke University. He completed his dissertation "A Cross-Cultural Comparison of Alzheimer's Disease Symptoms and Caregiving in the United States and Mexico" (2021) at the University of Massachusetts Amherst.

Ryan P. Harrod, PhD, is chief academic officer and dean at Garrett College in McHenry, Maryland. He is coeditor of this volume and has coauthored and coedited several books on bioarchaeology. His articles have appeared in journals such as the *Yearbook of Physical Anthropology, International Journal of Osteoarchaeology, Archeological Papers of the American Anthropological Association*, and *Cambridge Archaeological Journal*.

Julie Hemment, PhD, is associate professor in the Department of Anthropology at the University of Massachusetts Amherst. She is the author of *Empowering Women in Russia: Aid, NGOs and Activism* and *Youth Politics in Putin's Russia: Producing Patriots and Entrepreneurs*.

Vanessa Y. Hiratsuka, PhD, MPH, is assistant professor of clinical and translational research, and codirector of research and evaluation at the Center for Human Development at the University of Alaska Anchorage. She is coauthor of multiple articles on Alaska Native health in *Social Sciences, PLOS ONE*, and the *International Journal of Environmental Research & Public Health*.

Britteny M. Howell, PhD, CPG, CDP°, is assistant professor in the Division of Population Health Sciences, affiliate faculty for the National Resource Center for Alaska Native Elders, and founding director of the Healthy Aging Research Laboratory at the University of Alaska Anchorage. She is coeditor of this volume and has published multiple articles on healthy aging in *Journal of Applied Gerontology, Journal of Community Health, Ageing & Society*, and *Anthropology & Aging*.

Ankita Kansal, PhD, is a visiting scholar in the Department of Anthropology at the University of Delaware working on a study of public perceptions of the microbiome.

Kathryn E. Marklein, PhD, is assistant professor of anthropology and bioarchaeologist at the Center for Archaeology and Cultural Heritage at the University of Louisville. She has published multiple articles on skeletal frailty with human biology collaborators in *American Journal of Physical Anthropology, PLOS ONE*, and *Collegium Antropologicum*.

Melissa K. Melby, PhD, is professor of anthropology and codirector of the CIFAR Humans & the Microbiome program at the University of Delaware. She is coauthor of "The Hygiene Hypothesis, the COVID Pandemic, and Consequences for the Human Microbiome" in *PNAS* and "Are Noncommunicable Diseases Communicable?" in *Science*.

Mark Nichter, PhD, MPH, is Regents Professor emeritus in the School of Anthropology at the University of Arizona. He is the author of *Global Health: Why Cultural Perceptions, Social Representations, and Biopolitics Matter* and coeditor of *New Horizons in Medical Anthropology: Essays in Honour of Charles Leslie*.

Heather L. Norton, PhD, is associate professor of anthropology and director of the Skin Science & Technology Collaborative at the University of Cincinnati. She is the author and coauthor of multiple articles on the genetic architecture and evolution of pigmentary phenotypes published in *The American Journal of Physical Anthropology*, *The American Journal of Human Biology*, and *BMC Genetics*.

Joyce A. Parga, PhD, is associate professor of anthropology at California State University, Los Angeles. She is coauthor of the chapter "Primate Socioecology" in the volume *Primates in Perspective*, 2nd ed.

Cortney Hughes Rinker, PhD, is associate professor in the Department of Sociology and Anthropology and director of the Global Affairs Program at George Mason University. She is the author of *Actively Dying: The Creation of Muslim Identities through End-of-Life Care in the United States* and *Islam, Development, and Urban Women's Reproductive Practices*. She is also the coeditor of the volume *Applied Anthropology: Unexpected Spaces, Topics, and Methods*.

Peteneinuo Rulu is a PhD candidate in the Department of Anthropology at the University of Massachusetts Amherst. She is the coauthor of "Symptoms at Midlife among Women in Nagaland, India" in *The American Journal of Human Biology*.

Jean J. Schensul, PhD, is founding director of the Institute for Community Research in Hartford, Connecticut, and adjunct professor in the Department of Public Health Sciences at UCONN Health, University of Connecticut. She is the lead editor and coauthor of the *Ethnographer's Toolkit, Volumes 1–7* and first author of "Improving Oral Health in Older Adults and

People with Disabilities: Protocol for a Community-Based Clinical Trial (Good Oral Health)" in *JMIR Research Protocols*.

Sofiya Shreyer, MA, is a PhD student in the Department of Anthropology at the University of Massachusetts Amherst.

Lynnette Leidy Sievert, PhD, is professor of anthropology at the University of Massachusetts Amherst. She is the author of *Menopause: A Biocultural Perspective* and a coeditor of *Biological Measures of Human Experience across the Lifespan: Making Visible the Invisible*.

Jing Wang, PhD, is assistant professor at Panzhihua University in China. She is the author of "Keeping Quiet: Aging, Personhood, and Intergenerational Harmony in Rural Central Tibet" in *The Journal of Aging Studies*.

Nilüfer Korkmaz Yaylagül, PhD, is associate professor of gerontology and affiliate faculty of Health Sciences at Akdeniz University. She is coeditor of *Globalization and Aging: An Introduction to Critical Gerontology* [*Küreselleşme ve Yaşlılık: Eleştirel Gerontolojiye Giriş* in Turkish] and coauthor of "Assessing Liveable Cities for Older People in an Urban District in Turkey Using the Analytical Hierarchy Process" in *Journal of Urban Planning*.

Alyssa Willett, OTR/L, MOT, MA, is an occupational therapist at UCHealth Physical Medicine and Rehabilitation Clinic in Northern Colorado. Alyssa has coauthored articles in the *Journal of Western Archives* and book chapters in *New Developments in the Bioarchaeology of Care* and *Broken Bones, Broken Bodies: Bioarchaeological Approaches for Accumulative Trauma and Violence*.

Suzan Yazıcı, MD, is a medical doctor and gerontologist. She is coeditor of *Globalization and Aging: An Introduction to Critical Gerontology* [*Küreselleşme ve Yaşlılık: Eleştirel Gerontolojiye Giriş* in Turkish] and coauthor of "Use of Cross-Border Healthcare Services by Elderly Turkish Migrants in Denmark: A Qualitative Study and Some Critical Reflections about Public Health Concerns" in *Nordic Journal of Migration Research*.

Yan Zhang, PhD, is a postdoctoral research fellow in the Department of Global Health and Social Medicine at Harvard University. Her research interests include aging, caregiving, dementia, and gerontechnology in China.

Index

Page numbers in *italics* followed by the letters *t* and *f* indicate tables and figures.

Absent father archetype, 86, 90
Acceptance: of death, 181, 186–187, 199; of decline, 181
ACEs. *See* Adverse childhood experiences
Activities of daily living (ADLs), 32, 253; ADRD and, 300–301
AD. *See* Alzheimer's disease
Adaptation: to aging, 27, 38; occupational therapy as, 33; to reduced mobility, 36. *See also* Human adaptability theory
Adaptive capacity, 34
Adaptive strategies: for obtaining traditional foods, 160–164; role of, 153–154
ADLs. *See* Activities of daily living
Administration on Aging, 191
ADRD. *See* Alzheimer's disease and related dementias
Adulthood: older, 1, 271–273; perception of, 139
Adverse childhood experiences (ACEs): menopause and, 105
Age: ADRD and, 299; estimation accuracy, 316; initialization of, 136–137; meaning of, 6; perceived, 125–126; perception of, 121–122; prophylactic medical practices and, 147–148; PSS and, 103; relativity of, 136; stress hormones and, 16
Age at menopause: childhood stressors and, 99–100; intra-uterine stressors and, 98–99; median, 98; variation in, 98–100
Age perception: of facial skin, 121–122
Age registration: in Denmark, 137; impact of, 142; importance of, 146; inaccuracy of, 141–148; SES, 146; in Turkey, 138–140. *See also* Birth registration

Age spots, 120
Aged skin: care of, 123; as disease, 117–118; health-related implications of, 122–125; immune system and, 125; intrinsic *vs.* extrinsic, 120; tearing of, 123–124; views on, 128; wound healing in, 123. *See also* Skin
Ageism, 62, 315–316
Agency, aging and, 230, 272
Age-related changes to skin, 119–120
Age-related diseases, 28; frailty and, 29; microbiome and, 52*f*; stress and, 51. *See also* Geriatric syndromes
Aging, 175, 271; abnormal aging *vs.*, 308; adaptations to, 27, 38; additional support needs with, 32; as agba inira, 237, 240–242; agency and, 230, 272; in Alaska Native communities, 153; anthropological perspective on, 318–319; approaches to, 32–35; bioarchaeology and, 34; biocultural view of, 27, 314–315; biological perspective of, 5, 29–31; biology of, 27–28; biomedical view on, 316; bone formation and, 30; categories of, 3; cellular theory of, 3, 28; challenges of, 229; changes associated with, 64, 66–67*t*; conformity and, 229; contemporary, 198; as critical health issue, 192; cultural perspective on, 5, 314, 319; definitions of, 136; demographic, 141; diet and, 59, 66*t*; disease and, 47; disparities in, 3; effects of, 17, 33–34; enjoyment of, 187, 240–241; environmental exposure and, 48; evolutionary perspective of, 5, 316; exercise and, 66*t*; expectations of, 228, 242; fertility and, 5, 11; frailty and, 6–7; generativity and, 230–234;

Aging—*continued*
gut microbiome and, 47; holistic view of, 2, 4–5, 7, 241, 314; identity and, 200; influences on, 47; literature on, 192–193; longevity and, 34, 53, 263–264; longitudinal analysis of, 28–29; marginalization and, 240; medical perspective of, 5; medicalization of, 64; microbiota ecology and, 46, 50; among Muslim Americans, 193–196; myths of, 1–2; narrative shift, 315; neurodegenerative diseases and, 58; normal, 260; OA and, 30–31; obesity and, 65; osteoporosis and, 30–31; pace of, 1; physiological changes of, 17; political-economic theories on, 4; premature, 4; in primates, 5; QOL and, 63*f;* religion and, 196, 198–201, 205–206; research methods on, 5; senescence *vs.*, 28; SES and, 241; skeletal changes associated with, 29–30; skin and, 117, 119–120; social benefits of, 12; social interactions and, 53; social media campaign on, 315; social neglect and, 240; synergistic interactions of, 64; theories of, 2–4; treatment history for, 35–37; understanding, 271, 314, 316; as universal, 27; universal issues of, 36; vaccination and, 65, 67*t;* World Health Organization on, 174. *See also* Extrinsic aging factors; Good old age; Healthy aging; Intrinsic aging factors; Photoaging; Skeletal aging
Aging-in-place, 229, 231
Alaska Native peoples: cardiovascular disease in, 156; commonalities among, 154; diabetes in, 156; ethnographic work with, 159–160; healthy aging in, 157–158, 160; historical accounts of, 156; obesity in, 156; optimism in, 159; sharing among, 161–162; stress relief in, 159–160; traditional foods of, 155–157; on urban relocation, 160–161; urban *vs.* rural, 160–161
Alcoholism, 88, 90
Allostatic load, 253–254
Alzheimer's disease (AD): caregiver experiences, 298; diagnosis in Mexico, 306; diagnosis in US, 306; economic impact of, 299; family caregivers for, 301–304; gut microbiome and, 58; periodontitis and, 58; stigma of, 302
Alzheimer's disease and related dementias (ADRD): ADLs and, 300–301; age and, 299; demographic research challenges, 302–303; diagnostic criteria, 300; as disability, 306; education and, 305–308; ethical standards for research on, 301; family caregivers for, 301–304; misdiagnosis of, 300, 306, 308; QOL and, 303, 305; research barriers to, 298–300, 302–303; study recruitment crisis, 299–303, 306
American Occupational Therapy Association (AOTA), 32
Amyloid beta, 58
Anemia, 258
Anthropocene, 49
Anthropology: early focus of, 4. *See also* Biocultural anthropology
Antibiotics, 67*t;* bone health and, 54; need for, 62
Anxiety, 80–81, 240–241; grandmotherhood and, 84
AOTA. *See* American Occupational Therapy Association
Apes, 11; menopause and, 13; reproductive decline in, 14
Applied anthropology, 319
Applied gerontology, 272
Arthritis. *See* Osteoarthritis; Rheumatoid arthritis
Assisted care, 50, 53
Atresia, 98

Berry picking, 161
Bioarchaeology, 29, 249–250; aging and, 34; of culture, 36–37; on frailty, 251, 255, 265–266
Bioarchaeology of Care, 34
Biocultural anthropology, 1–2, 84, 316. *See also* Anthropology
Biocultural environment, 55*f*
Biological aging, 136, 253; microbiota and, 50
Biology of aging, 27–28
Biomarker, 250–251, 253–254, 257, 259–260, 261*t*, 265
Biomedical interventions, 117–118, 128–129, 316; for dementia, 215
Biomedical system, 140–141
Birth certificates, 138
Birth rates: of humans, 139; of primates, 11
Birth records: of deceased siblings, 143, 145; inaccuracies in, 137, 144–145
Birth registration, 144; culture and, 138; in

Denmark, 137, 142–143; inaccuracies in, 139. *See also* Age registration
Birth weight, menopause and, 99
Blat, 87
Blood-brain barrier permeability, 56
Blue Zones, 50, 62; physical exercise in, 59–60
Bolshevik state, 85–86
Bone balance, 55f
Bone health, antibiotics and, 54
Bone mineral density, 54
Bone remodeling, 30
Botox, 122
Brain health: gut-brain axis and, 56–59. *See also* Health
Breast cancer, menopause and, 106
Buddhism, 175; enlightenment in, 178; Four Noble Truths, 181; freedom to practice, 176; gaining merit in, 178; goal of, 178; harmony in, 182; impermanence in, 181; mental health and, 186; as passive, 177; prayer in, 179; recitations in, 179–180; six realms of, 177–178; tradition in, 179; on transience of life, 181. *See also* Manitso day

Cancer, 259; colon, 316
Capitalism, health-care and, 195
CAR. *See* Cortisol awakening response
Cardiovascular disease, 51, 52f; in Alaska Native peoples, 156; hot flashes and, 106; sitting and, 59–60
Caregiving, 5, 317; for AD, 298; female, 242; male, 302; as moral practice, 222. *See also* Family caregivers
Caring for karma, 177–178; collective activities in, 185; compared to successful aging model, 186–187; protective power of, 183
Case studies, 278; community decision making on medication management interventions, 284; on depression, 276; on loneliness, 283; of Muslim Americans, 201–203; on oral health, 285–286, 290; on social isolation, 287
CBPR. *See* Community-based participatory action research
CDC. *See* Centers for Disease Control
Centers for Disease Control (CDC), on falling, 30
Chanting, 173, 178–179
Child Trauma Questionnaire (CTQ), 105

Childcare: grandmotherhood and, 77; grandmothers' health and, 80–84; intergenerational, 78; role of, 5
Childhood: growth, 257; perception of, 139
Childhood stressors: menopause and, 99–100. *See also* Stress
Children, as social investments, 237
China: dementia in, 209, 211; elders in, 217–218; persons and nonpersons in, 214–215, 219, 222
Chronic stress: immune system and, 51; microbiome and, 62
Chronological aging, 136, 147–148
Circumambulations, 180, 186
Climate change, subsistence activities and, 164
Co-conduct of interventions, 283–285
Co-development, of interventions, 283–285
Cognitive system, 33
Co-involvement intervention studies, 272
Collaborative research, 272; ethical considerations of, 290–292
Collagen, 118–119, 123; degradation of, 120, 128–129
Colon cancer, 316
Commensal relationship, 46
Commerciogenic disease, 49
Communities, 273
Community belonging, 90
Community-based participatory action research (CBPR), 272
Community-based recruitment method, 308
Comorbidities, 302
Concept mapping, 281
Conformity, 228, 242–243; agba inira and, 244; aging and, 219
Consensus analysis, 281
Consent forms, 292
Consortium to Establish a Registry for Alzheimer's Disease Neuropsychological Battery, 304
Corneocytes, 118
Cortisol, 103–104
Cortisol awakening response (CAR), 104
Cosmeceuticals, 118, 122
Cosmetic surgery, 122
COVID-19, 64–65, 283, 301–302
C-reactive protein, 104
Cribra orbitalia, 258

Cross-cultural diversity, 155
Cross-sectional qualitative studies, 278
CTQ. *See* Child Trauma Questionnaire
Culture, 273; bioarchaeology of, 36–37; birth registration and, 138; health and, 35, 140–141; healthy aging and, 157–158; individual contributions to, 36; menopause and, 101; microbiota and, 48; occupational therapy and, 32; socioeconomic status and, 33; stress and, 103

DASH diet, 58
Data analysis, 288–289
Data collection methods, 279–280
Death, 173; acceptance of, 181, 186–187, 199; attitudes toward, 199; as good, 187; humor and, 199; as peaceful, 234; risk prediction, 253; successful aging and, 186–187
Decline, 186–187; acceptance of, 181
Dementia, 280, 284, 298–299, 309, 316; ages of care recipients, 213; aggressive, 210, 215–219, 222–223; amenable, 210, 219–223; biomedical construction of, 210, 223; biomedical interventions for, 215; childish behavior and, 220; in China, 209, 211; clinical diagnosis for, 210; cognitive ability and, 220; family caregivers and, 212–213; fear of, 222–223; folk understanding of, 218–219; in India, 211; inflammatory bowel disease and, 58; institutional care for, 218, 223–224; mutual dependency in, 221–222; personhood and, 210; public attitude toward, 215, 217; in Shanghai, 210, 212, 222–223; stigma of, 181, 211, 219, 304–305, 309; study recruitment crisis, 299–303, 306; symptoms of, 212; as threat to identity, 210; wen, 210, 219–223; wu, 210, 215–219, 222–223. *See also* Alzheimer's disease; Alzheimer's disease and related dementias
Demographic aging, 141, 317–318
Denmark: birth registrations in, 137, 142–143; first-generation immigrants to, 141–144
Depression, 34–35, 80–81; case study, 276; conceptual model, *278f*; menopause and, 96, 101
Dermis, 118–119
Developmental origins of health and disease (DOHaD) hypothesis, 98–99
Diabetes, 51, *52f*; in Alaska Native peoples, 156
Diademed sifaka post-reproductive life span, 13

Diet: aging and, 59, *66t*; effects of, 56; neurodegenerative diseases and, 58
Diffuse idiopathic skeletal hyperostosis (DISH), 29
Disease: aged skin as, 117–118; aging and, 47; commerciogenic, 49; illness *vs.*, 197; mortality and, 64–65; skeletal indicators of, 30; syndrome *vs.*, 28
DISH. *See* Diffuse idiopathic skeletal hyperostosis
Disinfection, 65
Divorce, in Russia, 88
DOHaD. *See* Developmental origins of health and disease
Donations, 180
Drug resistance, 62
Dysbiosis, 47, 51, *52f*; neurodegenerative disease and, 58

ECM. *See* Extracellular matrix
Ecomap, 282
Economies of gratitude, 89
Education: ADRD and, 305–308; menopause and, 97, 100
Elastin, 119–120
Elder care institution use: dementia and, 218, 223–224; in Islam, 195–196. *See also* Nursing homes
Elders, 154; adjusted personhood of, 219; in China, 217–218; community care of, 195; division of labor among, 178; as focal point, 163; knowledge transmission and, 164–165; lived experience of, 164; in Nigeria, 228–229; pilgrimages of, 180; prayer by, 179; recitations of, 179–180; religious focus of, 182–183; resilience of, 165; role of, 165; sharing with, 161–162; social position of, 228–229, 242; in Tibet, 176; uncertainty in, 198. *See also* Seniors
Elicitation techniques, 280–281
Emic perspective, 271
End-of-life care, 204, 206
Endurance, 250, 253
Enlightenment, 178
Epidemiological transition theory, 49
Epidemiological transitions, 48–49
Epidemiology, ecosocial approach to, 62
Epidermis, 118–119, 128
Epigenetics, 50, 62

328 Index

Epstein-Barr virus antibodies, 104
Estrogen, 96, 123
Ethnobotany, 37
Ethnographic surveys, 279, 282
Ethnographies, 278, 317; of Muslim Americans, 192–193
Ethnomedicine, 35, 37
Ethnopharmacology, 37
Eumelanin, 119–120
Executive function, 316
Exercise: aging and, 66t, effects of, 56
Extinction, of primates, 17–18
Extracellular matrix (ECM), 119, 123
Extrinsic aging factors, 119–120, 128. *See also* Aging

Facial rejuvenation, 118
Faith. *See* Religion
Falling: CDC on, 30; fractures and, 31; prevention of, 32
Families: as intergenerational, 77; in Islam, 195, 206
Family caregivers, 243, 318; for ADRD, 301–304; dementia and, 212–213; positive experience of, 219–222; reciprocity of, 238–239; toll on, 216–218; women as, 242. *See also* Caregiving
Fat-volume loss, 121–122
Female primates: reproductive aging in, 11–12; sexual behavior in, 11–12. *See also* Primates
Fertility, 317; aging and, 5, 11
Fetal growth restriction, 99
Fibroblasts, 119, 127
Filial piety, in Tibet, 181
Focus groups, 232–233
Folic acid deficiency, 258
Follicular loss, 99
Food procurement, 6
Food security, 164
Food sovereignty, 163–164
Food-sharing networks, 161–163
Four Noble Truths, 181
Fractures, 257, 261t; falling and, 31; healing of, 36; OA and, 31
Frailty, 249; age-related diseases and, 29; aging and, 6–7; bioarchaeological concept of, 251, 255, 265–266; biomedical concept of, 251; common assessment model for, 251; factors of, 253; gerontological models of, 251; health and, 266; indicators of, 252–253; among the living, 251–254, 257; in Medieval London, 260–265; monastic, *262t*, *263t*, 264; mortality and, 254–255; non-monastic, *262t*, *263t*, 264; OA and, 30; resilience and, 251, 259, 265–266; skeletal, 250–251, 254–265
Frontotemporal dementia, 299

Gender equality: in Soviet Union, 85–86
Gender roles: effects of, 85, 88–89; grandmotherhood and, 85–89; male, 86–87; in postsocialism, 90; skin and, 128
Gene expression studies, 127–128
Generativity, 6, 229, 243; agba inira and, 237; aging and, 230–234; good old age and, 230–234; healthy aging and, 158; motherhood and, 237–238; of parents, 238; practices of, 231; QOL and, 159–160; religion and, 235–236; role of, 159–164. *See also* Intergenerational teaching; Knowledge transmission
Genetics, 50; of skin aging, 125–128; variations in, 155–156
Genograms, 282
Genome-wide association study (GWAS), 126–128
Geographic information systems (GIS), 289
Geriatric, as negative term, 315
Geriatric pregnancy, 315
Geriatric syndromes, 28–29; adaptability and, 32, 35; biological consequences of, 36. *See also* Age-related diseases
Gerontology, 272, 318
GIS. *See* Geographic information systems
Global Clinical Frailty Scale, 253
Good old age: dimensions of, 233–234; fear of God and, 235–236; generativity and, 230–234; harmony and, 234–235, 241; particularity of, 233–234; social correctness of, 241. *See also* Aging
Grandmother hypothesis, 17, 78; in ring-tailed lemurs, 16
Grandmotherhood: anxiety and, 84; benefits of, 83–84; through biocultural lens, 84–89; childcare and, 77, 88; expectations about, 85; gender and, 85–89; mothering *vs.*, 83, 89; as primary identity, 84, 91–92; role of, 79; significance of, 91; uniqueness of, 78, 83, 91; views on, 82–83

Grandmothers: caretaking investment of, 80–81; contributions of, 78–79, 82; differential investment of, 79; maternal *vs.* paternal, 78–79, 81–82, 85, 89–92; mental health of, 80; mortality and, 78; need for, 90–91; as sanctuary, 82–83; in Soviet Union, 89; as stable support system, 87
Grandmothers' health, childcare and, 80–84
Group cohesion, 274
Gut microbiome: AD and, 58; aging and, 47; diversity of, 48; inflammaging and, 51; pathways of, 56; PD and, 58; serotonin regulation and, 56. *See also* Microbiome; Microbiota
Gut neuroendocrine cells, 57f
Gut neurons, 56
Gut-bone axis, 50, 55–56, 63f; microbiome and, 53; pathways of, 54. *See also* Osteoporosis
Gut-brain axis, 50, 62, 63f; brain health and, 56–59; microbiome and, 53; pathways of, 57f

Harmony: good old age and, 234–235, 241; religion and, 182
Health: culture and, 35, 140–141; definition of, 47; frailty and, 266; intervention studies for, 290, 292; marriage and, 60; physical exercise for, 36–37; religion and, 192; subsistence activities and, 155–157; traditional foods and, 155–157; understanding of, 35. *See also* Brain health
Health inequalities, 62, 317–318
Health transitions, 49
Health-care: capitalism and, 195; in Islam, 202–203; modern practices, 49; religion and, 194, 203; in Shanghai, 213; as siloed, 194–195; as social construct, 200; as wasted on seniors, 194–195. *See also* End-of-life care
Health-Related Quality of Life (HRQoL): menopause and, 105–106. *See also* Quality of life
Healthy aging, 6, 156, 174, 234, 315; Alaska Native Elders on, 152, 178; in Alaska Native peoples, 157–158, 160, 165; components of, 152–153; cross-cultural variation in, 152; culture and, 157–158; generativity and, 158; holistic framework of, 153, 158–159, 241; microbiome and, 50, 59–68; promotion of, 53; studies of, 61–62; subsistence activities and, 153–154, 158; traditional foods and, 158; views on, 154. *See also* Aging; Successful aging
Hermeneutic perspective, 271
Heterogeneous pigmentation, 122
Holobionts, 46
Hope, 198–199
Hormesis, 60
Hospice care, 191; Medicare and, 196
Hot flashes, 97, 101; cardiovascular disease and, 106; prevalence in India, 102t; PSS and, 103; severity of, 104; stress and, 102–104
HPA. *See* Hypothalamic-pituitary-adrenal axis
HRQoL. *See* Health-Related Quality of Life
HTCs. *See* Hunters and Trappers Committees
Human adaptability theory, 153–154, 160; biocultural approach to, 164; on genetic variation, 155–156. *See also* Adaptation; Resilience
Human Subjects Institutional Review Board (IRB), 290, 292
Human-environment interactions, 47
Humor, death and, 199
Hunters and Trappers Committees (HTCs), 164
Hygiene, 65
Hypercognitive culture, 211, 222
Hyperpigmentation, 120
Hypodermis, 118–119
Hypothalamic-pituitary-adrenal (HPA) axis, 103–105

ICR. *See* Institute for Community Research
Identity, 318; aging and, 200; crafting, 200; dementia as threat to, 210; grandmotherhood as, 84, 91–92; religion and, 199–200, 205
Illness: amodi, 235; disease *vs.*, 197
Immigrants, 140; in Denmark, 141–144
Immigration status, 302
Immune system, 57f; aged skin and, 125; chronic stress and, 51; inflammation and, 51
Immunosenescence, 51
Impermanence, in Buddhism, 181
Income inequality, 88
India, dementia in, 211
Individual choice, 174
Individualism, 182

Inequality: health, 62, 317; income, 88; structural, 4, 174–175; systemic, 314–315
Infant mortality rates, 2, 139
Infant survival, 12
Inflammaging: gut microbiome and, 51; senescence and, 51
Inflammation, 126; as immune response, 51; microbiome and, 50–53, *52f*, *63f*
Inflammatory bowel disease, dementia and, 58
Inflammatory cytokines, *52f*
Influenza, 64–65
Informant Questionnaire on Cognitive Decline in the Elderly Test, 304
Institute for Community Research (ICR), 272, 274–275
Interdependence, 186
Intergenerational competition avoidance, 183
Intergenerational teaching, 5. *See also* Generativity; Knowledge transmission
Intersectionality, 273–274
Interventions, 290, 292; co-conduct of, 283–285; co-development of, 283–285; multi-level design, 285
Intervertebral disc disease, 257, *261t*
Interviews, 232–233, 280, 292, 304
Intestinal wall permeability, 56
Intra-uterine stressors: age at menopause and, 98–99; menopause and, 98–99. *See also* Stress
Intrinsic aging factors, 119–120, 128. *See also* Aging
Inuit Food Security Project, 163–164
IRB. *See* Human Subjects Institutional Review Board
Islam, 238; elder care institution use in, 195–196; faith disconnection in, 204; family in, 195, 206; health-care guidance in, 202–203; interpretations of, 194; leadership in, 194; reconnection through death, 204–205; role in decision making, 200–201

Japanese macaques, 16

Karma, 177; purification, 178–179
Katz Activities of Daily Living Assessment, 303
Keratinocyte cells, 118–119, 123
Knowledge transmission, 5; elders and, 164–165; as stress relief, 159–160. *See also* Generativity; Intergenerational teaching

Langerhans cells, 118; morphological changes to, 124–125
Language barriers, 302
Langurs, 16
Lawton and Brody Instrumental Activities of Daily Living Scale, 303–304
LEH. *See* Linear enamel hypoplasia
Lewy body dementia, 299
Liberation, 178
Life course, 244, 271; critical windows in, *63f*; religion and, 198–199; theory, 4
Life expectancy, 317; increases in, 49–50, 141
Life history approach, 4
Life narratives, 282
Lifespan perspective: menopause and, 97, 107; midlife symptoms and, 104–105
Linear enamel hypoplasia (LEH), 258, *261t*, 262
Lipopolysaccharides (LPS), *52f*
Literacy, 139–140
Litter size, 12
Liver spots, 120
Living alliance of researchers, 274
Local biologies, 50; importance of, 53
Local theory, 277–278
Longevity, 314; aging and, 34, 53, 263–264; caloric restriction and, 59; SES and, 265; social networks and, 60–61

Male caregivers, 302
Male primates: reproductive aging in, 14–15; sexual behavior in, 14–15. *See also* Primates
Male-male competition, 15
Malignant social positioning, 211
Malnutrition, 36, 256–258
Mandrills, 15
Manitso day, 172–173, 179, 185. *See also* Buddhism
Mantra recitation, 178–180
Mapping, 281
Marginalization, aging and, 240
Marriage, health and, 60
Material security, 234
Mating behavior changes, 14–15
Maze Test, 304
Medical anthropology, 140–141, 146, 148–149
Medicare, 191; home hospice payment by, 196
Mediterranean diet, 50, 58; benefits of, 59

Melanin: photoaging and, 120–121; production of, 119
Melanocytes, 119
Melatonin, *57f*
Men, under socialism, 86
Menopause, 14, 78; ACEs and, 105; age variation and, 98–100; apes and, 13; attitude toward, 101; birth weight and, 99; breast cancer and, 106; culture and, 101; depression and, 96, 101; early onset of, 98; education and, 97, 100; famine and, 100; HRQoL and, 105–106; lifespan perspective and, 97, 107; monkeys and, 13; osteoporosis and, 106; physical exercise and, 105–106; prosimians and, 13; SES and, 98, 100; social significance of, 101, 106; stress and, 97; symptoms of, 96–97, 100–105; timing of, 96–97; variation in, 100–105. *See also* Age at menopause
Mental health, 50; Buddhism and, 186; of grandmothers, 80; social behavior and, 184–186
Mental illness: nonpersons with, 215; stigma of, 215
Merkel cells, 119
Metabolic disease, 65; sitting and, 59–60
Methods, 277–292
Mexico: AD diagnosis in, 306; diagnosis seeking in, 306; recruitment barriers in, 303–306; urban population of, 303
Microbes: benefits of, 46–47; biosocial network effect of, 60–61; exercise-induced changes to, 59–60
Microbial dysbiosis. *See* Dysbiosis
Microbiome, *55f*, *57f*; changes in, 50; chronic stress and, 62; family nuclearization influence on, 60; gut-bone axis and, 53; gut-brain axis and, 52; healthy aging and, 50, 59–68; inflammation and, 50–53, *52f*, *63f*; influences of, 50; neurodegenerative disease and, 53; polypharmacy effects on, 64; residence and, 61–62; roles of, 53–59, 65, 68; sharing of, 61. *See also* Gut microbiome
Microbiota, 46; aging and, 46, 50; culture and, 48; diversity of, 53, 60–61; evolutionary changes of, 48; impacts of, 61; as quantitative biomarkers, 61; roles of, 48. *See also* Gut microbiome
Milne-Edwards's sifaka, 12

MIND diet, 58
Mixed-methods studies, 278–279, 293
Mobility, 250, 253, 256–257
Monkeys, 11; menopause and, 13; reproductive decline in, 14
Moral agency, 222–223
Morbidity, 256; patterns of, 49–50
Mortality, 253, 314; disease and, 64–65; frailty and, 254–255; global causes of, 49; grandmothers and, 78; patterns of, 49–50; sitting and, 59–60
Mother-hero archetype, 86
Motherhood: generativity and, 237–238; grandmotherhood *vs.*, 83, 89; in Nigeria, 238; as political, 86; sacrifice of, 238–239; single, 88; in Soviet Union, 86
MsHeart Study, 105
Muscle changes, bone remodeling and, 30
Muslim Americans: aging among, 193–196; case studies of, 201–203; demographics of, 193; discrimination against, 205; diversity of, 193, 195, 205–206; ethnographies of, 192–193; minority experience of, 205–206; on nursing homes, 195–196, 202–203; stigma avoidance for, 200–201; in United States, 193
Mutual grooming, 16
Mutualistic relationships, 46

National Sleep Foundation Sleep Diary, 304
Neoplastic disorders, 259
Networks, 282
Neurodegenerative diseases, 50, *52f*; aging and, 58; diet and, 58; dysbiosis and, 58; microbiome and, 53
Neuropsychiatric Inventory, 304
Neurotransmitters, 56, *57f*
Night sweats, 97, 101
Non-human primates, 314, 316; aging in, 5. *See also* Primates
Nonpersons: Chinese perspectives on, 214–215, 219; with mental illness, 215
Normal, definition of, 47
Norms, 85
Nursing homes: Muslim Americans on, 195–196, 202–203. *See also* Elder care institution use
Nutrition: religion and, 263–264; of traditional foods, 155

OA. *See* Osteoarthritis
Obesity: aging and, 65; in Alaska Native peoples, 156
Occupational adaptation, 33
Occupational therapy: as adaptation, 33; culture and, 32; foundations of, 37; group level effects of, 34
Occupations, 37
OHRSA. *See* Older Adult Oral Health Research Strategic Alliance
Older Adult Oral Health Research Strategic Alliance (OHRSA), 274
Older Americans Act of 1965, 191
Oocytes, 98
Osteoarthritis (OA), 29, 256–257, 261t; aging and, 30–31; fractures and, 31; frailty and, 30; increases in, 37; prevention of, 33; sarcopenia and, 30; treatment of, 37
Osteochondritis dissecans, 30
Osteological paradox, 254–255
Osteoma, 259
Osteomalacia, 258, 261t; sarcopenia and, 30
Osteoporosis, 50, 52f, 253, 256–257, 261t; aging and, 30–31; drugs for, 56; menopause and, 106; microbiome and, 53; prevention of, 33. *See also* Gut-bone axis
Oxytocin production, 61

Paleodemography, 255
Paleoepidemiology, 255
Palliative care, 191
PAR. *See* Participatory action research
Parasympathetic nervous system, 56–58
Parkinson's disease (PD), gut microbiome and, 58
Participant observation, 279–281
Participant retention, 308
Participatory action research (PAR): approaches to, 272–273; benefits of, 286; criticism of, 287; entry to, 276–277; ethical considerations of, 290–292; with older adults, 286–287; volunteers for, 275
Partner agreements, 275, 277
Paternity, 15
Paternity certainty, 79
PD. *See* Parkinson's disease
Penn Ovarian Aging Study, 103
Perceived age, 125–127, 136. *See also* Age
Perceived Stress Scale (PSS), 103; age and, 103; hot flashes and, 103; VMS and, 103. *See also* Stress
Perimenopause, 96
Periodontitis, 261t; AD and, 58
Personhood: Chinese perspective on, 214–215; dementia and, 210–211; as dynamic, 223; of elders, 219; full, 219–220; gratitude and, 219; meanings attached to, 211–212; before and during modernization, 211; moral dimension of, 211–212, 214, 216–217, 222, 224; in Shanghai, 215–222, 224; sociopsychological dimension of, 210–211, 214
Phenotype, 249, 254–255, 265–266
Pheomelanin, 119
Photoaging, 120, 126; melanin and, 120–121. *See also* Aging
Photoprotection, 121
Photovoice, 287
Physical abuse, VMS and, 105
Physical exercise: in Blue Zones, 59–60; for health, 36–37; menopause and, 105–106; subsistence activities as, 156; in Tibet, 186
Pilgrimages, 184, 186; of elders, 180; as social behavior, 185
Political-economy, 4
Porotic hyperostosis, 258, 261t
Postsocialism, 87–89; gender roles in, 90. *See also* Socialism
Prayer: in Buddhism, 179; crop protection through, 179–180
Prayer wheel, 178–180
Pregnancy, geriatric, 315
Pressure ulcers, 123–124, 128–129
Primary care physician, 299–300
Primates, 314, 316; aged social behavior, 11; aging in, 5; behavioral differences in, 15–17; birth rates of, 11; extinction of, 17–18; as model organisms, 11, 17; post-reproductive life span in, 13–14; reproductive aging in, 11–12; senescence in, 11; social differences in, 15–17. *See also* Female primates; Male primates
Prosimians, 11; menopause and, 13
Prosthetics, 36
PSS. *See* Perceived Stress Scale
Psycho-social aging, 136
Psychosocial systems, 33

QOL. *See* Quality of life
Qualitative data, 288

Quality of life (QOL), 293; ADRD and, 303, 305; aging and, *63f*; generativity and, 159–160; intervention studies of, 290, 292; VMS and, 97. *See also* Health-Related Quality of Life
Quantitative data, 288
Qur'an, 194–195, 205

RA. *See* Rheumatoid arthritis
Race, 318; HRQoL and, 106; VMS and, 101
Rapport, 293
Rate of living hypothesis, 3
Reactive oxygen species (ROS), 119; cellular damage from, 120
Rebirth, 173, 178, 186
Reciprocal kin support, 90–91
Reciprocity, 238–239
Relationalism, 182
Religion: aging and, 196, 198–201, 205–206; belief *vs.* practice in, 200; burial status, 264–265; ceremony in, 200; gendered practices in, 241–242; generativity and, 235–236; harmony and, 182; health benefits of, 192; health-care and, 194, 203; as hope, 198–199; identity and, 199–200, 205; life course and, 198–199; nutrition and, 263–264; among seniors, 192; as social behavior, 173, 192; as support system, 198; varied effects of, 199; youth and, 177
Religiosity, 6, 192
Reproductive aging: in female primates, 11–12; in male primates, 14–15; in rhesus macaques, 14–15; in ring-tailed lemur, 14
Reproductive decline: in apes, 14; in monkeys, 14; tooth wear and, 12. *See also* Senescence
Research: COVID-19 and, 301–302; demographic challenges, 302–303; design, 277–292; model, 277–278; partnerships, 273–274, 293, 304; questions, 277; recruitment barriers, 304; underrepresentation in, 302
Resilience, 154–155, 271; of elders, 165; frailty and, 251, 259, 265–266. *See also* Human adaptability theory
Results sharing, 289
Rete ridges, 119, 124; attenuation of, 120
Rhesus macaques, reproductive aging in, 14–15
Rheumatoid arthritis (RA), 29–30; progression of, 31; sarcopenia and, 31
Rickets, 258, *261t*

Ring-tailed lemur, 12; grandmother hypothesis and, 16; reproductive aging in, 14
ROS. *See* Reactive oxygen species
Rotator cuff disease, 257, *261t*
Russia, divorce in, 88

Sanitization, 65
Sarcopenia, *52f*, 253, 256–257; inference of, 36; OA and, 30; osteomalacia and, 30; prevention of, 33; RA and, 31
Savanna baboon, reproductive success in, 15
SCFAs. *See* Short-chain fatty acids
Sebum changes, 129
Self-care, 32, 34
Senescence, 1, 3, 128, 154; aging *vs.*, 28; behavioral adjustments due to, 15–17; cellular, 28, 252, 254; dental, 12; disadvantages of, 17; inflammaging and, 51; in primates, 11; reproductive, 13–14, 78. *See also* Reproductive decline
Seniors: as growing demographic, 317; health-care as wasted on, 194; religion importance for, 192; support networks for, 229, 241. *See also* Elders
Sensorimotor system, 33
Sensory system function, 36
Serotonin regulation, *57f*; gut microbiome and, 56
SES. *See* Socioeconomic status
Sex steroid formation, 54
Sexual behavior: in female primates, 11–12; in male primates, 14–15
SFI. *See* Skeletal frailty index
Shanghai: dementia in, 210, 212, 222–223; health-care in, 213; pension system in, 213; personhood in, 215–222, 224
Short-chain fatty acids (SCFAs), 46, 51, *52f*, 53, 59
Silver tsunami, 317
Single motherhood. *See* Motherhood
Sitting: cardiovascular disease and, 59–60; metabolic disease and, 59–60; mortality and, 59–60
Situated biologies, 50, 53–54, 62
Skeletal aging, 2. *See also* Aging
Skeletal frailty, 250–251, 254–265; by cemetery, *263t*; patterns of, 265. *See also* Frailty
Skeletal frailty index (SFI), 256–260, *261t*, 266
Skeletal lesions, 250, 255, 257–258, 317

Skeletal record, 257
Skin: aging and, 5, 117, 119, 121–122; anatomy of, 118–119; appearance of, 121–122; consumer products for, 117–118; functions of, 117, 128; gender and, 128; genetics of, 125–128; pruritic, 123, 129; reduced barrier function, 123; thermoregulation and, 125; topography of, 121–122; UVR and, 120. *See also* Aged skin
Social aging, 136, 229
Social behavior, 67t; of aged primates, 11; benefits of, 185–186; longevity and, 60–61; mental health and, 184–186; moral status and, 217; pilgrimages as, 185; religion as, 173, 182
Social neglect, 240
Social networks, 282
Socialism: men under, 86. *See also* Postsocialism
Sociocultural standards, 228
Socioeconomic status (SES), 318; age registration and, 146; aging and, 241; culture and, 33; longevity and, 265; menopause and, 98, 100
Solar elastoses, 120
Solar lentigines, 120
Somatic frailty phenotype, 257
Soviet Union: collapse of, 87; cultural influences in, 91; grandmothers in, 89; male life expectancy in, 87
Spirituality, 229–230, 236, 243
Spontaneous abortions, 11–12
Stigma: AD and, 302; of dementia, 181, 211, 219, 304–305, 309; identification, 307; of mental illness, 215; reduction, 305; trigger avoidance, 308
Stillbirth, 11–12
Stratum basale, 118–119
Stratum corneum, 118; lipid content of, 123
Stratum granulosum, 118
Stratum spinosum, 118
Strength, 250, 253
Stress: age-related diseases and, 51; chronic, 253–254; culture and, 103; development and, 251–252; hot flashes and, 102–104; menopause and, 97; nutritional, 258; responses to, 258–259; self-reported, 104; VMS and, 97. *See also* Childhood stressors; Intra-uterine stressors; Perceived Stress Scale
Structural inequalities, 4; successful aging and, 174–175

Study problem identification methods, 274–275, 277
Subsistence activities, 6, 155; climate change and, 164; health impacts of, 155–157; healthy aging and, 153–154, 158; importance of, 152, 160; as physical exercise, 156; in Tibet, 175–176
Successful aging: biomedical definition of, 152–153; busy ethics of, 174; cost of, 174, 239; death and, 186–187; failure and, 153; individual responsibility for, 174; as oxymoron, 230; structural inequalities and, 174–175; in Tibet, 173, 180–181; Western concept of, 180. *See also* Healthy aging
Successful aging model: caring for karma compared to, 186–187; criticism of, 174–175; moral implications of, 175
Support network, 271, 282; grandmothers as, 87; religion as, 198; for seniors, 229, 241
Surveys, 279, 282
SWAN Mental Health Study, 105
Syndrome: disease *vs.*, 28
Systemic inequality, 314–315

Tamarins, 11
Testosterone decline, 14–15
Thalassemia, 258
Thermoregulation, skin and, 125
Tibet: elders in, 176; family harmony in, 182–183; filial piety in, 181; matrilocal inheritance in, 182; multigenerational living in, 182–184; pension scheme in, 176; physical exercise in, 186; subsistence activities in, 175–176; successful aging in, 173, 180–181
Tooth wear: reproductive decline and, 12
Traditional food, 159; adaptive strategies for, 160–164; of Alaska Native peoples, 155–157; consumption of, 156–157; health impacts of, 155–157; healthy aging and, 158; importance of, 152–153, 160; knowledge of, 163–164; nutrition of, 155; role of, 156–157; variation in, 155
Traditional Food Security Conceptual Framework, 164
Traditional knowledge: importance of, 159; of traditional food, 163–164
Transportation, 32
Trauma, skeletal indicators of, 30

Triadic agonistic support, 16
Tryptophan metabolism, 56
Turkey: age registration in, 138–140; illiteracy in, 139–140; migrants from, 141–142, 146–147; military service in, 140, 143

Ultraviolet radiation (UVR): exposure to, 119–120, 126; skin and, 120
United States: AD diagnosis in, 306
United States population: demographic shift in, 191; Muslim, 193
Urban harvesting, 161
UVR. *See* Ultraviolet radiation

Vaccination, 314; aging and, 65, *67t*
Vagus nerve, 56–58
Variables, 278
Vasomotor symptoms (VMS): physical abuse and, 105; PSS and, 103; QOL and, 97; race and, 101; stress and, 97
Vervet monkey, 17
Vignettes, 307–308
VMS. *See* Vasomotor symptoms

Walking tours, 281
Wellcome Osteological Research Database (WORD), 251, 260–265
Wen. *See* Dementia
Wildlife management, 164
Women: childbirth, 315; expectations of, 237–238; as family caregivers, 242
WORD. *See* Wellcome Osteological Research Database
Working mothers, 86. *See also* Motherhood
World Health Organization, on aging, 174
Wound healing, in aged skin, 123
Wu. *See* Dementia

X-chromosome relatedness, 79
Xerosis, 123, 129

Years: as Western concept, 139
Yoruba, Nigeria, 232, 234, 237, 243–244; elders in, 228–229; motherhood in, 238; systemic failures in, 239–240
Youth, 153; religion and, 177; value placed on, 118, 128

Printed in the United States
by Baker & Taylor Publisher Services